Writing in Foreign Language Contexts

PEFC
PEFC/16-33-111
CATG-PEFC-052
www.pefc.org

SECOND LANGUAGE ACQUISITION
Series Editors: Professor David Singleton, *Trinity College, Dublin, Ireland*

This series brings together titles dealing with a variety of aspects of language acquisition and processing in situations where a language or languages other than the native language is involved. Second language is thus interpreted in its broadest possible sense. The volumes included in the series all offer in their different ways, on the one hand, exposition and discussion of empirical findings and, on the other, some degree of theoretical reflection. In this latter connection, no particular theoretical stance is privileged in the series; nor is any relevant perspective – sociolinguistic, psycholinguistic, neurolinguistic, etc. – deemed out of place. The intended readership of the series includes final-year undergraduates working on second language acquisition projects, postgraduate students involved in second language acquisition research, and researchers and teachers in general whose interests include a second language acquisition component.

Full details of all the books in this series and of all our other publications can be found on http://www.multilingual-matters.com, or by writing to Multilingual Matters, St Nicholas House, 31–34 High Street, Bristol BS1 2AW, UK.

SECOND LANGUAGE ACQUISITION
Series Editor: David Singleton

Writing in Foreign Language Contexts

Learning, Teaching, and Research

Edited by
Rosa M. Manchón

MULTILINGUAL MATTERS
Bristol • Buffalo • Toronto

To the memory of my father, José Manchón.

Library of Congress Cataloging in Publication Data
A catalog record for this book is available from the Library of Congress.
Writing in Foreign Language Contexts: Learning, Teaching, and Research/Edited by Rosa Manchon.
Second Language Acquisition: 43
Includes bibliographical references and index.
1. Language and languages–Study and teaching. 2. Rhetoric–Study and teaching.
3. Second language acquisition. I. Manchón, Rosa.
P53.27.W75 2009
808′.0071–dc22 2009017380

British Library Cataloguing in Publication Data
A catalogue entry for this book is available from the British Library.

ISBN-13: 978-1-84769-184-2 (hbk)
ISBN-13: 978-1-84769-183-5 (pbk)

Multilingual Matters
UK: St Nicholas House, 31–34 High Street, Bristol BS1 2AW.
USA: UTP, 2250 Military Road, Tonawanda, NY 14150, USA.
Canada: UTP, 5201 Dufferin Street, North York, Ontario M3H 5T8, Canada.

The policy of Multilingual Matters/Channel View Publications is to use papers that are natural, renewable and recyclable products, made from wood grown in sustainable forests. In the manufacturing process of our books, and to further support our policy, preference is given to printers that have FSC and PEFC Chain of Custody certification. The FSC and/or PEFC logos will appear on those books where full certification has been granted to the printer concerned.

Typeset by Datapage International Ltd.
Printed and bound in Great Britain by the MPG Books Group.

Contents

Contributors

Christine Pearson Casanave taught full time at a Japanese university from 1990 to 2003 and part time most of those years at Teachers College, Columbia University's Japan campus in their MATESOL program. Between 2004 and 2007 she was affiliated with Temple University's Japan Campus, where she taught masters and doctoral students during fall semesters. She continues advising Temple doctoral students online from her home in California. Her speciality is issues in academic literacy.

M. Luz Celaya is Associate Professor in Applied Linguistics in the English and German Department at the University of Barcelona. Her main interests are the development of written production in EFL and the age factor, cross-linguistic influence and syntactic development in multilingual learners. She is the coordinator of the Masters 'Applied Linguistics and Language Acquisition in Multilingual Contexts' at her university and a member of the GRAL team that carried out the BAF project.

Alister Cumming is Professor and Head of the Modern Language Center at the Ontario Institute for Studies in Education, University of Toronto. He conducts research and teaches graduate courses on writing in second and foreign languages, language assessment, language policies and research methods. He is Executive Director of the journal *Language Learning*, as well as being on the editorial boards of numerous journals in applied linguistics and education.

John Flowerdew is a Professor in the Centre for Language Education Research, School of Education, University of Leeds, UK. As well as writing and editing a number of books, including four edited collections on academic discourse, he has published widely in the leading Applied Linguistics, Language Teaching and Discourse Analysis journals, focusing on academic and political discourse, His most recent edited book (with Vijay Bhatia and Rodney Jones) is *Advances in Discourse Studies* (Routledge, 2008).

Hiroe Kobayashi, Professor of English at Hiroshima University, earned her doctorate in TESOL at Teachers College, Colombia University. She teaches EFL, writing and pragmatics, and has taught ESL in the United States and the Philippines. Her primary interest is in development of L2 writing ability, including analysis of L1/L2 textual features and bidirectionality of transfer. She has published articles in *Language Learning* and the *Journal of Second Language Writing*, co-authored with Carol Rinnert.

Yongyan Li is currently a researcher at the City University of Hong Kong and a visiting scholar at the Centre of Asian Studies of the University of Hong Kong. She has published widely on the problems of Chinese scholars writing for publication in English and her work has appeared in journals such as *TESOL Quarterly, Journal of Second Language Writing, English for Specific Purposes* and *Asian Journal of English Language Teaching.*

Rosa M. Manchón is Associate Professor of Applied Linguistics, University of Murcia. Her research interests include the sociocognitive dimension of second language acquisition, particularly second language writing processes and research methods. Her work has appeared in leading Applied Linguistics and Second Language Writing journals such as *IRAL, Journal of Second Language Writing, Language Learning, Learning and Instruction* and the *Modern Language Journal*. Together with Ilona Leki, she edits the *Journal of Second Language Writing.*

Liz Murphy is Assistant Professor in the English Department, University of Murcia (Spain), where she teaches Academic Writing. Together with Julio Roca and Rosa Manchón she has published articles on foreign language writing processes in international journals including *Language Learning,* the *Modern Language Journal, Learning and Instruction* and the *Journal of Second Language Writing*. Her own particular research interest centres on the uses of the mother tongue in foreign language writing.

Teresa Navés is Assistant Professor in Applied Linguistics at the University of Barcelona. Her research interests include second language acquisition, content and language integrated learning, L2 writing and english language teaching methodology. She is a member of the GRAL research team that conducted the BAF project on the age factor. Her work has appeared in journals such as *International Journal of Multilingualism* and *EUROSLA Yearbook* and in books published by Multilingual Matters.

Lourdes Ortega is Associate Professor of Second Language Studies at the University of Hawai'i at Manoa. Her research interests include instructed SLA, tasks and interlanguage development, L2 writing, foreign language education, and research methods. Recent books are *Synthesizing Research on Language Learning and Teaching* (co-edited with John Norris; Benjamins, 2006), *The Longitudinal Study of Advanced L2 Capacities* (co-edited with Heidi Byrnes; Routledge, 2008) and *Understanding Second Language Acquisition* (Hodder Arnold, 2009).

Melinda Reichelt is Professor of English at the University of Toledo, where she coordinates the ESL writing program and teaches courses in TESOL and linguistics. Her research and publications focus on second language writing, including the role of English and English language teaching in Europe. Her work has appeared in journals such as the *Journal of Second Language Writing, Composition Studies, Issues in Writing,* the *Modern Language Journal* and *Foreign Language Annals.*

Carol Rinnert, Professor of International Studies, Hiroshima City University, earned her doctorate in linguistics at SUNY/Buffalo. She teaches sociolinguistics and English debate and writing, and has taught ESL/EFL in the USA and Yemen. Her research interests include comparative analysis of Japanese/English written and spoken discourse and development of L2 academic writing and pragmatic competence. She has published articles in the *Journal of Pragmatics* and *the Modern Language Journal*, co-authored with Hiroe Kobayashi.

Julio Roca de Larios is Associate Professor at the University of Murcia, Spain, where he works in initial EFL teacher education. His research interests include the analysis of writing processes, classroom interaction processes and the development of appropriate tools and strategies to foster reflective practice among student teachers. His work on foreign language writing has appeared in *Language Learning, the Modern Language Journal, Learning and Instruction* and the *Journal of Second Language Writing.*

Miyuki Sasaki is Professor in the Faculty of Foreign Studies at Nagoya Gakuin University, where she teaches graduate and undergraduate courses in EFL and applied linguistics. She received her MAs in TESL from Hiroshima University and Georgetown University, and her PhD in

Applied Linguistics from the University of California, Los Angeles. She is currently interested in the longitudinal development of L2 writing ability and motivation, as well as method factors in L2 testing.

Rob Schoonen is Associate Professor at the Amsterdam Center for Language and Communication, Faculty of Humanities of the University of Amsterdam. His main research interests are second and foreign language acquisition, psycholinguistics, research methodology and language testing, especially in relation to vocabulary knowledge and writing proficiency.

Patrick Snellings is Assistant Professor in the School of Psychology, Department of Psychology at the University of Amsterdam. His research interests include learning disabilities such as developmental dyslexia, (second) language acquisition, cognitive development, skill acquisition and school-based interventions.

Marie Stevenson lectures in applied linguistics and language education at the University of Sydney. Her main areas of research are second language reading and writing processes, and she has published in these areas in various international journals. She is a member of the TESOL Research Network.

Amos van Gelderen is Senior Researcher at the SCO-Kohnstamm Institute of the University of Amsterdam. His areas of interest include L1/L2 language learning and education, language awareness, and interrelations between the abilities of speaking, writing, reading and listening. He is currently involved in an international project investigating the literacy development of adolescents in multilingual contexts and a project into the effects of self-regulatory instruction and training in lexical fluency on writing in bilingual education.

Acknowledgements

All edited books are the result of a collective enterprise. This one has been so in very special ways and I would like to express my sincere gratitude to all the contributors for helping me shape the vision I had for our joint endeavour and for making the book a reality. I would also like to thank them for their diligence in writing and repeatedly rewriting their chapters, for always keeping to deadlines and for their generosity in reviewing each other's chapters. My sincere gratitude also goes to Ilona Leki for having accepted to write the Preface.

I am also grateful to the anonymous reviewer who read an earlier version of the manuscript and who helped us all to improve our chapters and the book as a whole. I wish to express my appreciation of the help and support by Multilingual Matters: the series editor David Singleton, Marjukka Grover, Tommi Grover, Anna Roderick, Sarah Williams and Elinor Robertson have all helped in different ways in the completion of this publishing project.

Lastly, my heartfelt thanks to my family, Chris, Laura, Beatriz and Helena, for their sustained, sincere and loving support and encouragement in all the projects I decide to undertake.

Preface

As language scholars, teachers and learners around the world increasingly focus their attention on issues related to writing in a second language (SL), the publication of *Writing in Foreign Language Contexts: Learning, Teaching, and Research* is a much needed and welcome bracer for L2 writing research. It firmly reminds us that L2 writing does not take place only in SL contexts, that is, where the target language is widely used outside the classroom. Far greater numbers of L2 writers reside, learn and write in foreign language (FL) environments. Ignoring the research contributions that come out of these contexts and failing to consider writing practices in FL settings badly distorts our understanding of L2 writing.

Writing in Foreign Language Contexts: Learning, Teaching, and Research is unique in its focus on FL writing, and that focus alone would make the collection an important contribution to the field of L2 writing research. But this volume is not the average edited collection with disparate and uneven contributions, some aimed too narrowly, some too broadly. Instead *Writing in Foreign Language Contexts: Learning, Teaching, and Research* is an unusually coherent, thorough and rigorous examination of research on FL writing. Rosa Manchón's fine editorial guidance is evident in the careful organization of the chapters of the text. Each chapter of the two main sections follows similar, though by no means monotonous or lockstep, patterns. In each chapter of the first section, the authors begin by retrospectively re-examining their own repertoire of research studies on FL writing (covering a variety of FL settings and learner proficiencies, ages and uses for L2 writing), then trace the methodological choices that guided that body of work, and, finally, use that contextualization to foreground their more recent studies or reflections. Readers will find the flexible regularity of this 'looking back, moving forward' approach innovative and helpful in drawing attention to the important trends and main findings of the high quality research on FL writing clearly and yet succinctly highlighted here.

A particularly innovative feature of *Writing in Foreign Language Contexts: Learning, Teaching, and Research* is the unique window it provides into the thinking processes of the researchers. Because the individual pieces of research discussed were often a part of long-term research projects (whether initiated that way or not), we are afforded insights not only into the kinds of methods that the researchers used, but also into their decision-making as each segment of the project yielded information that led the researchers toward the next methodologically appropriate step.

The chapters of the second part of *Writing in Foreign Language Contexts: Learning, Teaching, and Research* are broader reflections on and analyses of the findings of the first part, critically and imaginatively reshuffling them to bring out further perspectives made possible by this juxtapositioning. The authors' frequent references to the other chapters throughout the book contribute to a sense of unity without the artificiality that sometimes plagues this rhetorical move in other texts. The annotated and unannotated bibliography of the last section contributes a final piece that L2 writing scholars and students alike will find themselves turning to repeatedly.

Although language professionals and applied linguists have long noted the distinction between SL and FL learning contexts, it is a distinction that has been insufficiently heeded in L2 writing studies, which have instead been perhaps more concerned with marking the similarities and differences between L2 and L1 writing and writing instruction. Yet, many features of specifically FL writing contexts distinguish them from SL settings and vary across the FL contexts. These features are forcefully foregrounded in *Writing in Foreign Language Contexts: Learning, Teaching, and Research.* As the authors of the chapters of this book emphasize, among other features, in FL settings:

- It is likely that the linguistic, social, cultural and particularly educational backgrounds of the FL students are fairly uniform. This leveling may benefit research by reducing the linguistic and literacy variability among research participants.
- Some of these instructed learners will have had the opportunity to interact with and learn about L2 speakers and their cultures in, for example, study-abroad experiences; others will not have had any dealings with them at all. This differential opportunity has a likely impact on learner proficiency and motivation. Yet, that impact is shown here to play out differently for different groups of learners.
- Educational systems across the globe attend to L1 writing instruction to different degrees so that some students become fairly proficient L1 writers through schooling; others do not. L1 writing

proficiency is one of the many factors that correlate with L2 writing proficiency.

- The social value a particular society places on writing and on the role writing or learning to write is hoped to play in a given society differs. If, for instance, in North American SL settings, learning to write in L1 is conceived in school-sponsored writing mainly as taking and defending a position, then writers will develop certain approaches and attitudes toward writing that differ from the ones developed in cultures or societies where the ability to write or facility in writing is constructed primarily as, for instance, a general sign of a well-rounded education, the ability to self-reflect, personal originality or creativity, moral virtue, patriotic enthusiasm or any number of other orientations. Why a particular society wants its young people to learn to write in L1, if it does, influences the valuing of, approach to and interest in L2 writing that these learners absorb and reflect.
- As L2 writing is less likely to be a survival tool in FL than in SL contexts, motivation to write may be entirely extrinsic and explicit, never more than an obedient response to teacher-set assignments and perceived by the student writers as having no further role whatsoever in their lives.
- Contrary to dogma in SL writing, with its now-traditional de-emphasis of language learning, using writing to develop language proficiency may be a central aim of L2 writing in FL settings.

In considering these issues, the contributors explore FL writers' educational and social experiences in both L1 and L2 writing that drive learner attitudes, which, in turn, influence the variable efforts that the writers as agents are willing to expend to exploit the L2 writing resources available to them. Other influences on FL writing explored here include writers' access to the TL environment and the writers' potential creation of imagined TL communities; age of initiation into L2 literacy; attentional demands of writing tasks and writer allocation of cognitive resources while writing; and the impact of the spread of interest in L2 writing on different populations, such as scholars, English teachers and teacher educators, as well as ministries of education who determine education and language education policy. Consideration of these kinds of issues demonstrates the more comprehensive importance of FL writing studies to theory, research and learning. The chapters of this book explore these and many other subtle and sometimes forgotten or ignored aspects of FL writing that require approaches to research and pedagogy that cannot simply be imported in from SL writing domains.

In addition to challenging tenets of SL writing research and pedagogy, *Writing in Foreign Language Contexts: Learning, Teaching, and Research* responds to increased calls for an extension of second language acquisition (SLA) research beyond oral data to data from written sources. Such written sources arguably are especially well-suited to studying SLA because of their stability and their capacity for capturing the writer's hypotheses about and compensations for gaps in L2. Furthermore, they yield findings that are particular not only to FL versus SL settings, but also to written versus oral language forms. The findings touch on such issues as what might be the optimal age of exposure to L2 literacy (e.g. that late starting learners may outperform early starters not only initially, but also ultimately) or whether in producing the L2, overloaded cognitive capacities and linguistic capacities compete with or complement each other. These kinds of findings present a challenge to current assumptions about SLA that have been built from primarily oral data.

Like many calls to broaden research perspectives (from L1 writing to L2 writing, or from SLA in monolingual societies to SLA in multilingual societies), *Writing in Foreign Language Contexts: Learning, Teaching, and Research* invites us to step back and rethink what we believe we know about L2 writing. I feel I can say with confidence that even readers who have followed developments in FL writing closely, including those readers who are familiar with the published works the authors critically examine here, will be astonished at how much more they learn from this collection and how compelling the organization and presentation is. Each chapter reaches the highest standards of excellence. Given the high quality of the research discussed, the excellent writing and the carefully considered positions taken in this volume, accepting the book's invitation to thoroughly examine FL contexts brings not only enlightenment, but also true pleasure and even inspiration.

Ilona Leki
University of Tennessee

Introduction
Broadening the Perspective of L2 Writing Scholarship: The Contribution of Research on Foreign Language Writing

ROSA M. MANCHÓN

In 1997, Tony Silva, Ilona Leki and Joan Carson published a committed paper entitled 'Broadening the perspective of mainstream composition studies', in which they denounced the narrow and limited scope of the disciplinary inquiry in this area. Their main argument was that composition studies had neglected second language (SL) writing theory and research, a limitation that, in their view, had important theoretical and pedagogical implications. They reasoned that 'a theory of composition that looks only at English writers, readers, texts, and contexts is an extremely narrow one' (Silva *et al.*, 1997: 424), hence the need to overcome the monolingual and monocultural bias of composition studies by opening the field up to research that concerned itself with 'how different writers learn to deal with variable demands in various situations'. In their view, this research agenda entailed going beyond the 'political borders of North America' (Silva *et al.*, 1997: 424).

At this juncture in the history of the discipline, it might be appropriate to continue the disciplinary dialogue initiated by Silva, Leki and Carson over 10 years ago, this time exposing a similar limited perspective on writers, writing contexts and writing practices in mainstream SL writing research: just as composition research had neglected SL writing scholarship, so has the latter partly ignored foreign language (FL) writing theory and research. This is why voices have been raised to denounce a collegially tolerated SL-bias of official L2[1] writing discourse (cf. Manchón & DeHaan, 2008a; Ortega, 2004). In support of this contention, until recently, overviews of the field hardly accounted for the potential contribution of insights gained in FL writing studies to SL writing scholarship (for exceptions, see Cumming, 2001; Leki *et al.*, 2006, 2008; Silva & Brice, 2004). Similarly, mainstream pedagogical discussions have rarely debated whether or not instructional recommendations for SL contexts apply to FL settings, or acknowledged (much less endorsed) the right of those in charge of writing policies and practices in FL contexts to question, or resist (should this be the case), pedagogies developed for SL writing (see Casanave, this volume; Leki [2001] for educationally committed positions on this issue).

Important theoretical and pedagogical implications derive from this state of affairs. As noted by Ortega (2004: 8), the SL-bias of writing scholarship 'diminishes the capacity of L2 writing as a field to produce theoretically robust knowledge that can be useful in improving L2 writing across different settings'. Yet, as attested by several contributions to the present volume, the manner in which writing is learned and taught in FL contexts is dependent upon a whole set of material conditions and social practices that do not necessarily coincide with those of SL contexts. Particularly, FL contexts show their own idiosyncrasy regarding the role that writing plays (or can play) in the lives of students and teachers. In this respect, some groups of FL writers must *learn to write* for professional or academic reasons, just like many of their SL counterparts. This would be the case of academics who feel the imperative to publish internationally (see Flowerdew and Li, this volume); of university students for whom learning to write is crucial to success in their degree studies at home or in preparation for study-abroad experiences (see Rinnert & Kobayashi, and Sasaki, this volume); or of students educated in Content and Language Integrated Learning (CLIL) programmes, a popular educational approach across the world and certainly in Europe under the auspices of the European Centre for Modern Languages of the Council of Europe. However, in addition to these students and professionals who *learn to write*, another large number of FL writers *write to learn* (the language), and this may be a unique FL situation that stands in sharp contrast with writing practices in SL contexts, a setting in which 'writing to learn' is more specifically associated with learning content – not language – in 'writing across the curriculum' programs. The recognition of these distinctive characteristics of the FL context led Harklau (2002: 345) to the conclusion that 'it is important to investigate how L2 learners learn how to write, but it is just as important to learn more about the instrumental role that writing can play in the acquisition of a second language in educational settings'.

The situated and varied nature of writing practices in FL contexts also has important practical implications, especially in areas such as teacher education (as discussed by Casanave), as well as important ideological and ethical dimensions. In this respect, Leki (2001) recently drew our attention to the various institutional consequences of introducing writing into school programs in English non-dominant countries, such as 'the need to justify the large investment required on the part of institutions and individuals in order to teach L2 writing, the right to resist center imposed materials and methods, the need for a dialogue with students about the role of writing in their lives, and the need to make L2 writing enhance learner options rather than limit them' (Leki, 2001: 197).

In the article mentioned in the opening paragraph, Silva *et al.* (1997) suggested that the aim of our disciplinary inquiry is to search for answers to questions regarding how various student populations learn to deal with the demands of writing in a variety of contexts and situations. Therefore, it seems appropriate to 'cross the border' (to use their own words) of university-level and adult (professional) SL writers (the focal population in mainstream SL writing research), texts, contexts, writing practices and writing instruction in an attempt to open the field to critical discussions of a whole range of theoretical, applied and ethical dimensions of learning, teaching and researching writing in FL contexts. Various recent initiatives in this direction point to a shift in the field. For instance, the presence of FL studies in the *Journal of Second Language Writing* has substantially increased from the turn of the century onwards (see Ortega, this volume) and the Journal featured a special guest-edited issue on FL writing in 2008 (Manchón & DeHaan, 2008a). Similarly, the theme of the 2008 Symposium on Second Language Writing was 'Foreign Language Writing Instruction: Principles and Practices', a choice on the part of the organizers based on the recognition that SL research 'has overshadowed work on L2 writing done in the foreign language (FL) context', a situation that the Symposium attempted to remedy (http://www.sslw2008.org/).

This book is another initiative to put FL contexts on the scene. It pursues one basic aim: to reflect critically on where we are now and where we need to go next in our exploration of FL writing at the levels of theory, research and pedagogy. This justifies the two parts into which the book is divided: 'Looking back' and 'Looking ahead'. Regarding the looking-back perspective, although not sufficiently visible in the official discourse, we now have a substantial body of knowledge arising from empirical investigations undertaken by scholars with a continuous involvement in various research programs on learning and teaching writing in diverse geographical, educational and professional FL settings. These colleagues (whose contributions make up Part 1) kindly accepted the challenge to re-examine critically their own research, the ultimate aim of this collective critical reflection being to arrive at a *situated understanding of writing practices in FL instructional settings*. The book is also intended as an attempt to move forward, i.e. as a critical reflection on *what lies ahead in terms of theory, research and pedagogy*, a task that three colleagues with ample experience in the field also kindly agreed to undertake. Their contributions make up Part 2. In addition, the book features a comprehensive bibliography of empirical studies on FL writing in which Melinda Reichelt offers a panorama of the disciplinary inquiry in the area over the last 10 years, including works from geographical areas and educational levels that have not achieved sufficient visibility in mainstream discussions of L2 writing research.

In the overview that follows, I first summarize the orientation and content of the different chapters in the book, and then I highlight the main problems addressed by the contributors regarding the past and the future in the three areas that make up the title of the book.

An Overview of the Book

The chapters in Part 1 offer accounts of both the inquiry process followed and the main insights gained in various long-term programs of research. I asked each author or research team to focus on specific themes running across their studies, and they all follow a common pattern in the analysis of their research efforts over the years: they contextualize their research in L2 writing scholarship, present the rationale for their disciplinary inquiry, explain the methodology of their programs of research, fully discuss their main findings, and draw implications for theory, research and/or pedagogy. The result is that, as noted by Cumming in Chapter 8, these contributions 'tell us as much about foreign language writing as they do about the efforts, achievements, and challenges of doing research on this topic' (p. 222).

The first two chapters present the insights obtained in two programs of research conducted with Japanese English as a foreign language (EFL) writers. In Chapter 1, Carol Rinnert and Hiroe Kobayashi contribute an examination of their research on FL writing in order to explore the role of previous L1 (Japanese) and L2 (English) instruction and experience in the development of writing ability. This reanalysis of their empirical findings leads them to several observations in three main areas. First, their research reveals the significant influence that the writers' prior L1 and L2 writing experience and instruction exerts on both the development of writing ability and the shaping of the L2 writer's attitudes towards writing. Second, they explore their empirical data with respect to the transfer of skills across languages, which they found to take place in both directions and to depend on various individual and social factors. Third, they delve into the dynamic nature of writing practices in FL contexts, which they claim to be related to changing social conditions and the individual writer's perceptions of FL writing. Rinnert and Kobayasi also suggest a number of far-reaching theoretical and pedagogical implications of these findings. At the level of theory, they claim that past writing experience should be included as a major factor in a theoretical model of developing writing competence, whereas at the level of pedagogy, they emphasize the centrality of writing students' prior training in pedagogical decision making. In addition, an important contribution of Rinnert and Kobayashi's chapter is represented by the testable hypotheses they put forward regarding the manner in which multicompetent L2 users resort to their various languages and knowledge sources in L2 composing, an issue that runs through several other chapters (Celaya & Navés, Cumming, Manchón *et al.*, Ortega, Schoonen *et al.*).

In Chapter 2, Miyuki Sasaki first guides us through the dynamics of her disciplinary inquiry into FL writing in the last 10 years in terms of the issues she has looked into, the methodology she has employed, and the theoretical frameworks that have informed her research. She then presents an empirical study in which, in addition to testing hypotheses formulated on the basis of her previous research, she examined longitudinally the changes in L2 writing motivation and writing expertise of a group of Japanese EFL university student writers as a function of their educational experiences (comparing staying-at-home and study-abroad experiences) during a 3.5-year period. Based on her data, Sasaki concludes that writing development in a FL context appears to be dependent on the combination of two sets of factors: the possibility of acquiring metaknowledge about writing and engaging in writing practice, on the one hand, and the development of motivation to improve one's own writing, on the other. In line with some suggestions made by Rinnert and Kobayashi, Sasaki contends that in FL contexts, such motivation is dependent upon the formation of 'L2-related imagined communities', an outcome of overseas experience in her own research. The study therefore sheds light on three areas. First, we learn about the development of L2 writing competence in study-abroad programmes, a common educational experience in FL contexts that, surprisingly, has received only marginal attention in L2 writing scholarship. It should also be noted that equal scant attention has been paid to the study of writing in study-abroad research. Second, we gain insights into the influence of situational variables on the dynamics of motivation in FL contexts, a much-needed approach to understanding motivation in second language acquisition (SLA) (Dörnyei, 2005). Finally, Sasaki's research continues a recent line of inquiry into goals in L2 writing initiated by Cumming (2006), in her case shedding light on the same issue in a FL context.

Chapters 3 and 4 account for two programs of research that have investigated the processing dimension of composing, and both are representative of what Ortega and Carson (2009) term 'SLA-oriented writing research'. Another common characteristic is that these two groups of researchers approached the study of writing by comparing their EFL writers' composing processes in their L1 and L2.

In Chapter 3, Rob Schoonen, Patrick Snellings, Marie Stevenson and Amos van Gelderen contextualize and synthesize their research (the Nelson Project) into L1 and L2 writing by Dutch secondary school students. They describe a variety of complementary studies within the Project, including a large-scale longitudinal study, an in-depth think-aloud and keystroke study, and an intervention study intended to enhance lexical retrieval. When accounting for these various studies, they focus on the interplay between cognitive and linguistic resources in writing and relate their findings in this area to models of L1 and FL writing processes. One of the main outcomes of their research is the discovery that FL writing is more local and language-oriented than L1 composing. Based on their findings in this domain, they put forward the 'Inhibition Hypothesis', according to which the resource-demanding nature of linguistic processing in FL composing will limit the possibility of attending to other aspects of text production, such as content concerns or general textual features. In line with Rinnert and Kobayashi, and Sasaki, they also found that more general metacognitive knowledge about writing and text characteristics is also associated with proficient writing, both in L1 and FL; hence the strong correlation they obtained between L1 and FL writing proficiency. This finding is additional evidence in support of Rinnert and Kobayashi's claims regarding the interplay of L1 and L2 knowledge sources and skills in FL writing, this time with data from a younger population than the participants in Rinnert and Kobayashi's research and from a different FL context.

Further confirmation for Schoonen *et al.*'s findings regarding the more labor-intensive nature of L2 composing comes from the insights gained in the long-term programme of research on Spanish EFL learners at various proficiency and educational levels reported by Rosa Manchón, Julio Roca de Larios and Liz Murphy in Chapter 4. The main aim of this research was to investigate cognitive activity in L1 and L2 writing as a function of writer-related and task-related factors. The discussion revolves around two main themes: the problem-solving nature of composing activity, on the one hand, and the temporal dimension of writing processes, on the other. In accounting for their findings in these two areas, Manchón, Roca de Larios and Murphy delve into important issues in cognitively oriented accounts of writing, such as the internal structure of the process of converting ideas into language (which appears to be more time- and attention-consuming in the L2 condition), the purported recursive nature of composing (which was found to be proficiency-dependent), or the strategic behavior engaged in while writing (which in FL writing involves conspicuous recourse to the various resources in the L2 writer's linguistic repertoire). The researchers discuss their findings from various perspectives, one of them being the consideration of L2 writers as multicompetent language users (a perspective also adopted by Rinnert and Kobayashi) and conclude that FL writing is a truly bilingual event. They also stress the close interaction between the FL writer's composing and linguistic competence, an issue that in the FL context can be more fully explored, they maintain, when learner-internal and learner-external factors are jointly combined in the analysis.

Part I includes three more chapters that shed light on what Cumming (this volume) calls the 'macro-level of policy issues in foreign language education'. In Chapter 5, M. Luz Celaya and Teresa Navés report on their longitudinal inquiry into FL writing, thus complementing the longitudinal data reported in Sasaki's chapter, in their case from a 'macro' perspective. This research was part of a more general investigation on age-related differences in a multilingual, FL context, namely, the BAF Project, in which Catalan-Spanish EFL learners were investigated throughout their entire primary and secondary school education. Celaya and Navés frame their discussion around three issues. Two are theoretical in nature: the analysis of writing as a tool to gauge L2 development across different age groups (focusing on younger writers than those investigated in mainstream L2 writing research), and the examination of the use of the L1 in L2 writing (particularly lexical transfer). The other issue discussed (related to research methodology) is their search for the best instruments with which to measure written attainment by low proficiency school-age learners. As in the case of other chapters in the book, the insights gained in these three areas are relevant to both SLA and writing research. Thus, their findings add further support to (i) the empirical evidence in favor of 'the older, the better' in FL acquisitional contexts (since they found that those students who started their FL education at a later age systematically appeared to write better texts in their L2 than those who started at an earlier age); and (ii) what other chapters in the volume (and elsewhere) have discovered regarding multilingual L2 writers' recourse to their various languages while composing.

Chapter 6 includes the contribution by John Flowerdew and Yongyan Li, in which they take us into another geographical and sociocultural setting and another line of inquiry with their focus on the efforts of academics in mainland China and Hong Kong to publish in English as a necessary requisite for their professional advancement. Flowerdew and Li first explore in detail their inquiry process (which is characterized by multidimensional triangulations in terms of theoretical frameworks, issues and methods, a position related to the notion of 'glocalization') through a series of naturalistic case studies featuring academics writing for international publication. They then summarize the main findings of their research by noting that scholars in EFL contexts face particular challenges, not only because of a language barrier, but also from other sociopolitical and economic forces created in the processes of globalization. Flowerdew and Li discuss the theoretical, methodological and pedagogical implications of their findings, noting how their research contributes to opening the field of L2 writing to more grounded descriptions of new populations and contexts. In this respect, their chapter links up with other chapters in the book by highlighting the theme of the situatedness of writing (in this case, the sociopolitical nature of scholarly writing and publication) in EFL contexts, as well as the diversity inherent in FL writing, an issue further explored in Reichelt's chapter as well as in Cumming's and Ortega's contributions in Part 2.

The closing chapter in Part 1 contains Melinda Reichelt's wide-ranging account of FL writing instruction around the world, including a synthesis of her own program of research into FL writing teaching in North America and in some countries in Europe, as well as a summary review of the research conducted in other countries in Asia and Europe. Reichelt's analysis focuses on the impact of various sociohistorical and educational factors on both teaching policies/practices and teacher education, including the following: the role and status of the FL in the teaching context; local attitudes towards the FL; students' needs and goals regarding writing in the FL; cultural-specific educational values; L1 writing pedagogical practices; economic, cultural and political factors; and the availability of EFL writing materials, technology and qualified teachers. This analysis sheds light on the range of sociocultural factors that shape the purposes and values of FL writing instruction around the world, and, as argued by several contributors, is further evidence of the diversity that characterizes FL writing. Reichelt concludes that, in view of the accumulated evidence regarding the manner in which local factors shape FL instruction, 'FL specialists, curriculum developers and language planners should consider the specifics of their particular context in making decisions about FL writing instruction' (p. 202), a position also endorsed in the three chapters in Part 2.

As mentioned earlier, the chapters in Part 2 were conceived as a move forward in FL theory, research and pedagogy. Once the chapters in Part 1 were completed, they were passed on to the contributors of Part 2, who then incorporated their insights into their own chapters. Common to these three contributions is a retrospective look at the available empirical research (particularly the research reported in Part 1) and at professional experiences as a springboard to move forward in theory, research and pedagogy.

In Chapter 8, Alister Cumming first looks back to studies of FL education in the 1970s to establish how far research in the present volume has come in conceptualizing the complexities of writing in FL. Then, looking at the research reported in the seven chapters in Part 1, he observes how it asserts (i) the distinctiveness of FL writing (particularly regarding the nature of the interplay between contextual and individual factors, as well as the variability inherent in such interplay across diverse FL contexts and dimensions of writing); (ii) the importance of writing in English (and the concomitant expansion in expectations for and about writing in FL education); (iii) the multicomponential nature of writing and languages (including 'micro- and macro-components and processes that complement and interact with one another at multiple levels of texts, language systems, individual writers, and educational and social contexts'); and (iv) reflexivity about research (as manifested in the contributors' reflections on the dynamics of their enquiry processes over the years). Looking to future inquiry, Cumming suggests that it needs to continue to pursue the improvement of local educational policies and conditions, primarily by (i) using theories to interrelate the psycholinguistic and sociolinguistic dimensions of writing (a task that, in his view, entails adopting new theoretical perspectives and research perspectives); (ii) expanding definitions of literacy (of which, Cumming argues, composition writing in a FL is just one component); and (iii) reorienting the pedagogical functions of assessment, going beyond a testing approach so that a stronger link is established between assessment practices and pedagogical choices.

In Chapter 9, Lourdes Ortega looks back at both the body of available research on FL writing (including the publication patterns of flagship journals during the last 16 years, as well as the research programs synthesized in Part 1), and she offers a personal analysis of some threads that run through cognitive, textual-linguistic, social and educational dimensions of EFL writing. She then looks ahead and offers a critical reflection on the kinds of research that will be needed in the future in order to keep our knowledge of FL writing advancing at the levels of theory, research and pedagogy. Issues for further research include (i) researching the values and purposes of FL writing pedagogies (an area in which she discusses issues related to feedback, motivation, and the writing-to-learn and learning-to-write perspectives mentioned above); (ii) ascertaining the nature of FL writing instruction (along the explicit-implicit continuum) in view of the diversity inherent in FL contexts; and (iii) exploring the individual and social forces that shape the way FL writers make use of their knowledge sources and skills. She further argues that, in order for research on FL writing to advance theories and practices in L2 writing, work in the area must continue to employ the methods used up to now and also expand research methodologies, as well as to investigate a wider range of acquisitional contexts.

In the closing chapter, Christine Pearson Casanave focuses on FL writing pedagogy and, more precisely, on the question of FL writing teacher education, an issue almost absent in pedagogical discussions on L2 writing. Casanave analyzes some of the realities of teaching writing in FL contexts and the implications these realities have for the education of writing teachers in English-dominant teacher education programs. Informed by an ecological perspective on language teaching, Casanave maintains that there are benefits to be gained from balancing the local realities of EFL teachers and teacher educators with an idealistic view of their work. She argues her point by reviewing some existing literature on the issue, and by providing a vivid account of the views and experiences of a group of students in Teachers of English to Speakers of Other Languages (TESOL) programs who were also working teachers in Japan. To this she adds a reflection on her own efforts and values in teaching these TESOL programs. Based on this evidence, she concludes with some suggestions for language teacher education programs, particularly regarding (i) the actual content of MATESOL courses; (ii) the need to take principled decisions regarding what to teach and how to teach in FL writing programs; and, in line with the suggestions of other contributors,

(iii) the need to decenter L2 research from its traditional English-dominant university settings, and to open it to new contexts and peoples. The idea, as Casanave puts it, would be for 'EFL writing educators and teachers to observe closely the local needs and realities of their particular settings rather than prescribing fixed teacher education curricula for future EFL writing teachers'.

Learning, teaching and researching writing in FL contexts: Looking back and looking ahead

Different messages emerge from the book regarding where we are now and where we need to go next in our search for answers in the realms of learning, teaching and researching FL writing.

Learning FL writing: Looking back

The accumulated empirical evidence allows us to reach some conclusions in three main domains. First, we must acknowledge *the diversity that characterizes FL writing in terms of writing processes, textual outputs and pedagogical approaches*: FL writing is learned for multiple purposes, in various sociocultural contexts, each one shaped by its own sociohistorical factors and educational purposes and values, and by different writers who must learn to deal with variable demands in various educational and professional situations. This is why Ortega (this volume) rightly warns us that 'we should take great care to avoid the pitfall of treating teachers, writers, and writing contexts across studies as belonging to an undifferentiated, homogeneous contextual class of "FL" or "EFL"' (p. 250).

Second, various chapters in the book shed light on the *range and interplay of social, linguistic and cognitive variables that appear to shape the development of writing ability over time in FL contexts*. The contexts in which FL writers write and learn to write shape their metacognitive knowledge about composing and textual conventions, their conception of writing, motives for writing and, consequently, their approach to writing. Some educational factors that appear to mediate the development of writing ability include the kinds and amount of instruction received, as well as the type and amount of writing practice engaged in. Particularly relevant in this respect are the insights gained in the research conducted by Sasaki and by Rinnert and Kobayashi into the influence exerted by study-abroad experiences on students' goals and motivation for writing, and in the development of their confidence in their own capabilities. In line with these findings, it is important to stress, as Ortega does, the dynamics of change in the texts produced by FL writers depending on the sociocultural contexts in which they write and learn to write, as opposed to viewing 'what our students know as a static knowledge base deterministically stemming [...] from their cultural affiliation' (Ortega, this volume).

As for the interplay of linguistic and cognitive factors in the development of writing ability, the empirical evidence shows that FL writing is a true problem-solving task. This labor-intensive nature of L2 composing entails the solution of numerous linguistic problems (thus making FL writing much more language-oriented than L1 writing) and, at least at some levels of L2 proficiency, creates a tension in attentional demands. Understanding this problem-solving activity has certainly contributed to theorizing in the field (as noted in various contributions), but the issue also has an important ethical dimension (as noted, for instance, in the discussion of academics' publishing efforts), as well as crucial implications for pedagogy, particularly regarding the content of FL writing instruction and the preparation of FL writing teachers and EAP specialists.

Third, another main conclusion to be drawn from the research reported in the book relates to *the multilingual nature of FL writing*. We learn in various contributions that transfer is an ever-present phenomenon in FL writing, that transfer is bidirectional, and that it includes transfer of knowledge, skills and, very importantly, the use of the writer's total linguistic repertoire at product and process levels. This general conclusion has important implications for a theory of L2 writing (which cannot obviate the multicompetent nature of FL writers and the multilingual nature of FL writing) and also for the long-standing study of transfer in language production within SLA research, an area of inquiry in which claims about transfer derive in great part from research on oral communication.

Learning FL writing: Moving forward

Various avenues for future research are suggested in the book. One relates to the investigation of new languages, new contexts and new uses of writing from those so far investigated. Cumming advocates expanding conceptualizations of 'literacy that link conventional school-based and academic tasks to new technologies, multimedia communications and diverse notions of literacy at work and in society', as well exploring the relationship between reading and writing in FL contexts. Ortega claims that future research must explore 'a wide range of school, university, workplace, and virtual settings across diverse geographical and institutional FL contexts'. Flowerdew and Li remind us of the relevance that grounded investigation of advanced academic literacy experiences in various parts of the world may have for theory building. Finally, Casanave argues in favor of opening up L2 writing research to new populations and contexts.

Another area of future research relates to the instrumental role that writing can play in the language learning experience of FL writers. From a theoretical perspective, investigating the language learning potential of writing in FL contexts is not only relevant in L2 writing research, but also in SLA research, particularly in relation to the theory and research on the role of output practice in the acquisition of an additional language (as discussed recently in Manchón [forthcoming], Manchón & Roca de Larios [2007] and Muranoi [2007]. See also Ortega, this volume).

In addition to these new research avenues, future research must also delve further into some of the issues investigated up to now. For instance, Schoonen *et al.* contend that the Inhibition Hypothesis must be put to empirical test with more proficient writers and more cognitively demanding tasks. The explicit or implicit nature and content of the metaknowledge acquired by FL writers in their learning experiences (see Ortega) also merits further exploration. Various contributors (particularly Rinnert and Kobayashi, and Manchón *et al.*) suggest some empirical questions worth investigating in relation to the manner in which FL writers (at various levels of L2 proficiency and writing expertise) resort to their various languages and the purposes for which they do so. Finally, the research program initiated by Flowerdew and Li on the scholarly publication experiences of academics has opened up various avenues worth exploring in the future regarding the ethical, linguistic, cultural and sociopolitical dimensions of the discursive activities of these EFL writers. As noted by Flowerdew and Li, and Ortega, an important area of future research would be the study of academics' attempts 'to contribute their voice in international academia, despite potential discursive and non-discursive obstacles' (Flowerdew & Li: 170).

Teaching FL writing: Looking back

As mentioned earlier, a general consensus of the research reported in Part 1 is that FL writing instruction appears to be varied and locally situated, and thus shaped by various sociohistorical and educational values. Reichelt's review of teaching practices around the world reveals the various purposes of FL writing instruction, including the development of language skills as well as intellectual abilities related to critical thinking and cultural literacy. FL writing instruction, therefore, has to be understood as situated practice, which in essence means, as several contributors point out (Casanave, Cumming, Ortega, Reichelt), that theoretical and pedagogical discussions in the area need to acknowledge the diversity and variability that characterizes the range of contexts in which a variety of student and teacher populations learn and teach FL writing.

Various contributors have also shed light on the question of writing teacher preparation, an area that has attracted very little attention in official pedagogical discourse. Reichelt documents the variability observed in the professional training for FL writing that teachers in various settings receive and the influence that such instruction may have on these teachers' pedagogical decision making. To this, Casanave adds an analysis (perhaps the first ever) of the challenges faced by those writing teachers who do receive such professional training, when they try to accommodate what they have learned in their teacher education programs to the local realities of the FL contexts in which they teach. As she explains, the result is more often than not a mismatch between the teachers' pedagogical ideas and the pedagogical and political realities of local EFL contexts.

Teaching FL writing: Moving forward

A whole research program for the future emerges from the book. This includes questions in three main areas: the joint work between teachers and learners, the nature and purposes of writing instruction and questions of writing teacher education.

Regarding the first dimension, areas worthy of further exploration are the development of FL students' motivation to write, feedback issues, and the purposes and functions of assessment. As for motivational issues, Sasaki's findings call for a search for ways to induce long-lasting motivation in FL instructional contexts. In addition, given the beneficial effects of study-abroad experiences on the development of motivation to improve FL writing, and given also that not all FL writers can enjoy these overseas experiences, an ethical commitment would be to look for ways to create similar potentially motivating learning environments in the home contexts where FL writers live and write. Regarding the question of motivation, Ortega also points out that future research must disclose the possible dilemmas between attempts to increase the learners' motivation to write, and similar attempts to foster L2 development via writing practice.

Feedback is another area in which many open questions exist, as noted by Ortega and Cumming. In contrast to the attention that it has enjoyed in SL writing research, the study of feedback is certainly an under-researched area in FL writing. Future studies therefore need to explore feedback issues specifically in relation to sociocultural contexts other than those within the borders of university-level writing centers and writing courses in English-dominant countries. What is more, the question of 'focus on form' (cf. Doughty, 2001; Doughty & Williams, 1998) – of which the issue of feedback is an important part – acquires special significance in the FL context, a setting in which the L2 input made available to the L2 learner is limited in quality and quantity, and a context in which attempts to speed up language learning via intentional (versus incidental) learning makes much pedagogical sense.

Closely related to the learner's motivation and the forms and functions of feedback is the new orientation of the purposes and values of assessment suggested by Cumming, an issue that also bears upon another macroarea for further exploration: that of teacher education. Casanave deals with the issue in depth and she offers a number of proposals that, in essence, advocate informing professional development by ecological approaches to language teaching. This approach would entail reorienting the content of teacher education programs so that prospective writing teachers become fully aware of the realities of the varied teaching contexts subsumed under the umbrella term of FL classrooms, develop abilities to cope with these varied realities, acting flexibly as reflective practitioners and, ultimately, engage in pedagogical decision making aimed at enhancing learner's options. In this respect, Flowerdew and Li add a further suggestion, this time regarding academics' publishing efforts with the help of English for academic purposes (EAP) professionals acting as 'mediators of literacy'.

Closely linked to the issue of teacher professional development are the various areas for future study suggested in relation to the nature and purposes of writing instruction. The general message is a plea for locally appropriate practices. When deciding on these, questions to be considered include the dual option of writing-to-learn and learning-to-write instructional approaches (Casanave, Ortega); the question of the explicit-implicit nature of instruction (Ortega); and various issues related to the functions of feedback and assessment practices mentioned above. Cumming adds the investigation of the political dimensions of individual writing and mass education as further items on the research agenda.

Researching FL writing: Looking back

One of the possible merits of this collection is the wide variety of contexts and language combinations investigated in the research reported in Part 1. The book features empirical studies that exemplify how FL writing is learned (by FL learners with Eastern and Western native languages, including different age groups, as well as various L2 proficiency levels and degrees of writing expertise) and practised in different geographical (in Asia, America and Europe) and instructional contexts (covering the whole spectrum of primary, secondary and university education). The programs of research reported also vary in the research designs and methods employed, as well as in the theoretical perspectives adopted. Reflecting on this diversity, Cumming and Ortega make two important observations. First, they argue that varied research approaches are needed in the exploration of diverse aspects of FL writing, which include psycholinguistic, textual-linguistic, sociolinguistic and educational dimensions. Second, they contend that some approaches are more suited to the exploration of these various dimensions of EFL writing; hence, the relevance of continuing to use all the methodologies employed in research to date, as documented in the studies reported in Part 1.

One important merit of the available research resides in the fact that, as the authors in Part 2 note, we are concerned with sustained, long-term programmes of research that have involved successive and deeper investigations into various facets of FL writing through a series of empirical studies. This must have certainly contributed to the credibility and robustness of the knowledge accumulated so far about FL writers, contexts and texts.

Researching FL writing: Moving forward

Despite the merits and achievements of available research on FL writing, a message we can begin to draw from the book is that future advancement in theory, research and pedagogy is dependent upon the investigation of new themes, the adoption of new theoretical frameworks and the employment of new methodologies.

The new *themes* that await further investigation have been mentioned in the previous sections on learning and teaching. Perhaps it is worth adding that the necessary visibility of FL writing research depends in part on an acceptance by journal editors and reviewers that certain topics and methods may need to be investigated anew across FL contexts, even if they have already been widely addressed in SL contexts. This would be the case of some of the items on the research agenda mentioned earlier, such as the study of voice in academic writing, feedback and assessment issues, or the influence of particular FL educational experiences in writing development. This is so because the SL bias of scholarly work in the field mentioned in the opening paragraphs means that the bounds of claims of official discourse have not been sufficiently tested across diverse contexts (much less across widely varying EFL contexts).

Regarding *theoretical approaches*, an overwhelming message from the book is that FL writing is certainly a sociocognitive endeavor, hence the need to combine cognitive and social perspectives in future research. The insights reported in Part 1 make it clear that FL writing is certainly a mental process that individual writers engage in. However, this activity takes place in a given sociocultural context and, therefore, FL writers develop their metaknowledge about writing, attitudes, motivation, confidence and writing abilities as a function of their previous learning experiences within specific cultures of practice. Accordingly, both cognitive and social perspectives are needed in the analysis, although, as noted by Cumming, this is not an easy task. Yet, as he suggests, sociocultural and goal theories can be appropriate frameworks to reconcile the two perspectives.

Hinted at in various contributions is the need to adopt what Ortega (this volume and elsewhere) calls the 'multicompetence lens' in the investigation of L2 writers (both SL and FL writers) and their texts. FL writers are not deficient users of an L2, but rather possessors of a distinct form of multicompetence that allows them to resort to their various linguistic and cognitive resources in their attempts to express themselves in writing in one of the languages that form their linguistic repertoire. What future research must uncover are the 'hows' and 'whys' of their behavior.

The investigation of new themes under the umbrella of new theoretical approaches requires travelling along new avenues in the area of *research methodology*, particularly regarding analytic methods, research instruments and research designs. Further research needs to adopt valid and reliable measures of writing processes (see Manchón *et al.*, Schoonen *et al.*) and writing products (see Celaya & Navés, Rinnert & Kobayashi), as well as to make use of new statistical techniques (Schoonen *et al.*). The field also requires more longitudinal studies, and more grounded, in-depth investigations of FL writers, and of FL writing teachers and classrooms. Interpretive-qualitative case studies of teachers and learners, ethnographic studies, learner autobiographies and life histories are suitable future options suggested by various contributors (Casanave, Cumming, Flowerdew & Li, Ortega). Interestingly, some contributors maintain that future research must also move in the other direction. For instance, Schoonen *et al.* argue that the investigation of the open questions that still exist in the cognitive domain of FL writing requires both descriptive online studies of writing processes and further experimental studies.

I mentioned earlier that this book attempts to make visible the insights gained in research conducted on L2 writing in FL contexts. In addition to putting FL writing on the scene, it is hoped that the book also achieves its aim of revealing the situated nature of FL writing practices. I would also like to think that this collective effort can make a valuable general contribution to L2 writing scholarship in terms of writing theories, research and pedagogies. Finally, it is hoped that the book is also a contribution in terms of the understanding of writers, texts and contexts that it may bring to the general field of language learning studies, a field in which research on L2 writing has much to add to the insights obtained so far in input-based and oral-based empirical research.

The book is therefore intended for a wide readership in different areas of applied linguistics. First, it may appeal to *academics* in L2 writing studies in search of an updated and critical account of the past, present and future of FL writing research. The book may also be of value to researchers in SLA and composition studies, regardless of their interest in FL writing issues. Second, *doctoral students* pursuing a principled engagement with the field of FL writing may find it useful. Third, the book should be of interest to *language teaching professionals, curriculum developers* and *policymakers* wishing to have an informed opinion on the findings and implications of writing research conducted in different FL settings.

I would like to invite the reader to initiate a journey through the book to discover how the ideas presented in this opening chapter are fully explored in the various contributions that make up this collective reflection on the output and value of past and future FL writing research.

Note

1. L2 is used to refer to both second and foreign languages.

References

Cumming, A. (2001) Learning to write in a second language: Two decades of research. In R.M. Manchón (ed.) *Writing in the L2 Classroom. Issues in Research and Pedagogy.* Special issue of *International Journal of English Studies* 1 (2), 1–23.

Cumming, A. (ed.) (2006) *Goals for Academic Writing: ESL Students and Their Instructors.* Amsterdam: John Benjamins.

Dörnyei, Z. (2005) *The Psychology of the Language Learner. Individual Differences in Second Language Acquisition.* Mahwah, NJ: Lawrence Erlbaum.

Doughty, C. (2001) Cognitive underpinnings of focus on form. In P. Robinson (ed.) *Cognition and Second Language Instruction* (pp. 206–257). New York: Cambridge University Press.

Doughty, C. and Williams, J. (eds) (1998) *Focus on Form in Classroom Second Language Acquisition*. New York: Cambridge University Press.

Harklau, L. (2002) The role of writing in classroom second language acquisition. *Journal of Second Language Writing* 11, 329–350.

Leki, I. (2001) Material, educational, and ideological challenges of teaching EFL writing at the turn of the century. In R.M. Manchón (ed.) Writing in the L2 Classroom: Issues in Research and Pedagogy. *The International Journal of English Studies* 1 (2), 197–209.

Leki, I., Cumming, A. and Silva, T. (2006) Second-language composition teaching and learning. In P. Smagorinski (ed.) *Research on Composition. Multiple Perspectives on Two Decades of Research* (pp. 141–169). New York: Teachers College Press, Columbia University.

Leki, I., Cumming, A. and Silva, T. (2008) *A Synthesis of Research on Second Language Writing in English*. London: Routledge.

Manchón, R.M. (forthcoming) The language learning potential of writing in foreign language contexts. Lessons from research. In M. Reichelt and T. Chimasko (eds) *Foreign Language Writing*. West Lafayette, IN: Parlor Press.

Manchón, R.M. and DeHaan, P. (2008a) Writing in foreign language contexts: Research insights. *Journal of Second Language Writing* 17 (1), 1–6.

Manchón, R.M. and DeHaan, P. (2008b) Writing in foreign language contexts: An introduction. *Journal of Second Language Writing* 17 (1).

Manchón, R.M. and Roca de Larios, J. (2007) Writing-to-learn in instructed language contexts. In E. Alcón and P. Safont (eds) *The Intercultural Speaker. Using and Acquiring English in Instructed Language Contexts* (pp. 101–121). Dordrecht: Springer-Verlag.

Muranoi, H. (2007) Output practice in the L2 classroom. In R. DeKeyser (ed.) *Practice in a Second Language. Perspectives from Applied Linguistics and Cognitive Psychology* (pp. 51–84). Cambridge: Cambridge University Press.

Ortega, L. (2004) L2 writing research in EFL contexts. Some challenges and opportunities for EFL researchers. *ALAK Newsletter*, Spring.

Ortega, L. and Carson, J. (2009) Multicompetence, social context, and L2 writing research praxis. In T. Silva and P.K. Matsuda (eds) *Practicing Theory in Second Language Writing*. West Lafayette, IN: Parlor Press.

Silva, T. and Brice, C. (2004) Research in teaching writing. *Annual Review of Applied Linguistics* 24, 70–106.

Silva, T., Leki, I. and Carson, J. (1997) Broadening the perspective of mainstream composition studies. Some thoughts from the disciplinary margins. *Written Communication* 14 (3), 398–424.

Part 1

Looking Back. Research Insights

Chapter 1

Situated Writing Practices in Foreign Language Settings: The Role of Previous Experience and Instruction

CAROL RINNERT and HIROE KOBAYASHI

Introduction

An English as a foreign language (EFL) setting epitomizes the situated nature of writing. The writing of EFL students is affected not only by their first language (L1), but also by the educational context where they learn to write. This socially and culturally characterized context provides metaknowledge about writing (i.e. view of audience and goals of writing) as well as linguistic and textual knowledge, affecting the ways in which students process and produce writing.

Recognizing that L1 writing instruction/experience plays an important role in the development of students' writing in an EFL situation, for the last decade we have conducted a number of studies to examine possible effects of such experience. These studies have evolved under the influence of major writing theories in the field of second language (L2) writing, including contrastive rhetoric, cognitive-process approaches, genre theory and sociocognitive theory. Along with this evolution, the methods adopted have changed from large-scale experimental and questionnaire survey studies to a case-study approach based on a variety of data sources, including in-depth interviews.

In order to elucidate this evolution, we have selected the 12 studies shown in Table 1.1. These studies focus primarily on two of the three dimensions of L2 writing that characterize the knowledge that students are expected to acquire: the features of texts they produce, and the sociocultural context where writing takes place (Cumming, 2001). The studies highlight a relationship between these two dimensions; that is, the students' perceptions and use of L1 and L2 rhetorical patterns tend to

Table 1.1 Main studies for analysis

	Reference	*Title*
Stage 1		
1	Kobayashi (1984a, 1984b)	Rhetorical patterns in English and Japanese
2	Kobayashi and Rinnert (1996)	Factors affecting composition evaluation in an EFL context: Cultural rhetorical pattern and readers' background
3	Rinnert and Kobayashi (2001)	Differing perceptions of EFL writing among readers in Japan
Stage 2		
4	Kobayashi (2002)	L1 Japanese high school literacy training: Student and teacher perspectives
5	Kobayashi and Rinnert (2002)	High school student perceptions of first language literacy instruction: Implications for second language writing
6	Rinnert and Kobayashi (2004)	Japanese university teachers' perceptions of L1 academic writing across disciplines
7	Rinnert and Kobayashi (2005)	Borrowing words and ideas: Insights from Japanese L1 writers
Stage 3		
8	Kobayashi and Rinnert (2004a)	Composing competence: How L1 and L2 writing experience interact
9	Kobayashi (2005)	Rhetorical decisions in L1 and L2 writing: How do novice writers differ?
10	Rinnert and Kobayashi (2007)	L1 and L2 preuniversity writing experience: What effects on novice Japanese EFL writers?
11	Kobayashi and Rinnert (2008)	Task response and text construction across L1 and L2 writing
12	Kobayashi and Rinnert (2007)	Transferability of argumentative writing competence from L2 to L1: Effects of overseas experience

change through writing training and experience, as well as with changing social-cultural contexts. While the chosen studies do not deal directly with composing processes such as planning and revising (a third dimension in Cumming's [2001] terms; see contributions by Manchón *et al.* and Schonnen *et al.*, this volume), those conducted at the latest stage show how EFL students in Japan respond to given writing tasks and construct texts in Japanese and English. The conceptual, linguistic and rhetorical choices individual writers make when writing essays constitute part of the composing process, which reflects 'ideational, interpersonal and textual positions arising from the writer's experience in participating in genres and discourses' (Roca *et al.*, 2002: 47). From a sociocognitive approach, the studies have looked at both macro- and micro-level discourse/rhetorical choices that students have made in constructing L1 and L2 texts.

In relation to the acquisition of EFL students' academic writing ability, we are greatly concerned with the issue of transfer of writing skills across languages, not only from L1 to L2, but also the reverse direction, from L2 to L1. A number of studies have investigated the transfer of writing ability from L1 to L2 (Cumming, 1989; Kobayashi, 2005; Sasaki & Hirose, 1996), and also from L2 to L1 (Berman, 1994; Shi & Beckett, 2002). However, few studies have approached the issue to clarify how previous writing instruction and experience affect the occurrence of transfer and even fewer have taken a close look into the direction of such influence.

In this chapter, we categorize our studies into three stages, which constitute a logical continuum, and attempt a critical examination of the research conducted in each stage. In the sections below, we summarize, evaluate and reinterpret the major findings of the studies shown in Table 1.1, while drawing logical connections among them. In the conclusion, we synthesize the findings and discuss their significance in relation to L2 writing theory, research and pedagogy.

Stage 1

The initial studies, especially two evaluation studies (2 and 3 in Table 1.1), were framed in terms of traditional contrastive rhetoric, which assumed that the rhetorical aspects of each language are culturally unique and preferred (Kaplan, 1966) and suggested that differences in organizational patterns between students' first and second languages cause difficulties for L2 learners (Casanave, 2004; Kubota, 1997). These two evaluation studies were designed on the basis of the findings of Kobayashi's (1984a, 1984b) study, which compared four groups of students (American college students, advanced Japanese ESL students in America and two groups of Japanese college students in Japan) in their use of rhetorical patterns. The study found a consistent tendency among the four groups: Whereas American students writing in English often used a general-to-specific ('deductive') pattern, Japanese students writing in Japanese frequently employed a specific-to-general ('inductive') pattern, and the two Japanese groups writing in English differed from each other, the group in Japan being substantially close to the group writing in Japanese and the group in the USA, relatively close to the American group. These findings confirmed what contrastive rhetoric had argued, but they also clearly suggested that the writing instruction and experience the Japanese advanced ESL students in the USA received influenced their frequent use of the general-to-specific pattern. In terms of research design, the study has strongly affected our subsequent research, in that we have continued to assume that a multiple group comparison can provide more insight than a single or two-group comparison in the investigation of the effects of such factors as writing experience on EFL students' writing.

Method

Whereas Kobayashi's (1984a, 1984b) study investigated the use of culturally preferred rhetorical patterns in the L1 and L2 writing of Japanese EFL students, the two evaluation studies examined the perceptions of L2 writing containing such patterns in a Japanese EFL context. More specifically, these large-scale experimental studies investigated how readers' background (differing L1, academic status and amounts of writing instruction) influenced the evaluative judgments of essays with contrasting rhetorical patterns. We assumed that the findings of the studies would benefit both sides (students and teachers) instructionally, in that students might learn about reader's expectations, and teachers could find out what features need to be taught in class on the basis of students' perceptions.

In these studies, the term 'culturally preferred patterns' was carefully rephrased as 'culturally influenced patterns' as an attempt to avoid essentializing cultural rhetorical patterns (Kubota, 1997, 1998a). Each of the two 'culturally influenced patterns' was a collection of rhetorical features taken from a variety of sources, including research findings, professional writing and composition textbooks (e.g. for Japanese, 'inductive' with loose transitions among paragraphs; for American, 'deductive' with explicit transitional markers). In addition to these rhetorical differences, the two other features of coherence breaks and language use errors were also included as text characteristics, and four groups of readers with different backgrounds ($n = 465$) were asked to evaluate two essays, one with a Japanese rhetorical pattern and one with an American pattern.

Findings

The analyses of the readers' evaluative judgments in the two studies yielded the same overall tendencies among the four groups. The 1996 study found that on one of the expository topics (*TV's effects on family life*), Japanese EFL students who had not received English writing instruction ('inexperienced students') preferred the Japanese rhetorical pattern; native English teachers favored the American rhetorical pattern; Japanese teachers and Japanese EFL students who had received English writing instruction ('experienced students') valued features of both patterns. The 2001 study went further to analyze both evaluative criteria and comments by the same readers and showed clear parallel tendencies between the two sets of data: while inexperienced students attended predominantly to content in judging and commenting on essays, experienced students and Japanese teachers focused on clarity, logical connection and organization. The experienced groups' perceptions tended to be more similar to the perceptions of the native English-speaking teachers, which may suggest that with more L2 writing experience, EFL readers' perceptions of English essays change gradually from preferring L1 writing features to preferring many of those of L2 writing.

Whereas the method of using manipulated compositions in the evaluation studies drew both criticism and approval (Casanave, 2004; Kubota, 1998a), the three studies (1–3 in Table 1.1) together evidenced that cultural preferences for certain rhetorical features exist. They also showed that writing experience and more exposure to English rhetorical features change student writers' perceptions, implying that such perceptions or preferences are not static, but dynamic. This part of the findings should have been more strongly stressed, as it was by Kubota and Shi (2005: 101), who took it as suggesting 'a dynamic and varied nature of cultural and rhetorical perceptions'. The finding, in fact, supports the central criticism against the concept of traditional contrastive rhetoric that emphasizes the uniqueness of culture (Kubota, 1997; Kubota & Lehner, 2004; Matsuda, 1997) and accords with the concept of a new contrastive rhetoric, characterized by Connor (2002, 2005) as being concerned with dynamic interlinguistic/cultural influences.

Although the findings suggest that the writing instruction/experience students receive affects their changing rhetorical perceptions, the studies did not provide any insight into the effects of specific amounts and kinds of previous writing instruction/experience on L2 writing. Thus, we felt it necessary to find out more about Japanese EFL students' writing training before entering universities. This turned our attention particularly to the current status of L1 literacy being practiced in higher education in Japan, including high schools and universities.

Stage 2

We conducted four large-scale questionnaire surveys to clarify the nature of Japanese students' L1 writing experience and instruction in both high school and university (studies 4–7 in Table 1.1). In addition to our own research interest, these studies responded to social needs for investigating students' previous educational training in two academic contexts, Japan and North America. In Japan, many educators have been concerned with how to articulate high school education to the university level in order to deal with the recent problem of declining academic ability among university students (Arai, 2000). Similarly, those in North America have become increasingly concerned with obtaining information about the L1 educational background of their non-native students to assist them with academic difficulties they are likely to face at the university level (e.g. Leki & Carson, 1994).

These questionnaire studies were theoretically grounded in the view of writing as a situated act, which emphasizes the actual performance of writing in a particular context, focusing attention on 'the experiences of writers and... their understandings of the local features of context they deal with as they write' (Hyland, 2002: 30). Through the use of a variety of data sources such as questionnaires, observation and in-depth interviews, this approach allows researchers to attain a detailed description of the context that characterizes local writing.

Method

Two of the four surveys (4 and 5 in Table 1.1) elicited Japanese students' ($n = 389$) and teachers' ($n = 179$) perceptions of current L1 reading and writing instruction in high school, while the other two (6 and 7 in Table 1.1) collected perceptions of students ($n = 791$) and teachers ($n = 90$) toward L1 academic writing at university.[1] The sample sizes for the four questionnaire studies were large enough for statistical analyses; however, the method of sampling had a limitation: although the survey for high school teachers employed stratified random sampling to obtain responses nationwide, the other three used convenience sampling, in which questionnaires were distributed through personal contacts around the country, and hence may be less representative. Along with the questionnaire surveys, in-depth interviews were also conducted with university students to take a close look at their writing instruction/experience in high school and university.

Findings

The quantitative and qualitative analysis of the high school responses indicated parallels between the students' and teachers' perceptions, particularly that the most important goal of *kokugo* (Japanese) instruction is to develop an ability to read and understand '*bunshou*' (texts), and much more time is spent on reading than writing instruction. The overwhelming emphasis on reading over writing appears to be related in part to educational policies stressing historical and cultural heritage through reading classics and modern prose, and also to many teachers' belief that reading trains the basic human abilities to think and judge. However, the findings also revealed that many high schools (85% of the 79 schools that responded) provide special writing training, often as individual tutoring outside regular *kokugo* classes, to help students prepare to write short essays for university entrance exams. According to the students interviewed ($n = 21$), the training was given on a short-term basis consisting of 1–4 months of intensive, individualized instruction, and the common task was to write opinion-stating essays in which they were instructed to take a clear position, for example, for or against the author's assertion or on a social issue presented in a text, and to provide support from such sources as personal experience, observation or factual knowledge. In short, the present L1 literacy instruction in high school offers two kinds of writing training, one for all the students in regular *kokugo* classes and another for a selected group of students.

These findings were significant regarding the following points: (1) against the commonly held view that Japanese students do not learn to write in high school (Liebman, 1992; Mok, 1993), it appears that increasing numbers of students experience intensive L1 writing outside their formal classes, and (2) L1 specialized writing training emphasizes a type of text in which a particular position with supporting evidence is provided. Although essay-writing for college entrance exams may be one specific 'genre' in which students are expected to write to convince particular readers (i.e. professors judging their qualifications for admission), the findings suggest that the kind of writing that students are trained to produce in such special training sessions attaches importance to logical argumentation, which seems to echo the typical characteristics of English academic writing (e.g. Langan, 2000; Reid, 1988), as well as the emphasis on opinion writing in recent writing textbooks in Japan (Kubota & Shi, 2005).

Like the high school surveys, the university questionnaire responses showed that students and teachers shared similar perceptions of L1 academic writing. One of the most significant findings was that both groups perceived a strong need for more instruction in appropriate citation conventions (Rinnert & Kobayashi, 2005). Japanese students were found to have little knowledge of citation of sources and also to perceive the borrowing of words or ideas without citing the source to be not entirely negative. Another related finding was that academic discipline was a more influential factor than academic level (undergraduate versus graduate) in affecting student knowledge and attitudes toward the borrowing, with more concern shown in humanities/social sciences than in physical/information sciences.

While the evaluation studies in Stage 1 suggested that L2 writing instruction/experience and exposure to English rhetorical features contributed to Japanese EFL readers' changing perceptions of culturally influenced patterns in English writing, the high school questionnaires and interviews showed that L1 writing instruction promotes rhetorical conventions similar to those of English opinion-writing. These rhetorical similarities may reflect common characteristics of opinion-writing across languages or changes occurring in Japanese L1 writing instruction to help students express ideas clearly and logically in order to cope with the rapidly changing world. Whatever the source, rhetorical perceptions continue to evolve in a dynamic way, being influenced by social and educational changes. However, it is not certain whether changes in L1 writing instruction affects actual writing in both L1 and L2, as claimed in the interviews by some of the students. This became a new inquiry for our research at the next stage.

Stage 3

As a natural outgrowth from the earlier stages, we decided to look more specifically at the role of writing instruction/experience in the development of Japanese EFL students' writing ability. Unlike Stage 1, Stage 3 investigates the effects of specific kinds of instruction: preuniversity short-essay writing training, EFL writing instruction in a Japanese university setting and varying kinds of L2 writing experience overseas. The studies in this stage were undertaken from a sociocognitive perspective (Flower, 1994; Riazi, 1997; Roca & Murphy, 2001; Villamail & de Guerrero, 1996), which sees writing as a primarily mental activity by an individual writer within a particular socially mediated context and assumes that writers construct their own writing abilities and practices at least partly on the basis of their previous experiences and perceptions. We chose to employ a case-study approach, based on in-depth qualitative analysis of individual writers' texts and perceptions and drawing comparisons among small groups, to attempt to capture the relationship between text features and the sociocultural context affecting the writers' choices of such features. Although small-scale studies are limited in terms of how far the findings can be generalized, we agree with Hirose (2006) that such studies can provide deeper insights about aspects of writing that cannot easily be accessed through large-scale quantitative studies.

The two sets of studies in Stage 3 involved novice writers and more experienced writers, respectively, to examine the effects of particular kinds of previous writing training/experience on L1 and L2 writing. In this stage, we have looked not only at English, but also at Japanese writing, focusing on essay-level and paragraph-level discourse/rhetorical features, to explore the issue of transfer across languages.

Studies with novice writers

The first set of studies (8–11 in Table 1.1) investigated the transfer of knowledge from L1 to L2 writing. We were looking in more depth at the specific effects of intensive training for university entrance exams, identified in Kobayashi and Rinnert (2001b), on the writing of novice university writers.

Method

We compared four groups of first-year Japanese EFL students ($n = 27$), all at an intermediate English proficiency level: (1) those with both L1 and L2 intensive training; (2) those with only L1 training; (3) those with only L2 training; and (4) those with no intensive training in either L1 or L2. They wrote Japanese and English essays in response to two open-ended topics: what students thought about living alone or with family, and what they thought about traveling alone or in a group. The wording of the prompts left the writers free to decide how to frame their responses, rather than requiring a specific discourse type, such as argumentation or exposition. Immediately following the writing, in-depth interviews were conducted to probe the students' perceptions of their writing in both languages.

Findings

Analysis of the text structure supplemented by analysis of the interview data showed that the intensive instruction affected text construction in both L1 and L2. Moreover, transfer was found from L1 to L2, and to some extent from L2 to L1.

Identification of the task responses revealed four discourse types in the essays. The first was argumentation, defined as taking a position, such as 'I think that it is much better to travel with friends or family' or 'I think that university students should start to live by themselves', usually placed near the beginning of the essay, and supporting it. The second was exposition, which generally involved comparing the two sides of the issue, without taking a position in favor of either one, but stating a thesis such as 'Which type of travel to choose would depend on what you seek in the journey' or making a general statement like 'They both have their merits'. The third was self-reflection, in which the writer narrates and reflects on personal experiences related to the issue, without stating a position, thesis or general statement. The last was a mixed pattern, which consisted mainly of combinations of either exposition and argumentation or self-reflection and argumentation. Major differences in the frequencies of discourse types across languages were found. Overall, argumentation was the most frequent discourse type in the English essays (48% for all students combined, and 71% for those with only L2 training). In contrast, there were more expository (37%) and mixed (33%) than argumentation (22%) essays in Japanese. In particular, the students who received L1 training alone used exposition most often in L1 (56%) and tended to transfer this response to the L2 essays (28%) (Kobayashi & Rinnert, 2008). In sum, it was found that the L2 instruction strongly promoted the use of an argumentation discourse type in the L2 essays, whereas the L1 training was associated with a more diverse choice of discourse types. These findings suggest that compared to the English training, which tended to concentrate on argumentation, the intensive Japanese training presented more varied models of effective texts, as was also seen in the junior high school textbooks analyzed by Kubota and Shi (2005).

In relation to discourse types, we also found that students' early experiences with *sakubun* (expressive writing) in their *kokugo* (Japanese language) classes throughout their elementary and secondary school years led to frequent use of self-reflection, either as a single discourse type or as part of a mixed type (with either argumentation or exposition).

Most notably, students who had no intensive L1 training tended to rely heavily on this earlier L1 writing experience, using personal reflection and evidence in their L1 and L2 essays (Kobayashi & Rinnert, 2008; Rinnert & Kobayashi, 2007).

One methodological weakness in our analysis of text types was the fact that it depended entirely on textual analysis to interpret the writer's intention. As pointed out by Kubota and Shi (2005: 122), the determination of text types, especially for hybrid (mixed) texts, requires a determination of the purpose of the writing in the context, but we were not able to confirm our interpretations with the students, mainly because of the time lag between the data collection and the completion of the analysis. A fruitful area for future research would be the exploration of the whole notion of discourse type, particularly how it is addressed in L1 Japanese training.

A second main finding was that while the internal structure of the English essays was rather simple, the structure of the Japanese essays by the students with L1 training tended to be more complex, with a substantial number (over 30%) containing an original or extended perspective (Kobayashi & Rinnert, 2008). One student, for example, first compared and contrasted the two sides of the given topic (*Should college students live alone or with family?*) and then gave an extended perspective, in which the student writer pointed out that ways students live are similar to those of the elderly, as follows (translated from Japanese):

> an increasing number of senior citizens have begun living together after they became alone or lost living partners, forming a new type of family. I think living alone for [X University] students is closer to this type of living arrangement. When someone gets hurt or ill, we can come and take care of him or her immediately.

After this extended perspective, the writer ended with a statement of a position. This difference between English and Japanese essays apparently resulted from a strong emphasis on the importance of demonstrating originality in the Japanese entrance examination essays.

This result may be related to earlier findings from Stages 1 and 2. In the Stage 1 evaluation studies, the inexperienced students (with no university EFL writing instruction) tended to focus much more on the content and originality of the essays than either the experienced students or the Japanese teachers (though not more than the native English-speaking teachers). This could be at least partially explained by the finding from Stage 2 that Japanese high school *kokugo* classes place major emphasis on content for reading and writing, which may also be related to the genre of university entrance exam essays.

A third major finding concerned the striking effects of the interaction between L1 and L2 specialized training. Most notably, whereas L1 training clearly led to greater use of metadiscourse markers such as 'There are three main reasons', 'First' and 'In conclusion', students who had a combination of both L1 and L2 training tended to produce coherently structured L2 essays with a wide variety of discourse markers and rich elaboration of content, particularly specification in the form of concrete examples (Kobayashi & Rinnert, 2004a; Rinnert & Kobayashi, 2007). This strong positive interaction between the L1 and L2 training apparently resulted from the increased amount of writing practice, which was substantial enough to allow them to activate the linguistic and discourse knowledge they had acquired and apply it in their L2 writing. Furthermore, some students who had received both types of training were found to have transferred their knowledge of such features as discourse markers from L2 training to L1 writing, even though most of the transfer observed in the study was from L1 to L2. This bidirectional transfer could occur across languages when common features are perceived to be shared between tasks (L1 and L2 writing, in this case), just as Singley and Anderson (1989) observed a high level of positive transfer between similar line text editing tasks. At the same time, this group of students can be considered 'multicompetent writers' who are developing the capacity to draw on abilities across the languages they know as they learn to write effectively for various communities (Ortega & Carson, 2009).

One possible criticism of our above interpretations of some essays as being 'coherently structured' or containing 'rich elaboration of content' is that these positive characterizations have not been confirmed through independent evaluation of the quality of the essays. Although we attempted such an evaluation, we were unable to use the assessments because of unacceptably low inter-rater reliability in the judgments of essay organization, which we attributed to the difficulty of evaluating different discourse types in relation to each other. This is one reason we decided to concentrate on only one main discourse type in the next set of studies.

Studies with more advanced writers

The second set of studies[2] (12 in Table 1.1) aims at investigating the effects of writing instruction/experience Japanese EFL students received in overseas school settings, including a variety of academic levels from high school to postgraduate, on text construction in Japanese and English. One main reason for undertaking these studies is the social phenomenon of a large number of Japanese students going overseas to study in institutions where English is the medium of instruction (see Sasaki, this volume). This phenomenon led us to go beyond our investigation of L1 to L2 transfer in the preceding studies to consider the effect of L2 writing experience on L1 writing in this set of studies. Extrapolating from previous studies of L1 to L2 transfer (e.g. Cumming, 1989; Hirose, 2003; Kobayashi, 2005; Kubota, 1998b) and L2 to L1 transfer (Berman, 1994; Eggington, 1987; Shi, 2003), as well as cases of transfer in both directions among the novice writers as explained above, we posited a bidirectionality of transfer of writing features across languages. This perspective conforms with that of Manchón and Roca (2007), who found evidence of bidirectional transfer, including features of text organization, in the Spanish and English writing by the higher-proficiency students in their study.

Method

In this set of studies, we have been focusing on possible influences of L2 training/experience on L1 argumentation essays. We chose the discourse type of argumentation because many similarities have been identified between Japanese and English argumentation essays (e.g. Hirose, 2003; Kobayashi & Rinnert, 2004a; Kubota, 1998a), and we were interested in exploring these similarities in relation to the influences of L1 and L2 instruction. The first study (12 in Table 1.1) included three groups of more experienced Japanese EFL writers ($n = 25$): two groups of third and fourth year undergraduate students, one with no overseas experience and one with two semesters of study in English-speaking countries; and one group of postgraduate students and teachers who had spent at least three years engaged in academic work in English-speaking countries. The participants wrote essays in both Japanese and English on relatively challenging argumentation topics: for/against foreign language education for elementary students, and for/against elderly parents living with their family. The writing sessions were followed by in-depth retrospective interviews that probed the writers' perceptions of the textual structure and writing process, in relation to their previous writing experiences.

Findings

One main finding was that in both L1 and L2 essays, the overall argumentation structure, particularly placement of a position statement at the beginning and end of the essay, resulted mainly from L2 training. A second feature of the argumentation essays that could more often be traced to L2 than to L1 training was the inclusion of a counterargument component within the body of the essay, which occurred most frequently in the L1 essays of those writers with overseas experience, particularly those with two semesters' overseas college experience (L1: 60%; L2: 33%) as opposed to students without overseas experience (L1: 30%; L2: 30%) (Kobayashi & Rinnert, 2007). Moreover, the interview data clearly indicated that the content of the instruction played a role, in that those who had not been taught to use counterarguments did not include them. It was also found that learning about making a counterargument from L2 training did not necessarily lead to the inclusion of counterarguments in L2 essays (due to risk avoidance strategies, lack of confidence and difficult formulation), but this knowledge could be transferred to L1 essays, most likely because the use of L1 allowed the mental capacity to cope with a cognitively challenging task (Berman, 1994).

Another major effect from L2 experience, identified mainly in the L1 essays by participants who had spent long periods overseas, was elaboration of the introductions to include a preview of the content of the paper, specification of both sides of the issue, clarification of the topic and definition of terms. The following excerpt from an elaborated introduction from an English essay by a long-term overseas resident illustrates clarification of the topic (*Should elderly people live with family?*) and definition of terms [the underline indicates the clarification; the underlined italics, the definition of terms]

> Furthermore, it is a quite personal, complex issue that has to take lots of things into consideration. A should-or-shouldn't debate is thus unrealistic. Based on this point of view, I will discuss some major possible pros and cons for old people to live with their family members. *In this essay, "old people" refers to single old people and "family member(s)" to sons or daughter's family member(s).*

Such elaboration features apparently resulted mainly from disciplinary knowledge and/or training the participants acquired in their specialized areas, which appears to represent a clear instance of expertise acquired through extensive experience of situated writing practice (Carter, 1990).

A final influence of L2 training was seen in the conclusions of the L1 essays. Most of the L1 essays by the participants with no overseas experience included an extended idea or future concerns (L1: 90%; L2: 20%), in which the writer went one step beyond a summary to relate the topic to a broader context or a future perspective such as a suggestion. These elements appeared much less frequently in the L1 conclusions of the overseas groups (L1: 20%; L2: 20%). An example of an *extension* is seen in the following excerpt from a conclusion by a writer without overseas experience (written on the topic *Should foreign language education begin in elementary school?*) [translation of original Japanese; the underline indicates the extension part of the Japanese conclusion]

> As seen above, the implementation of early foreign language education has many advantages and it is expected to help improve the English ability of Japanese. *As the world goes more global, chances of Japanese taking an active role in the world must be increasing. In such cases, the need for speaking foreign languages will be remarkably high. Regrettably, Japan now has only a handful of people with good command of English. In order to change this situation and turn Japan into a new and open country,* we should move ahead with early foreign language education.

The interview data suggest that the infrequent use of such components by the writers with overseas experience resulted from explicit L2 instruction that conclusions summarize an essay and contain 'no new ideas', descriptions that match the characteristics of English conclusions in English writing textbooks (e.g. Langan, 2000; Reid, 1988). Interestingly, even those writers with overseas experience who reported that English and Japanese conclusions differ tended to transfer this L2 feature (suppression of extended ideas/future concerns) to their L1 conclusions.

Implications for Theory, Research and Pedagogy

The studies we have reviewed demonstrate a positive role of previous writing instruction/experience in the development of writing ability, providing evidence that both the kinds and the amount of instruction/experience affect writers' acquisition of textual features and also help shape their perceptions/attitudes toward writing (see Sasaki, this volume, for similar results). When writers construct texts, such perceptions play a large role in the uptake/choice of textual features from among those they have acquired through L1 and L2 training.

In this concluding section, we will first synthesize the findings reported in this chapter in relation to the role of previous experience and instruction, and then discuss the bidirectionality of transfer of writing features across L1 and L2 writing.

Kinds of instruction and experience

L1 and L2 writing instruction and particular kinds of writing experience were found to be associated with specific features of Japanese writers' L1 and L2 texts. First, extensive early L1 experience/training in *sakubun* (personal expressive writing), when not combined with any other training, led to the use of self-reflection and personal accounts in L1 and L2 essays by novice writers. Second, novice writers who had received intensive L1 training wrote more coherently organized L1 and L2 essays (consisting of introduction, body and conclusion, with discourse markers signalling connections among the parts) than those without such training. Third, novice writers with L2 writing training adopted a basic schema to place the main idea or opinion statement at the beginning and end of the L2 essay and present reasons in support of the position. Fourth, among more advanced writers, L2 writing experience overseas strengthened the tendency to adopt L2 rhetorical features for not only the overall structure, but also the development of the body of the L1 essays (e.g. inclusion of a counterargument and explicit topic sentences at the beginnings of paragraphs). This may be related to the findings by Sasaki (this volume) that overseas experience can lead students to reconceptualize the task of writing through imagination of a possible audience that motivates them to refine their writing. Finally, those who had received disciplinary training in overseas academic institutions were found to elaborate their introductions through clarification and definition, which reflects such training.

One major finding was that in both L1 and L2 settings, writing instruction tends to be varied and locally situated. Related to this finding, the diversity of discourse types found in the L2 essays of novice writers with only L1 training may be explained by the kinds of instruction students had received. According to interview reports, some teachers emphasized exposition, focusing on the structure of raising a problem in the introduction and discussing it through comparison or illustration in the body, while others stressed argumentation, with the structure of an opinion statement followed by supporting reasons. Although Kobayashi and Rinnert (2002) suggested that opinion writing was predominant in the specialized essay writing practice, a closer look at the later findings indicates that the discourse frames of both exposition and argumentation were emphasized in the L1 short-essay training. Diversity was also found in the instruction on argumentation writing, with some L1 and L2 training stressing the need for strong support reasons, and other instruction, emphasizing the importance of including a counterargument. The findings also suggest that unless such knowledge is taught, writers are unlikely to employ these specific features when writing L1 or L2 essays. At the same time, diverse instruction affects EFL writers' ways of constructing L2 texts if they transfer what they were taught in the L1 instruction, as was evidenced in our studies.

Amount of instruction/experience

While different kinds of instruction provide knowledge about composing processes and textual conventions, the amount of training and experience appears to affect writers' perceptions and acquisition of both kinds of knowledge through repeated practice. First, the progression from inexperienced students, to experienced students, to Japanese teachers in the Stage 1 evaluation studies showed that longer experience with L2 writing led to changes in perceptions/evaluations of features of L2 writing, mainly placing more importance on logical connection than on content development. Second, the novice writers who had written many papers in both languages made the most frequent and varied use of metadiscourse markers; when the same text features are shared across L1 and L2 writing, training and practice in both languages apparently enhances the likelihood of the features being internalized by individual writers. Third, even though it was found that one year of overseas experience was not enough to register much influence on students' texts, a period of three or more years was associated with large effects, particularly on the construction of essay introductions.

All these findings confirm that without extensive writing practice, text features cannot be transformed from what Anderson termed 'declarative knowledge (verbalizable data gathered from previous experience)' to become 'procedural knowledge (internalized knowledge about working within a specific domain)' (cited in Carter, 1990: 273). As widely discussed by DeKeyser (1998, 2001, 2007), according to skill learning theory in cognitive psychology, knowledge becomes proceduralized through 'engaging in the target behavior' (DeKeyser, 1998: 49), and then the procedural knowledge can be refined and automatized through repeated practice.

Perceptions/attitude toward L1 and L2 writing

Writing training and experience received through past schooling influenced students' perceptions/attitude toward writing, and the Stage 3 studies found that writers' views of similarities and/or differences between Japanese and English writing related to their choices of particular text features across languages. Some novice writers viewed L1 and L2 writing as being very similar and used the same rhetorical structures (i.e. opinion statement → support reasons) regardless of the language they were writing in, while others reported some different features in L1 and L2 writing and opted for different ways of structuring their essays in the two languages (e.g. for L1, general statement → comparison; for L2, opinion statement → support reasons).

Throughout the three stages, there have also been some indications that writers' perceptions of rhetorical features taught in L1 or L2 instruction affected their uptake of particular textual features. For example, several experienced students in Stage 1 and one novice writer in Stage 3 explicitly rejected the L2 logical structure consisting of an opinion and support reasons because they viewed it as 'too formulaic'. On the other hand, another novice writer consciously used discourse markers learned from L2 training in both L1 and L2 writing because she found the device useful for communicating her ideas clearly to the reader. Another more advanced writer, who had learned a deductive movement of ideas from L2 and an inductive movement from L1, chose to write in an inductive way in both languages because she thought it would be 'more persuasive' and 'get the reader's understanding easily'. In these cases, the writers' perceptions greatly influenced their text construction and transfer or nontransfer of features across languages.

These individual differences in perceptions/attitudes that lead to differences in writing behaviors are reflections of the writers' agency in constructing texts. For example, as implied in critical contrastive rhetoric (cf. Kubota & Lehner, 2004), writers can decide to accept or reject features of the dominant discourse conventions in a particular setting, instead choosing other features that are characteristic of subordinate or less widely taught rhetorical patterns. Moreover, as mentioned above, writers' attitudes can be considered important factors in whether or not transfer occurs across languages. For instance, one recent study (Kobayashi & Rinnert, 2007) found that some constituent elements of introductions and conclusions differed between Japanese and English texts by the same writers. Even with the same overall L1 and L2 essay structures, what features writers chose to include in the introduction and conclusion of each essay apparently depended upon individual factors, such as their perceptions of L1 and L2 writing, and also the contexts where the writers were situated while acquiring their instruction/experience.

In relation to the acquisition of academic writing skills, this finding also implies that although the writers reported in the interviews that they were more influenced by L2 than L1 writing, they could still end up choosing L1 rhetorical features when they had to deal with some specific rhetorical aspects (e.g. elements of introductions and conclusions) they had studied in L2 classes, but not yet acquired. Thus, it appears that past L1 writing training and experience may still exert an influence after EFL students have become more advanced writers.

Bidirectional nature of transfer across languages

Regarding the issue of transfer, the findings of our studies confirm that novice writers tend to transfer L1 textual features to L2 writing, whereas more advanced writers are more likely to depend upon L2 textual features in the development of L2 writing skills (Ferris & Hedgcock, 1998). While this observation generally holds true, our findings clearly indicate that the transfer of textual features takes place not only from L1 to L2, but rather in both directions even at novice-writer levels. For example, novice EFL writers who had received only preuniversity writing training tried to construct texts in both Japanese and English by relying on the knowledge they obtained from L1 or L2 writing instruction or their combination, as specifically illustrated in the case of students who used the same rhetorical features in the two languages (see Table 1.2). Similarly, more advanced EFL writers' greater use of counterargument in their L1 texts than their L2 texts shows the transfer of L2 knowledge to L1 writing, while their choice of some specific elements for introductions (general rather than specific preview) and conclusions (general rather than specific summary) for L2 writing indicates the reverse transfer, from L1 to L2. Whereas the novice and more advanced writers differed in the degree to which they chose L1 or L2 textual features, they basically utilized what they had learned from either L1 or L2 experience, or both. Although individual differences within each group should not be dismissed, as mentioned above, our research findings appear to lend empirical support to the bidirectionality of transfer across languages, which can be discussed within the proposed notion of 'multicompetence', referred to as 'the knowledge of more than one language in the same mind' (Cook, 2002: 10).

As implied above, the issue of transfer is a complex one. Based on the findings of our studies, we would like to propose a schematic representation, shown in Figure 1.1, of the salient factors that have been identified as affecting the transfer of rhetorical features across languages. The factors include L1 and L2 writing instruction/experience; disciplinary knowledge/training; individual factors (perceptions,

Table 1.2 Shared rhetorical features across L1 and L2 writing by five novice writers

Writer#	*Training*	*Discourse type*	*Rhetorical features**
Yoko	L1 and L2	Mixed (Exp → Arg)	Inductive approach (L1) Similar overall structure (L1) Use of discourse markers (L2) Avoiding repetition of the same expression (L2)
Noriko	L1 and L2	Arg	Deductive approach (L2) Overall and internal structure (L2) Prioritizing ideas (L1) Use of discourse markers (L2) Avoiding absolute statement of ideas (L1)
Koichiro	L1	Arg	Deductive approach (L1) Overall structure with counterargument (L1) Use of discourse markers (L1)
Motoko	L1	Exp	Deductive approach (L1) Overall structure (L1) Original thesis (L1) Use of discourse markers (L1) Stating important ideas in a definite form (L1) Concrete examples (L1)
Harue	L2	Mixed (Self → Exp)	Inductive approach (L1)** Loosely structured frame (L1) Anecdotes and quotations (L1) Reflecting feelings and thoughts (L1)

Source: Kobayashi (2005).

Notes: Arg: argumentation, Exp: exposition, Self: self-reflection; Mixed: two modes combined, →: direction of overall movement.

#The writers' names are all pseudonyms.

*Information in parentheses indicates the reported source of knowledge, i.e. whether it was obtained from L1 or L2 special writing training.

**In Harue's case, the knowledge was received from nonintensive writing training.

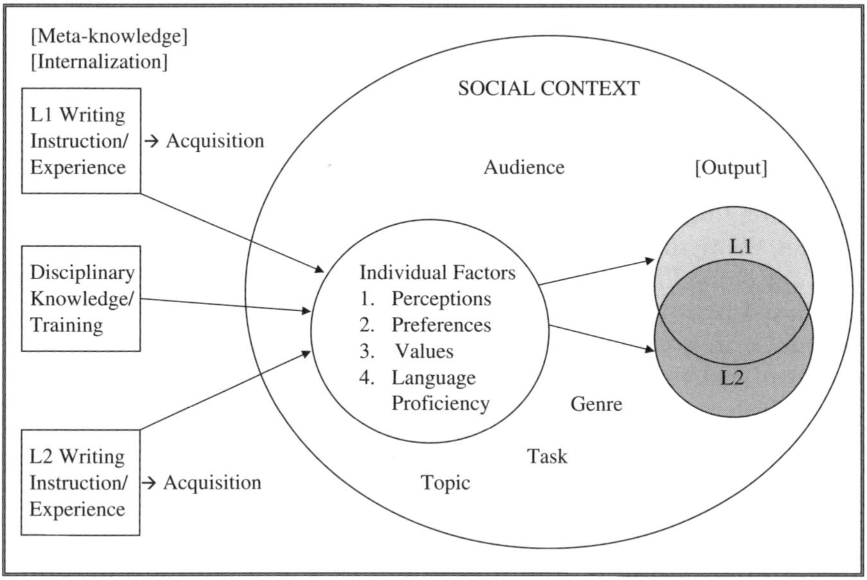

Figure 1.1 Factors influencing transfer of writing features across languages

preferences, values and language proficiency); and social context, including audience, genre, task and topic. Although language proficiency has not been discussed in this chapter, our studies indicate that this factor is important. In particular, the less frequent use of counter-argument in the L2 texts of relatively advanced writers (with one year overseas experience) was due to a language factor, as they clearly stated in the interviews.

In the schema shown in Figure 1.1, the boxes (left) represent the writer's literacy background, including writing training and experience received in L1 and L2, along with related disciplinary knowledge. This background knowledge, accrued through experience, contributes to the formulation and implementation of the writing task by the writer. The notations above and beside the boxes indicate that it is not enough to be exposed to metaknowledge about writing; instead, it is necessary to receive sufficient writing practice and experience for the knowledge to become internalized, leading to acquisition. Arrows lead from the boxes to a circle representing the individual writer, whose perceptions are shaped by training/experience. Based on such individual factors as perceptions, values and language proficiency, the writer can choose which features to uptake or transfer according to the context of the writing, indicated by the larger circle, which includes the social setting, audience, genre, task and topic. The overlapping circles on the right, representing L1 text and L2 text, indicate output from the writer. The overlap between the circles, depicting the shared features of the L1 and L2 texts, could vary from almost entire overlap to little or none, depending upon how individual factors interact with L1 and L2 writing instruction/experience. Thus, in addition to showing factors affecting transfer, the figure attempts to capture a major theme of this chapter: the dynamic nature of writing practices related to changing social conditions and individual writers' perceptions. At the same time, it indicates how L1 and L2 are connected to a greater or lesser degree, depending upon a variety of factors. This schema can be taken as representing interconnection between languages, which Cook (2002) refers to as one type of integration continuum model consisting of multicompetence.

In order to confirm the viability of this representation of the factors, we are currently working in several new directions. In particular, we are including an evaluation component with experts in *kokugo* (L1 Japanese) and EFL writing to ascertain which textual features are associated with assessments of higher quality in L1 and L2 argumentation essays; adding a comparison with more advanced Japanese writers who have had little exposure to English writing instruction or experience; and testing the generalizability of the findings by extending the study to include native English-speaking learners of Japanese as a foreign language writing English and Japanese essays in North America.

As discussed by Ortega and Carson (2009), evidence has been accumulating that multicompetent writers are able to draw on diverse sources of knowledge of L1 and L2 writing while developing their ability to construct texts in either language. In this chapter, we have attempted to clarify some of the ways that previous experience and instruction contribute to the development of writing knowledge and practices in a foreign language setting. At the same time, we have reconfirmed the necessity of combining cognitive and social perspectives in order to understand situated practices of writing.

Acknowledgements

Most of these studies were supported by research grants from the Japanese Society for the Promotion of Science (Grant-in-Aid for Scientific Research [C2], Research Codes 11680263, 1458029 and 1650343). We would like to thank Rosa Manchón for her valuable suggestions for improvement of this chapter.

Notes

1. For comparison purposes, a small number of North American high school ($n=66$) and university students ($n=76$) were administered corresponding English questionnaires. Their responses indicated that American high school language classes provided significantly more instruction in writing and less emphasis on reading than Japanese classes, and American college students wrote more frequently and received relatively more formal writing instruction than Japanese students.
2. Although only one of these studies has been reported to date, several more are in progress.

References

Arai, K. (2000) Koukou kyouiku to daigaku kyouiku tono setsuzoku [Articulation between high school and university education]. In K. Arai (ed.) *Gakusei wa koukou de naniwo manandekuruka* [*What Have College Students Learned in High School?*] (pp. 1–24). Tokyo: National Center of University Entrance Examination.

Berman, R. (1994) Learners' transfer of writing skills between languages. *TESL Canada Journal* 12 (1), 29–46.

Carter, M. (1990) The idea of expertise: An exploration of cognitive and social dimensions of writing. *College Composition and Communication* 41 (3), 265–286.

Casanave, C.P. (2004) *Controversies in Second Language Writing: Dilemmas and Decisions in Research and Instruction*. Ann Arbor, MI: University of Michigan Press.

Connor, U. (2002) New directions in contrastive rhetoric. *TESOL Quarterly* 36 (4), 493–510.

Connor, U. (2005) Comment by Ulla Connor. *Journal of Second Language Writing* 14 (2), 132–136.

Cook, V. (2002) Background to the L2 user. In V. Cook (ed.) *Portraits of the L2 User* (pp. 1–28). Clevedon: Multilingual Matters.

Cumming, A. (1989) Writing expertise and second-language proficiency. *Language Learning* 39 (1), 81–141.

Cumming, A. (2001) Learning to write in a second language: Two decades of research. In R.M. Manchón (ed.) *Writing in the L2 Classroom. Issues in Research and Pedagogy*. Special issue of *International Journal of English Studies* 1 (2), 1–23.

DeKeyser, T. (1998) Beyond focus on form: Cognitive perspectives on learning and practicing second language grammar. In C. Doughty and J. Williams (eds) *Focus on Form in Classroom Second Language Acquisition* (pp. 42–63). Cambridge: Cambridge University Press.

DeKeyser, R. (2001) Automaticity and automatization. In P. Robinson (ed.) *Cognition and Second Language Instruction* (pp. 42–63). Cambridge: Cambridge University Press.

DeKeyser, R.M. (2007) Study abroad as foreign language practice. In R.M. DeKeyser (ed.) *Practicing in a Second Language: Perspectives from Applied Linguistics and Cognitive Psychology* (pp. 208–226). New York: Cambridge University Press.

Eggington, W.G. (1987) Written academic discourse in Korean: Implications for effective communication. In U. Connor and R.B. Kaplan (eds) *Writing Across Languages: Analysis of L2 Text* (pp. 153–167). Reading, MA: Addison-Wesley.

Ferris, D.R. and Hedgcock, J.S. (1998) *Teaching ESL Composition: Purpose, Process, and Practice*. Mahwah, NJ: Lawrence Erlbaum.

Flower, L. (1994) *The Construction of Negotiated Meaning: A Social Cognitive Theory of Writing*. Carbondale, IL: Southern Illinois University Press.

Hirose, K. (2003) Comparing L1 and L2 organizational patterns in the argumentative writing of Japanese EFL students. *Journal of Second Language Writing* 12 (2), 181–209.

Hirose, K. (2006) Dialogue: Pursuing the complexity of the relationship between L1 and L2 writing. *Journal of Second Language Writing* 15 (2), 142–146.

Hyland, K. (2002) *Teaching and Researching Writing*. New York: Pearson Education.

Kaplan, R.B. (1966) Cultural thought patterns in intercultural education. *Language Learning* 16 (1), 1–20.

Kobayashi, H. (1984a) Rhetorical patterns in English and Japanese. Unpublished doctoral dissertation, Teachers College, Columbia University.

Kobayashi, H. (1984b) Rhetorical patterns in English and Japanese. *TESOL Quarterly* 18 (4), 737–738.

Kobayashi, H. (2002) L1 Japanese high school literacy training: Student and teacher perspectives. *Language and Culture Study* (Hiroshima University, Integrated Arts and Sciences) 28, 1–29.

Kobayashi, H. (2005) Rhetorical decisions in L1 and L2 writing: How do novice writers differ? *Language and Culture Study* (Hiroshima University, Integrated Arts and Sciences) 31, 43–73.

Kobayashi, H. and Rinnert, C. (1996) Factors affecting composition evaluation in an EFL context: Cultural rhetorical pattern and readers' background. *Language Learning* 46 (3), 91–116.

Kobayashi, H. and Rinnert, C. (2001a) Factors relating to EFL writers' discourse level revision skills. In R.M. Manchón (ed.) *Writing in the L2 classroom. Issues in Research and Pedagogy.* Special issue of *International Journal of English Studies* 1 (2), 71–102.

Kobayashi, H. and Rinnert, C. (2001b) *The Role of Academic Writing in Higher Education in Japan: Current Status and Future Perspectives*. Report for the Japan Society for the Promotion of Science, Research Code 11680263.

Kobayashi, H. and Rinnert, C. (2002) High school student perceptions of first language literacy instruction: Implications for second language writing. *Journal of Second Language Writing* 11 (2), 91–116.

Kobayashi, H. and Rinnert, C. (2004a) Composing competence: How L1 and L2 writing experience interact. In M. Baynham, A. Deignan and G. White (eds) *Applied Linguistics at the Interface. British Studies in Applied Linguistics* (pp. 105–118). London: Equinox.

Kobayashi, H. and Rinnert, C. (2004b) *Transferability of Composing Competence Across Languages: From L1 to L2.* Report for the Japan Society for the Promotion of Science, Research Code 148580292.

Kobayashi, H. and Rinnert, C. (2007) Transferability of argumentative writing competence from L2 to L1: Effects of overseas experience. In M. Conrick and M. Howard (eds) *From Applied Linguistics to Linguistics Applied: Issues, Practices,*

Trends. British Studies in Applied Linguistics (pp. 91–110). London: British Association for Applied Linguistics.

Kobayashi, H. and Rinnert, C. (2008) Task response and text construction across L1 and L2 writing. In R.M. Manchón and P. De Haan (eds) *Writing in Foreign Language Contexts: Research Insights*. Special issue of the *Journal of Second Language Writing* 17 (1), 7–29.

Kubota, R. (1997) Reevaluation of the uniqueness of Japanese written discourse: Implications for contrastive rhetoric. *Written Communication* 14 (4), 460–480.

Kubota, R. (1998a) An investigation of Japanese and English L1 essay organization: Differences and similarities. *The Canadian Modern Language Review* 54 (4), 475–507.

Kubota, R. (1998b) An investigation of L1–L2 transfer in writing among Japanese university students: Implications for contrastive rhetoric. *Journal of Second Language Writing* 7 (1), 69–100.

Kubota, R. and Lehner, A. (2004) Toward critical contrastive rhetoric. *Journal of Second Language Writing* 13 (1), 7–27.

Kubota, R. and Shi, L. (2005) Instruction and reading samples for opinion writing in L1 junior high school textbooks in China and Japan. In X. Li and C.P. Casanave (eds). *Journal of Asian Pacific Communication, Special Issue* 15 (1), 97–123.

Langan, J. (2000) *College Writing Skills* (5th edn). Boston, MA: McGraw-Hill.

Leki, I. and Carson, J. (1994) Students' perceptions of EAP writing instruction and writing needs across thee disciplines. *TESOL Quarterly* 28 (1), 81–101.

Liebman, J.D. (1992) Toward a new contrastive rhetoric: Differences between Arabic and Japanese rhetorical instruction. *Journal of Second Language Writing* 1 (2), 141–165.

Manchón, R. and Roca de Larios, J. (2007) On the temporal nature of planning in L1 and L2 composing: A study of foreign language writers. *Language Learning* 57 (4), 549–593.

Matsuda, P.K. (1997) Contrastive rhetoric in context: A dynamic model of L2 writing. *Journal of Second Language Writing* 6 (1), 45–60.

Mok, W.E. (1993) Contrastive rhetoric and the Japanese writer of EFL. *JALT Journal* 15 (2), 151–161.

Ortega, L. and Carson, J. (2009) Multicompetence, social context, and L2 writing research praxis. In T. Silva and P.K. Matsuda (eds) *Practicing Theory in Second Language Writing*. West Lafayette, IN: Parlor Press.

Reid, J. (1988) *The Process of Composition*. Englewood Cliffs, NJ: Prentice Hall Regents.

Riazi, A.M. (1997) Acquiring disciplinary literacy: A social-cognitive analysis of text production and learning among Iranian graduate students of education. *Journal of Second Language Writing* 6 (2), 105–137.

Rinnert, C. and Kobayashi, H. (2001) Differing perceptions of EFL writing among readers in Japan. *The Modern Language Journal* 85 (2), 189–209.

Rinnert, C. and Kobayashi, H. (2004) Japanese university teachers' perceptions of L1 academic writing across disciplines. *Hiroshima Journal of International Studies* (Faculty of International Studies, Hiroshima City University) 10, 151–170.

Rinnert, C. and Kobayashi, H. (2005) Borrowing words and ideas: Insights from Japanese L1 writers. *Journal of Asian Pacific Communication* 15 (1), 31–56.

Rinnert, C. and Kobayashi, H. (2007) L1 and L2 pre-university writing experience: What effects on novice Japanese EFL writers? *Hiroshima Journal of International Studies* (Faculty of International Studies, Hiroshima City University) 13, 65–92.
Roca de Larios, J. and Murphy, L. (2001) Some steps towards a socio-cognitive interpretation of second language composition processes. In R.M. Manchón (ed.) *Writing in the L2 classroom. Issues in Research and Pedagogy.* Special issue of *International Journal of English Studies* 1 (2), 25–46.
Roca de Larios, J., Murphy, L. and Marín, J. (2002) A critical examination of L2 writing process research. In S. Ransdell and M. Barbier (eds) *New Directions for Research in L2 Writing* (pp. 11–47). Boston, MA: Kluwer Academic.
Sasaki, M. and Hirose, K. (1996) Explanatory variables for EFL students' expository writing. *Language Learning* 46 (1), 137–174.
Shi, L. (2003) Writing in two cultures: Chinese professors return from the West. *The Canadian Language Review* 59 (3), 369–391.
Shi, L. and Beckett, G.H. (2002) Japanese exchange students' writing experiences in a Canadian university. *TESL Canada Journal* 20 (1), 38–56.
Singley, M.K. and Anderson, J.R. (1989) *The Transfer of Cognitive Skill*. Cambridge, MA: Harvard University Press.
Villamail, O. and de Guerrero, M. (1996) Peer revision in the L2 classroom: Social-cognitive activities, mediating strategies, and aspects of social behavior. *Journal of Second Language Writing* 5 (1), 51–75.

Chapter 2

Changes in English as a Foreign Language Students' Writing Over 3.5 years: A Sociocognitive Account

MIYUKI SASAKI

Introduction

In this chapter, I present an empirical longitudinal study of 22 foreign language (FL) writers, with a special focus on the dynamics of their second language (L2) writing ability and motivation over 3.5 years. The study is a follow-up of another recent longitudinal study (Sasaki, 2004), and it was also motivated by the findings of five other studies (Hirose & Sasaki, 1994; Sasaki & Hirose, 1996; Sasaki, 2000, 2002, 2007) that I have conducted over the past 15 years. In line with the other contributions in Part 1, I will first present a synthesis of these studies, which will serve as the contextualization for the present study.

The six studies (including Sasaki, 2004) can be categorized according to their purpose, theoretical framework, data type and empirical approach (Table 2.1). The first four studies are divided into two pairs in that the earlier ones in each pair (Hirose & Sasaki, 1994; Sasaki, 2000) were exploratory with smaller sample sizes and more research targets analyzed, and the later ones (Hirose & Sasaki, 1996; Sasaki, 2002) were confirmatory, statistically testing hypotheses obtained on the basis of the previous exploratory studies. In the first pair, Keiko Hirose and I examined explanatory factors for Japanese learners' English writing ability. In Hirose and Sasaki (1994), L2 proficiency and first language (L1) writing ability significantly explained 74.5% of the 19 Japanese students' L2 composition score variance. In Sasaki and Hirose (1996), in addition to L2 proficiency (52%) and L1 writing ability (18%), L2 writing meta-knowledge significantly explained 11% of the L2 composition score variance. We also found that good L2 writers were different from poor

Table 2.1 Relationships among six studies

The target of analysis	*Theoretical framework*	*Data type used*	*Exploratory*	*Confirmatory*
Explanatory factors for the quality of L2 writing	Psychometric (causal-comparative)	Cross-sectional (*etic*)	Hirose and Sasaki (1994)	Sasaki and Hirose (1996)
L2 writing processes	Cognitive models of L1 writing	Cross-sectional/ longitudinal (*etic*)	Sasaki (2000)	Sasaki (2002)
Changes in L2 writing behavior and motivation	Cognitive models of L1 writing	Longitudinal (*etic* + *emic*)	Sasaki (2002)	
Effect of study-abroad experiences	Cognitive models of L1 writing	Longitudinal (*etic* + *emic*)	Sasaki (2007)	

writers in terms of L2 writing strategy use, previous L2 writing experiences and L2 writing confidence.

After we conducted these two studies examining *what* factors determined the quality of Japanese students' L2 writing, I became interested in *how* the end-product of such writing was actually achieved. Thus, in Sasaki (2000) and (2002), the second pair of the studies in Table 2.1, I investigated the English writing processes among three different pairs of Japanese English as a foreign language (EFL) writers: experts versus novices; more- versus less-skilled student writers; and novice writers before and after two semesters of writing instruction. For the theoretical framework, I drew on studies that had originally been employed for building 'cognitive models of L1 writing' (Manchón *et al.*, 2007) both in Japanese (Anzai & Uchida, 1981) and in English (e.g. Flower & Hayes, 1981), and later in L2 (e.g. Cumming, 1989). In Sasaki (2000) and (2002), I also added a longitudinal design comparing the same novice writers before and after two semesters of L2 writing instruction in order to examine how such instruction would affect the same participants' L2 writing processes. In Sasaki (2000), the eight novice writers did not become either better or more fluent in L2 writing over two semesters, but in Sasaki (2002), another 22 participants did become significantly better if not more fluent. The results of Sasaki (2002) also revealed that the experts paid significantly more attention to rhetorical refining, and less attention to local planning than the novices, and that the novices paid significantly less attention to local planning at the end of the second semester.

In these four previous studies, I dealt mainly with the cognitive aspects of L2 writing product/processes from an *etic* perspective. It was not until Sasaki (2004) that I became interested in the participants' *emic* perspective as well as possible effects of external factors on their L2 writing ability and its development. After I conducted Sasaki (2002), I was able to continue to observe 11 out of the 22 participants for the following 2.5 years (i.e. for 3.5 years including the first year in Sasaki [2002]). In Sasaki (2004), I thus reported these participants' changes over 3.5 years in terms of L2 proficiency, L2 writing quality/fluency, the use of L2 writing strategies and confidence in L2 writing. Because six (the English as a second language [ESL] students) of the 11 participants chose to spend some time in English-speaking environments during the observation period, I could also examine the effects of these experiences. The scarcity of such longitudinal studies and the small sample size made the study exploratory in nature. As mentioned above, at the end of my 3.5-year observation period, I decided to ask each participant about their own views of their changes in these different variables over the period because, having looked at *what* and *how* these students learned to write in L2, I became interested in exploring *why* they changed the way they did.

The results of Sasaki (2004) revealed that most participants improved their L2 writing quality, fluency and confidence over 3.5 years. The students who remained in Japan (the EFL students) attributed their improvement mainly to the English classes they took at the Japanese university. In contrast, the ESL students explained that their overseas experiences made the greatest impact on their L2 writing ability. Furthermore, it was only the students who went abroad that became more motivated to write better compositions, and they all attributed such motivation increase to their overseas stay.

Because the factor of study-abroad (SA) experiences was so influential on the participants' L2 writing development in Sasaki (2004), I did a follow-up study (Sasaki, 2007) to confirm these findings. I thus compared the L2 writing ability/fluency and the use of L2 writing strategies of seven Japanese university students (the SA group) who spent four to nine months in English-speaking countries with six students (the at-home [AH] group) who remained in Japan over one year that covered all the

SA students' overseas stay, but not extending too long after that. The results showed that only the SA group improved their L2 writing ability, although both groups improved their general L2 proficiency. In terms of motivation, as with the ESL students in Sasaki (2004), only the SA students became more motivated to make efforts to write better L2 compositions. For this study, I also included students' interviews and reports representing their *emic* perspective. Such data revealed that the AH students attributed the deterioration in their L2 writing ability to the extensive job-hunting activities they had been engaged in over the one year, and that the SA students again mainly credited their L2 writing improvement to their overseas experiences. These results confirmed the importance of examining the participants' cognitive development as situated in their sociocultural environments. At this point, as a researcher, I redirected myself toward a larger theoretical framework than the 'main-stream' (Thorne, 2005: 393) exclusively cognitivistic research perspective.

The Present Study

In the present study, using a new set of data, I therefore examined both the cognitive and social aspects of the participants' changes in L2 writing ability and motivation, the two variables that played important roles in my previous studies as explained above. Because many of the participants spent some time in L2 speaking environments during the 3.5-year observation period, and because these experiences had varying degrees of impact on their L2 writing ability development and motivation according to the length of their overseas stays, the study also investigated the effects of different lengths of such SA experiences. Unlike in Sasaki (2004) where the social aspects were by-products of its research design, in the present study, I adopted a sociocognitive design, which guided me in investigating the participants' L2 writing development in a more socially situated manner. This 'socio-cognitive' orientation corresponds to Riazi's (1997: 110) 'social-cognitive perspective' in its belief that the cognitive aspects of L2 writing are better explained when considered with the social situations that the learners interact with.

Below are brief summaries of the results of previous studies that have targeted the three relevant factors for the present study: L2 writing ability development, L2 writing motivation, and effects of SA experiences on L2 writing.

Influential factors for L2 writing ability development

Researchers have investigated potentially influential factors for L2 writing development both cross-sectionally and longitudinally. Cross-sectionally, the construct of L2 writing ability has usually been measured by L2 writing quality. Researchers to date have found that the quality of L2 writing tends to be high if the writers have high L2 proficiency (e.g. Pennington & So, 1993) and/or high L1 writing ability (e.g. Cumming, 1989), if they use good writers' strategies (e.g. 'planning' in Jones & Tetroe, 1987), if they possess a sufficient amount of metaknowledge (e.g. Kobayashi & Rinnert, 2001) and/or if they have practiced L2 writing sufficiently (e.g. Sasaki & Hirose, 1996). The findings of these cross-sectional studies are insightful, but we cannot assume any causal relationship between these factors and the participants' L2 writing ability because their characteristics were examined synchronically with L2 writing quality. In other words, they might have just co-occurred with good L2 writing.

In contrast, longitudinal studies, although scarce in number, can allow us to establish more confidently a causal relationship between various factors and L2 writing development (Asher, 1983). This is especially true when students are receiving L2 writing instruction while studies are being conducted. In Sasaki (2002), for example, participants significantly improved their L2 composition scores while taking a freshman composition class over two semesters. I thus speculated that such instruction probably brought about the students' L2 writing development. Furthermore, when I had access to the participants' own views, I became even more confident in the effects of the instruction (Sasaki, 2004, 2007). In these studies, students who went abroad added that having written much and often in their overseas classes was also useful. These accounts confirm the results of cross-sectional studies (e.g. Sasaki & Hirose, 1996) suggesting that L2 writing practice and metaknowledge can influence L2 writing ability development.

L2 writing motivation

In the 1970s, Robert Gardner and his colleagues initiated modern L2 motivation studies in Canada. Their models usually included factors affecting L2 acquisition, such as attitude and anxiety, in addition to (sometimes different types of) motivation (e.g. Gardner & MacIntyre, 1993). Their studies were typically psychometric, utilizing correlations among scores for these variables, and the target variable tended to be general L2 proficiency. The fact that the research target was general L2 proficiency remained true even after the 1990s when some other constructs such as self-confidence (e.g. Clément *et al.*, 1994) started to be introduced into L2 motivation research from the fields of education and psychology, and even after qualitative studies started to investigate how learners' motivational changes interacted with their sociocultural environments over time (e.g. Ushioda, 2001).

The particular construct of L2 writing motivation was thus rarely investigated until the beginning of 2000 when Alister Cumming and his colleagues started a series of inquiries into the nature and development of L2 writing goals and motivation. Their participants were all ESL students in university settings in Canada. Because the studies were conducted after the field of L2 motivation research had been challenged to include the perspective of 'context and time' (Dörnyei, 2001: 47), Cumming and his colleagues responded to this challenge by employing longitudinal and situated data. Yang *et al.* (2004), for example, provided a microlevel detailed analysis of six ESL students' L2 motivational changes over the course of one ESL program. As the means of explaining the qualitative changes in the participants' L2 writing motivation, Yang *et al.* (2004) used Engeström's (1987) expanded activity system, believing that 'individual students are active, responsive agents with their own individual goals, orientations, values, beliefs, and histories' (Yang *et al.*, 2004: 14). In addition to this activity theory perspective, Cumming (2006: ix) employed goal theory from the field of psychology for its 'multiple theoretical frames' in seven collaborative studies focusing on both students' and their teachers' goals for learning and teaching L2 writing. Cumming's (2006) results are insightful, showing how L2 students'/teachers' motivation constantly interacted with environmental factors. And yet, from the perspective of FL writing research, investigation of students' goals for learning L2 writing may not be applicable because FL students do not always have to set goals to survive in their L2 learning situations. However, no study to date has been conducted to investigate such general L2 writing motivation in an FL setting.

Effects of study-abroad experiences

Research on the effects of SA experiences has become increasingly popular, especially during the past two decades. Researchers have discovered that (1) compared with their AH counterparts, SA students made greater improvement in their L2 speaking ability (e.g. Lafford, 2004), L2 listening ability (e.g. Allen, 2002), L2 reading ability (e.g. Dewey, 2004) and in their sociolinguistic use of L2 (e.g. Barron, 2006); (2) the sociocultural environments of the L2 community (e.g. how they were treated) played an important role for such changes (e.g. Churchill, 2006); and (3) there were great individual differences in terms of these changes (e.g. Isabelli-García, 2006).

Despite these findings, there are many other aspects of SA experiences that still need further investigation. For example, compared with speaking, listening and reading skills, very few studies have investigated the effects of SA experiences on L2 writing skills (Churchill & Dufon, 2006). Another area that remains to be studied and is also relevant to the present study is motivation. Very few studies have examined the effects of overseas stay on L2 learning motivation. When they were investigated at all, the findings were mixed, with SA experiences working positively (e.g. Simões, 1996) or negatively (e.g. Allen, 2002). Furthermore, no study to date has examined how the particular variable of L2 writing motivation might be affected by SA experiences. A third area that needs further studies concerns the effects of the length of stay overseas. Very few studies have been conducted to examine such effects on any variable of skill and knowledge. Although researchers admit that longer stays tend to produce better results, 'the question of how long is needed to make significant gains in specific skills remains unanswered' (Churchill & Dufon, 2006: 23). Lastly, practically no study has reported long-term effects (e.g. six months after) of SA experiences on any skill and knowledge.

Informed and motivated by the results of these previous studies as well as my own studies described in the introductory section, I undertook the present study with the following four questions in mind:

(1) How does the students' L2 writing ability change over 3.5 years?
(2) How does their L2 writing motivation change over 3.5 years?
(3) How do their motivational changes interact with changes in their L2 writing ability?
(4) Do the different lengths of the students' SA experiences have differential impacts on their L2 writing ability and motivational changes?

Method

Participants

At the beginning of the present study, the 22 participants were all 18-year-old university freshmen, majoring in British and American studies at the same university in Japan. They had studied English for six years by the time the study began. They had received little L2 writing instruction while at high school. By the time they graduated from the university, however, they had taken at least one ESL class where they obtained some knowledge about how to prepare texts for what Johns (1997: 46) calls 'the pedagogical genres', such as 'the essay examination responses, the term paper, or the pedagogical summary'. Their mean score ($M = 122.82$ for a maximum of 200, $SD = 17.01$) for an argumentative composition was not significantly different from that ($M = 134.55$, $SD = 17.43$) of the participants of Sasaki (2004) when they were freshmen ($t(31) = 1.85$, $p = 0.07$). They all received compensation for participating in this study.

Between their sophomore and senior years, 17 of the 22 students participated in SA programs provided by the university, spending different lengths of time in Canada, the USA or in New Zealand. All participants were subsequently divided into four groups according to the length of their overseas stay. The SA-2 group ($n = 6$) participated in two-month SA programs, the SA-4 group ($n = 3$) in four-month SA programs, the SA-8/11 group ($n = 8$) in eight- to eleven-month SA programs and the AH group ($n = 5$) remained in Japan during my 3.5-year observation period. In addition to such length differences, the three SA programs also differed in prior requirements: only five applicants (out of a total of 150 students) with the top institutional Test of English as a foreign language (TOEFL) scores were allowed to attend the 8/11 SA program, and only the next 10 best were allowed to attend the SA-4 programs, but there was no such requirement for the SA-2 programs. Consequently, most SA-4 and SA-8/11 students studied hard to obtain high TOEFL scores before going abroad. In this sense, these four groups might have been motivationally different from the very beginning of their university life. However, when they were freshmen, neither their general English proficiency (measured by the sum of Listening and Structure section scores of *Comprehensive English Language Test*; see Harris and Palmer [1986]; $F(3, 18) = 1.15$ for a maximum of 200) nor their English writing ability (see the Results and Discussion section) was significantly different.

Table 2.2 presents the mean hours of ESL and regular-subject classes the participants took overseas and in Japan. The SA-2 students only took ESL classes whereas the SA-4 and SA-8/11 students took both ESL and regular-subject classes. At the Japanese university, the AH students generally took more English classes than the SA students simply because they were in Japan longer. The number of English classes these four groups took at the Japanese university drastically decreased for their

Table 2.2 Four different groups' English-related educational experiences over the four university years

Group	*Mean class hours per week when abroad*	*Mean English class hours per week when in Japan*
At-home ($n = 5$)	None	Freshman: 9
		Sophomore: 6.5
		Junior: 6.6
		Senior: 0.2
SA-2 ($n = 6$)	ESL: 25.4	Freshman: 9
		Sophomore: 5.1
		Junior: 3.8
		Senior: 1.5
SA-4 ($n = 3$)	ESL: 12.4 Regular subject: 5.7	Freshman: 8.9
		Sophomore: 4.8
		Junior: 6.6
		Senior: 1.9
SA-8/11 ($n = 8$)	ESL: 10.9 Regular subject: 6.2	Freshman: 9
		Sophomore: 4.1
		Junior: 4.5
		Senior: 0.4

senior year because, like many other university students in Japan, they were busy job-hunting during that year (see Sasaki, 2007).

Data

As shown in Table 2.3, I collected L2 writing and motivation data at four different points: in the first month of the participants' freshman year (pre-freshman period), and the third month of their sophomore, junior and senior years (mid-sophomore, mid-junior, mid-senior periods). In addition, in the eighth month of their senior year (post-senior period), I interviewed them again to collect their own accounts of changes in their L2 writing ability and motivation.

Table 2.3 Types of data collected at different periods of observation

Type of data collected (month, year)	*Pre-freshman (month 1, year 1)*	*Mid-sophomore (month 4, year 2)*	*Mid-junior (month 4, year 3)*	*Mid-senior (month 4, year 4)*	*Post-senior (month 9, year 4)*
L2 writing score	x	x	x	x	
Student interviews about L2 classes and motivation	x	x	x	x	
Student interview about changes in L2 writing ability and motivation					x

Composition scores

The participants wrote an argumentative composition on a randomly selected topic from among seven prompts concerning such issues as living in a city or in the country, or abolishing school uniforms (see Sasaki [2004] and the Appendix). The prompts were selected in such a way that the participants wrote about different topics on four different occasions, and that similar ratios of the participants in the four groups addressed the same topics. No participant wrote about the same topic twice.

Two EFL writing specialists scored all the compositions, following Jacobs *et al.*'s (1981) English Composition Profile (an analytical rating scale for EFL compositions involving five evaluation criteria: content, organization, vocabulary, language use and mechanics). The raters had not been informed of the purposes of the present study, when each composition had been written or from which participant group it came. The inter-rater correlation (Pearson correlation coefficient) for the content subscore was 0.88; the organization subscore, 0.83; the vocabulary subscore, 0.75; the language use subscore, 0.80; the mechanics subscore, 0.48 (probably caused by the very narrow range of 1 to 5); and the total score, 0.91. I judged that these correlations were acceptable for the study.

Interviews about L2 writing strategies, L2 classes and motivation given after each composition session

After the participants wrote the compositions described above, I interviewed them about the L2 writing strategies they used for the compositions they had just written (see Sasaki, 2007), the English classes they had taken before and on which aspect of English writing they wanted to improve, if any. The sessions lasted about 60 minutes.

Post-senior interviews on changes in L2 writing ability and motivation

Four months after the participants wrote their mid-senior compositions, I interviewed them individually to collect accounts of their changes between their pre-freshman and mid-senior periods in terms of their L2 writing ability/fluency and strategy-use. During the interviews, I showed the participants a table or a figure containing the actual changes in these variables. In terms of their motivational changes, I showed them the transcription of what they had said when asked which aspects of English writing they wanted to improve in each of the four data-collection sessions. Concerning these accounts, I also asked them additional questions about what other aspects, if any, they might have wanted to improve for the given year, why they had these particular goals and what they did to achieve these goals. When they did not mention any aspect they wanted to improve, I showed them a list (written in Japanese) of possible areas to be improved in L2 writing based on the Cumming's (2006) scheme to probe L2 writing motivation. The entries on the list had been revised as the result of a pilot trial with five students from the same population, and the final list included grammar, vocabulary, organization, planning/revising, speed, quantity, content, various types of writing (e.g. letters, reports), various genres (e.g. narrative, exposition), resistance against writing L2, and personal growth. The entire post-senior interview session lasted for 30–40 minutes. The participants' spoken accounts were all tape-recorded and subsequently transcribed.

Analysis of all the interview data

When analyzing the transcribed interview data, I basically followed Miles and Huberman's (1994: 245) data synthesis tactics, especially those of 'noting patterns, themes, seeing plausibility, and clustering', and 'making contrasts/comparisons'. As in Sasaki (2004), I used the interview data related to the participants' L2 writing ability changes to better interpret the quantitative data of their L2 composition score changes. For the participants' motivational changes, however, I analyzed the data for their own sake following Yang *et al.*'s (2004) research framework based on Engeström's (1987) expanded activity system. The basic principles of activity theory originated from Vygotsky's (e.g. 1978) idea that artifacts or sociocultural entities mediate human thought processes and actions when humans (subjects) operate on objects. This idea was further developed by Leont'ev (e.g. 1981) who focused more on the human relationships and development entailed by activities 'in the process of cooperative labor and social interaction' (Leont'ev, 1981: 56). More recently, Leont'ev's theory was expanded into Engeström's (1987) model of activity system, incorporating additional concepts such as 'rules', 'communities' and 'division of labor'. The model is graphically represented as a triangle with community, roles and division of labor affecting both subject and object (and possible outcomes outside the triangle), which are mediated by mediating artifacts (e.g. Figure 1.2 in Engeström, 1999). Yang *et al.*'s (2004: 15) example below is helpful to understand this model:

> To take an example of second language (L2) learning, a student (subject) in an ESL class aims to improve her competence in academic English writing (object). This student may follow the teacher's instruction, do assignments, read a textbook, talk with friends, surf the Internet, refer to dictionaries and so on (mediating artifacts). After a period of practice this student may achieve her goal such as getting a high grade on her essays (outcome). This activity happens in the ESL class (community), and the student intends to grasp the conventions of academic English writing (rules). In this ESL class, the teacher provides model instruction, gives assignments, and offers feedback, and students follow their teacher and do the assignments (division of labor).

In addition to the categories originally used by Yang *et al.* (2004), in the present study I included two more categories of 'imagined L2-related community' and 'imagined non-L2-related community' because in the process of analyzing the interview data, I realized that they were also important for understanding the participants' motivational changes. Consequently, I changed the term 'community' in Yang *et al.*'s scheme to 'actual L2-related community' to distinguish it from the two imagined communities. For the term 'imagined community', I followed Kanno and Norton's (2003: 241) definition of 'groups of people, not immediately tangible and accessible, with whom we connect through the power of imagination'.

Results and Discussion

L2 writing ability

I present the participants' changes in L2 composition scores for descriptive purposes. In addition, I used analysis of variance (ANOVA) to check the degree of the changes between the pre-freshman and mid-senior periods, using SPSS Version 6.1 (SPSS Incorporated, 1994). Because of the small sample sizes, however, the results of the ANOVA analyses should not be generalized.

As shown in Table 2.4, the changes in the four groups' total composition scores increased until their sophomore year, but the AH group's score decreased after that, and dropped below their freshman level for their senior composition. In contrast, the three SA groups' senior year composition scores were all higher than those of their freshman compositions, although the SA-8/11 group was the only one that kept improving until their senior year (see the Appendix for examples of their improvement). A two-way ANOVA comparing the four groups' differences between their freshman and senior years indicated a significant interaction between the time and group effects ($F(3, 18) = 6.77, p < 0.01$).

The results of subsequent *post-hoc* simple effects analyses (Tanaka & Yamagiwa, 1992) revealed that the four groups were not significantly

Table 2.4 Mean total composition scores (Total Possible = 200) at the four different observation periods

Group	*Pre-freshman (M (SD))*	*Mid-sophomore (M (SD))*	*Mid-junior (M (SD))*	*Mid-senior (M (SD))*
At home ($n = 5$)	125.20 (14.02)	140.40 (13.07)	138.60 (13.76)	123.20 (7.89)
SA-2 ($n = 6$)	109.17 (18.68)	128.00 (21.84)	126.67 (17.24)	130.17 (26.72)
SA-4 ($n = 3$)	123.33 (1.15)	153.00 (8.19)	169.67 (7.51)	163.67 (16.86)
SA-8/11 ($n = 8$)	131.38 (16.08)	155.63 (10.06)	159.38 (15.17)	162.00 (6.85)

different when they were freshmen, but that they were significantly different as seniors ($F(3, 18) = 8.22$, $p < 0.01$ for their freshman year; and $F(1, 20) = 33.59$, $p < 0.01$ for their senior year). Furthermore, the time effect was significant for the composition score changes for all three SA groups ($F(1, 18) = 9.67$, $p < 0.01$ for the SA-2 group; $F(1, 18) = 35.67$, $p < 0.01$ for the SA-4 group; and $F(1, 18) = 20.56$, $p < 0.01$ for the SA-8/11 group), but not for the AH group. That is, the three SA groups significantly improved their composition scores over 3.5 years, but the AH group did not. Subsequent multiple comparisons by the Least Significant Difference Method ($MSE = 89.27$, $p < 0.05$) indicate that when they were seniors, the SA-4 and SA-8/11 groups' scores were significantly higher than those of the AH and SA-2 groups, but that the pair of the AH and SA-2 groups, and the pair of the SA-4 and the SA-8/11 groups were not significantly different from each other.

At the individual level, two of the AH students' English composition scores decreased over 3.5 years, and the other three students' scores slightly increased. However, just like the AH students in Sasaki (2007), all of them felt that their English writing ability deteriorated especially after their junior year because they had had fewer English classes and fewer opportunities to write in English. In contrast, all of the SA students' English composition scores improved over the 3.5 years. Two SA-2 and three SA-4 students attributed their score increase mainly to the English writing classes they took at the Japanese university, four SA-8/11 students attributed their score increase to the English writing classes they took abroad, one SA-2 student and five SA-8/11 students attributed their increases to both the classes they took in Japan and abroad, one SA-2 student said that writing emails to friends she made abroad was the only helpful factor and the last SA-2 student said that the junior and senior compositions were simply easier to write.

The 10 SA students who attributed their score increase to their overseas L2 writing classes all added that the experiences of learning how to write (e.g. how to organize an effective paragraph), and having to write much and often (both for ESL and other classes) were especially helpful. These results concur with those of previous cross-sectional and longitudinal studies (e.g. Kobayashi & Rinnert, 2001; Sasaki, 2004) in that the two factors of L2 writing metaknowledge and practice influenced L2 writing development. In contrast, the AH students all felt that their English writing ability worsened after their junior year because they had fewer English classes. This is especially noteworthy when we recall that many of the SA students whose scores increased for their senior compositions, also had fewer English classes after becoming seniors

(Table 2.2). In spite of what they claimed, the perceived and actual deterioration of the AH students' L2 writing ability as seniors could be better explained by their low motivation rather than reduced L2 contact hours (see also the next section).

L2 writing motivation

Table 2.5 presents the changes in the four group members' L2 writing motivation in terms of the relevant components of the revised version of Yang *et al.*'s (2004) research scheme based on Engeström's (1987) expanded activity systems. The descriptions presented in the table are the tendencies shared by more than half of the members of each group. In the activity of studying L2 writing over 3.5 years, the components of 'rules' and 'division of labor' basically remained the same. That is, the participants studied how to write in the genre of academic writing, and the teachers taught the English classes where they learned these rules. The participants' changes in the other components are shown in Table 2.5.

The first four rows of Table 2.5a show the characteristics of the four groups' L2 writing motivation when they were freshmen. Under the column for object (i.e. what they wanted to improve), we can see that the four groups were all motivated to improve some aspects of their L2 writing. The only difference is that, as can be seen in the column of mediating artifacts (i.e. what were involved in the participants' trying to attain their objects), except for the AH group, all the other groups used textbooks, dictionaries and teachers to achieve their goals. In other words, unlike the other three groups, the AH group remained in what Dörnyei and Ottó (1998) call the 'preactional phase', without crossing the 'metaphorical "Rubicon" by actually embarking on the task' (Dörnyei, 2001: 88). In fact, 60% of them reported doing nothing to improve their L2 writing throughout the 3.5-year observation period. Such low motivation of the AH group helps us better explain why their L2 composition scores decreased after their junior year, whereas the other three groups' scores did not, despite the fact that they all took similar numbers of L2 classes as seniors.

The four groups' characteristics presented in Table 2.5b for their sophomore year were similar to those for their freshman year except that 10 (58.8%) of the SA students had a SA experience in that year. Recall that even before going abroad, the SA-4 and SA-8/11 groups had to study hard to achieve high TOEFL scores. In addition, the three SA groups' overseas experiences in their sophomore year influenced their

Table 2.5 Students' L2 writing motivation and related components

Group	*Object*	*Mediating artifact*	*Actual L2-related community*	*L2-related imagined community*	*Non-L2-related imagined community*	*Outcome*
(a) Freshman year						
At-home ($n = 5$)	Grammar (60%); vocabulary (60%)	Nothing (60%)	EFL classes (100%)			Improved L2 writing ability (60%)
SA-2 ($n = 6$)	Grammar (66.7%); vocabulary (83.3%); quantity (50%); confidence (50%)	Textbooks, dictionary, teachers (83.3%)	EFL classes (100%)			Improved L2 writing ability (100%)
SA-4 ($n = 3$)	Grammar (100%); vocabulary (100%); quantity (66.7%)	Textbooks, dictionary, teachers (100%)	EFL classes (100%)			Improved L2 writing ability (100%)
SA-8/11 ($n = 8$)	Vocabulary (87.5%); quantity (62.5%)	Textbooks, dictionary, teachers (87.5%)	EFL classes (100%)			Improved L2 writing ability (100%)
(b) Sophomore year						
At-home ($n = 5$)	Grammar (60%)	Nothing (60%)	EFL classes (100%)			Improved L2 writing ability (60%)

Table 2.5 (*Continued*)

Group	*Object*	*Mediating artifact*	*Actual L2-related community*	*L2-related imagined community*	*Non-L2-related imagined community*	*Outcome*
SA-2 ($n = 6$)	Grammar (83.3%); vocabulary (66.7%); quantity (66.7%)	Books (66.7%)	ESL classes (33.3% for two months) EFL classes (100%)			Improved L2 writing ability (83.3%)
SA-4 ($n = 3$)	Grammar (100%); vocabulary (100%); quantity (66.7%)	Grammar reference books (66.7%)	ESL classes (33.3% for four months) EFL classes (100%)			Improved L2 writing ability (100%)
SA-8/11 ($n = 8$)	Vocabulary (50%); quantity (50%)	Textbooks, dictionary, teachers (87.5%)	ESL classes (62.5% for 8–11 months) EFL classes (100%)			Improved L2 writing ability (62.5%)
(c) Junior year						
At-home ($n = 5$)	Grammar (80%)	Nothing (60%)	EFL classes (100%)			Improved L2 writing ability (40%). Decreased L2 writing ability (40%)

Table 2.5 (*Continued*)

Group	*Object*	*Mediating artifact*	*Actual L2-related community*	*L2-related imagined community*	*Non-L2-related imagined community*	*Outcome*
SA-2 ($n = 6$)	Grammar (100%); vocabulary (50%); quantity (66.7%)	E-mail (66.7%)	ESL classes (50.0% for two months) EFL classes (100%)	NES/foreign e-mail-pals/ pen-pals (66.7%)		Decreased L2 writing ability (83.3%)
SA-4 ($n = 3$)	Vocabulary (100%); organization (66.7%); planning (66.7%); content (66.7%)	Teachers (66.7%)	EFL classes (100%)	ESL classes (100%)		Improved L2 writing ability (100%)
SA-8/11 ($n = 8$)	Content (50%)	TOEIC[a]/ TOEFL (62.5%); NES friends (62.5%)	ESL classes (37.5% for 8–10 months) EFL classes (100%)	ESL classes (87.5%)		Improved L2 writing ability (50%). Motivated to write better in L2
(d) Senior year						
At-home ($n = 5$)	Grammar (60%)	Nothing (60%)	EFL classes (100%)		The community of the professionals of their choice (80%)	Decreased L2 writing ability (80%). Lost interest in studying L2 writing (80%)

Table 2.5 (*Continued*)

Group	*Object*	*Mediating artifact*	*Actual L2-related community*	*L2-related imagined community*	*Non-L2-related imagined community*	*Outcome*
SA-2 ($n = 6$)	Grammar (100%); how to write e-mail/letters (50%); vocabulary (50%)	E-mail (83.3%)	ESL classes (16.7% for two months) EFL classes (100%)	NES/foreign e-mail-pals/pen-pals (88.3%)	The community of the professionals of their choice (83.3%)	Improved L2 writing ability (83.3%)
SA-4 ($n = 3$)	Vocabulary (66.7%)	TOEIC[a]/Step Test[b] (100%)	EFL classes (100%)	ESL classes (66.7%)	The community of the professionals of their choice (100%)	Decreased L2 writing ability (66.7%). Motivated to write better in L2 (100%)
SA-8/11 ($n = 8$)	Content (75%)	Self-directed writing (62.5%); dictionary, reference books (50%)	EFL classes (100%)	ESL classes (87.5%)	The community of the professionals of their choice (87.5%)	Improved L2 writing ability (50%). Motivated to write better in L2 (87.5%)

[a]Test of English for International Communication.
[b]Society for Testing English Proficiency.
Note. The descriptions in the cells in (a) to (d) are given if they were shared by more than half of the participants.

subsequent motivational behavior for L2 writing. One noticeable consequence of such influences is that the three SA groups as juniors and seniors formed some kind of 'L2-related imagined communities' that had not existed before. That is, after they became juniors, when they studied L2 writing, many of them came to imagine communities where people would use L2 for actual communicative purposes. For example, many SA-2 group members kept in touch with the L1 English-speaking or foreign friends they had become acquainted with while abroad, and corresponded with them through email after coming home. Although they did not receive emails from such friends every day, they imagined their life through received emails, and spent time thinking how best to reply to them. Many of them said that they used such email letter writing to improve their L2 writing. Interestingly, when they became seniors, writing good email letters even became one of their L2 writing goals.

In contrast, the other two SA groups mainly imagined ESL and other overseas class communities when they wrote in L2. Unlike the SA-2 students, they did not imagine email pen pals when writing in L2, although all of them used email to keep in touch with their overseas friends. This might be because these two groups had more opportunities to write in classes than the SA-2 group while abroad. In the ESL and/or other writing classes, they learned how to organize effective compositions, and in both ESL and regular classes, they wrote different types of texts (e.g. term papers, speech drafts) much and often. When they had to write in L2 after coming home, 100% of the SA-4 group and 87.5% of the SA-8/11 group remembered the time they were writing for the classes they took abroad, and they still expressed their desire to write better in L2, as exemplified in Sayuri's remarks in Example 1.

Example 1

Sayuri (who spent nine months in the USA was explaining how her motivation to write better in English had emerged): When I was in the USA,

Miyuki: Yes?

Sayuri: There was an institute where teachers read my term papers before I turned them in.

Miyuki: Uh, huh.

Sayuri: Having my papers revised there was useful.

Miyuki: Yeah, it must be useful.

Sayuri: I always tried to write better so that the revision there would be minimal. And even now I always try to make such revision minimal when I write in English.

Such motivation is qualitatively different from the SA-2 students' motivation to simply improve one particular aspect (i.e. email letter writing) of their L2 writing. The difference may also be reflected in the fact that only SA-4 and SA-8/11 groups were motivated to improve the 'content' of their L2 writing after their junior year (Table 2.5c,d). Furthermore, the post-senior interviews asking about changes in specific L2 strategy-use reveal that after coming home, one (33.3%) SA-4 student and four (50%) SA-8/11 students started to pay more attention to rhetorical refinement even when translating from L1 to L2 while writing in L2. None of the AH and SA-2 groups reported such changes. These findings imply that the task of writing may no longer have been the same for the four groups of students after becoming juniors. For the AH and SA-2 groups, the writing task was something they would do when asked to do so, but they were not particularly motivated to do a good job. In contrast, those who had been abroad for more than four months could imagine the possible audience and how to write well, and they often spent much time and energy refining their expressions. In other words, over 3.5 years, 'the same task' of L2 writing became 'different activities' (Coughlan & Duff, 1994: 173) for those four groups of students.

Lastly, related to their senior year (see Table 2.5d), the most noticeable difference from the other years was that many participants formed imagined communities consisting of the professionals of their choice (e.g. an information technology community). That is, when they became seniors, they had some kinds of professional communities they wanted to be members of. Out of the 22 participants, however, only four (one AH, one SA-4, two SA-8/11) had L2-related imagined communities (e.g. a community of English teachers). Although their major (British and American studies) was related to L2 (English), not many graduates at this university (e.g. only 16% in 2006) actually obtained directly L2-related jobs. Consequently, their imagined communities did not always encourage L2 writing improvement. In fact, 80% of the AH group and 66.7% of the SA-4 group had a decrease in their senior L2 composition score, and in the post-senior interviews, all of them attributed this decrease to their intensive job-hunting. And yet, 62.5% of the SA-8/11 group still voluntarily practiced L2 writing (e.g. writing for different topics) to improve the 'content' of their L2 writing, even though such actions did not directly benefit their future career. This indicates that their motivation had become more intrinsic in that they were engaged in 'an ongoing process of seeking and attempting to conquer optimal challenges' (Deci & Ryan, 1985: 32).

These participants' changes in L2 writing motivation in relation to their L2 writing ability development over 3.5 years suggest characteristics unique to FL writers. Recall that all participants, including the AH students, took a relatively large number of English classes until their junior year at the university (Table 2.2). This can explain why even the AH students with low motivation kept improving their L2 compositions until their junior year. Table 2.4 shows that as long as they were exposed to L2 and asked to write in L2, their L2 writing ability could develop even when they made no extra efforts outside the classrooms. As I discussed in the previous section, the two factors of L2 writing metaknowledge and writing practice they gained in L2 writing classes were especially helpful. When that external force of L2 classes diminished, however, students seem to have needed to imagine L2-related communities to keep improving. Considering that the SA-4 and SA-8/11 students improved significantly more than the other two groups over 3.5 years, the former groups' motivation to write better content, imagining the actual L2 writing classrooms might have provoked stronger motivation than the SA-2 students' simply imagining email pen pals. Furthermore, when an impeding factor such as job-hunting entered into their lives, only the SA-8/11 students, who became intrinsically motivated, continued to develop. This group might be the only one expected to improve in the future because such improvement is often not crucial for the learners' social survival in the type of FL situations targeted in the present study.

These findings are in sharp contrast with those of the studies conducted by Cumming and his colleagues (e.g. Cumming, 2006) targeting SL students in Canada. Their participants not only set various objects in terms of L2 writing goals, but also actually took action to act on those goals. Given that many of them were preparing for their university studies, they had immediate needs, such as class assignments to complete, in order to survive in such situations. The participants in the present study, on the other hand, could afford not to pursue improvement in their L2 writing ability as long as they passed their English classes. Such a lack of action to achieve higher-level goals seems a particular characteristic of the FL students represented by the AH group in the present study.

Conclusion

The present study illustrates how FL students' L2 writing ability and motivation changed over 3.5 years, and how individual changes were significantly affected by various sociocultural factors. The study was also unique in examining the long-term effects of SA experiences on L2 writing ability development. The findings reveal that (1) the two factors of gaining L2 metaknowledge and L2 writing practice were especially helpful for developing L2 writing ability; (2) only those students who spent some time abroad formed an L2-related 'imagined community' that potentially motivated them to improve their L2 writing ability; (3) only those students who spent more than four months abroad became motivated to write better in L2, imagining the writing classes they took abroad; (4) after external factors started to impede their studying L2 writing, students needed intrinsic motivation to continue to improve. These findings exemplify the merits of investigating FL phenomena in a socially situated manner.

Despite these findings, however, the present study is still limited in many ways, and should be followed by future studies. First, the study should be replicated, and the findings should be confirmed by studies with larger sample sizes. Because the sample size for each group was small in the present study, individual differences may have masked general patterns that might have emerged if the sample sizes had been larger. On the other hand, however, we also need more in-depth studies of how each individual's changes are affected by various sociocultural factors in order not to overlook critical individual differences, which might be washed away in a search for generalizable patterns. For example, we need to investigate why and how each student chooses (or does not choose) to spend different lengths of time abroad in the first place. Furthermore, after students spend some time abroad, we need to know how (differently) such SA students possibly form L2-related imagined communities, and how such communities help to motivate the students to write better in L2. This seems especially important if we consider that not all FL students can afford to spend time abroad (Dörnyei, 2001). Pedagogically, it would be ideal if we could find a way to create L2-related imagined communities in students' minds without necessarily sending them abroad. Exploring a similar implication, Yashima (2007) reported that Japanese students became more willing to communicate in English by being introduced to an 'imagined international community' (e.g. a Model United Nation) through a 'cognitively and emotionally involving' content-based English class. Applying such a method might be a promising way to increase students' motivation to write in L2 in FL settings. Finally, we also need to investigate why and how only the SA-8/11 group became intrinsically motivated to keep studying L2 writing in a rather autonomous manner. Because more than one year had passed since most of them (70.6%) came home, their SA experiences may not have been directly relevant. Further in-depth studies of SA-8/11 types of learners' changes over time in a motivational research framework (Dörnyei, 2001) may provide a key to inducing long-lasting motivation in FL learners such as those studied in the present research.

Acknowledgements

An earlier version of this manuscript was presented at the Conference on Social and Cognitive Aspects of Second Language Learning and Teaching, The University of Auckland, in New Zealand on 13 May 2007. I would like to thank Ryu Itoh for coding the protocol data and scoring the compositions, Harumi Oishi for scoring the compositions, Takashi Shimokido for his statistical advice, and Rosa Manchón, Chris Casanave, Lourdes Ortega, Phillip Morrow, William Herlofsky and Eton Churchill for their valuable comments and suggestions. The preparation of this manuscript has been aided by a research grant for the 2007 academic year from Nagoya Gakuin University, and by Research Grants No. 18520461 and No. 20520533 for the 2006 to 2008 academic years from the Ministry of Education, Culture, Sports, Science and Technology in Japan.

References

Allen, H.W. (2002) Does study abroad make a difference? An investigation of linguistic and motivational outcomes. PhD thesis, Emory University, 2002. *Dissertation Abstracts International*-A 632 (4), 1279.

Anzai, Y. and Uchida, N. (1981) Kodomo wa Ikani Sakubun o Kakuka [How children produce writing]. *Japanese Journal of Educational Psychology* 29 (4), 323–332.

Asher, H.B. (1983) *Causal Modeling*. Newbury Park, CA: Sage.

Barron, A. (2006) Learning to say 'you' in German: The acquisition of sociolinguistic competence in a study abroad context. In M.A. Dufon and E. Churchill (eds) *Language Learners in Study Abroad Contexts* (pp. 59–88). Clevedon: Multilingual Matters.

Churchill, E. (2006) Variability in the study abroad classroom and learner competence. In M.A. Dufon and E. Churchill (eds) *Language Learners in Study Abroad Contexts* (pp. 203–227). Clevedon: Multilingual Matters.

Churchill, E. and Dufon, M.A. (2006) Evolving threads in study abroad research. In M.A. Dufon and E. Churchill (eds) *Language Learners in Study Abroad Contexts* (pp. 1–27). Clevedon: Multilingual Matters.

Clément, R., Dörnyei, Z. and Noels, K.A. (1994) Motivation, self-confidence, and group cohesion in the foreign language classroom. *Language Learning* 44 (3), 417–447.

Coughlan, P. and Duff, P.A. (1994) Same task, different activities: Analysis of SLA task from an activity theory perspective. In J.P. Lantolf and G. Appel (eds)

Vygotskian Approaches to Second Language Research (pp. 173–191). London: Ablex.

Cumming, A. (1989) Writing expertise and second language proficiency. *Language Learning* 39 (1), 81–141.

Cumming, A. (ed.) (2006) *Goals for Academic Writing: ESL Students and Their Instructors*. Amsterdam: John Benjamins.

Deci, E.L. and Ryan, R.M. (1985) *Intrinsic Motivation and Self-determination in Human Behavior*. New York: Plenum Press.

Dewey, D.P. (2004) A comparison of reading development by learners of Japanese in intensive domestic immersion and study abroad contexts. *Studies in Second Language Acquisition* 26 (2), 303–327.

Dörnyei, Z. (2001) *Teaching and Researching Motivation*. Harlow: Pearson Education.

Dörnyei, Z. and Ottó, I. (1998) Motivation in action: A process model of L2 motivation. *Working Papers in Applied Linguistics* (Thames Valley University, London) 4, 43–69.

Engeström, Y. (1987) *Learning by Expanding: An Activity-theoretical Approach to Developmental Research*. Helsinki: Orienta-Konsultiti.

Engeström, Y. (1999) Activity theory and individual and social transformation. In Y. Engeström, R. Miettinen and R-L. Punamäki (eds) *Perspectives on Activity Theory* (pp. 19–38). Cambridge: Cambridge University Press.

Flower, L. and Hayes, J.R. (1981) The pregnant pause: An inquiry into the nature of planning. *Research in the Teaching of English* 15 (3), 229–244.

Gardner, R.C. and MacIntyre, P.D. (1993) On the measurement of affective variables in second language learning. *Language Learning* 43 (2), 157–194.

Harris, D.P. and Palmer, L.A. (1986) *CELT: Examiners' Instruction and Technical Manual*. New York: McGraw-Hill.

Hirose, K. and Sasaki, M. (1994) Explanatory variables for Japanese students' expository writing in English: An exploratory study. *Journal of Second Language Writing* 3 (3), 203–229.

Isabelli-Garcia, C.L. (2006) Study abroad social networks, motivation and attitudes: Implications for second language acquisition. In M.A. Dufon and E. Churchill (eds) *Language Learners in Study Abroad Contexts* (pp. 231–258). Clevedon: Multilingual Matters.

Jacobs, H.L., Zinkgraf, S.A., Wormuth, D.R., Hartfiel, V.F. and Hughey, J.B. (1981) *Testing EFL Composition: A Practical Approach*. Rowley, MA: Newbury House.

Johns, A.M. (1997) *Text, Role, and Context: Developing Academic Literacies*. Cambridge: Cambridge University Press.

Jones, S. and Tetroe, J. (1987) Composing in a second language. In A. Matsuhashi (ed.) *Writing in Real Time: Modelling Production Processes* (pp. 34–57). Norwood, NJ: Ablex.

Kanno, Y. and Norton, B. (2003) Imagined communities and educational possibilities: Introduction. *Journal of Language Identity, and Education* 2 (4), 241–249.

Kobayashi, H. and Rinnert, C. (2001) Factors relating to EFL writers' discourse level revision skills. In R.M. Manchón (ed.) *Writing in the L2 Classroom. Issues in Research and Pedagogy*. Special issue of *International Journal of English Studies* 1 (2), 71–101.

Lafford, B.A. (2004) The effect of the context of learning on the use of communication strategies by learners of Spanish as a second language. *Studies in Second Language Acquisition* 26 (2), 201–225.

Lave, J. and Wenger, E. (1991) *Situated Learning: Legitimate Peripheral Participation*. New York: Cambridge University Press.

Leont'ev, A.N. (1981) *Problems of the Development of the Mind*. Moscow: Progress Press.

Manchon, R.M., Roca de Larios, J. and Murphy, L. (2007) Second and foreign language writing strategies: A review of empirical research. In A.D. Cohen and E. Macaro (eds) *Language Learner Strategies: 30 Years of Research and Practice* (pp. 229–250). Oxford: Oxford University Press.

Miles, M.B. and Huberman, A.M. (1994) *Qualitative Data Analysis: An Expanded Sourcebook* (2nd edn). Thousand Oaks, CA: Sage.

Pennington, M.C. and So, S. (1993) Comparing writing process and product across two languages: A study of 6 Singaporean university student writers. *Journal of Second Language Writing* 2 (1), 41–63.

Riazi, A. (1997) Acquiring disciplinary literacy: A social-cognitive analysis of text production and learning among Iranian graduate students of education. *Journal of Second Language Writing* 6 (2), 105–137.

Sasaki, M. (2000) Toward an empirical model of EFL writing processes: An exploratory study. *Journal of Second Language Writing* 9 (3), 259–291.

Sasaki, M. (2002) Building an empirically based model of EFL learners' writing processes. In S. Ransdell and M-L. Barbier (eds) *New Directions for Research in L2 Writing* (pp. 49–80). Amsterdam: Kluwer Academic.

Sasaki, M. (2004) A multiple-data analysis of the 3.5-year development of EFL student writers. *Language Learning* 54 (3), 525–582.

Sasaki, M. (2007) Effects of study-abroad experiences on EFL writers: A multiple-data analysis. *Modern Language Journal* 91, 602–620.

Sasaki, M. and Hirose, K. (1996) Explanatory variables for EFL students' expository writing. *Language Learning* 4 (1), 137–174.

Simões, A.R.M. (1996) Phonetics in second language acquisition: An acoustic study of fluency in adult learners of Spanish. *Hispania* 79 (1), 87–95.

SPSS Incorporated (1994) *SPSS 6.1 Base System: User's Guide, Macintosh Version*. Chicago, IL: SPSS.

Tanaka, S. and Yamagiwa, Y. (1992) *Yuuzaa no tameno kyouiku-shinritoukei to jikkenkeikakuhou*. [*Statistics and Research Methodology for Users in the Fields of Education and Psychology*.] Tokyo: Kyouikushuppan.

Thorne, S.L. (2005) Epistemology, politics, and ethics in sociocultural theory. *Modern Language Journal* 89 (3), 393–409.

Ushioda, E. (2001) Language learning at university: Exploring the role of motivational thinking. In Z. Dörnyei and R. Schmidt (eds) *Motivation and Second Language Acquisition* (Technical Report No. 23, pp. 93–125). Honolulu: University of Hawai'i, Second Language and Curriculum Center.

Vygotsky, L. (1978) Mind in Society: The Development of Higher Psychological Processes. Cambridge, MA: Harvard University Press.

Yang, L., Baba, K. and Cumming, A. (2004) Activity systems for ESL writing improvement: Case studies of three Chinese and three Japanese adult learners of English. *Angles on the English-Speaking World* 4, 13–33.

Yashima, T. (2007) *Willingness to communicate as a goal for EFT in Japan: International posture and English using self*. Paper presented at the International Symposium on English Education in Japan. Kansai University, Japan.

Appendix

Freshman and senior compositions written by Makoto, a SA-8/11 student

Makoto's freshman composition (given 67 points)

PROMPT: There has been a heated discussion in an English newspaper about introducing English as an elementary-school subject in Japan. Some people think that English should be taught at the elementary-school level, whereas others believe that it is too early. Suppose you are writing for the readers' opinion column. Take one of the positions described above and write your opinion within 30 minutes. [Original in Japanese, translated by the author.]

I agree with the suggestion that it is early to teach English for erementary school student. Because both English and Japanese are difficult. When I was student, I though why school classes are so difficult. And I became slow learner. I can't understand classes. So there are many slow learners like me. They were thinking that that were same to me. If erementary school student have to study English, they confuse their brain. And they'll be not able to understand classes more and more. I think it makes Japanese student bad. The more study hard, the more become bad. English isn't so easy. It will be pain for person who isn't good at Engilsh. I think English must not study hard. Only student who is interest in English must study. Erementary school only teach human life is good.

Makoto's senior composition (given 162 points)

PROMPT: There has been a heated discussion in an English newspaper about university student life. Some people think that university students should not have part-time jobs, whereas others believe that it is advisable for them to work part-time. Suppose you are writing for the readers' opinion column...

University students have too much free time people usually believe. It might or might not be true because university is a place where students learn a lot of things which are more advanced than they have done. There are many argument about the way university students spend time, but I think they are missing something important. Working as a part time job will not help students' future.

The most important thing is that part-time job is completely different from that of full time workers. Part-time workers are not responsible for the sales, which is the biggest difference between them. Some people even commited suicide to take responsibility of his failure in contract with other company. It is much harder to work as a full time job. For the reason, people should stop thinking that working as a part-time job is a kind of experience for their future.

In addition, there are much more important things only university students can do, such as club activity, research, volunteer and so on. Since university course normally finishes in four year, students have experience those things before graduating. That will be more significant than anything, working, even taking a class, because students can learn how people become adult through those experiences that students get involved in social activity. That is why I don't think students should work.

Chapter 3

Towards a Blueprint of the Foreign Language Writer: The Linguistic and Cognitive Demands of Foreign Language Writing

ROB SCHOONEN, PATRICK SNELLINGS, MARIE STEVENSON and AMOS VAN GELDEREN

Introduction

In the past decades, the focus of many foreign language (FL) writing studies has been more on the pedagogical aspects than on the psycholinguistic aspects of FL writing. Although in recent years a number of very interesting studies examining cognitive aspects of first (L1) and second (L2) or FL writing have been published (e.g. Chenoweth & Hayes, 2001; Kellogg, 1996; Levy & Ransdell, 1996; Roca de Larios *et al.*, 2006; Sasaki, 2002), it is perhaps telling that in a comprehensive book on the neurocognition of language (Brown & Hagoort, 1999), we can find chapters about the blueprint of the speaker (Levelt, 1999), the listener (Cutler & Clifton, 1999) and the reader (Perfetti, 1999), but no such chapter about the writer. This might indicate that cognitively oriented research on writing is still relatively young and results are not yet widespread.

One of the core questions of cognitively oriented writing research is, of course: *What's involved in writing?* or *What would the 'blueprint of the writer' look like?* Many recent studies have contributed building blocks for this blueprint, some of which we will discuss below. In a four-year research programme, called NELSON,[1] we have tried to contribute to this blueprint from different perspectives and methodologies: a large-scale correlational study of L1 and FL writing in relation to linguistic knowledge and psycholinguistic skills; an in-depth, think-aloud and keystroke study of a smaller sample of L1 and FL writers; and, finally, an experimental study into the effects of lexical retrieval fluency on FL writing performance. The

FL context offers an especially interesting setting to study the interaction between higher order skills and lower order linguistic skills, the understanding of which is important for developing a blueprint of the writer.

A blueprint of the writer

In the 1970s and 1980s, a number of researchers and theorists were carefully studying the writing process and the skills involved in writing (e.g. Emig, 1971; Flower & Hayes, 1981). However, it is only in the last two decades that many more researchers have become involved and that approaches to studying writing have become more advanced and more cognitively oriented (Bereiter & Scardamalia, 1987; Chenoweth & Hayes, 2001; Hayes, 1996; Kellogg, 1996; Levy & Ransdell, 1996; Manchón *et al.*, this volume; Stevenson *et al.*, 2006). As writing is a form of language production, we can look for parallels with speaking (cf. Grabowksi, 1996). The language production process, as described in Levelt's model of spoken language production (1989, 1999), can be subdivided into three major components. These components are conceptual preparation (including planning), linguistic formulation and physical production (note: for writing transcription is the counterpart of articulation for speaking) (cf. Chenoweth & Hayes, 2001; Levelt, 1989, 1999), with each component having its own subcomponents. Output of the production processes can be monitored by language perception processes matching the output with intended results.

Generating and/or planning a message is generally considered preverbal and, as such, has drawn relatively little attention within the field of applied linguistics (however, see Ellis, 2005; Hayes & Nash, 1996; Manchón & Roca de Larios, 2007). The content writers convey through their writing can be self-selected, but is sometimes prescribed by the writing assignment. In either case, the writer needs to have knowledge about the topic to be able to develop an appropriate text. The world or encyclopaedic knowledge resources of a writer can be considered to be part of the blueprint. It is well recognized that the topic of writing and the writing task greatly influences the quality of the ultimate written product (Schoonen, 2005). Such task effects most likely consist of a mixture of topic knowledge, genre-familiarity and conceptual complexity of the writing task (see Robinson [2001], Skehan & Foster [2001] and Kuiken & Vedder [2008] for a discussion about task complexity and its effect on L2 language production). Task effects often contaminate the assessment of a writer's linguistic writing proficiency in research.

Preparation of a message includes planning the text, which can be considered to be a *pre*linguistic or conceptual process. The quality of this conceptual process can affect the quality of the ultimate written product (Hayes & Nash, 1996) and, as such, it is important that the writer is able to allocate enough time and cognitive resources to this subprocess (Bereiter & Scardamalia, 1987; Kellogg, 1987; Manchón & Roca de Larios, 2007). In studies of writing, planning refers mostly to the planning of larger text parts and less to very local planning of (short) utterances (cf. Levelt's [1989] micro- and macroplanning). However, this does not imply that planning is restricted to the initial stages of writing. Planning is a cyclically reoccurring process (Flower & Hayes, 1981; Van den Bergh & Rijlaarsdam, 1996). In planning a written message or part of it, writers can use their (metacognitive) knowledge about texts, writing processes and writing contexts to develop their writing plan and goals. This knowledge can help orchestrate the writing processes. However, writers differ in terms of the (metacognitive) knowledge they have about writing and also in terms of which knowledge they can put into use. In FL writing contexts, it might be the case that available knowledge about, for example, text structure (developed from L1 writing experience) cannot be used, due to the fact that the writer has to allocate cognitive resources to other subprocesses, particularly when writing under time pressure (Manchón & Roca de Larios, 2007).

So far, we have not systematically distinguished L1 and L2 or FL writing, but when it comes to formulating a message, linguistic skills and knowledge become prominent in the writing process (Chenoweth & Hayes, 2001). In formulating, a writer transforms the propositional content of the message into language. The propositions in the preverbal message trigger the selection of appropriate forms from the mental lexicon. The selection of these forms can involve morphosyntactic restrictions that need to be taken into account in framing a grammatically correct sentence, and which will also be affected by other content-related parameters, such as the required style or register and rhetorical considerations. In Levelt's model, formulating consists of two major subcomponents: grammatical and phonological encoding. Grammatical encoding pertains to the construction of clauses and sentences in terms of vocabulary selection and sentence building. In order to translate the propositions into language, the words selected from the mental lexicon have to be put together in a grammatically correct and pragmatically adequate way, so that coherence and cohesion are maintained. Usually these requirements of adequacy are felt more strongly in written language than in spoken language, the latter generally being more tolerant of 'errors' or sloppy wording. It goes without saying that a writer needs to have a large repertoire of words, collocations, sentence frames and morphological options to get the intended messages across. Preferably, this repertoire should be easily accessible.

In speaking, phonological encoding produces the phonetic word forms. The counterpart in writing would be orthographic encoding. The 'abstract' language needs to be spelled, that is, the writer needs to choose between 'nation' and *'nashion', or, if writing in Dutch, between the homophonic expressions *'hij word' and 'hij wordt' ('he becomes'). The grammatically encoded message has to be transformed into graphemic form.

The formulation process (consisting of both grammatical and orthographic encoding) strongly depends on the availability and accessibility of linguistic means. Therefore, writing in an L2 or FL is much harder and more time consuming than in the native language (Chenoweth & Hayes, 2001; Roca de Larios *et al.*, 2006), and the problems an L2/FL writer has to deal with are often more language-specific, narrowing attention to a local scope (Roca de Larios *et al.*, 2006; Stevenson, 2005).

The writer's graphemic representation of the message triggers motor-muscular actions that move a pen across paper or fingers across a keyboard with a text as the end product of this complex writing process. The text should convey the intended message to a reader, be it an independent reader reading the text at another time and another place or the writer himself/herself rereading his/her own text. With the writer alternating between generating, formulating, spelling, transcribing or typing and generating or formulating again, the writing process (as a whole) is not linear, but cyclical. The (result of the) writing process and its subprocesses can be monitored by the writer applying (metacognitive) knowledge to judge the appropriateness of the writing, and this monitoring may lead to revisions at different levels of the text. Revisions in writing are often more intentional and elaborate than self-repairs in speaking, they may pertain to all levels of the texts and they can even be made some time after the moment of writing. Therefore, revisions are an interesting source of information about the writing monitoring process and revising is sometimes considered to be a separate component in writing process models (cf. Chenoweth & Hayes, 2001; Hayes & Flower, 1980).

Compared to speaking, writing is relatively slow, not only at the final stage of the actual production (typing/writing down versus articulating), but also at the earlier stages. A writer probably does not feel the 'pressure' to produce language instantaneously, and usually has time to (re)consider both content and wording (see Grabowski [1996] for a more extensive comparison between speaking and writing). However, this difference in the time scale of writing and speaking should not be interpreted as meaning that fluency is not an issue in writing. Irrespective of time available for the writing task, writers are restricted by the limitations of their working memory (Kellogg, 1996; McCutchen, 1996; Ransdell & Levy, 1999). To be able to formulate fluently, the retrieval of words, collocations and sentence frames must be easy and not burden working memory, because memory resources should remain available for keeping track of the discourse as a whole, as well. A piece of paper or a computer screen can be considered as a temporary extension of working memory, but it is still likely that burdening working memory with vocabulary searches and morphosyntactic considerations will affect the focus of a writer's attention (Kellogg, 1996; McCutchen, 1996). If the writer becomes overburdened with such considerations, attentional resources will be narrowed down to local problems in a text, ignoring the overall features of the text as part of a larger discourse.

The requirements for successful writing are often difficult to meet for young or inexperienced writers in their L1 (Bereiter & Scardamalia, 1987; Graham & Perin, 2007). The level of linguistic proficiency and metacognitive knowledge needed is higher than for speaking, and the lack of context and conversational feedback demands a higher level of explicitness. In FL writing, things get even harder. Although we can assume that adolescent writers bring some (metacognitive) knowledge about writing and writing experience from their L1 to FL writing situations, it is suggested that the limited linguistic knowledge of the FL can hinder the use of this (metacognitive) knowledge and writing experience (Jones & Tetroe, 1987; Whalen & Ménard, 1995; see also Schoonen *et al.*, 2003). Below a certain threshold of FL linguistic knowledge, the writer will be fully absorbed in struggling with the language, inhibiting writing processes such as planning or monitoring. One of the foci in FL writing research has been the interplay between FL writing proficiency, FL linguistic knowledge and L1 writing proficiency or expertise (cf. Cumming, 1989; Jones & Tetroe, 1987; Manchón *et al.*, this volume; Sasaki & Hirose, 1996; Schoonen *et al.*, 2003). Seen from the perspective of developing a blueprint of an FL writer, it seems that L1 writing expertise and metacognitive knowledge can be used for conceptual (prelinguistic) preparation. However, the use of this L1 expertise and knowledge comes under pressure at other stages of the writing process, that is, during formulation, when the writer might be struggling with the constraints of his/her limited FL linguistic knowledge. As writing is far slower and more cyclical than speaking, it offers more opportunities for monitoring and interaction between subprocesses, and thus lack of sufficient FL linguistic resources might feed back to conceptual preparation, triggering content in which complex formulations are avoided or triggering the use of other compensatory strategies. The relationship between L1 and FL writing proficiency is without doubt mediated by FL linguistic knowledge, but the issue of how and to what extent these three constructs interact is still not settled.

In the remainder of this chapter, we will draw together some of our own work on L1 and FL writing. First, we will evaluate the correlations between L1 and FL writing proficiency, on the one hand, and metacognitive knowledge, constituent linguistic knowledge and psycholinguistic processing skills, on the other, providing some insights that should be useful in developing the blueprint of a writer. Second, we will focus on L1 and FL writing processes as they unfold during writing: how and when do writers use their linguistic resources? Finally, we will explore to what extent training (FL) lexical retrieval affects writing.

Linguistic and Metacognitive Resources and Writing Performance in L1 and FL

Nearly 400 Grade 8 students from secondary schools in the Netherlands participated in a large-scale study about reading and writing in their L1 and FL (Schoonen *et al.*, 2003; van Gelderen *et al.*, 2004). Of this sample, 281 students were speakers of Dutch as a first language, and for these students English was a foreign language (EFL) (Schoonen *et al.*, 2003).[2] In this section, we will discuss the performance of this subsample.

Students performed three 'functional' writing tasks in Dutch and three similar tasks in English, and panels of raters holistically rated their performances. In addition to these writing tasks, a large number of linguistic tests of Dutch and English were administered. These linguistic tests measured vocabulary knowledge, grammatical knowledge and spelling knowledge; metacognitive knowledge of reading and writing; and tests for the speed (reaction times: RTs) of lexical retrieval and grammatical sentence building. With the paper-and-pencil tests, we tried to tap some of the metacognitive and linguistic knowledge resources that are likely to be used during planning, grammatical encoding, orthographic encoding and monitoring. With the speed tests, we assessed the accessibility of lexical and grammatical resources (see Schoonen *et al.* [2003] for more detailed information).

The relationships between these constituent variables and writing performance in L1 and FL were studied using structural equation modeling (SEM) techniques, that is, an integration of multiple regression and factor analysis. The results showed that, as was expected, (almost) all variables were substantially related to writing proficiency, that is, the more metacognitive and linguistic knowledge a writer has, and the faster this lexical and grammatical knowledge can be retrieved, the better the writing performance (see Table 3.1). These cognitive and linguistic variables together could 'explain' 56% ($R=0.75$) of the variance in L1 writing proficiency and 80% ($R=0.89$) of the variance in FL writing proficiency.[3]

Table 3.1 shows that both the correlations between linguistic knowledge and writing performance and between fluency (RTs[4]) and writing performance are generally higher for English than for the mother tongue. Correlations between metacognitive knowledge and L1 and FL writing scores, respectively, are quite similar to each other (0.63 and 0.73). Together with the difference in the amount of variance explained in the two languages (Dutch: 56% versus English: 80%), these results suggest that FL writing is more dependent on the level of linguistic knowledge and fluency (i.e. speed of processing words and sentences, RTs) than L1 writing. Examples a and b (Table 3.2) show two student texts for the same assignment, that is, 'Write to an English music magazine (*Music Maker*) to complain about their ignoring your favorite group'. Student A performed poorly on the English grammar test and received low gradings for his/her text, whereas Student B scored high on both the grammar test and the writing assignment. Among other things, the examples show an enormous difference in grammatical repertoire.

The analyses also showed that the fluency measures (RTs) strongly overlap with the knowledge measures in 'predicting' writing proficiency. It turned out that they did not make a *unique* contribution to the prediction of the writing scores. This might not be surprising considering that, for example, a large vocabulary is probably related to large exposure and frequent use of the language, which, in turn, will lead to faster accessibility of the knowledge.

Finally, our results show that the correlation between L1 and FL writing scores is very high (0.93). This might be due to the SEM technique we used, which might give more accurate estimates of correlations (see Table 3.1 and Methodological considerations section).

Although we were able to do a large-scale study using advanced statistical techniques, basically, we are dealing with a correlational study of test scores that does not allow us to describe the nature of the cognitive

Table 3.1 Correlations between (latent) writing proficiency in L1 and FL variables, respectively, and the corresponding component variables

	Metacognitive knowledge	*Vocabulary knowledge*	*Grammatical knowledge*	*Orthographic knowledge*	*Lexical retrieval (RT)*	*Sentence building (RT)*	*L1 writing proficiency*
Dutch L1 writing proficiency	0.67	0.47	0.63	0.58	−0.10	−0.48	–
English FL writing proficiency	0.73	0.63	0.84	0.85	−0.38	−0.60	0.93

Source: Reprinted from Schoonen *et al.* (2003) with permission from Blackwell Publishing.
Note: Only within-language correlations are reported. For example, Dutch vocabulary with Dutch writing proficiency (r=0.47) and English vocabulary with English writing proficiency (r=0.63); metacognitive knowledge is one and the same general test. The final column provides the correlation between Dutch and English writing proficiency. Correlations can be considered 'true' correlations (i.e. not attenuated by measurement error).

Table 3.2 Two writing samples of grade 8 students (see text for further explanation)

Example a (Student A)	*Example b (Student B)*
Name (ID 810)	Name (ID211)
Dear Music Maker,	Dear Music Maker,
I ben fan of Five.	I'm very dissappointed in your magazin.
I thinks stupid that not picters and interviews, but i can not new poster hang of Five op my room.	For the past five months there haven't been any interviews or posters about Another Level.
I hope that er picters and interviews come in the Misic Maker.	I buy your magazin every week and it's a nice magazin to read but there is nothing about Another Level in it.
	In the last interview which was over five months from now you said there would be an other interview soon but it still didn't come. If there won't be an interview soon in your magazin I'm bound to never buy your magazin ever again and I'm sure I'm not the only one. I would also be very pleased if you would place an poster in your magazin. I hope you will do something about my problem.

processes involved. It also means that we must refrain from causal interpretations of relations between variables (cf. Cook & Campbell, 1979). In order to obtain detailed information concerning how writers actually process texts during the act of writing – that is about online writing processes – it is highly desirable to be able to look over the writer's shoulder as he or she writes. This is what we did in the study we report next.

Looking over the Writer's Shoulder: Online Writing Processes

This section provides the reader with an over-the-shoulder look at FL writing by reporting the results of a small-scale study comparing how 22 junior high school writers, aged 13–14 years, wrote texts in Dutch L1 and English as a FL (Stevenson, 2005). Although different students, they were the same age as the students in the study reported in the previous section.

As we have seen, writing involves both conceptual and linguistic processing. We have also argued that in a FL, writers can become so absorbed in linguistic processing, that is, in searching for the right words, the right sentence structures and the right spelling, that they have little eye for conceptual processing, that is, for the global content and structure of the text (e.g. Chenoweth & Hayes, 2001; Schoonen *et al.*, 2003; Whalen & Ménard, 1995). Our first study showed that linguistic processing plays a role in FL writing, as both linguistic knowledge and fluency variables correlated more strongly with writing proficiency in FL than in L1. However, the role that fluency in linguistic processing plays in FL writing can only be investigated by examining writers' actual writing processes in detail. Therefore, in this study (Stevenson, 2005; Stevenson *et al.*, 2006) we addressed the question: *is conceptual processing in FL writing inhibited compared to similar processing in L1 writing?* If so, *to what extent is inhibition of conceptual processing in FL writing related to lack of fluent FL linguistic processing?*

These questions were addressed by comparing writing processes in L1 and FL using two kinds of analyses: an analysis of online revisions during writing and an analysis of think-aloud protocols. The two analyses and the results are briefly described below, followed by a discussion of the results (see Stevenson [2005] and Stevenson *et al.* [2006] for more extensive information).

Online revisions

As we explained in our blueprint of the writer, writing is a cyclical process in which writers move back and forth between generating ideas, formulating these ideas into language and transcribing these ideas into writing (Flower & Hayes, 1981; Hayes & Flower, 1980). The cyclical nature of writing means that there are many opportunities for making changes to the text before the ultimate product is shared with a reader. Writers make 'online' revisions at different stages of writing a text. A writer can return to an earlier part of the text to make a change, or revisions can be made as soon as something has been written, as happens in quick self-repairs in speaking, or even prior to writing something down, as writers sometimes mentally rehearse formulations, changing them before they appear on the page. A writer can make online revisions to various aspects of the text, including surface linguistic elements (such as spelling and grammar) and also conceptual aspects (such as the information that the text contains and the order in which this information is presented). The particular kinds of revisions that a writer makes will be dependent on the writer's (metacognitive) knowledge and on the particular features of the text on which he/she is focusing.

In the revision analysis (Stevenson, 2005; Stevenson *et al.*, 2006), online revisions made by the 22 students were examined using keystroke-logging software. Keystroke logging provides information about writers' online writing processes by recording the step-by-step creation of computer-written texts. The students produced four argumentative texts: two in Dutch and two similar ones in English. While writing these texts, the students' keystrokes were registered in a log-file. This log-file was later exported to the keystroke analysis program, called *Trace-it* (Kollberg, 1998). *Trace-it* has a function with which a text can be played either forwards or backwards revision-by-revision, which greatly facilitates the coding of revisions (see Kollberg, 1998; Lindgren & Sullivan, 2002). The interpretation of this data was supplemented by information obtained from the think-aloud protocols that were collected simultaneously (see next section).

The revisions which the students made while writing the texts were manually coded according to four dimensions: (1) Orientation: the orientation of the revisions (i.e. whether they are conceptual, linguistic or typographic); (2) Domain: the size of the unit of text that is revised (i.e. whether they are below word, below clause or above-clause revisions); (3) Location: place where a revision is made (i.e. at the end of the current text, at an earlier point in the text, or only in the think-aloud protocol, meaning that the revision did not make it into the actual text); and (4) Action: the action that the writer performs (i.e. addition, deletion or substitution).

The results of the study showed that for each of the four dimensions there was a higher frequency of one or more categories in FL compared to L1, while the frequencies of the revisions in the remaining categories were roughly equal in both languages. As was expected, in terms of the orientation of the revisions, more attention was devoted to linguistic revision processes in FL than in L1. The writers made more language revisions and also more typographic revisions in FL. However, this increase in attention to linguistic problems did not seem to be associated with less attention being devoted to conceptual revision processes, as although writers made more revisions to linguistic aspects of the text, they made a similar number of conceptual revisions in both L1 and FL. These results seemed to indicate that there was little competition for cognitive resources between conceptual and linguistic processes.

A similar pattern of results emerged for the other three dimensions (i.e. Domain, Location and Action). Although the writers made more revisions within a restricted textual domain (i.e. below word and below clause level), more immediate revisions and more of particular actions (i.e. substitutions and deletions) in their FL writing than in their L1 writing, the frequencies of revisions made within larger units of text, more distant revisions and other kinds of Action revisions were similar in L1 and FL.

The observed pattern would seem to indicate that while there was some redistribution of revising resources in FL, this did not lead to the inhibition of other kinds of revising in FL. Rather, the results of the analyses appear to point to the compensatory role that revising plays in FL writing. In FL, the writers compensated for lack of linguistic knowledge and/or processing fluency by spending more time solving language problems in their writing. They were able to do this without affecting their ability to make conceptual revisions.

However, on the basis of this analysis it is premature to conclude that no inhibition of processing has taken place. Firstly, perhaps due to their age or lack of writing experience, the writers in this study did not make many higher-level revisions in either Dutch or English, and perhaps for this reason they had no difficulty in maintaining their writing behavior in both languages.

Secondly, this analysis was in terms of revision frequencies, and takes no account of either the amount of time spent on particular writing subprocesses, such as conceptualising or formulating (cf. Roca de Larios *et al.*, 2006), or the actual level of fluency of the writers.

Fluency and writing strategies

The second analysis involved an examination of the same texts written by these students in terms of both the time devoted to writing subprocesses and the level of writing fluency (Stevenson, 2005). In order to examine real-time, online text production processes, writing fluency was examined using an online measure. The online measure was the average number of intact, recognizable words transcribed by a writer between pauses of two seconds or more, regardless of whether the words occurred in the final product (see Spelman Miller, 2002). The log-files (see above) allowed this information to be recorded. In order to allow comparison, a more traditional offline measure of fluency was also included: namely, the number of words occurring in the final text divided by the total time on the task.

Think-aloud data was used to examine how much time the writers spent on the writing subprocesses (conceptualising, formulating and reading) when developing their L1 and FL texts. In order to examine whether the level of fluency and attention to particular writing subprocesses affected the final writing product, the fluency and writing strategy measures were correlated with both global text quality scores and a measure of rhetorical text structure (i.e. number of arguments, subarguments, etc.) for each of the four texts written by the students.

The results of this analysis corroborated the finding of the online revision study that the writers paid more attention to linguistic processing in FL than in L1. This attention to linguistic processes manifested itself in more localized (re)reading of the text and in greater use of strategies to solve language problems. Moreover, conceptual processes seemed to be inhibited in FL. This inhibition manifested itself in both the writing process and the written product: less attention was devoted to conceptualising in FL than in L1, and the FL texts were rhetorically less well developed than the L1 texts. The writers produced less rhetorical content in FL in a period very similar in length to total task time in L1. There was also some indication that writers' global reading processes were inhibited, as greater attention to highly localized rereading of the writers' own texts (i.e. reading the current clause) was accompanied by less attention to more global reading of the texts. Although it is not possible to directly equate the distinction between global and local rereading with the dichotomy between conceptual and linguistic processing, this finding does show that there is a narrowing of focus in writers' rereading of their FL texts. This narrowing of focus is possibly a reflection of the greater effort involved in FL formulation processes, with writers rereading the clause they are working on over and over again in an attempt to find appropriate words to express their ideas.

Despite the evidence for both extra attention to linguistic processes and less attention to conceptual processes in FL writing, it was not possible to establish clearly that this inhibition was related to actual lack of fluency of linguistic processes. As expected, the writers were less fluent in FL than in L1, in terms of both the size of the chunks of text produced without pausing and the number of words produced per minute. However, no significant relationship was found between the level of fluency and the level of rhetorical development in the FL texts. Nor was there evidence of a relationship between level of fluency and text quality in either Dutch or English.

Inhibition or not?

In support of cognitive capacity accounts of writing (e.g. Kellogg, 1996; McCutchen, 1996), it appears that some inhibition of conceptual processing can occur in FL writing. However, the two analyses were divergent in the degree of support they provided for the hypothesis that conceptual processing is inhibited in FL writing. The fluency and writing subprocess analysis provided partial support for the hypothesis, while the online revision analysis did not. A possible explanation for the divergent results of the two analyses may be found in the fact that the revision analysis counts frequencies while the subprocess analysis measures duration of processing episodes. It may be that time is a more appropriate process measure than frequencies. Thus, inhibition of conceptual processing in FL writing manifests itself in terms of the time spent conceptualising rather than in terms of the numbers of conceptual revisions that writers make.

To gain more specific insight into how particular subprocesses affect the overall writing process, more experimentally controlled studies may be needed. To what extent can constituent processes be manipulated or be the target of interventions? And, how does this affect the writing performance as a whole? As an example, we will take a closer look at fluency of lexical retrieval during grammatical encoding as part of the formulation process.

Enhancing Fluency and Writing Quality

In our blueprint of the writer, we indicated that propositional content has to be transformed into language. The process of formulation is facilitated when lexical resources are easily accessible. Lexical retrieval is an important subprocess in formulating, which has attracted relatively little attention in research on L2 writing and L2 writing instruction. As pointed out above, correlational research (Schoonen *et al.*, 2003) found a relationship between lexical retrieval and writing proficiency. In addition, online writing research (Stevenson, 2005) showed that smaller chunks and fewer words per minute are produced in the FL than in the L1. In the study reported next, we took an experimental approach to investigating whether there is a causal relationship between the fluency of FL lexical retrieval and the ultimate written product.

Lexical retrieval in L1 writing

Kellogg (1994) showed that lexical retrieval during writing is highly effortful, even for native speakers. Demands made by lexical retrieval on cognitive resources were measured by RT interference on a secondary (auditory probe) task. A number of other studies have also shown a relationship between resource demands and writing by experimentally increasing the cognitive loads in writing tasks (Alamargot & Chanquoy, 2001). Brown *et al.* (1988) showed that when lexical material had to be retrieved from memory, this process usurped attention from execution processes, resulting in reduced legibility and a greater number of errors in written texts. Correlational studies have also served to emphasize the importance of lexical retrieval for writing. McCutchen *et al.* (1994) found that proficient writers had shorter latencies and higher accuracy rates on lexical decision tasks than less proficient writers.[5] McCutchen *et al.* followed Flower and Hayes (1980) in arguing that writers have to handle a number of constraints simultaneously, which could place a strain on attentional resources. The results may be that the more attention devoted to formulating and lexical retrieval, the less can be devoted to other processes such as planning, generating ideas and reviewing (for a review see McCutchen, 1996).

Flower and Hayes (1980) suggested the possibility of providing training to increase efficiency of sentence production processes in the L1, for example, through sentence-combining exercises, the ultimate aim of which would be to enable writers to concentrate more on other important writing processes. In fact, a number of studies have established the effects of training fluency in sentence construction on the quality of L1 writing (Graham & Perin, 2007; van Gelderen & Oostdam, 2005).

Lexical retrieval in L2 writing

Lexical retrieval is more attention demanding in an FL than in the L1 (Chenoweth & Hayes, 2001). Therefore, fluency of lexical retrieval is likely to have a larger effect on quality of writing in FL than in L1. Roca de Larios *et al.* (2006) have demonstrated the formulation difficulties writers have when writing in the FL, with writers spending twice as much time on formulation problems in the FL than in the L1. However, despite the importance of lexical retrieval for writing, there has been – to the best of our knowledge – no research trying to improve FL writing by enhancing the fluency of lexical retrieval.

An experimental study on enhancing FL lexical retrieval and writing

Our study investigated the effects of computerized training on the fluency of lexical retrieval in an FL (Snellings *et al.*, 2002, 2004a). A total of 100 Dutch Grade 9 students were randomly assigned to one of two similar training conditions. Each training condition used a different set of FL stimulus words (60 and 64, respectively). Students in condition A were trained with a set of words (A-words) that were thought to be helpful in writing a narrative, cartoon-based text (text A). Students in condition B were trained with an alternative set of words (B-words) that were instrumental in writing an alternative text (text B). The training consisted of five 50-minute sessions in a four-week period. After training, all students were tested on their lexical retrieval skills of both A- and B-words. Results showed that training aimed at speeding up lexical retrieval resulted in both higher levels of accuracy and faster RTs: the students in condition A outperformed the B students on the A-words, while these B students had superior scores on the B-words compared to the A students. These findings indicated that training learners to focus on speed and providing them with immediate feedback on both speed and correctness effectively altered and improved an essential cognitive subprocess involved in FL production, potentially reducing the cognitive demands of lexical retrieval in FL writing.

Next, we examined the effects of enhanced lexical retrieval on several aspects of the written narratives. We investigated whether the lexical retrieval training resulted in more frequent use of the trained words in the writing tasks and whether the training resulted in learners being better able to express the details of the story and the desired content. Finally, we explored whether the enhanced lexical retrieval had an effect on the global quality of the texts. Both experimental groups wrote two cartoon-based narrative texts, one about topic A and one about topic B. Thus, for one topic the students had been trained in the lexical retrieval of relevant words, whereas for the other one they had not. Results showed that students in condition A used more trained words in the A narrative than students of condition B and, reversely, B students used more B words in the B narrative than the students of condition A. In addition, students in condition A used more content elements in narrative A than the condition B students. Although the reverse for the B condition was not statistically significant, the pattern of differences for narrative B was in the expected direction.

Our assumption was that if lexical retrieval proceeded with less effort, this would benefit other writing processes, such as planning and reviewing. The results of our study did not, however, support these assumptions unequivocally. One possibility is that the link between the trained words and the content to be expressed in narrative B was less strong than in narrative A. It is possible that the content elements in narrative B could easily be expressed using words other than the trained words, thus reducing the influence of training the retrieval of those particular words. Indeed, correlations showed there was a closer relationship between the use of trained words and expression of content elements in narrative A than in narrative B. Another possibility could be that the content of narrative B was more difficult to express. It could be that retrieving the trained B words with less effort did not help in expressing the contents in a more detailed way. In accordance with this explanation, we found that students with greater vocabulary knowledge were better at expressing content elements and telling the story of narrative B.

As to the effect on global text quality, our results showed that even though the data were in the expected direction in the case of narrative A, the scores on global text quality of the students in the two conditions did not significantly differ from each other. This suggests that the quality of processes like generating ideas, planning and monitoring contribute to global text quality at least as much as lexical retrieval, and our (short) training intervention did not stand out sufficiently against those other contributing factors. Clearly, fluency of lexical retrieval is but one skill that may influence global text quality (see the blueprint). Even though the subprocess of lexical retrieval has become faster and more efficient, other processes essential to writing have not. Glynn *et al.* (1982) raised a similar issue when their study showed that only undergraduates with average verbal ability profited from reducing resource demands by producing more arguments in their texts. They found no effects in the case of students with low verbal ability and concluded that 'additional capacity can provide writers only with the *opportunity* to increase their pool of persuasive arguments; it cannot remediate deficiencies in ideational fluency' (Glynn *et al.*, 1982: 565). In the present study, enhanced lexical retrieval may have provided the *opportunity* to plan, monitor or use metacognitive knowledge, but it could not make up for lack of such knowledge.

Our finding that students used more trained words implies that the effect of the computerized training transferred to a real writing task, leading to a change in the writing process that can be detected in the writing product. This is an important finding, especially in view of our earlier finding (see above) that FL writers pay more attention to local linguistic problems. Training of lexical retrieval may help to overcome these local word-finding problems. Apart from the increased use of trained words, the relationship between enhanced lexical retrieval and the expression of detailed content in FL writing is of interest. Research has demonstrated that writers sometimes refrain from using certain wordings because of lexical problems (Roca de Larios *et al.*, 1999). Once lexical retrieval proceeds effortlessly, it could facilitate writing in two different ways. In the first place, it may help students to retrieve the necessary vocabulary directly, without having to simplify the wording of the concepts they want to express. In this case, the quality of the formulation improves directly and attention does not need to be devoted to 'tentative formulations', that is formulations that do not make it to actual text as, for example, the two italicized constituents in 'off-piste skiing was *a very nice experience* ...*a great experience* ...an exhilarating experience' when the intention is to say that the experience makes you feel very excited and happy. Alternatively, enhanced lexical retrieval may enable a faster retrieval process, whereby a number of tentative formulations can be generated rapidly, freeing the writer to select the most appropriate formulation for use (cf. Zimmerman, 2000). In this case, not all of the trained words may appear in the written output because some tentative formulations will have been replaced by a more appropriate formulation (see also van Gelderen & Oostdam, 2004). In both scenarios, formulating proceeds more smoothly and students do not become bogged down in retrieving tentative formulations. As a result, more attention can be devoted, for instance, to monitoring whether the information provided in the text is clear and detailed enough for the intended audience.

General Conclusions

In the NELSON project, we were able to combine several approaches to studying the L1 and FL writing of junior high school students and to provide insights into some of the building blocks of the blueprint of the writer. With respect to the knowledge resources and the accessibility of these resources, our large-scale study showed that both speed of processing and linguistic knowledge are substantially related to writing proficiency, but knowledge more so than speed. Grammatical knowledge and processing speed seem to be more strongly related to writing proficiency than their lexical counterparts. These relationships exist in both L1 and FL, but proficiency in FL writing is more strongly associated with the linguistic resources than proficiency in L1. This might indicate that the formulation process in FL writing is less self-evident or less fluent than in L1 writing. Linguistic knowledge and skills are very determinative in FL writing. However, more general metacognitive knowledge about writing and text characteristics is also associated with proficient writing, both in L1 and FL. This might (partly) explain the strong correlation between L1 and FL writing proficiency.

To take a closer look at the processes using these linguistic and more general knowledge resources, we conducted two in-depth studies. Looking at writing strategies, fluency and revision processes showed that in FL writing, compared to L1 writing, writers pay more attention to the linguistic features of their developing text. They seem to be forced to narrow their focus (more local re-readings) and to become less fluent (smaller chunk size, fewer words per minute). There are some indications that narrow focus and lack of fluency affect other components in the blueprint, for example, less attention for conceptual issues during writing, producing texts that are rhetorically less well developed. However, these effects do not show in a correlation with the holistic rating of the texts. This might be due to compensatory strategies employed in FL writing. FL writers showed an increase in linguistic revisions, but not at the cost of other kinds of revisions; these remained equally frequent in FL in comparison to L1 writing.

In the second in-depth study, we aimed at exploring the relation between one of the writing subprocesses, speed of lexical retrieval, and FL writing performance. The retrieval of FL words could be speeded up by a computer-based training, which led to an increase in the use of these words in a related text. However, effects on the propositional content of the texts and the overall quality were harder to establish, although the results were in the expected direction. Longer training of lexical retrieval of more words might have induced larger effects.

Drawing a detailed blueprint of the writer requires further studies. So far, our measures of metacognitive knowledge, FL knowledge and speed measures could 'explain' 80% of the variance in FL writing proficiency, which means that other variables, which we did not measure, are involved as well. Most likely, these variables relate to the preverbal stages of writing, for instance, planning and structuring, and skills related to monitoring the actual writing process and developing text. To find out *how* all these components contribute to the writing process and the ultimate written product requires further online studies of processes. Keystroke-logging in combination with think-aloud protocols proved to be very informative. In combination, these methods were able to show at what stages the writer appeals to what kind of metacognitive and linguistic knowledge and how easy or hard this appeal turns out to be and whether it leads to alternative formulations or not. Such descriptive studies should be supported by experimental studies to investigate whether interventions on subprocesses cause the expected improvement of the process as a whole. So far, we have focused on training lexical retrieval, but in future research it might be both interesting and promising to study in a similar way the effect of training multiple word structures or sentence frames on the ease of processing and possible reduction of cognitive effort (cf. Weinert, 1995).

Apart from investigating more potential building blocks and their interactions in the writing process, we should also try to improve our methodologies in order to increase the validity of our findings and conclusions.

Methodological considerations

One of the major challenges in writing research is the assessment of the core construct itself, 'writing proficiency'. It is relatively easy to collect written products and to achieve high inter-rater reliabilities. However, generalizability of scores across tasks is generally low (Schoonen, 2005). This low generalizability attenuates correlations between writing and, for example, language tests and, even more so, correlations between *two* measures of writing (e.g. L1 and FL writing). This might explain why some studies – contrary to our findings – report low correlations between L1 and FL writing. Multiple assignments to assess writing proficiency seem to be a prerequisite in this kind of research. Using statistical techniques that take into account (differences in) reliability of measures, such as SEM, might also contribute to valid comparisons of correlations.

Furthermore, we opted for independent measures of linguistic knowledge and skills instead of inferring the linguistic abilities from the written product, for example, rating lexical or grammatical features of the written text. Using independent assessments avoids confounds in the study of the relationship between writing performance and linguistic knowledge and skills.

In the two in-depth studies, we went beyond the mere description of behavior during writing. The ultimate goal of studying writing is not only to understand the process, but also to be able to inform teaching; therefore, it is important to relate writing behavior to the quality of the resulting text. However, not all differences in processing showed up in the ultimate text. This might be due to the small scale of the in-depth studies (in number of subjects, tasks and duration of the intervention, respectively). However, these issues are not easily settled in a single study. A series of studies accumulating insights in the writing process is needed.

Another important insight from our (think-aloud) study is that the use of percentages, convenient as they are for standardization purposes, may also hide similarities between L1 and FL writing processes (cf. Stevenson, 2005) when they are not complemented with the raw numbers. For example, if the percentage of language-oriented processes increases and the percentage of content-oriented processes decreases, without raw frequencies it remains unclear what has caused these changes in percentages; this could be a higher frequency of language-oriented processes, lower frequency of content-oriented processes or both.

All in all, we think that the use of different approaches and methods of data collection has been fruitful. Combining information from large-scale assessments and more in-depth examination of both actual writing processes and the effects of experimental intervention paints a more interesting and valid blueprint of the writer.

Notes

1. The NELSON project was not restricted to the study of L1 and FL writing, but also focused on L1 and FL reading of the same population, that is, adolescents in secondary education (see van Gelderen *et al.*, 2004). The Netherlands Organization of Scientific Research (NWO) funded the project (Grant No. 575-36-001). Besides the current authors, the research team consisted of Kees de Glopper, Jan Hulstijn, Ruben Fukkink and Annegien Simis.
2. The students for whom Dutch was not the L1 were still educated in Dutch. Their performances, in comparison to those of the L1 students, are described in Schoonen *et al.* (2002).
3. These correlations are higher than generally found in the literature, which is probably due to the use of multiple assignments for the assessment of writing proficiency, which strongly increases the reliability of the assessment (Schoonen, 2005). Moreover, in SEM, estimations of correlations are not attenuated by error variance.
4. Negative correlations with RT measures were as expected, because a low RT means a fast response.
5. Although lexical retrieval is more demanding than lexical access and the two processes are not equivalent (see Snellings *et al.*, 2004b), lexical access as measured with lexical decision tasks provides an indication of lexical retrieval skills.

References

Alamargot, D. and Chanquoy, L. (2001) *Through the Models of Writing*. Dordrecht: Kluwer.

Bereiter, C. and Scardamalia, M. (1987) *The Psychology of Written Composition*. Hillsdale, NJ: Lawrence Erlbaum.

Brown, C.M. and Hagoort, P. (eds) (1999) *The Neurocognition of Language*. Oxford: Oxford University Press.

Brown, J.S., McDonald, J.L., Brown, T.L. and Carr, T.H. (1988) Adapting to processing demands in discourse production: The case of handwriting. *Journal of Experimental Psychology: Human Perception and Performance* 14, 45–59.

Chenoweth, N.A. and Hayes, J.R. (2001) Fluency in writing. Generating text in L1 and L2. *Written Communication* 18 (1), 80–98.

Cook, T.D. and Campbell, D.T. (1979) *Quasi-Experimentation. Design and Analysis Issues for Field Settings*. Boston, MA: Houghton Mifflin.

Cumming, A. (1989) Writing expertise and second-language proficiency. *Language Learning* 39 (1), 81–135.

Cutler, A. and Clifton Jr, Ch. (1999) Comprehending spoken language: A blueprint of the listener. In C.M. Brown and P. Hagoort (eds) *The Neurocognition of Language* (pp. 123–166). Oxford: Oxford University Press.

Ellis, R. (ed.) (2005) *Planning and Task Performance in a Second Language*. Amsterdam: John Benjamins.

Emig, J. (1971) *The Composing Processes of Twelfth Graders*. Urbana, IL: National Council of Teachers of English.

Flower, L.S. and Hayes, J.R. (1980) The dynamics of composing: Making plans and juggling constraints. In L.W. Gregg and E.R. Steinberg (eds) *Cognitive Processes in Writing* (pp. 31–50). Hillsdale, NJ: Lawrence Erlbaum.

Flower, L.S. and Hayes, J.R. (1981) A cognitive process theory of writing. *College Composition and Communication* 32 (4), 365–387.

Glynn, S.M., Britton, B.K., Muth, D. and Dugan, N. (1982) Writing and revising persuasive documents: Cognitive demands. *Journal of Educational Psychology* 74 (4), 557–567.

Grabowski, J. (1996) Writing and speaking: Common grounds and differences toward a regulation theory of written language production. In C.M. Levy and S. Ransdell (eds) *The Science of Writing: Theories, Methods, Individual Differences and Applications* (pp. 73–91). Mahwah, NJ: Lawrence Erlbaum.

Graham, S. and Perin, D. (2007) A meta-analysis of writing instruction for adolescent students. *Journal of Educational Psychology* 99 (3), 445–476.

Hayes, J.R. (1996) A new framework for understanding cognition and affect in writing. In C.M. Levy and S. Ransdell (eds) *The Science of Writing: Theories, Methods, Individual Differences and Applications* (pp. 1–27). Mahwah, NJ: Lawrence Erlbaum.

Hayes, J.R. and Flower, L.S. (1980) Identifying the organization of writing processes. In L.W. Gregg and E.R. Steinberg (eds) *Cognitive Processes in Writing* (pp. 3–30). Hillsdale, NJ: Lawrence Erlbaum.

Hayes J.R. and Nash, J.G. (1996) On the nature of planning in writing. In C.M. Levy and S. Ransdell (eds) *The Science of Writing: Theories, Methods, Individual Differences and Applications* (pp. 29–55). Mahwah, NJ: Lawrence Erlbaum.

Jones, S. and Tetroe, J. (1987) Composing in a second language. In A. Matsuhashi (ed.) *Writing in Real Time. Modelling Production Processes* (pp. 34–57). Norwood, NJ: Ablex.

Kellogg, R.T. (1987) Effects of topic knowledge on the allocation of processing time and cognitive effort to writing processes. *Memory & Cognition* 15 (3), 256–266.

Kellogg, R.T. (1994) *The Psychology of Writing*. New York: Oxford University Press.

Kellogg, R.T. (1996) A model of working memory in writing. In C.M. Levy and S. Ransdell (eds) *The Science of Writing: Theories, Methods, Individual Differences and Applications* (pp. 57–71). Mahwah, NJ: Lawrence Erlbaum.

Kollberg, P. (1998) S-notation – a computer-based method for studying and representing text composition. Licentiate thesis, Royal Institute of Technology, Stockholm.

Kuiken, F. and Vedder, I. (2008) Cognitive task complexity and written output in Italian and French as a foreign language. *Journal of Second Language Writing* 17 (1), 48–60.

Levelt, W.J.M. (1989) *Speaking. From Intention to Articulation.* Cambridge, MA: The MIT Press.

Levelt, W.J.M. (1999) Producing spoken language: A blueprint of the speaker. In C.M. Brown and P. Hagoort (eds) *The Neurocognition of Language* (pp. 83–122). Oxford: Oxford University Press.

Levy, C.M. and Ransdell, S. (eds) (1996) *The Science of Writing: Theories, Methods, Individual Differences and Applications*. Mahwah, NJ: Lawrence Erlbaum.

Lindgren, E. and Sullivan, K.P.H. (2002) The LS graph: A methodology for writing revision. *Language Learning* 52 (3), 565–595.

Manchón, R.M. and Roca de Larios, J. (2007) On the temporal nature of planning in L1 and L2 composing. *Language Learning* 27 (4), 549–593.

McCutchen, D. (1996) A capacity theory of writing: Working memory in composition. *Educational Psychology Review* 8 (3), 299–325.

McCutchen, D., Covill, A., Hoyne, S.H. and Mildes, K. (1994) Individual differences in writing: Implications of translating fluency. *Journal of Educational Psychology* 86 (2), 256–266.

Perfetti, C.A. (1999) Comprehending written language: A blueprint of the reader. In C.M. Brown and P. Hagoort (eds) *The Neurocognition of Language* (pp. 167–208). Oxford: Oxford University Press.

Ransdell, S. and Levy, C.M. (1999) Writing, reading, and speaking memory spans and the importance of resource flexibility. In M. Torrance and G.C. Jeffery (eds) *The Cognitive Demands of Writing. Processing Capacity and Working Memory in Text Production* (pp. 99–113). Amsterdam: Amsterdam University Press.

Robinson, P. (2001) Task complexity, task difficulty, and task production: Exploring interactions in a componential framework. *Applied Linguistics* 22 (1), 27–57.

Roca de Larios, J., Manchón, R.M. and Murphy, L. (2006) Generating text in native and foreign language writing: A temporal analysis of problem solving formulation processes. *The Modern Language Journal* 90 (9), 100–114.

Roca de Larios, J., Murphy, L. and Manchón, R.M. (1999) The use of restructuring strategies in EFL writing: A study Spanish learners of English as a foreign language. *Journal of Second Language Writing* 8 (1), 13–44.

Sasaki, M. (2002) Building an empirically based model of EFL learners' writing processes. In S. Ransdell and M-L. Barbier (eds) *New Directions for Research in L2 Writing* (pp. 49–80). Dordrecht: Kluwer.

Sasaki, M. and Hirose, K. (1996) Explanatory variables for EFL students' expository writing. *Language Learning* 46 (1), 137–174.

Schoonen, R. (2005) Generalizability of writing scores. An application of structural equation modeling. *Language Testing* 22 (1), 1–30.

Schoonen, R., van Gelderen, A., De Glopper, K., Hulstijn, J., Simis, A., Snellings, P. and Stevenson, M. (2003) First language and second language writing: the role of linguistic fluency, linguistic knowledge and metacognitive knowledge. *Language Learning* 53 (1), 165–202.

Schoonen, R., van Gelderen, A., De Glopper, K., Hulstijn, J., Snellings, P., Simis, A. and Stevenson, M. (2002) Linguistic knowledge, metacognitive knowledge and retrieval speed in L1, L2 and EFL writing. A structural equation modelling approach. In S. Ransdell and M-L. Barbier (eds) *New Directions for Research in L2 Writing* (pp. 101–122). Dordrecht: Kluwer.

Skehan, P. and Foster, P. (2001) Cognition and tasks. In P. Robinson (ed.) *Cognition and Second Language Instruction* (pp. 183–205). Cambridge: Cambridge University Press.

Snellings, P., van Gelderen, A. and De Glopper, K. (2002) Lexical retrieval: An aspect of fluent second-language production that can be enhanced. *Language Learning* 52 (4), 723–754.

Snellings, P., van Gelderen, A. and De Glopper, K. (2004a) The effect of enhanced lexical retrieval on L2 writing: A classroom experiment. *Applied Psycholinguistics* 25 (2), 175–200.

Snellings, P., van Gelderen, A. and De Glopper, K. (2004b) Validating a test of second language written lexical retrieval: A new measure of fluency in written language production. *Language Testing* 21 (2), 174–201.

Spelman Miller, K. (2002) Units of production in writing: Towards a discourse perspective. In S. Burgess (ed.) *Revista Canaria de Estudios Ingleses* (pp. 115–140). Tenerife: University of La Laguna.

Stevenson, M. (2005) Reading and writing in a foreign language. A comparison of conceptual and linguistic processes in Dutch and English. Doctoral dissertation, University of Amsterdam.

Stevenson, M., Schoonen, R. and De Glopper, K. (2006) Revising in two languages: A multi-dimensional comparison of online writing revisions in L1 and FL. *Journal of Second Language Writing* 15 (3), 201–233.

Van den Bergh, H. and Rijlaarsdam, G. (1996) The dynamics of composing: Modeling writing process data. In C.M. Levy and S. Ransdell (eds) *The Science of Writing: Theories, Methods, Individual Differences and Applications* (pp. 207–232). Mahwah, NJ: Lawrence Erlbaum.

van Gelderen, A. and Oostdam, R. (2004) Revision of form and meaning in learning to write comprehensible text. In L. Allal, L. Chanquoi, P. Largy and Y. Rouiller (eds) *Revision: Cognitive and Instructional Processes* (pp. 103–123). Dordrecht: Kluwer.

van Gelderen, A. and Oostdam, R. (2005) Effects of fluency training on the application of linguistic operations in writing. *L1 Educational Studies of Language and Literature* 5 (2), 215–240.

van Gelderen, A., Schoonen, R., De Glopper, K., Hulstijn, J., Simis, A., Snellings, P. and Stevenson, M. (2004) Linguistic knowledge, processing speed and metacognitive knowledge in first and second language reading comprehension; A componential analysis. *Journal of Educational Psychology* 96 (1), 19–30.

Weinert, R. (1995) The role of formulaic language in second language acquisition: A review. *Applied Linguistics* 16 (2), 180–205.

Whalen, K. and Ménard, N. (1995) L1 and L2 writers' strategic and linguistic knowledge: A model of multiple-level discourse processing. *Language Learning* 44 (3), 381–418.

Zimmerman, R. (2000) L2 writing: Subprocesses, a model of formulating and empirical findings. *Learning and Instruction* 10 (1), 73–99.

Chapter 4

The Temporal Dimension and Problem-solving Nature of Foreign Language Composing Processes. Implications for Theory

ROSA M. MANCHÓN, JULIO ROCA DE LARIOS and LIZ MURPHY

Introduction

In 1995, we initiated a programme of research entitled *A crossectional study of EFL writing processes*, whose ultimate aim was theoretical in orientation: we planned our research as an inquiry into the regularities that govern cognitive activity while writing, attempting at the same time to shed light on how our writers' processes and strategies varied when they tackled writing tasks in the languages that constituted their linguistic repertoire. This issue was particularly relevant in the context we were investigating, given that (i) our student writers' literacy experience included writing practice, but not specific instruction in either native language (L1, Spanish) or foreign language (L2, English) writing; and (ii) their L1 and L2 writing experience and their second language acquisition (SLA) process had been almost synchronous.

In this chapter, our aim is to try to paint the picture that emerges from this research programme as well as to draw theoretical implications from it. We shall proceed by first offering a theoretical background to our research, and then summarizing the main methodological decisions taken in the design and implementation of the different studies conducted within the project. The main part of the chapter will be devoted to synthesizing our most outstanding findings, and to exploring their theoretical relevance.

Contextualizing the Research Programme

In two recent reviews, Cumming (2001) and Hedgcock (2005) distinguish three central strands of research in L2 writing scholarship, namely, (i) the ways in which L2 writers approach writing; (ii) the distinct nature of L2 writers' texts; and (iii) the various socioeducational contexts in which L2 writing takes place. According to this tripartite distinction, our research falls within [illegible] tegory, given its focus on cognition and writi[illegible] what Ortega and Carson (2009) call 'SLA [illegible]

The develop[illegible] as led to a search for answers in two [illegible] on of writing processes, on the one hand, [illegible] of composing activity, on the other. The [illegible] light of basic tenets in cognitive accoun[illegible] of composing as a recursive, cogniti[illegible] task.

L1 writing mo[illegible] Hayes, 1981) see composing as recursive in natur[illegible] due to the cyclical interplay of writing processes (planning, formulation and revision) that characterize the construction of texts. This implies that writing processes are dynamic, allowing writers to shift continually among them. Bearing also in mind that the fact that composing processes take place in time, we concluded that it was worth looking into the temporal dimension of text production in order to ascertain whether all processes are equal candidates to be activated during writing, and hence equal candidates for interacting with any other. In addition, we also speculated that the time-based character of composing might be constrained by individual differences, such as level of writing ability or L2 proficiency, an issue clearly overlooked in previous empirical research. Our research agenda, therefore, included an inquiry into the allocation of attentional resources (operationalized as the time spent on different composing activities) by focusing on the whole L2 composing activity (Roca de Larios *et al.*, 2008), or just on one macrowriting process in L1 and L2 writing, be it formulation, i.e. text-generating activity (Roca de Larios *et al.* 2001, 2006) or planning (Manchón & Roca de Larios, 2007) (see Appendix 1 for an overview of the different studies in our research programme).

Another central tenet in cognitive accounts of writing is the consideration of composing as a cognitively demanding, problem-solving activity, with expert and novice writers differing in the type of problems they pose themselves, and in the range of (and control over) the strategies used to solve them (see review in Manchón *et al.*, 2007; Roca *et al.*, 2002). In this context, a crucial empirical question was whether or not writing in a second language imposes further constraints on the learner that may create additional competing demands for attention and also influence the type of problems attended to and the strategies used to solve them. This issue had been investigated with second language writers, but little research had been conducted in foreign language settings when we initiated our research programme. What is more, to our surprise, scant attention had been paid in empirical research to the process of formulation in contrast to that devoted to planning and revision. This explains our decision to make a priority of this area in our own research agenda. Our speculation was that this text-generating activity would be the process in which L2 writing could show its own specificity with regard to the writer's problem-solving activity because of the obvious differences in the nature and accessibility of L1 and L2 knowledge (see Roca *et al.*, 2001, 2006).

In view of these issues, our enquiry into the problem-solving nature of composing has materialized in several studies (all of them framed in the problem-solving paradigm in cognitive psychology) in which we have attempted to delve into both the problems faced by our student writers, and the strategies employed in their problem-solving behavior, particularly the strategies of Backtracking (Manchón *et al.*, 1998, 2000a, 2000b), Restructuring (Roca *et al.*, 1999), and the Use of the L1 (Murphy *et al.*, 2002, 2007).

In the next section, we explain the main methodological decisions that guided our inquiry process into the various areas just mentioned (see also Appendix 1).

Method

In our attempt to a[illegible] fit between the cognitive orientation and [illegible]t and its design and implementatio[illegible]n. First, we opted for think-aloud [illegible]e in which subjects verbalize their [illegible]s our data-elicitation procedure beca[illegible]ose as possible to our participants' onli[illegible]nt protocols are thought to offer the closest co[illegible]inking and its verbalization, and to be more valid t[illegible]orms of verbal reports because the verbalizations are not c[illegible]ned by memory (Ericsson, 1998).

Second, we chose a within-writer design (i.e. having the same participants writing in their L1 and L2) in the belief that this would allow us to compare across languages and within proficiency levels. In retrospect, we are pleased to discover that this approach is thought to put researchers in a better position to contribute to theory building (which was actually our ultimate aim) and to move research forward in the treatment of L2 writers as *multicompetent* individuals, such treatment being considered a fruitful and promising approach to understanding L2 writers (see Ortega & Carson, in 2009).

Further methodological details are briefly summarized below. The reader is referred to Manchón *et al.* (2005) for a fuller account, particularly regarding issues of validity in the use of concurrent protocols.

Participants

A total of 21 Spanish English as a foreign language (EFL) participants took part in the research programme. They varied in terms of educational level, L2 proficiency and previous writing experience and instruction. Our writers were seven secondary school pupils (Level 1) with a preintermediate level of English proficiency, seven university students of Education (Level 2) at an intermediate proficiency level and seven recent graduates in English (Level 3) with an advanced command of English. All were native speakers of Spanish, with classroom exposure to English that ranged from five to 12 years. As mentioned earlier, the three groups had received some writing guidance as part of their language courses, but no instruction specifically aimed at developing their writing skills. The more advanced participants had had both greater contact with English (as this was the medium of instruction in the last three years of their degree course) and substantially more L2 writing practice, particularly academic writing.

Data sources

Two main data sources were used in the project: think-aloud protocols while writing argumentative and narrative tasks, and retrospective questionnaires.

Argumentative and narrative tasks were chosen given their different cognitive demands (see prompts in Appendix 2 and extracts of the students' writing in Appendix 3). We opted for similar topics in the L1 and L2 tasks to reduce the influence of confounding variables, as well as for familiar topics in an effort to facilitate the participants' degree of involvement. Our choice of prompts also aimed to encourage their engagement in problem-solving behavior while completing the tasks, in the belief that such problem-solving activity would elicit more useful and informative data (see Manchón *et al.*, 2005).

Retrospective questionnaires were administered after each writing task to overcome the incompleteness of think-aloud protocols (see

Jourdenais, 2001). These questionnaires attempted to tap the participants' attitudes about the topics of the compositions, the rhetorical situation, the writing environment and their perceptions of their own composing processes (see Manchón & Roca, 2007; Manchón *et al.*, 2005).

Procedures

We followed standard procedures for the elicitation of protocol data with respect to the nature of the instructions and the trial run (see Manchón *et al.*, 2005). Before the first session, our participants were instructed in Spanish to verbalize all thinking while composing. They were then given the opportunity to practice thinking aloud with a mock composition and, after this trial run, they were allowed an hour to complete the task. This means that our findings and conclusions only apply to time-compressed writing.

Data analysis

The data analysis entailed the transcription of the participants' verbalizations, on the one hand, and the setting up of the coding schemes guiding the different studies, on the other. Regarding the latter, we followed basic principles for the analysis of protocol data suggested in the relevant literature and, in particular, the tenet that encoding must have a theoretical basis (Ericsson & Simon, 1993; Kasper, 1998), in our case cognitive, problem-solving theories of writing. Accordingly, the analysis of our participants' problem-solving activity has always been guided by the conceptualization of 'problems' and 'strategies' in the problem-solving literature (cf. Hayes, 1989; Newell, 1980; Newell & Simon, 1972). Our conceptual definition of a problem was the existence of a gap (between an initial state and an intended goal or final state) that cannot be bridged without a search process. Similarly, the participants' behavior was coded as an instance of problem solving whenever an attempt was made to engage in a search process to cross this gap. Writing strategies were defined as the sequence of operations implemented while engaged in problem-solving activity.

With respect to the analysis of the temporal dimension of writing processes, we decided to use the time spent on the different writing activities as percentages of total composition time in an effort to neutralize variability across informants regarding the number of processes verbalized and the time spent on the task. As for the analysis of the temporal distribution of writing activity throughout the composing process, the total amount of time spent on each writing task was divided into three equal periods. We were thus able to calculate how much time our writers devoted to a given composing activity (say revision) at the beginning, middle and end stages of their individual composing process.

Main Findings

We shall next provide a synthesis of the main results obtained in the two macro areas investigated (i.e. temporal dimension of writing process and problem-solving behavior). Whenever data are available, this analysis will account for any similarities or differences observed in L1 and L2 writing, as well as across proficiency levels.

The temporal dimension of writing processes

Important insights were obtained regarding how L2 proficiency appears to constrain the allocation of attentional resources to various composing activities, both globally and at different times in the composing process.

Global time allocation

As can be seen in Figure 4.1, one general pattern was for a gradual increase in the time devoted to planning and revision along with an increase in L2 proficiency, with a parallel decrease in the attention paid to formulation (Roca de Larios *et al.*, 2008). This means in effect that as proficiency grows, a more balanced allocation of attentional resources to different processes takes place, which concurs with previous findings in both L1 and L2 writing research that associate successful writing with an

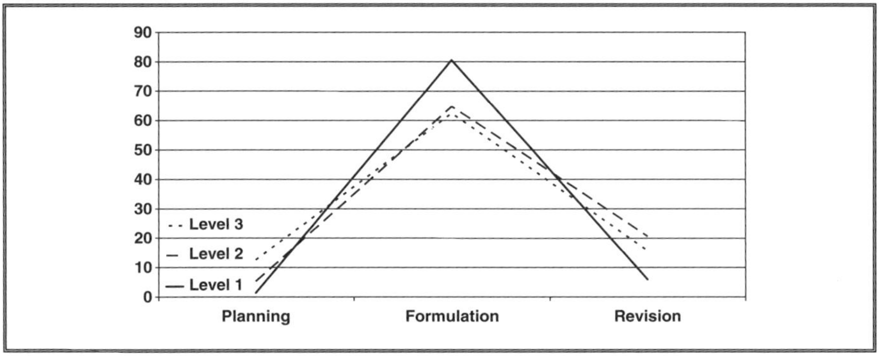

Figure 4.1 Percentage of total composition time devoted to different composing activities

appropriate balance among writing processes (cf. Hayes & Nash, 1996; Pennington & So, 1993; Raimes, 1987).

Regarding *formulation* (i.e. the process of converting ideas into language), the lower the proficiency level, the more dominant formulation was in the writing process (Roca de Larios *et al.*, 2001). Another fairly robust finding was that for all participants, regardless of their proficiency level, this process took up most of their composition time, occupying around 60% (Levels 2 and 3) to 80% (Level 1) of the total time (Roca *et al.*, 2001, 2008).

Regarding *planning* (Manchón & Roca de Larios, 2007), the opposite trend was observed (see Figure 4.1): the higher up the proficiency scale the writers were situated, the more time they devoted to constructing their pragmatic and ideational representations before putting pen to paper, and the greater their ability to activate and incorporate them into the text. In addition, it is important to note that, in contrast to formulation, differential effects were observed for planning in L1 and L2 writing depending on the participants' L2 proficiency. Thus, the Level 1 and Level 2 participants – the two lower levels – planned more in the L1 task than in the L2 task (although this was not statistically significant), whereas the Level 3 group – the more advanced level – did the reverse, engaging in more planning in the L2 task.

Time allocation throughout the composing process

One important finding was that the various composing activities our participants engaged in did not stand an equal chance of being activated at any given time in the composing process. As might be expected, across languages and proficiency levels, planning episodes tended to concentrate in the first period, whereas formulation reached its peak in the second period. Revision, in contrast, gradually increased from the beginning to the end of the composition process.

The picture, however, was rather more complex given that this general tendency was mediated by proficiency, as seen in the statistically significant triple interaction found between proficiency, process and period (Roca de Larios *et al.*, 2008). Basically, with greater competence, L2 writers appeared to be able to strategically decide what attentional resources to devote to which composing activities at any particular point in the writing process. In support of this contention, the Level 1 participants (see Figure 4.2) maintained the same pattern of time allocation throughout the different stages of their text production process: these participants put pen to paper, and when they ran out of ideas (towards the end of the composition process), a gradual increase in

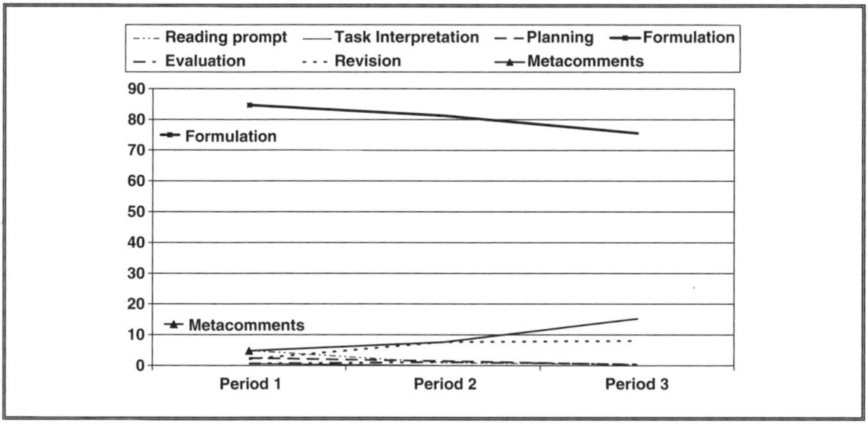

Figure 4.2 Allocation of attentional resources throughout the writing process (Level 1)

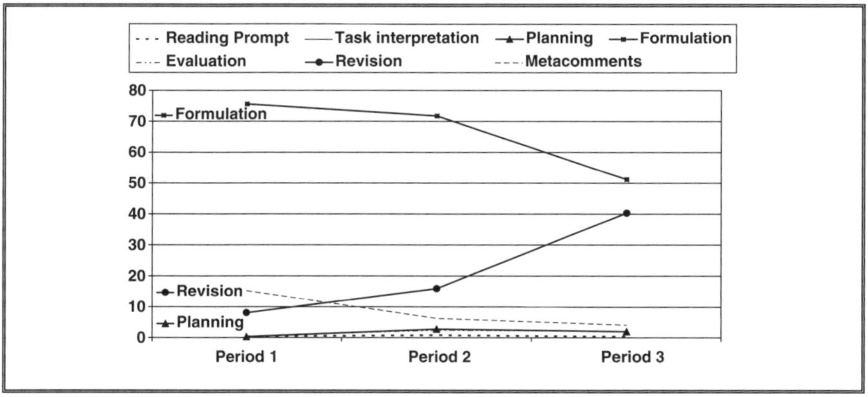

Figure 4.3 Allocation of attentional resources throughout the writing process (Level 2)

off-task comments was observed, though this may well have been an artefact of the instruction to think aloud.

In contrast, in the case of Level 2 (see Figure 4.3), we can see the beginning of a more diversified allocation of time to different processes more directly related to the act of composing properly, a clearly visible tendency in the data of the Level 3 participants (see Figure 4.4): the time devoted to planning was concentrated mainly in the first period and progressively decreased in the second and third periods, whereas

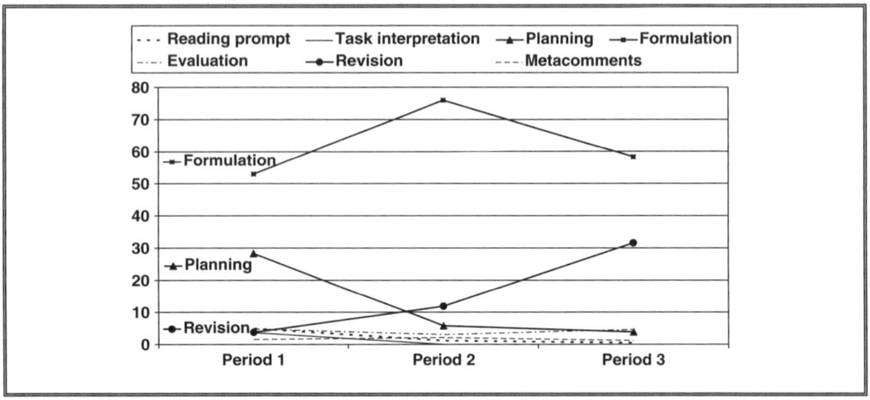

Figure 4.4 Allocation of attentional resources throughout the writing process (Level 3)

revision showed the opposite tendency. Formulation reached its peak in the second period.

The problem-solving nature of composing

We have been able to shed light on three main aspects related to the problem-solving nature of composing: (i) the more labor-intense nature of text-generating activity in L2 composing; (ii) the variation in problem-solving activity as a function of proficiency and across languages; and (iii) the strategies used in L2 composing.

More problem-solving activity in L2 writing

To put it briefly, L2 writing involves more problem solving than L1 writing because of the greater density and more varied nature of the problems tackled in this condition.

We observed (Roca de Larios *et al.*, 2001) that the internal structure of text-generating activity entailed the combination of episodes in which writing developed without having to tackle problems (fluent formulation), and episodes that clearly involved having to solve various kinds of problems (problem-solving formulation) (see exemplification in Appendix 4). To our surprise, fluent formulation was more frequent than problem-solving formulation for all groups and tasks. However, the ratio between fluent and problem-solving formulation varied in L1 and L2 writing – 5:1 in L1 as opposed to 2:1 in L2 – which means that the density of problems to be tackled in L2 writing is significantly higher.

Although these findings can be explained from the perspective of the availability and accessibility of L1 and L2 knowledge, when we looked into the text-generating episodes that entailed problem-solving, we further realized that the density of formulation problems was not just a question of interlanguage deficits. In fact, our writers engaged in the solution of two main types of problems: 'compensatory' and 'upgrading' (see examples in Appendix 3). The former are attempts to compensate for lack of (accessibility to) the necessary linguistic resources, whereas the latter are attempts to improve lexical, stylistic and rhetorical options. As might be expected, compensatory problems were practically nonexistent in L1 writing, which means that L2 writing involves a wider range of problems.

Let us exemplify these issues with data from one study (Roca *et al.*, 1996) in which we investigated the nature and frequency of lexical problems in L1 and L2 writing. We found that the total number of problems tackled in the L2 was more than double that in L1 writing, which confirms again that writing in a second language imposes a heavier burden on writers. Data also showed that our participants struggled with various types of lexical problems, including (i) those that arose from addressing higher-level co[illegible]s (lexical and stylistic precision and appropriacy); (ii) search f[illegible]ion equivalents (in cases in which the intended meaning h[illegible] in the L1); (iii) problems due to lack of access to rel[illegible]h which to express the intended meaning, or [illegible]t the correctness or appropriacy of the [illegible] intended meaning. All these probl[illegible]hereas in the L1 condition the pa[illegible] range of lexical problems because [illegible] in activities such as searching to find tra[illegible]

Variation in the problems [illegible]unction of proficiency and across languages

As expected, the lower the [illegible] proficiency of the writers, the more they were found to engage in compensating for interlanguage deficits *vis à vis* ideational or textual preoccupations (Roca *et al.*, 2006).

As for *planning* (Manchón & Roca de Larios, 2007), the picture that emerges from the protocol and questionnaire data is one in which the type of higher- and lower-level concerns that guided our participants' planning activity varied across proficiency levels. Thus, when asked in the follow-up questionnaire about the kind of constraints they had in mind before engaging in writing, the three proficiency groups mentioned 'topic', whereas 'text organization' was a concern only for the Level 2 and 3 students. The gradual increase in textual concerns (other than mere quantity of words, a concern only mentioned by the two lower proficiency groups) as we move up the proficiency scale is indicative of a more sophisticated approach to writing in that it involves deeper processing than the mere noting down of ideas as they come to mind.

Interestingly, the protocols of Level 1 and Level 2 participants showed evidence of performance loss in the management of ideas in the L2 task, as seen, for instance, in the structuring of ideas, or the choice of personal narration in the L2 task as against the well-developed network of ideas generated in the L1 task, which could be an indication of problem avoiding rather than problem-solving behavior. In contrast, the Level 3 writers not only planned significantly more in the L2, but they also showed no signs of performance loss in this condition.

Regarding *formulation* in both languages, the Level 1 group spent twice as much time on compensatory problems as on upgrading ones, while the Level 2 group did exactly the opposite. The Level 3 group continued this tendency by devoting around nine times more time to improving the quality of their ideas, their way of expressing them and the coherence of their texts than to compensating for their linguistic deficiencies. These findings were also applicable to another study (Roca *et al.*, 1999) in which we focused on how our participants solved problems via the use of Restructuring strategies in L2 writing. Our student writers restructured their texts at all three levels of discourse (ideational, textual and linguistic; see examples in Appendix 3) for both compensatory and upgrading purposes, although clear proficiency-related tendencies were observed: the lower proficiency group in this study (Level 2 in the general research programme) spent seven times longer on restructuring their texts for compensatory purposes than the advanced group (Level 3 participants). In contrast, the advanced group allotted twice as much time as the lower group to restructuring for textual and ideational purposes. This lends further support to the idea that the automatization of language skills that comes with increased L2 proficiency frees up cognitive resources to be deployed in the solution of higher-level writing problems.

These tendencies were also apparent in our participants' L2 revision behavior. Although no statistical differences were observed regarding the amount of time devoted to revision by the three groups (perhaps because we are dealing with a time-compressed task), a significant interaction between proficiency and purposes of revision was found. Thus, in contrast to the two lower proficiency groups, the Level 3 participants engaged four times more often in revision processes related to the elaboration and clarification of ideas, and to the solution of discourse and stylistic problems, than to compensatory language problems.

Writers use a range of strategies

In addition to the study of Restructuring that we mentioned earlier (Roca *et al.*, 1999), we have looked into two very characteristic L2 writing strategies, namely, Backtracking and the Use of the L1 (see Appendix 1).

Backtracking. Anybody who writes can attest to the fact that the process of text creation involves continuous movements backward and forward between what we have written and what we will write next. Our interest in this phenomenon emerged, however, when we realized that backtracking was an ever-present phenomenon in our data, and also that our writers' backtracking behavior seemed to show a degree of complexity that was worth examining. This complexity relates to the forms that backtracking takes and the purposes it serves (Manchón *et al.*, 1998, 2000a, 2000b; see Appendix 1).

Regarding *forms*, our writers rescanned their texts, notes/outlines and the prompt by resorting to different forms of Backtracking that varied according to whether backtracking was implemented (i) through the writer's L1 or L2; and (ii) in a linear or in a selective fashion (see Appendix 3). When done in a linear way, writers either reread or back-translated previous fragments literally. Selective Backtracking, however, involved reprocessing, rather than merely reiterating, a previous written fragment or the prompt through paraphrasing, skimming-and-dipping or summarizing (in either their L1 or L2).

As for the *purposes* Backtracking serves, our participants resorted to Backtracking for both retrospective and prospective uses. The retrospective uses involved an attempt on the part of the writer to check or improve the solutions given to problems in relation to (i) the fulfilment of task requirements; (ii) the appropriacy of the ideas in the plan intended to guide the composing process; (iii) the match between the original plan and its implementation; and (iv) the correspondence between their communicative intention and their linguistic expression. In our data, however, Backtracking was mainly used as a way of moving forward through the text, which might be related to the fact that our participants wrote under time constraints. When used prospectively, they resorted to rescanning the prompt, their plans and their texts to (i) focus their attention on the requirements of the task at hand; (ii) keep on generating ideas to be incorporated into the text; and (iii) find a way to solve the different linguistic problems tackled while formulating their texts.

In short, as we suggested in Manchón *et al.* (2000a), backtracking may be a useful writing strategy that appears to help L2 writers at all proficiency levels to lower the processing load, which, in turn, creates more favorable conditions for moving forward through the text.

Use of the L1. Switching to the L1 is without doubt one of the most characteristic features of L2 writing. In our review of the empirical literature on the use of this strategy (Manchón *et al.*, 2007), we noted that it appears in various forms, serves different purposes, is influenced by different learner- and task-related variables, and is deployed by writers while planning, writing and revising, as well as serving as a control mechanism for the writing process.

Our own research in this area (Murphy *et al.*, 2002, 2007) has offered empirical evidence of the rich array of strategic purposes to which the L1 is put. Thus, our participants reverted to their L1 for a variety of purposes associated with (i) conceptualizing the task at hand; (ii) planning, formulating and revising their texts; and (iii) monitoring their composing process. At the level of planning, the L1 appeared to serve ideational, textual, linguistic, procedural and pragmatic purposes, whereas while formulating, the L1 was mainly used for idea generation, involving both backtracking as a springboard to move forward (see above), and also generating ideas via the L1 to be incorporated into their L2 texts. As mentioned earlier, writers also resorted to Backtracking through their L1 while revising their texts. Finally, when used for monitoring purposes, the L1 was used to evaluate their texts at ideational, textual and linguistic levels, as well as for procedural, pragmatic and conceptual purposes.

We also observed proficiency-related differences in the use of the L1, which we have explained with reference to two different roles that writers play in the composing process: Controller and Writer. The Writer needs to formulate ideas and convert them into text, using rereading (via the L1) to help with this process. The Controller directs the processes. Planning and monitoring are the realm of the Controller, and in our data the use of the L1 for this control function increased along with L2 competence. As we mentioned in our discussion about the temporal dimension of writing processes, the Level 1 writers needed all their cognitive resources (and task time) to struggle along in their role of Writer. As a result, they used their L1 strategically in their linguistic struggle by, for instance, generating ideas or searching for synonyms in Spanish. Consequently, they used their L1 to plan and monitor less than more advanced writers. For the latter, the formulating process was much less problematic at the lexico-grammatical level (recall that they used only 60% of their time in text-generating activity; Roca *et al.*, 2001, 2008) and, in many cases, they could carry it out directly in English because they had automatized many procedures. Thus, they had extra cognitive capacity to be used for planning, revising and monitoring purposes. The interesting finding was that they resorted to their L1 for these purposes in the realm of the Controller. In other words, they were using different languages for different roles: the L1 for that of the Controller and the L2 for that of the Writer, a division that, we would speculate, assisted them in their problem-solving activity.

Discussion

Given the general aims of our programme of research, it is worth ascertaining what it has uncovered about the recursive and problem-solving nature of composing propounded in classical cognitive models of writing. In addition, we consider it relevant to re-examine our data with respect to two crucial issues in SLA-oriented L2 writing research: the manner in which L2 linguistic expertise appears to constrain and/or expedite the development of FL composing abilities; and the way multicompetent users exploit their varied linguistic abilities and cognitive resources in the completion of writing tasks in the languages that form their linguistic repertoire.

The recursive and problem-solving nature of composing

We feel that our findings can be considered to constitute a step forward in cognitively oriented theorizing on composing.

Regarding the classical cognitive conception of *writing as a purely recursive process*, three issues are worth mentioning. First, although L2 composing in a time-compressed mode cannot be conceived as a kind of linear progression from planning to formulation and then to revision, neither can it be seen as an activity in which time can equally be allocated to any process at any stage of the composition: whatever the language and the proficiency level involved, planning episodes in our data tended to concentrate in the first period, whereas formulation reached its peak in the second period, and revision increased as the writing process progressed. Second, our research has also revealed that the recursive nature of L2 composing is mediated by proficiency: increased command of the L2 brings with it the possibility of sharing attentional resources among various composing processes, thus increasing the likelihood of their cyclical interplay as propounded in classical cognitive accounts of writing. Third, the recursive nature of writing also involves the movements backwards and forwards between the already written and the emerging text, a component of writing that was part of the L1 writing model proposed by Flower and Hayes (1981) and of the most recent one propounded by Hayes (1996). What we have learned about the strategy of Backtracking leads us to suggest some qualifications. In particular, Hayes (1996) argues that writers go back over what they have written as a way of shaping what they will write next. While further confirming this position as far as time-compressed L2 writing tasks are concerned, our data has made us realize that the picture is rather more complex on account of (i) the variety of purposes of Backtracking that emerge from our data (which include both prospective and retrospective purposes); and (ii) the range of linguistic, rhetorical and ideational problems that L2 writers attempt to solve by resorting to Backtracking while planning, formulating and revising their L2 texts.

We feel that our research has also allowed us to shed light on the purported *problem-solving nature* of the only nonoptional writing process: *text-generating activity*. Put most simply, L2 writing entails more problem solving than L1 writing as far as problem density and the range of problems to be tackled are concerned. However, an interesting finding of our research was that, both in L1 and in L2 writing, our writers were able to transform their ideas into language without any signs of problem solving much more frequently than they had to engage in problem-solving behavior (5:1 in L1 and 2:1 in L2). This internal structure of formulation processes reveals that the representation of writing as problem solving in classical cognitive models does not fully account for all the processes involved in FL composing. According to our data, when writing under time limits, FL writers appear to construct their sentences through a process in which bottom-up, largely automatic processing episodes alternate with others in which writers have to tackle various lexical and syntactic problems that entail either upgrading their options (in L1 and L2 writing) or compensating for linguistic deficits (in L2 composing). Finally, as in the case of recursiveness, problem-solving behavior in L2 writing is mediated by proficiency: the likelihood of attending to higher-level concerns while writing increases as writers become more capable of using the L2, and this applies to the problems writers pose themselves while planning, formulating and revising their texts.

The proficiency-dependency of writing activity

One of the aims of our research was to delve into the proficiency-dependency of cognitive activity while writing. We have already mentioned that with increased L2 proficiency, writers appear to be able to (i) make strategic decisions as to the allocation of attentional resources to various composing activities throughout the writing process; and (ii) tackle ideational, textual and stylistic problems in addition to those that derive from having to compensate for language deficits.

Seen from a different angle, these data can be interpreted to mean that increased language expertise brings with it the gradual development of a more multidimensional model of writing, by which we mean the set of beliefs, goals and intentions that guide writing performance (Devine *et al.*, 1993). It could be argued that the Level 1 participants were guided by a monodimensional mental model of writing, as evidenced in their sole concern with language and text-length problems. In contrast, the performance of the more advanced participants can be interpreted as evidence of a more multidimensional mental model according to which writing is a complex task that requires both (i) attending to various higher- and lower-level concerns (of a linguistic, ideational and textual nature); and (ii) making decisions as to how to allocate attentional resources to these problems at any given point in the course of text production.

The crucial question is, however, whether this development towards a more multidimensional model of writing is just a question of increased command in the L2 and/or the result of the writer's literacy experience. Recall that the population studied, both developed at the same time as part of their education. Recall also that these EFL writers had not had any writing instruction as such, although the Level 3 participants had had plenty of actual practice in academic writing as part of their degree studies. This practice, we would speculate, brought with it repeated engagement with writing assignments and some form of response from their teachers. These two factors together must have helped our writers to develop (implicitly, we would argue) a mental model of writing that gradually became more complex and that guided the writer's performance towards the pursuance of more sophisticated goals. Given also that this coincided in time with the concomitant development of their L2 language abilities, it may be safe to assume that the more proficient writers in our research were more able to engage in deeper problem-solving activity as a result of the combined forces of their literacy and language learning experience. The question, therefore, is whether or not the situation would have been the same had these writers received just language learning experience but no writing experience. We are tempted to think that the answer would be a negative one. Ultimately, this speaks to the need to go inside the learners' heads to understand cognition in writing, but also to study writing and writing development in foreign language contexts as the result of literacy experiences, an approach that would be in line with the attempt to understand writing as situated practice, as repeatedly claimed by L2 writing specialists (see Atkinson, 2003; Ortega & Carson, 2009).

The way multicompetent users exploit their linguistic and cognitive abilities

There is a further piece to fit into the puzzle that we are trying to solve, which is the interpretation of our writers' performance in their two languages. We shall approach this issue from the theoretical stance of multicompetence. Ortega and Carson (2009) defend the position that L2 writers should be seen as *multicompetent writers*, which means that rather than viewing them as two monolinguals in one, they ought to be seen as possessing a 'psycholinguistically distinct form of "multicompetence"'.

Two aspects of our data are worth discussing from a multicompetence point of view: the way in which our writers made use of their whole linguistic repertoire, and the cross-linguistic similarities and differences observed.

Recourse to L1 in L2 composing

Multicompetent writers are also multilingual, which, as empirical evidence has revealed, has consequences at writing product and process levels. From a processing perspective, the writers we investigated appeared to have found a facilitating effect in making use of their whole linguistic repertoire. This was evident in the division of roles (i.e. those of Writer and Controller) and languages (Writer > L2; Controller > L1) mentioned earlier. Along the same lines, we also know that these writers resorted to their L1 while rescanning their texts, a facilitating, strategic value of L1 use in L2 writing that Leki (2000: 103) interpreted as follows:

> Such a role for the L1 may be particularly significant in L2 writing since the Already Written Text is constrained by the writer's L2 proficiency and yet has the burden of representing not only the actual or instantiated texts, but also the intended one. In other words, if any Already Written Text is, in a sense, always impoverished in relation to the "unwritten possibilities" and "plans, goals and alternatives" in

> the mind of the author, the L2 Already Written Text can be expected to be even more strapped, making reliance on those "unwritten possibilities" through the use of L1 eminently sensible.

We also noticed that not all writers used their two languages in the same way, and we could discern a slight developmental trend in this respect. This starts with the L1 being used as a compensatory strategy in the early stages of learning in order to deal with the multiple language problems that arise for low proficiency students while trying to convey their ideas through the means of the L2. In our data for these students, almost all writing activities took place in the mother tongue, which allowed them to generate ideas (generating the intended message in the L1 and then translating) and access language (using the L1 in their lexical search process), and then evaluate the match between their communicative intentions and their linguistic expression through rescanning via their L1. As we move up the proficiency scale, our writers gave signs that their text-generation process required fewer attentional resources and with this came the possibility of devoting free cognitive capacity to higher levels of processing-planning, organization and solving rhetorical and discourse problems. These may continue to take place in the mother tongue because of the deeper processing involved, particularly where the task presents great cognitive demands (see Centenero-Cortés & Jiménez-Jiménez [2004] for similar findings). This could explain the facilitating role of resorting to the L1 when performing the Controller role: even at high levels of proficiency, some of our writers continued to use their L1 for such activities as task conceptualization, planning ideas and organization, monitoring the writing process or evaluating their task performance.

In short, the insights obtained in our research provide further evidence for the specificity of multicompetent writers' strategic behavior in that their linguistic knowledge sources (and probably textual/ideational resources too; Ortega, personal communication), which are wider than those of the monolingual writer, can and are brought to bear when composing. This adds to claims derived from cognitive accounts of transfer that posit a strategic role for the mother tongue in L2 learning and use (Manchón, 2001; Odlin, 2003).

Crosslinguistic similarities and differences

A common finding in L2 writing process-oriented studies is that writers show a qualitatively similar approach to L1 and L2 task completion, although important quantitative differences are also noticeable (see review in Roca *et al.*, 2002). Such differences have been explained as a function of the learner's L2 proficiency.

We would like to go one step further and venture the hypothesis that this mediation of proficiency is related to the compulsory or optional nature of the writing actions L2 writers engage in. Let us explain what we mean. Having been asked to complete a writing task within one hour, all our multicompetent writers had to end up with a text written down. In order to get this done, first, the amount of composition time devoted to text-generation was maintained across tasks, and, second, more time was devoted to fluent formulation than to problem-solving formulation in the two conditions.

Anything else that they did, apart from struggling to get a text on the blank page, was optional and the consequence of whatever decisions they took regarding whether or not to engage in deeper processing. This applied, for instance, to whether or not writers engaged in planning and, if so, which type of planning, and whether or not they added upgrading concerns (and to what extent) in the L2 condition. In this respect, we observed important cross-linguistic differences related to the ratio between fluent and problem-solving formulation in the two conditions, and between compensatory and upgrading problems. These two important differences can be easily explained if we remember that our writers were much more proficient in one language (their L1) than in the other (their L2). However, when we look at the ratio between compensatory and upgrading problems across proficiency levels, we are able to fit in another piece of the puzzle. Thus, whereas the Level 1 and the Level 3 participants showed a similar behavior across languages, the Level 2 participants gave signs of performance loss in the L2 condition. Our interpretation is that the Level 1 participants showed cross-linguistic similarities simply because the presence of upgrading problems was practically nonexistent in either language. However, when upgrading concerns are an issue, we have two distinct situations: the Level 3 participants did not show signs of performance loss in the L2 condition because their language expertise allowed them to maintain their approach to task completion. The Level 2 participants, in contrast, had not reached the threshold level that is meant to facilitate the transfer of writing skills across languages.

Exactly the same interpretation can be adduced in the analysis of our participants' planning behavior. As in the case of compensatory and upgrading problems, the concerns guiding their planning was more expert-like in the case of the Level 2 and 3 participants. But we see again the mediation of language proficiency in maintaining goals across tasks: the Level 2 participants planned more in the L1 task (perhaps as a result of not having to tackle compensatory problems), but gave signs of performance loss in the L2 task. The Level 3 participants, in contrast, not only planned more in the L2 task, but they were also able to maintain their planning goals in the two conditions. Variation in language development can easily explain these differences.

In short, multilingual writers' writing performance shows a complexity that can be more fully understood when the joint combination of language availability and language expertise, writing expertise and educational experience are jointly combined in the analysis.

Concluding Remarks

To conclude, we feel that our programme [illegible] tributed to expanding the empirical eviden[illegible] ects of composing with data from for[illegible] one of the most outstanding conclusion[illegible] orted in the chapter is that FL writing [illegible]. As noted by Woodall (2002: 23), th[illegible] nce [between L1 and L2 writing] is that [illegible] be at work at the same time. This is [illegible] less) of something; it is a different experie[illegible] mphasis in the original).

Another important finding from our [illegible] search is the close interaction between the FL writer's composing and linguistic competence, an issue that in the FL context can be more fully explored (as argued in an earlier section) when learner-internal and learner-external factors (particularly educational experiences) are jointly combined in the analysis.

Finally, we hope that our general findings regarding the problem-solving nature of composing and the temporal dimension of writing processes represent a relevant building block to be used in the construction of the blueprint of the L2 writer that Schonnen *et al.* discuss in their contribution to this volume.

Acknowledgements

This research was supported by a grant from the Spanish Ministry of Education (SE2005-04266). We are grateful to Carol Rinnert and Lourdes Ortega for their very helpful and insightful suggestions on an earlier draft of this chapter, and to Laura Mayhew-Manchón for her help with the figures.

References

Atkinson, D. (ed.) (2003) L2 writing in the post-process era. Special issue of the *Journal of Second Language Writing* 12 (1), 3–15.

Centenero-Cortés, B. and Jiménez-Jiménez, A.F. (2004) Problem-solving tasks in a foreign language: The importance of L1 in private verbal thinking. *International Journal of Applied Linguistics* 14, 7–35.

Cumming, A. (2001) Learning to write in a second language: Two decades of research. In R.M. Manchón (ed.) *Writing in the L2 Classroom: Issues in Research and Pedagogy.* Special issue of *International Journal of English Studies* 1, 1–23.

Devine, J., Railey, K. and Boshoff, P. (1993) The implications of cognitive models in L1 and L2 writing. *Journal of Second Language Writing* 2 (3), 203–225.

Ericsson, K.A. (1998) Protocol analysis. In W. Bechtel and G. Graham (eds) *A Companion to Cognitive Science* (pp. 425–432). Oxford: Oxford University Press.

Ericsson, K.A. and Simon, H.A. (1993) *Protocol Analysis: Verbal Reports as Data* (revised edn). Cambridge, MA: MIT Press.

Flower, L. and Hayes, J.R. (1981) A cognitive process theory of writing. *College Composition and Communication* 32, 365–387.

Hayes, J.R. (1989) *The Complete Problem Solver* (2nd edn). Hillsdale, NJ: Lawrence Erlbaum.

Hayes, J.R. (1996) A framework for understanding cognition and affect in writing. In C.M. Levy and S. Ransdell (eds) *The Science of Writing: Theories, Methods, Individual Differences and Applications* (pp. 1–27). Mahwah, NJ: Lawrence Erlbaum.

Hayes, J.R. and Nash, J.G. (1996) On the nature of planning in writing. In C.M. Levy and S. Ransdell (eds) *The Science of Writing: Theories, Methods, Individual Differences and Applications* (pp. 29–55). Mahwah, NJ: Lawrence Erlbaum.

Hedgcock, J.S. (2005) Taking stock of research and pedagogy in L2 writing. In E. Hinkel (ed.) *Handbook of Research in Second Language Teaching and Learning* (pp. 597–628). Mahwah, NJ: Lawrence Erlbaum.

Jourdenais, R. (2001) Cognition, instruction and protocol analysis. In P. Robinson (ed.) *Cognition and Second Language Instruction* (pp. 354–375). Cambridge: Cambridge University Press.

Kasper, G. (1998) Analysing verbal protocols. *TESOL Quarterly* 32 (2), 358–363.

Leki, I. (2000) L2 writing: A commentary. *Learning and Instruction* 10 (1), 101–105.

Leki, I. (2001) Material, educational, and ideological challenges of teaching ESL writing at the turn of the century. In R. Manchón (ed.) *Writing in the L2 Classroom: Issues in Research and Pedagogy.* Special issue of *International Journal of English Studies* 1 (2), 197–209.

Manchón, R.M. (2001) Un acercamiento psicolingüístico al fenómeno de la transferencia en el aprendizaje y uso de segundas lenguas. *ELUA*, Anexo 1, 39–72.

Manchón, R.M., Murphy, L. and Roca de Larios, J. (2005) Using concurrent protocols to explore L2 writing processes: Methodological issues in the collection and analysis of data. In P.K. Matsuda and T. Silva (eds) *Second Language Writing Research. Perspectives on the Process of Knowledge Construction* (pp. 191–205). Mahwah, NJ: Lawrence Erlbaum.

Manchón, R.M. and Roca de Larios, J. (2007) On the temporal nature of planning in L1 and L2 composing: A study of foreign language writers. *Language Learning* 57 (4), 549–593.

Manchón, R.M., Roca de Larios, J. and Murphy, L. (1998) Language ability, writing behaviours and the use of backward operations in L2 writing. Paper given at the AAAL Conference, Seattle, WA.

Manchón, R.M., Roca de Larios, J. and Murphy, L. (2000a) An approximation to the study of backtracking in L2 writing. *Learning and Instruction* 10 (1), 13–35.

Manchón, R.M., Roca de Larios, J. and Murphy, L. (2000b) The strategic value of backtracking in L2 writing. Paper given at the AAAL 2000 Conference, Vancouver, Canada.

Manchón, R.M., Roca de Larios, J. and Murphy, L. (2007) Second and foreign language writing strategies: Focus on conceptualizations and impact of the first language. In A.D. Cohen and E. Macaro (eds) *Language Learner Strategies: 30 Years of Research and Practice* (pp. 229–250). Oxford: Oxford University Press.

Murphy, L., Manchón, R.M. and Roca de Larios, J. (2002) *Recourse to the native language in foreign language composing. An exploratory study of Spanish EFL learners*. Paper presented at the XX Conference of the Spanish Association of Applied Linguistics, Jaén, Spain.

Murphy, L., Roca de Larios, J. and Manchón, R.M. (2007) *Investigating the strategic use of the L1 in composing. The case of lexical searches in EFL writing*. Paper given at the BAAL Conference, Edinburgh, UK.

Newell, A. (1980) Reasoning, problem solving and decision processes: The problem space as a fundamental category. In R.S. Nickerson (ed.) *Attention and Performance* (Vol. 8; pp. 693–719). Hillsdale, NJ: Lawrence Erlbaum.

Newell, A. and Simon, H.A. (1972) *Human Problem Solving*. Englewood Cliffs, NJ: Prentice Hall.

Odlin, T. (2003) Cross-linguistic influence. In C. Doughty and M. Long (eds) *The Handbook of Second Language Acquisition* (pp. 436–486). Oxford: Blackwell.

Ortega, L. and Carson, J. (2009) Multicompetence, social context, and L2 writing research praxis. In T. Silva and P.K. Matsuda (eds) *Practicing Theory in Second Language Writing*. Mahwah, NJ: Lawrence Erlbaum.

Pennington, M.C. and So, S. (1993) Comparing writing process and product across two languages: A study of 6 Singaporean university student writers. *Journal of Second Language Writing* 2 (1), 41–63.

Raimes, A. (1987) Language proficiency, writing ability, and composing strategies: A study of ESL college student writers. *Language Learning* 37 (3), 439–468.

Roca de Larios, J., Manchón, R.M. and Murphy, L. (1996) Strategic knowledge in L1 and L2 writing. Strategic knowledge in L1 and L2 composing: A cross-sectional study. *Proceedings of the European Writing Conference, SIG Writing*, Barcelona Autonomous University.

Roca de Larios, J., Manchón R.M. and Murphy, L. (2006) Generating text in native and foreign language writing: A temporal analysis of problem-solving formulation processes. *The Modern Language Journal* 90 (1), 100–114.

Roca de Larios, J., Marin, J. and Murphy, L. (2001) A temporal analysis of formulation processes in L1 and L2 writing. *Language Learning* 51 (3), 497–538.

Roca de Larios, J., Murphy, L. and Manchón, R.M. (1999) The use of restructuring strategies in EFL writing: A study of Spanish learners of English as a foreign language. *Journal of Second Language Writing* 8 (1), 13–44.

Roca de Larios, J., Murphy, L. and Marín, J. (2002) A critical examination of L2 writing process research. In S. Ransdell and M-L. Barbier (eds) *New Directions for Research in L2 Writing* (pp. 11–47). Dordrecht: Kluwer.

Roca de Larios, J., Manchón, R.M., Murphy, L. and Marín, J. (2008) The foreign language writer's strategic behaviour in the allocation of time to writing processes. In R.M. Manchón and P. de Haan (eds) *Writing in Foreign Language Contexts. Research Insights*. Special issue of *Journal of Second Language Writing* 17 (1), 30–47.

Woodall, B.R. (2002) Language-switching: Using the first language when writing in a second language. *Journal of Second Language Writing* 11 (1), 7–28.

Appendix 1

Overview of studies conducted within the programme of research

Study	*Method*							*Area investigated*		*Focus of the study*
	Participants			*Tasks*						
	Level 1	*Level 2*	*Level 3*	*ARG L1*	*ARG L2*	*NARR L1*	*NARR L2*	*Temporal dimension of writing processes*	*Problem-solving nature of composing*	
Manchón *et al.* (1998)	●	●	●		●				●	Backtracking
Manchón *et al.* (2000a)		●			●		●		●	Backtracking
Manchón *et al.* 2000b)	●	●	●		●				●	Backtracking
Manchón and Roca (2007)	●	●	●	●	●			●		Planning
Murphy *et al.* (2002)	●	●	●		●		●		●	L1 use in L2 writing
Murphy *et al.* (2007)			●		●		●		●	L1 use in L2 writing (lexical searches)
Roca *et al.* (1996)	●	●			●				●	Lexical problems

(*Continued*)

Appendix 1 (*Continued*)

Study	*Method*							*Area investigated*		*Focus of the study*
	Participants			*Tasks*				*Temporal dimension of writing processes*	*Problem-solving nature of composing*	
	Level 1	*Level 2*	*Level 3*	*ARG L1*	*ARG L2*	*NARR L1*	*NARR L2*			
Roca *et al.* (1999)	●	●	●						●	Restructuring strategies
Roca *et al.* (2001)	●	●	●	●	●			●	●	Formulation
Roca *et al.* (2006)	●	●	●	●	●			●	●	Formulation
Roca *et al.* (2008)	●	●	●	●	●			●		Planning, formulation and revision

Appendix 2

Tasks

Argumentative L1	*School failure is more a result of teachers' lack of responsibility in carrying out their teaching than of the attitude, effort, aptitude and motivation of the pupils. Do you agree or disagree?*
Argumentative L2	*Success in education is influenced more by the student's home life and training as a child than by the quality and effectiveness of the educational program. Do you agree or disagree? (taken from Raimes, 1987)*
Narrative L1	*Write about something that went right in your life. Write about what happened, when, where, how you felt then and how you feel about it now.*
Narrative L2	*Write about something that went wrong in your life. Write about what happened, when, where, how you felt then and how you feel about it now.*

Appendix 3

Exemplification of students' writing
Prompt: *Success in education is influenced more by the student's home life and training as a child than by the quality and effectiveness of the educational program. Do you agree or disagree?*
(We reproduce the first 150 words of the students' essays)

Level 1 student:
I am agree because I think that your family influenced then you learn in the school. My parents always told me that I had to study more. When I waa a child my mother and my father had teached me to study and they has always helped me. When I was in school my parents helped me to do my homework, but when I began the instituto they don't help me as before.

I think that when people don't help in their home they don't feel well, they think that they don't have to study and they aren't sure that they have to study. In my experience this doesn't happen because my parents always help me.

When people don't have help they think that can't study in the university. If a child his/her family help him since he begins to go to the school, he/she feelins well.

Level 2 student:

As regards to the success of a person in the education, everybody know that there are 2 factors: the students home life and the quality of the teaching and the effectiveness of the educational program.

Some people say that the first idea is more important than the second one and however there are other people who think the other way round. So we can't say that one is better than the other one; it depends on the point of view of each one.

In my opinion I agree with the first idea. I believe that if a person has problems in his/her life, he/she can't have the same results as other person who doesn't have any problem. I think so because of my experience. I have rarely had serious problems which have not let me study.

Level 3 student:

It is easy to realise that both factors can be very influential on the educational success of a given subject. What is not so easy is to determine which of the two or whether one of the two is actually much more influential than the other.

Since a lot of what you learn is learnt at home, the environment under which you study when you are there is obviously to be considered carefully because there may be factors or conditions encouraging or preventing a successful learning.

Among the conditions that are good for studying we might include a quiet room of your own in which you can read and write without being continuously disturbed or put off by noises or other members of your family. Of course, if you cannot find this piece and quiet at home you can always try study room at university or in the library.

Appendix 4

Exemplification of some coding categories

Fluent formulation	*..can be determinated for them a lot* a causa de ellos for them by them (Level 2)
Problemsolving formulation	*a more delicate teaching* that is (4) proporcionada.. otorgada..impartida (3) que tiene lugar..that has placed through the educational program.." (Level 2)
Upgrading problems	I dont like don't include the word essay (4) *the issue the issue* (9) *the issue* concerning [...] let's see *the issue under consideration* in this piece of writing (Level 3)

Appendix 4 (*Continued*)

Compensatory problems	if the members of their homes don't pay attention to them..*pay attention to them* (3) they aren't..vamos que les da igual el colegio..pero es que..¿cómo puedo poner yo eso? les da igual.. *if the members of their homes don't pay attention to them* they..que les da igual pero yo no sé cómo se escribe que les da igual..*if the members of their homes don't pay attention to them* they do all they want.. (Level 2)
Restructuring (ideational)	so in this stage is clear that success is in the children's homelife but it doesn't mean that an effective educational program is bad or not important because it's not true..no it's not true no (deletes "it's not true") *because* it can improve many skills in children but it's less important than the love of the family and the need of children of feeling this love (Level 3)
Restructuring (textual)	so for example (3) no (crosses out 'so for example') although los únicos ejemplos the only examples that I know are based on bad programs.. (Level 2)
Restructuring (linguistic)	.. it's a long no (crosses out 'it's a long').. a long time ago she told me that.. (Level 2)
Backtracking (via L2)	The issue under consideration (9) no *the issue under consideration* no *the issue* considering this... essay (6) no I dont like don't include the word essay (4) *the issue the issue* (9) *the issue* concerning [...] let's see *the issue under consideration* in this piece of writing (Level 3)
Backtracking (via L1)	*I think that education is important* and (4) education (3) should.. depender depend *should* depend of specialized *specialized* people (5) *specialized people it should depend of specialized people...* aunque *pienso que la educación es importante y la educación debe depender de gente especializada* and and (Level 1)

Chapter 5

Age-related Differences and Associated Factors in Foreign Language Writing. Implications for L2 Writing Theory and School Curricula

M. LUZ CELAYA and TERESA NAVÉS

Introduction

The first studies on second language (L2) writing were largely influenced by the body of knowledge and theory in the field of first language (L1) writing. The idea that findings from L1 writing could be applied to L2 writing was taken for granted, and it has taken some time to decide what findings from L1 writing could be extended to L2 writing and which concepts needed to be revised.

One issue that has received a great deal of attention in the studies of L2 learning and that is the focus of the present chapter is onset age. As will be discussed later, in L2 contexts it was found that the sooner learners were exposed to the target language, the better chances they had of succeeding in learning the language effectively. This chapter aims to shed some light on this issue in relation to writing in a foreign language (FL). There are several reasons for investigating the potential benefits of an early start in a FL and in FL writing in particular. From a language policy point of view, it is important to determine whether the long-term benefits of an early start, which have been found in naturalistic settings, also hold true in a FL context. From a writing theory perspective, the influence of writing in one language on writing in other languages is still being debated. From an L2 writing angle, further research is needed on the best measures to ascertain both L2 and FL learners' interlanguage (IL) in writing needs.

The BAF Project

The BAF (Barcelona Age Factor)[1] project at the University of Barcelona was started in 1995 with the main goal of analyzing the effects of lowering the age for starting to learn English as a Foreign Language (EFL) in an instructional context (see Muñoz, 2006a). All over the world, and in Europe in particular, it is becoming increasingly common to commence the learning of EFL earlier. While most European curricula used to introduce English between the ages of 11 and 12, nowadays English is started between the ages of 7 and 9, and it is becoming more popular to have kindergartens introducing English to 3 or 4 year old children.

From the very beginning, an important area of study in BAF has been the analysis of writing as a tool to gauge IL development across different age groups. This objective led us to a second, closely related aim, i.e. the search for the best instruments with which to measure written attainment by very low proficiency school-age learners (see Method section). Finally, age-related differences have also been investigated by examining the use of the L1 in writing, mainly lexical transfer, as we believe that the analysis of cross-linguistic influence (CLI) in multilingual settings, like that of our studies, may offer important insights about the FL acquisition process. As Juzwik *et al.* (2006) state in their overview of research on writing, in comparison with other issues, minimal attention has been paid to studies on middle and high school students and to bi- or multilingualism within the population up to Grade 12. We think, therefore, that our studies may help to fill this gap.

This chapter is structured around three main areas of concern: the effects of an early start in FL contexts as measured on a written task; CLI in EFL writers; and the analytical measures used to assess FL learners' language in writing. An overview of the age factor, CLI and measures for the analysis of writing will be provided before presenting and discussing our own findings. The studies on writing from the BAF that will be reported in this chapter are summarized in Table 5.3.

Review of the Literature

Findings on the age factor in the acquisition of L2 are still controversial; most research in naturalistic settings confirms the picture presented by Krashen *et al.* (1979) and Long (1990) after examining the short- and long-term effects of an early start. The consensus view in the 1980s and 1990s was that older L2 learners are faster and achieve higher levels of proficiency in the short term, but that in the long run, Early

Starters (ES) will catch up with Late Starters (LS) (see Birdsong [2005] and Singleton & Ryan [2004] for an updated state of the art).

It was soon suggested (Long, 1990; Singleton & Lengye, 1995) that findings from L2 contexts could also be extended to FL settings. Some researchers (see Ellis [1994] among others) questioned this supposition, and more recently, other researchers have written along the same lines (see, for instance, Muñoz, 2006b, 2007). In naturalistic contexts, the picture synthesized by Krashen *et al.* (1979) and Long (1990) is consistent with studies such as that of Patkowski (1980) and the classic, frequently cited study by Johnson and Newport (1989).

Patkowski (1980) studied immigrants who had lived in the USA for at least five years and found that those who were exposed to the L2 before the age of 15 achieved a higher syntactic command than those who arrived later. Almost a decade later, Johnson and Newport (1989) correlated the age of arrival to the USA with proficiency in English, as measured by grammatical judgment tests, and concluded that age of arrival was the best predictor of L2 learners' proficiency.

The studies in FL settings from the 1960s and 1970s analyzing the results of introducing a FL in primary school showed that, as in naturalistic contexts, older learners were faster than younger learners, especially in grammar and cognitively demanding tasks, but, in contrast to the case in naturalistic contexts, children did not outperform older learners in the mid or long term (see, for instance, Bland & Keislar, 1966; Ekstrand, 1978; Stankowski-Gratton, 1980). After five or 10 years of instruction, when exposure was kept constant, it was the older learners who outperformed the younger learners in overall proficiency, in grammar tests and in reading and writing tasks. A large-scale project ($n = 1700$) by Burstall (1975) found that children who started studying French as a FL at the age of 11 learnt French more efficiently than younger children (starting at 8) when it came to morphosyntax and cognitively demanding tasks such as clozes, reading and writing tasks. Despite the fact that these studies were soon dismissed as inconclusive and have been severely criticized on methodological grounds – because during the last years of schooling some ES and LS were mixed in the same classrooms – one may wonder whether they should not be replicated in light of the fact that more recent findings with improved methodological designs have led to extremely similar results.

In Spain, the studies conducted by García-Mayo and García-Lecumberri (2003) and the studies from the BAF project collected in Muñoz (2006a) found that less than 1000 hours of instruction in FL contexts may not provide enough opportunities for ES to catch up with

LS except in a few oral tasks. In this research, ES and LS who had received the same total number of hours of instruction were compared on leaving high school after seven to ten years of learning EFL. It was the LS who significantly outperformed the ES in most domains, especially in cognitively demanding tasks such as that of writing (Torras *et al.*, 2006). Therefore, the researchers concluded that, in the long run, later is better.

One specific aspect on which some of our studies on writing have focused is the use of the L1, our second concern in this chapter. The decision to analyze lexical transfer in writing was taken because of its frequency and communicative relevance in multilingual learners in BAF. Besides, studies dealing with CLI mainly analyze oral production; CLI in writing has often been neglected because, given the lack of spontaneity with which learners confront a written task as compared to an oral one, it is assumed that instances of CLI are scarce. We hope to be able to show that writing can also offer an interesting area for CLI research. It is worth noting the change from the 1960s, when the L1 was seen as the cause of errors (interference), and the 1970s, when almost all errors were considered as developmental and there was no role left for the L1 in SLA, to the 1980s, when it became possible to disentangle the notion of transfer from behaviorism (see Odlin [2003] for a recent review). More recently, the study of multilingual speakers has identified another process, that of interlanguage transfer (ILT) or the influence of languages other than the first between one another (see Cenoz *et al.* [2001] for studies on CLI in third language acquisition). The findings reported below may help us to understand writing done by multilingual learners.

The relationship between age and writing necessarily led us to our third area of concern: the measures used to assess writing and its development as proficiency in the L2 increases. In BAF, we attempted to create an instrument of analysis that could gauge the production by young, low-proficiency learners and could discriminate between groups at different ages and proficiency levels.

Larsen-Freeman (1978: 439) defines the index of development as 'an independent yardstick by which we can expediently and reliably gauge proficiency in a second language'. The underlying assumption is that these indices develop in tandem, i.e. as learners become more proficient, they write more fluently, more accurately and produce more grammatically and lexically complex texts (Wolfe-Quintero *et al.*, 1998). However, as Skehan and Foster (1999) claim, attentional resources are limited and attending to one aspect of performance may mean that other dimensions are neglected (see Schoonen *et al.*, this volume). They propose that for language development to proceed optimally, a balance needs to be established between the performance dimensions of fluency, accuracy and complexity, because, they hypothesize, when faced with a cognitively demanding production task, L2 learners will attend to conveying meaning first and to accuracy and linguistic complexity of their output last. This perspective suggests not only that there is individual variability at any given point in time, but also that one aspect of development may progress at the expense of another. Foster and Skehan (1996) maintain that complexity in L2 learners' use of language indicates a greater willingness to experiment and to take risks, whereas accuracy reflects a focus on form to achieve freedom from errors. They argue that complexity and accuracy are two competing goals for L2 learners.

Contrary to Skehan and Foster's Limited Attentional Capacity Model, Robinson (2001) proposes that L2 learners can access multiple and noncompetitional attentional pools. Tasks that make increasing conceptual/communicative demands engage cognitive resources that progressively exploit learning mechanisms leading to greater analysis, modification and restructuring of IL with consequent performance effects. Robinson's proposal is consistent with the hypothesis on cognition found in Long (1996) and Schmidt (2001). The Cognition Hypothesis, integrating information-processing and interactionist explanations of L2 task effects, predicts that increasing the cognitive demands of the tasks in the developmental dimension will push learners toward greater accuracy and complexity in L2 production. Some of the studies in our project (see Table 5.3 for details) examined the assumption questioned by Wolfe-Quintero *et al.* (1998) that the four areas will develop in parallel.

Method

Participants

The participants in BAF (see Table 5.1) were learners of English from different state schools in Barcelona (Spain). They were all Catalan-Spanish bilinguals. The ES began learning English at the age of 8 in Grade 3 and the LS began learning English at the age of 11 in Grade 6. In order to carefully control the amount of exposure received, most of the short- and mid-term BAF studies focused exclusively on students whose entire exposure was limited to the school instruction. At Time 3 of data collection, with learners from Grades 11 and 12, only 20% had received their exposure solely in the school setting; 40% had attended out-of-school classes and another 40% had repeated one of their last years of high school. This explains why some of our long-term studies include

Table 5.1 Participants

Grade		3	*4*	*5*	*6*	*7*	*8*	*9*	*10*	*11*	*12*
Age		*8*	*9*	*10*	*11*	*12*	*13*	*14*	*15*	*16*	*17*
ES (AO = 8)	AO	8									
	Time			T1		T2				T3	
	C h			200		416				726	
	AT			10.9		12.9				16.9	
	Gr			1		3				5	
	Y	1	2	3	4	5	6	7	8	9	
LS (AO = 11)	AO				11						
	Time					T1		T2			T3
	C h					200		416			726
	AT					12.9		14.9			17.9
	Gr					2		4			6
	Y				1	2	3	4	5	6	7

Note: AO: age of onset; AT: age at testing; Gr: BAF groups; C h: curricular hours of instruction at time of data collection; Y: number of years of instruction of EFL.

learners with out-of-school exposure, but unless explicitly indicated otherwise, instructed exposure was kept constant.

As Table 5.1 shows, ES started learning English when they were 8, in Grade 3. At Time 1, after 200 hours of instruction, they were 10.9 years old, in Grade 5, and had already received three years of instruction. At Time 2, now aged 12.9 years in Grade 7, they had had two more years of school and 416 hours of English instruction. At Time 3, the 16.9-year-old learners in Grade 11 had received four more years of EFL instruction. In contrast, the LS started three years later than their younger peers, in Grade 6, when they were already 11. At Time 1, the older group had only received instruction for two years – not three like the ES. At Time 1, the older group was 12.9 years old on average and they were in Grade 7. At Time 2, LS had been learning English for two more years, as had the ES group. They were now in Grade 9 and they were 14.9 years old. At Time 3, LS were in Grade 12 and about to leave high school and enter university or get a job.

It is important to notice that for LS the last period of instruction was concentrated into three years instead of four, as was the case for their younger peers. This can be seen in Table 5.1, which also shows the differences in intensity and how the instruction was distributed to account for exactly the same amount of instruction when the two groups of learners were compared. The difference in age between ES and LS at Times 1 and 2 was two years, but there was a difference of only one year at Time 3. ES received instruction over a total of nine years, while the LS received the same amount of instruction in only seven. At Time 3, the ES were 16.9 years old and in Grade 11 while the LS were one year older, 17.9, and were in Grade 12. It is important to remember that in the BAF design, the total amount of instruction was carefully kept constant. ES and LS were compared in the short run, after just 200 hours of instruction; in the mid run, after 416 hours of instruction and in the long run, after 716 hours of instruction.

Instruments and procedure

The data came from a written composition, which was administered to participants in their own classroom by a BAF researcher. Both teachers and researchers made it clear to the students that the task would not be assessed as an exam and instructions were also given in the learners' L1s (Catalan and Spanish) to avoid misunderstandings. They were not allowed to use dictionaries or grammar books and could not ask the teacher or researcher for help.

All the participants were given the same amount of time (15 minutes) to write on the topic 'Introduce yourself: Me, my past life and my future' (see Appendix for examples) – although younger learners did not use more than 10 minutes. In this way, both time and topic constraints were controlled for in order to make results comparable (Wolfe-Quintero *et al.*, 1998).

Instruments for data analysis

The review of existing measures that had been used in previous studies showed that there was a need to adapt and even create new measures that could gauge our learners' IL in a reliable way. We realized that the fact that our learners were much younger and less proficient than the subjects of most previous studies required a careful decision-making process and thorough piloting before proposing a reliable instrument. The review of previous work by other researchers in Celaya *et al.* (2001b) focused on Long (1991), one of the first reports on measures to gauge written competence with examples and good descriptions of the measures, Polio (1997) on measures of linguistic accuracy and, finally, Wolfe-Quintero *et al.* (1998) where more than 100 measures to analyze written competence in a L2 are reviewed. The first instrument proposed in Celaya *et al.* (2001b) included 17 measures used for the short-term studies with the youngest and least proficient learners. When the three groups of learners were compared, the initial set of measures was expanded to 40 measures (see Navés *et al.*, 2003), as reflected in Table 5.2.

Results and Discussion

The main features of the studies on writing from the BAF project are summarized in Table 5.3.

Results from studies on writing from the BAF project focusing on the age effects

The short- and mid-term effects of age of onset were analyzed and discussed in Pérez-Vidal *et al.* (2000) and in Celaya *et al.* (2001a), while the long-term effects of an early start are the main focus of Navés *et al.* 2003, Navés (2006) and Torras *et al.* (2006). Overall, these studies found that as far as writing was concerned, in the short run, i.e. after 200 hours of instruction, it was the older learners who wrote significantly better compositions than their younger peers. The mid-term comparisons, after 416 hours of instruction, showed that it was still the LS who did significantly better in the writing task. In the long run, at Time 3, after 726

Table 5.2 Analytical measures in the four writing components

Accuracy	*Fluency*	*Syntactic complexity*	*Lexical complexity*
1. Error-free sentences	4. Total number of words	12. Number of subordinate clauses	28. Noun tokens
2. Error-free sentences in %	5. Total number of words in English	13. Number of coordinated clauses	29. Noun types
3. Number of rejected units	6. Total number of nodes	14. Number of combined clauses	30. Adjective tokens
	7. Total number of clauses	15. Coordination Index	31. Adjective types
	8. Total number of sentences	16. Number of nonfinite nodes	32. Adverb tokens
	9. Words per clause	17. Ratio of nonfinite nodes per clause	33. Adverb types
	10. Mean sentence length (words per sentence	18. Ratio of nonfinite nodes per sentence	34. Lexical verb tokens
	11. Mean clause length (words per clause)	19. Ratio of clauses per sentence	35. Lexical verb types
		20. Ratio of subordinate clauses per clause	36. Primary verb types
		21. Ratio of coordinated clauses per clause	37. Open class words
		22. Ratio of combined clauses per clause	38. Lexical density
		23. Ratio of subordinate clauses per sentence	39. Total number of words in L1 (borrowings)

Table 5.2 (*Continued*)

Accuracy	*Fluency*	*Syntactic complexity*	*Lexical complexity*
		24. Ratio of coordinated clauses per sentence	40. Total number of lexical inventions
		25. Ratio of combined clauses per sentence	
		26. Ratio of nodes per sentence	
		27. Auxiliary modal verbs	

Source: Adapted from Navés *et al.* (2003).

hours of instruction over a period of either seven (LS) or nine years (ES), it was the older learners who still significantly outperformed their younger peers. These findings are consistent with the results of research on writing competence with a similar population of Basque-Spanish bilingual children conducted at the University of the Basque Country (see Lasagabaster & Doiz, 2003).

The analysis of short- and mid-term effects of an early start showed that age of onset had a clear influence on the scores obtained in the written compositions (see Celaya *et al.*, 2001a; Pérez-Vidal *et al.*, 2000). At Time 1, after 200 hours of instruction, the LS, who were 12.9 years of age, showed better results than the ES (who were 10.9) in the four areas of fluency, accuracy, lexical and syntactic complexity. At Time 2, after 416 hours of instruction, some of the measures in both lexical and syntactic complexity yielded significant differences in favor of the LS aged 14.9, but the ES, aged 12.9, were able to catch up in accuracy and fluency. These results were consistent with those found in naturalistic settings, in which older learners are reported to be faster in the initial stages of learning. It was hypothesized that differences in cognitive maturity might account for these results. To probe further into this finding, writing by learners at the same biological age (12.9 years) but different starting ages (ES at 8 and LS at 11) was analyzed. The two groups of learners, aged 12.9 when tested, had received 200 and 416 hours of instruction, respectively. Results in Pérez-Vidal *et al.* (2000) and Celaya *et al.* (2001a)

Table 5.3 Summary of BAF studies on writing

BAF studies on writing reviewed	*Topic*			*OA*		*Term*			*Age at testing*						*Grade at testing*						*Type*		
	A	*T*	*W*	*B*	*O*	*S*	*M*	*L*	*10*	*12*	*14*	*16*	*17*	*18+*	*5*	*7*	*9*	*11*	*12*	*U*	*C*	*L*	*B*
Pérez-Vidal *et al.* (2000)	✓	✓	✓	✓		✓	✓		✓	✓					✓	✓	✓				✓		
Celaya *et al.* (2001a)	✓	✓	✓	✓		✓	✓		✓	✓					✓	✓	✓				✓		
Navés *et al.* (2003)	✓	✓	✓	✓		✓	✓	✓	✓	✓	✓	✓	✓		✓	✓	✓	✓	✓		✓		
Navés (2006)	✓	✓	✓	✓				✓				✓	✓					✓	✓		✓		
Celaya and Torras (2001)	✓	✓	✓		✓				✓	✓				✓	✓	✓				✓	✓		
Navés *et al.* (2005)	✓	✓	✓	✓											✓	✓	✓	✓	✓		✓		
Celaya (2006)	✓	✓	✓	✓		✓	✓	✓	✓	✓		✓			✓	✓		✓				✓	
Muñoz and Celaya (2007)	✓	✓	✓		✓	✓	✓	✓						✓	✓					✓	✓		
Celaya *et al.* (2001b)	✓	✓	✓	✓		✓			✓	✓					✓	✓					✓		
Torras and Celaya (2001a)	✓	✓	✓	✓		✓	✓		✓	✓					✓	✓	✓				✓		

Table 5.3 (*Continued*)

BAF studies on writing reviewed	*Topic*			*OA*		*Term*			*Age at testing*						*Grade at testing*						*Type*		
	A	*T*	*W*	*B*	*O*	*S*	*M*	*L*	*10*	*12*	*14*	*16*	*17*	*18+*	*5*	*7*	*9*	*11*	*12*	*U*	*C*	*L*	*B*
Torras and Celaya (2001b)	✓	✓	✓	✓		✓	✓		✓	✓					✓	✓	✓					✓	
Torras *et al.* (2006)	✓	✓	✓	✓		✓	✓	✓	✓	✓	✓	✓	✓		✓	✓	✓	✓	✓		✓		
Navés (2007)	✓		✓	✓				✓				✓	✓					✓	✓		✓		

Note: BAF main onset ages: 8 and 11.

O: other onset age; A: study on age factor effects; T: study on cross-linguistic influence and transfer in particular; W: study on writing measures; S: short-term study; M: mid-term study; L: long-term study; C: cross-sectional study; L: longitudinal study; B: both cross-sectional and longitudinal study; U: university students.

showed that LS with 200 hours still outperformed ES with 416 hours in some variables, specifically in the domain of syntactic complexity, while ES performed significantly better on those measures related to lexical complexity and in the area of fluency. It was concluded that in the initial stages of language acquisition, a higher number of hours of instruction, together with earlier age of onset, may result in an increase in lexical complexity and in fluency, but not in either grammatical complexity or accuracy. A more intense pattern of exposure for the LS (200 hours of instruction over a period of two years in contrast with the five years for ES) might be a key factor in explaining the results. In other words, 11-year-old starters manage to maximize the learning concentrated in two academic years, while eight-year-old starters do not seem to have benefited from having started earlier in spite of having received twice as much formal exposure as their older peers.

The long-term effects of an early start in writing were analyzed with learners from Grades 11 and 12 in Navés *et al.* (2003), Navés (2006) and Torras *et al.* (2006). The main objective was to determine whether ES (AoO = 8) would have caught up with LS (AoO = 11) in the long run within the school system, i.e. when the oldest group was about to leave high school while the younger peers with the same amount of instruction were one grade behind them. ES had been studying EFL for nine years while LS had been studying EFL for seven years. ES and LS were measured after the same number of hours of instruction, 726 hours of school instruction in the case of Navés *et al.* (2003) and Torras *et al.* (2006) and either 726 or 850 hours of instruction in Navés (2006) (See Table 5.1).

The results revealed that after 726 hours of instruction, when Grade 12 learners were compared with Grade 11 learners, LS' writing was still significantly better than that of ES. The writing components of fluency, accuracy, and lexical and syntactic complexity were examined by means of analytical measurements. LS' accuracy in writing, as measured by the *percentage of error-free sentences*, was significantly higher than that of younger learners. The older learners also significantly outperformed the younger learners in *mean sentence length*, as measured by the *total number of words per sentence*, and in *lexical complexity* (see Table 5.2). As for syntactic complexity, LS' grammatical complexity was significantly higher as measured by *subordination*, *coordination index* and other ratios involving *finite subordination*, all of which, as will be discussed later, are regarded as highly sophisticated indices. ES only managed to outperform LS in less sophisticated indices of grammatical complexity involving *nonfinite nodes* (*nonfinite subordination*) measures. In other words, in the long run, within the school system, at Time 3, after 726 hours of EFL instruction, LS' writing is still significantly better than that of ES. ES have only managed to catch up with LS on fluency as measured by *essay length* and most *production unit measures*.

When learners with an extra exposure of 125 hours were also included in the long-term analyses, the same results were found. Navés (2006) analyzed the writing of two large groups of learners ($n = 406$) after the same number of hours of instruction: 726 and 850, respectively. For the analytical analysis of the writing, 85 measures were used. Navés (2006) classified the measures in each of the four domains as highly sophisticated and less sophisticated measures in light of research on L1 and L2 acquisition and studies in L2 writing, and suggested considering *mean production units* as belonging to a construct other than fluency that has to do with syntactic complexity but behaves somewhat differently. She found that LS, after receiving either 726 or 850 hours of instruction, significantly outperformed ES in all domains except fluency when examined by highly sophisticated indices.

Cummins (1980) has argued that older learners show higher mastery of L2 syntax, morphology and other literacy-related skills, such as vocabulary and reading comprehension, due to their greater cognitive maturity. We concluded that the limited amount of input and input quality that characterize FL contexts might explain the different results from those found in naturalistic settings. DeKeyser (2000) has argued that very young learners benefit the most from implicit learning, something which requires massive contact with the language and which FL learning contexts do not provide, while older learners benefit the most from explicit language learning. Therefore, in a FL context, with very limited contact with the target language, older learners will have a greater opportunity to succeed.

Finally, as claimed in Navés *et al.* (2003), the intensity of the instruction learners received and the way instruction was distributed in the two groups might also account for the differences found. The amount of instruction received by ES is spread out much more over the three collection times than that of the LS. Research examining intensity suggests that more intensive courses are more effective (Collins, 1999; Serrano & Muñoz, 2007). Navés (2006) proposed that in an instructional FL setting, the expected long-term benefits of an early introduction should be checked at the end of high school, just before learners enter university, because of the nature of the context. In overall EFL proficiency, in grammar-oriented tests and in cognitively demanding tasks such as writing, it is the older learners, the LS, who show a clear and statistically significant advantage in the long run, i.e. when they have finished their high school education.

Cross-linguistic influence

The analysis of CLI in relation to age in BAF has focused mainly on lexical transfer from the L1. Two moderating variables we have dealt with are language dominance in our bilingual learners and the effect of L2 proficiency (see Table 5.3 for a summary). Our main findings can be summarized as follows: age seems to have an effect on the types of lexical transfer analyzed and there is a clear effect of L2 proficiency. However, language dominance has no effect.

Lexical transfer errors were classified in Celaya and Torras (2001) adapting James's classification (1998), into *misspellings* (e.g. *braun*), *borrowings* (e.g. The school is *bonica* [*bonica* = nice, from Catalan]), *coinages* (e.g. I am good *deportis* [from Spanish *deportista* = sports person]) and, finally, *calques* (e.g. The best of my life I *passed* it there [from Spanish *pasé* = lived]). The participants were three groups of learners of different ages (10 years old, 12 years old, and 18+), who had received the same number of hours of instruction (200 hours). Results showed differences both in the number and the types of lexical transfer due to age. Children seem to draw more on the L1 but this difference appears only when the type of transfer is more direct (as in *borrowings*); adults and preadolescents were found to draw on the L1 more than children in *coinages*, that is, in that process which combines L1 and L2 knowledge. We concluded that age seems to be strongly related to CLI and that this may be due to the fact that, because of differences in cognitive maturity, the same amount of instruction may be more effective in older learners, making them more proficient than younger learners. If this is the case, we can claim that learners with different levels of proficiency fall back on the L1 in different ways.

Two of the types of lexical transfer mentioned above were the focus of Naves *et al.* (2005). The participants belonged to the six BAF groups of learners with ages ranging from 10.9 to 17.9 (from school grades 5–12). The first question analyzed whether CLI (as measured through the use of borrowings and lexical inventions) changed in relation to age and amount of instruction in the FL. The second question aimed to analyze how the amount of instruction influenced the transfer of content and function words in young low-proficiency learners from Grades 5 and 7. The third research question focused on the impact of language dominance and hours of instruction and age on the use of borrowings and lexical inventions, respectively. In contrast to Cenoz (2003), but in agreement with previous research studies on transfer as a compensatory strategy (e.g. Celaya, 1992; Möhle, 1989; Poulisse, 1990; Ringbom, 1987), it was found that young learners in lower grades used these strategies more extensively. Statistical differences were only found at the end of the age span and only for borrowings, not for lexical inventions.

The answer to the second research question showed that the youngest groups transferred a similar percentage of content and function words, thus corroborating the results in Miralpeix and Celaya (2003), but not those found in Poulisse and Bongaerts (1994). Finally, our results on the effect of language dominance indicated that Catalan-dominant learners and balanced-bilinguals used fewer borrowings and lexical inventions than Spanish-dominant learners (independently of age and amount of instruction), but the differences between the groups as regards language dominance did not reach statistical significance.

L1 influence and proficiency effects on writing were the focus of Celaya (2006). The written production of 16 learners was followed longitudinally and collected at ages 10, 12 and 17 (from fifth grade in primary school to first noncompulsory year in high school), which means, according to the design of data collection in BAF, 200, 416 and 726 hours of instruction respectively. Results show that nonstandard words due to L1 influence show a remarkable decline at the second measuring time, when learners are 12 (Grade 7). The second finding was that L1 influence, proficiency and age interrelate in different ways depending on the type of nonstandard word, that is, depending on whether the influence of the L1 is more direct as in *borrowings* or whether the L1 and the L2 are activated simultaneously as in *lexical inventions*. Maturational factors and language awareness may have something to do with the explanation for these results, as pointed out in Torras and Celaya (2001b) and Celaya and Torras (2001).

The analysis of adult learners ($n = 69$) after the same number of hours of instruction as above yields similar findings (see Muñoz & Celaya, 2007). Results show three different patterns of L1 and L2 influence depending on the type of lexical transfer and a predominance of L1 influence over other L2 in lower levels (200 hours), which gradually disappears in favor of a more varied use of other languages at higher levels (416 and 726 hours).

Finally, the qualitative analysis of *rejected units* (Pérez-Vidal *et al.*, 2000), a very relevant measure in the case of beginner young learners in a FL learning context, revealed interesting uses of the L1. In our studies, rejected units are incomprehensible units, telegraphic speech or whole units in the L1, as in *myself waterpol; the favourite very very vevery the swim; the bodi larn erg lang fotball me*. With the same number of hours of instruction (416 hours), LS who were 14 at the time of data collection did not produce any rejected units, whereas ES who were 12 still produced this type of unit. This finding led us to conclude that learners need to have reached a certain age in order to be able to realize that the target language operates as a code that is different from the L1.

These studies have shown that the analysis of CLI offers interesting insights to understand the development of writing in a FL. CLI was found to be affected by age and proficiency but not by language dominance in our bilingual learners. However, it is true that the two first languages of our learners are typologically close, which may explain this finding. Further research is in progress with immigrant learners with L1s distant from Spanish and Catalan in our school context.

Measuring learners' writing in an EFL context

A wide variety of analytical measures have been used in the BAF project. Commonly used measures were first included, but it soon became evident that there was a need to develop and use other measures suitable for the production of very young EFL writers. For example, the Coordination Index, a widely used measure of syntactic complexity, could not be used in the first studies on the short- and mid-term effects of an early start because those very young, low proficiency, inexperienced writers used almost no subordination.

English language teaching methodology, second language acquisition (SLA) and L2 writing use accuracy, fluency, lexical and syntactic complexity as useful constructs. Measurement of these language components, however, is still far from clear. Confirmatory factor analyses, correlations and principal component analyses are among the statistical procedures employed in testing, and in our studies on writing, several of these statistical analyses have been used.

The third issue to be considered when reflecting on the instruments used is whether those components develop in parallel or not, that is to say, whether becoming a better writer involves being more accurate, fluent, and also more lexically and syntactically complex. If the four components do not develop in line with one another, it might be appropriate to further explore whether, as suggested by Skehan and Foster (1999), accuracy is achieved at the expense of both lexical and syntactic complexity or if, as suggested by the work of Robinson (2001), a highly demanding task will trigger both accuracy and lexical and syntactic complexity at the expense of fluency. Several of our studies have partially addressed these last issues.

Navés (2007) conducted an exploratory factor analysis with older school-age students from Grades 11 and 12 who had received exactly the same number of hours of instruction (either 726 or 850 hours) and found that most of the variance could be best described using five, not just four components, as in the first principal component analysis in Celaya *et al.* (2001b). Four of the components were easy to label because in one component all the measures dealing with *error-free production units* could be found. In a second component, well-established measures of syntactic complexity involving finite subordination were found. *Essay length* constituted another of the components, while classical lexical variety measures such as McClure's (1991) *lexical variety* constituted another. Interestingly enough, however, *mean production units* such as *words per clause*, *words per sentence* and *words per t-unit* represented a fifth factor for which the literature has not yet suggested a name. While the two latter measures, *mean sentence length* and *t-unit length*, were also partially loaded on the factor with measures of syntactic complexity, *mean clause length* was only found in this new component. It was suggested that *mean sentence length* and *mean t-unit length* had to do more with syntactic complexity than with fluency, as Ortega (2003) had also suggested in contrast to Wolfe-Quintero *et al.*'s (1998) initial proposal. However, it remains to be seen whether these mean production unit measurements were not of a rather different nature, i.e. did not measure a dimension different from grammatical complexity, in light of those preliminary studies.

In view of the results presented in the first part of this chapter, it could be concluded that our studies found that older learners significantly outperformed the younger learners in all the four domains studied. However, if *mean sentence length* and *clause length* were to be regarded as measures of syntactic complexity, as suggested by Ortega (2003), then the LS would still be significantly outperforming ES in the domains of accuracy, lexical and syntactic complexity, but ES would have caught up with LS in fluency.

The development of writing shows that after 200 hours of instruction, complexity and accuracy develop closely to each other and that they both develop less than fluency in both ES and LS. After 416 hours (T2), fluency is still more highly developed than the other two areas, especially complexity, which is the lowest of the three (see Torras & Celaya, 2001a). Similarly, in the longitudinal study presented in Torras and Celaya (2001b), both intragroup and intergroup longitudinal analyses revealed that not all the areas of writing proficiency develop in parallel and that an earlier start does not seem to show clear advantages in the development of EFL written production.

The results of the analysis of the Mann–Whitney tests performed in Navés *et al.* (2003) arrange development in the four areas of writing (accuracy, fluency, lexical and syntactic complexity) into two patterns. The variables representing these four areas cluster together in the above-mentioned patterns, which are presented in Figures 5.1 and 5.2. Figure 5.1 shows almost no IL development in complexity as measured

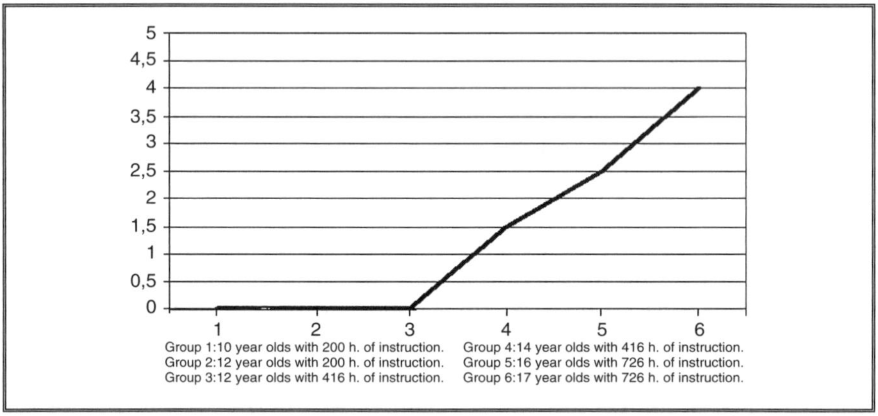

Figure 5.1 IL development in syntactic and lexical complexity

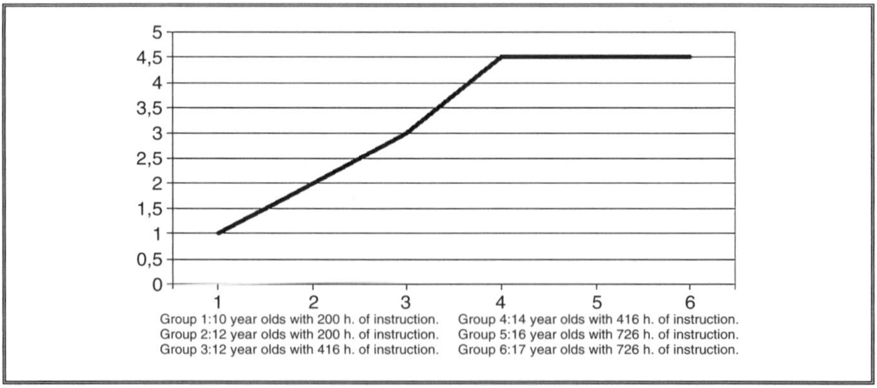

Figure 5.2 IL development in accuracy and fluency (and less sophisticated lexical metrics)

by syntactic complexity measures involving *subordination* and sophisticated measures of lexical complexity such as *adverbs* (tokens and types) and *lexical verbs* (types) in the first three groups of younger learners (aged under 14 with up to 416 hours of instruction). The pattern also shows a steady rise in syntactic complexity involving *subordination* and in *adverbs* (tokens and types) and *lexical verbs* (types) in learners in groups 4–6 (learners over 12 years of age with at least 416 hours of instruction). In short, no syntactic or lexical complexity is found in groups 1–3 (learners under 14 with up to 416 hours of instruction), while syntactic and lexical complexity steadily increases in groups 4–6 (learners over 14 with either 416 or 726 hours of instruction).

Figure 5.2 shows a steady development in accuracy (*error-free sentences*), fluency (*essay length*) and less sophisticated lexical metrics involving *nouns* and *adjectives* in the first four groups of younger learners (those under 16 years of age after 200 and 416 hours of instruction). This development suddenly stops in the two older groups (over 16 with 726 hours of instruction). In short, accuracy and fluency increase steadily in groups 1–4 but stop improving in groups 5 and 6.

Interestingly enough, the behavior of learners in group 3, the 12-year-old learners with 416 hours of instruction, shows that they seem to cope with the demands not only of accuracy and fluency, but also of syntactic and lexical complexity. Group 3 learners' writing pattern shows that the four language domains (accuracy, fluency, syntactic and lexical complexity) are developing in tandem.

It could be concluded from an examination of the first four groups of learners (aged under 14 with up to 416 hours of instruction) that accuracy and fluency develop in tandem. There seems to be no lexical or syntactic complexity development in the first stages of writing. However, an examination of the two older groups of learners (groups 5 and 6 aged over 16 with 726 hours of instruction) reveals that syntactic and lexical complexity is achieved at the expense of accuracy and fluency.

Summary of Findings and Conclusions

When taken as a whole, the studies reported in the last section lead to the following two main conclusions: first, in a FL school context, in the long run, i.e. after more than 700 hours of instruction over a period of seven or nine years, it is the older learners, not the ES, who still significantly outperform the younger learners in most writing domains; second, the trade-offs of accuracy and syntactic complexity predicted by the Limited Attentional Capacity Model were found for the older and more proficient learners in groups 5 and 6 (aged 16 and 17 who had received 726 hours of instruction). Their writing complexity is still steadily improving while accuracy and fluency have already stopped. Learners in groups 5 and 6 seem to increase their syntactic and lexical complexity at the expense of accuracy and fluency. Interestingly enough, the behavior of learners in group 3, however, corroborates the Cognition Hypothesis, because the 12-year-old learners with 416 hours of instruction in group 4 seem to cope with the demands not only of accuracy and fluency, but also of syntactic and lexical complexity. Group 3 learners' writing pattern shows that the four language domains (accuracy, fluency, syntactic and lexical complexity) are developing in tandem for these 12-year-olds with 416 hours of instruction.

The development of the various aspects of writing shown by the younger groups of learners with fewer hours of instruction (groups 1–3 aged under 14 with up to 416 hours of instruction) can be explained by both hypotheses. For the Limited Attentional Capacity Model, it would be clear evidence that accuracy and fluency are achieved at the expense of complexity. For the Cognition Hypothesis, however, it would show that for complexity to develop, learners need to be sufficiently proficient.

We fully agree with Muñoz (2006b, 2007) that there are fundamental differences between L2 and FL learning with respect to the amount and quality of the input learners receive. These differences have a significant influence on the effects that the starting age has on the rate and outcome of the learning process. In other words, the assumption that learning age will have the same effect on students of a FL, when they are exposed to limited speakers of the target language in only one setting (the classroom) and only for very limited amounts of time, is not confirmed by empirical research. Empirical studies in L2 contexts have shown that individuals who begin to learn a L2 very early in life are slower at first but generally attain higher levels of proficiency than those who start at a later stage. Our results show that, similar to L2 contexts, in a FL context older learners are faster at first, and, as regards the focus of the present chapter, i.e. writing, they do better than their younger peers. However, contrary to what was found in L2 contexts and predicted by Krashen *et al.* (1979) and Long (1990), in the long run (after 7 or 9 years) in a formal FL context, after the same amount of instruction it is still the LS who outperform their peers in writing. The long-term advantage of an early start found in L2 contexts does not appear in FL settings in schools for cognitively demanding tasks such as writing. Differences between empirical research conducted in naturalistic and in FL contexts can be explained by two factors:

(1) The same length of time, 10 years, for example, entails an intensity and quality of exposure to the target language that is radically different in foreign versus second language learning contexts. As predicted by researchers such as DeKeyser (2000, 2001) and DeKeyser and Larson-Hall (2005), with the limited exposure to the language provided in the EFL context, the possible benefits of an early start are not confirmed.
(2) The findings in the BAF studies on age-related factors and writing can be interpreted in light of the differences between implicit and explicit learning which is characteristic of children and young adults, and the superior cognitive maturity of the older learners (DeKeyser, 2000, 2001).

The second general finding of our studies shows an effect of age on the use of the L1 in writing, as younger learners resort to the L1 in more direct ways than older learners.

Finally, our studies have confirmed that the areas of accuracy, fluency, lexical and syntactic complexity do not develop in parallel. The development of the older and more proficient learners' writing (groups 5 and 6 aged over 16 with 726 hours of instruction) matches the prediction of the Limited Attentional Capacity Model, as syntactic and lexical complexity seem to be achieved at the expense of accuracy and fluency. However, the writing pattern observed in group 3 at 12 years of age with 416 hours of instruction seems to corroborate the Cognition Hypothesis, as both accuracy and complexity are achieved. The preliminary factor analyses conducted showed that instead of the traditional four writing components, we might need to consider a new construct that will account for mean production unit measures. The measurement of learners' language in writing by means of analytical measures calls for further methodological studies, not only in order to allow comparison between more proficient and less proficient, older and younger learners and between L2 and FL learners, but also because what some measures gauge is still unclear.

Note

1. The BAF Project was funded by the Spanish Ministry of Education for nine consecutive years (PB 94-0944, PB 97-0901, BFF2001-3384).

References

Birdsong, D. (2005) Interpreting age effects in second language acquisition. In J.F. Kroll and A.M.B. DeGroot (eds) *Handbook of Bilingualism: Psycholinguistic Perspectives* (pp. 109–127). New York: Oxford University Press.

Bland, M. and Keislar, E. (1966) A self-controlled audio lingual program for children. *French Review* 40, 266–276.

Burstall, C. (1975) Primary French in the balance. *Educational Research* 17, 193–198.

Celaya, M.L. (1992) *Transfer in English as a Foreign Language: A Study on Tenses.* Barcelona: PPU.

Celaya, M.L. (2006) Lexical transfer and second language proficiency: A longitudinal analysis of written production in English as a foreign language. In A. Alcaraz, C. Soto and M.C. Zunino (eds) *Proceedings of the 29th AEDEAN International Conference* (CD format). Universidad de Jaén.

Celaya, M.L. and Torras, M.R. (2001) L1 influence and EFL vocabulary. Do children rely more on L1 than adult learners? *Proceedings of the 25th AEDEAN International Conference* (CD format). Granada: Universidad de Granada.

Celaya, M.L., Torras, M.R. and Pérez-Vidal, C. (2001a) Short and mid-term effects of an earlier start. An analysis of EFL written production. In S. Foster-Cohen and A. Nizegorodcrew (eds) *EUROSLA Yearbook* (Vol. 1; pp. 195–209). Amsterdam: John Benjamins.

Celaya, M.L., Pérez-Vidal, C. and Torras, M.R. (2001b) Matriz de criterios de medición para la determinación del perfil de competencia lingüística escrita en inglés. *Revista Española de Lingüística Aplicada (RESLA)* 14, 87–98.

Cenoz, J. (2003) Factors determining the acquisition of an L3: Age, cognitive development, and exposure. *AILE: Acquisition et Interaction en Langue Etrangere* 18, 37–51.

Cenoz, J., Hufeisen, B. and Jessner, U. (eds) (2001) *Cross-linguistic Influence in Third Language Acquisition: Psycholinguistic Perspectives.* Clevedon: Multilingual Matters.

Collins, L. (1999) Time and the distribution of time in L2 instruction. *TESOL Quarterly* 33, 655–680.

Cummins, J. (1980) The construct of language proficiency in bilingual education. In J.E. Alatis (ed.) *Georgetown University Round Table on Language and Linguistics pages?* (pp. 81–103). Washington, DC: Georgetown University Press.

DeKeyser, R.M. (2000) The robustness of critical period effect in second language acquisition. *Studies in Second Language Acquisition* 22 (4), 499–534.

DeKeyser, R.M. (2001) The differential role of comprehension and production practice. *Language Learning* 51 (1), 81–112.

DeKeyser, R.M. and Larson-Hall, J. (2005) What does the critical period really mean? In J.F. Kroll and A.M.B. DeGroot (eds) *Handbook of Bilingualism: Psycholinguistic Perspectives* (pp. 88–108). New York: Oxford University Press.

Ekstrand, L.H. (1978) *English Without a Book Revisited: The Effect of Age on Second Language Acquisition in a Formal Setting.* Didakometry 60. Malmö: Department of Education and Psychological Research.

Ellis, R. (1994) *The Study of Second Language Acquisition.* Oxford: Oxford University Press.

Foster, P. and Skehan, P. (1996) The influence of planning and task type on second language performance. *Studies in Second Language Acquisition* 18 (3), 299–323.

García Mayo, M.P. and García Lecumberri, M.L. (eds) (2003) *Age and the Acquisition of English as a Foreign Language: Theoretical Issues and Fieldwork.* Clevedon: Multilingual Matters.

James, C. (1998) *Errors in Language Learning and Use.* London: Longman.

Johnson, J.S. and Newport, E.L. (1989) Critical period effects in second language learning: The influence of maturational state on the acquisition of English as a Second Language. *Cognitive Psychology* 21 (1), 60–99.

Juzwik, M.M., Curcic, S., Wolbers, K., Moxley, K.D., Dimling, L.M. and Shankland, R. (2006) Writing into the 21st century. An overview of research on writing, 1999 to 2004. *Written Communication* 23 (4), 451–476.

Krashen, S., Long, M. and Scarcella, R. (1979) Age, rate and eventual attainment in second language acquisition. *TESOL Quarterly* 13 (4), 573–582.

Larsen-Freeman, D. (1978) An ESL index of development. *TESOL Quarterly* 12 (4), 439–448.

Lasagabaster, D. and Doiz, A. (2003) Maturational constraints on foreign-language written production. In M.P. García-Mayo and M.L. García-Lecumberri (eds) *Age and the Acquisition of English as a Foreign Language: Theoretical Issues and Fieldwork* (pp. 136–160). Clevedon: Multilingual Matters.

Long, M.H. (1990) Maturational constraints on language development. *Studies in Second Language Acquisition* 12 (3), 251–285.

Long, M. (1991) Measuring classroom language change. University of Hawai'i at Manoa. Unpublished manuscript.

Long, M.H. (1996) The role of linguistic environment in second language acquisition. In W.C. Ritchie and T.K. Bhatia (eds) *Handbook of Second Language Acquisition* (pp. 413–468). San Diego, CA: Academic Press.

McClure, E. (1991) A comparison of lexical strategies in L1 and L2 written English narratives. *Pragmatics and Language Learning* 2, 141–154.

Miralpeix, I. and Celaya, M.L. (2003) The use of P_Lex to assess lexical richness in compositions written by learners of English as an L3. *Proceedings of the 26th AEDEAN International Conference* (pp. 399–406). Santiago de Compostela: Universidad de Santiago de Compostela.

Möhle, D. (1989) Multilingual interaction in foreign language production. In H.W. Dechert and M. Raupach (eds) *Interlingual Processes* (pp. 179–194). Tübingen: Gunter Narr.

Muñoz, C. (ed.) (2006a) *Age and the Rate of Foreign Language Learning*. Clevedon: Multilingual Matters.

Muñoz, C. (2006b) The effects of age on foreign language learning: The BAF Project. In C. Muñoz (ed.) *Age and the Rate of Foreign Language Learning* (pp. 1–40). Clevedon: Multilingual Matters.

Muñoz, C. (2007) Aprender un idioma no es sólo una cuestión de edad. Plenary talk at 25th AESLA International Conference. Universidad de Murcia.

Muñoz, C. and Celaya, M.L. (2007) 'When I have holidays'. Influència entre llengües i producció escrita. Un estudi amb aprenents adults d'anglès coma llengua estrangera. *Llengua, Societat i Comunicació* (LSC) 5. On WWW at http://www.ub.edu/cusc/LSC_set.htm.

Navés, T. (2006) The long-term effects of an early start in writing in foreign language learning. Unpublished PhD dissertation. Universitat de Barcelona. On WWW at http://www.ub.edu/GRAL/naves/.

Navés, T. (2007) An early start. Does it make a difference in EFL writing? Paper presented at the Symposium of Second Language Writing, Nagoya, Japan.
Navés, T., Miralpeix, I. and Celaya, M.L. (2005) Who transfers more... and what? Cross-linguistic influence in relation to school grade and language dominance in EFL. *International Journal of Multilingualism* 2 (2), 1–22.
Navés, T., Torras, M.R. and Celaya, M.L. (2003) Long-term effects of an earlier start. An analysis of EFL written production. In S. Foster-Cohen and S. Pekarek (eds) *EUROSLA-Yearbook. Annual Conference of the European Second Language Association* (Vol. 3; pp. 103–130). Amsterdam: John Benjamins.
Odlin, T. (2003) Cross-linguistic influence. In C.J. Doughty and M.H. Long (eds) *The Handbook of Second Language Acquisition* (pp. 436–486). Oxford: Blackwell.
Ortega, L. (2003) Syntactic complexity measures and their relationship to L2 proficiency: A research synthesis of college-level L2 writing. *Applied Linguistics* 24 (4), 92–518.
Patkowski, M. (1980) The sensitive period for the acquisition of syntax in a second language. *Language Learning* 30 (2), 449–472.
Pérez-Vidal, C., Torras, M.R. and Celaya, M.L. (2000) Age and EFL written performance by Catalan /Spanish bilinguals. *Spanish Applied Linguistics* 4 (2), 267–290.
Polio, C. (1997) Measures of linguistic accuracy in second language writing research. *Language Learning* 47 (1), 101–143.
Poulisse, N. (1990) *The Use of Compensatory Strategies by Dutch Learners of English*. Dordrecht: Foris.
Poulisse, N. and Bongaerts, T. (1994) First language use in second language production. *Applied Linguistics* 15 (1), 36–57.
Ringbom, H. (1987) *The Role of the First Language in Foreign Language Learning*. Clevedon: Multilingual Matters.
Robinson, P. (2001) Task complexity, task difficulty, and task production: Exploring interactions in a componential framework. *Applied Linguistics* 22 (1), 27–57.
Schmidt, R. (2001) Attention. In D.W. Robinson (ed.) *Cognition and Second Language Instruction* (pp. 3–32). Cambridge: Cambridge University Press.
Serrano, R. and Muñoz, C. (2007) Same hours, different time distribution: Any difference in EFL? *System* 35 (3), 305–321.
Singleton, D. and Lengye, Z. (eds) (1995) *The Age Factor in Second Language Acquisition: A Critical Look at the Critical Period Hypothesis*. Clevedon: Multilingual Matters.
Singleton, D. and Ryan, L. (2004) *Language Acquisition: The Age Factor* (2nd edn). Clevedon: Multilingual Matters.
Skehan, P. and Foster, P. (1999) The influence of task structure and processing conditions on narrative retellings. *Language Learning* 49 (1), 93–120.
Stankowski-Gratton, R. (1980) An experimental study on German instruction from the first grade of elementary school. *Rassegna Italiana di Linguistica Applicata* 12 (3), 119–141.
Torras, M.R. and Celaya, M.L. (2001a) El desarrollo de la producción escrita en inglés lengua extranjera en alumnos con diferentes edades de inicio en el aprendizaje. In A.I. Moreno and V. Colwell (eds) *Perspectivas Recientes sobre el Discurso* (pp. 1–10). León: Universidad de León.

Torras, M.R. and Celaya, M.L. (2001b) Age-related differences in the development of written production. An empirical study of EFL school learners. In R.M. Manchón (ed.) *Writing in the L2 Classroom: Issues in Research and in Pedagogy.* Special issue of *International Journal of English Studies* 1 (2), 103–126.

Torras, M.R., Navés, T., Celaya, M.L. and Pérez-Vidal, C. (2006) Age and IL development in writing. In C. Mũnoz (ed.) *Age and Rate of Foreign Language Learning* (pp. 156–182). Clevedon: Multilingual Matters.

Wolfe-Quintero, K., Inagaki, S. and Kim, H-Y. (1998) *Second Language Development in Writing: Measures of Fluency, Accuracy and Complexity. Technical Report* 17. Manoa, HI: University of Hawai'i Press.

Appendix

Sample from learners' compositions

My life is like a narrow road. I've passed my whole life learning. I can imagine that everybody has lived like me, but I feel like an animal in a jail. It's quite pathetic but it's true. Although I've had my 'glory' moments, such as the day my brother was born. He was born the fourth of December of 1996, and this has been an spectacular experience for me. However I've always been a happy girl and now I'm becoming a happy woman. After finishing HS I want to become a Social Assistant, which is not the dream I've had ever since as I've always expected to become a nurse like my mother. The situation, and especially my marks made me change and I've decided that becoming a Social Assistant is what I really want. I can't say more about my future because I'm not as Rappel, so these are my earlier projects.

(ID: 699; ES aged 17 from Grade 11 with 726 hours of instruction)

When I was a child, I was a friendly girl who was always playing. I liked animals and I used to play with dogs and cats. Now, I haven't got time to dedicate it to animals. I have to study a good career and can to be an independent woman. Although I haven't got a lot of time in my free time, I play basketball, I go out with my friends and I ride bike because I like to fun.

On the other hand, I also like to stay with my family we do trips with ours friends and we do camping in summer. We like the beach and sea very much and on holidays go to the coast.

(ID: 671; ES aged 17 from Grade 11 with 726 hours of instruction)

Chapter 6

The Globalization of Scholarship: Studying Chinese Scholars Writing for International Publication

JOHN FLOWERDEW and YONGYAN LI

In this chapter, we present a review of the first two stages (1996–2006) of our on-going research project on Chinese scholars writing for publication. We may note at the outset that viewing our work in terms of a very long-term project consisting of several stages, or a connected series of several smaller projects, is derived from hindsight rather than initial design. The first stage of our project, conducted by Flowerdew, focused on Cantonese-speaking Hong Kong scholars writing for scholarly publication in English (see Flowerdew [2005] for a review of this stage of the research); the second stage, investigating Mandarin-speaking Mainland Chinese novice scientists (doctoral science students) in the same endeavour, was first conducted by Li as a PhD thesis project under the supervision of Flowerdew and then at a later point Flowerdew assumed a larger role in this work; the present third stage of our project, not covered in this chapter, is devoted to examining the publication endeavours of Chinese scholars in the humanities and social sciences (HSS) at both the local and international levels, with a comparative perspective between Hong Kong and the Mainland.

In the following, we begin by contextualizing our research at the global, national and institutional levels. In doing so, we highlight the globalization of scholarship and internationalization of higher education institutions. We then raise the notion of 'glocalization' and note how the idea bears upon our research objectives and methodological orientations. Following this, we then present a narrative of our research process in the first two stages of our project, focusing on a characterization of our reiterative workings with theories, methods and issues and summarizing some of the key findings. Finally, we discuss the theoretical, methodological and pedagogical implications of our research with regards to the teaching and researching of English as a second language/English as a foreign language (ESL/EFL) writing. We emphasize that our main goal is not to present a summary of our findings (although this is done briefly – readers can refer to the original publications for more detail), but to reflect on the research process as we have developed it and consider what implications this might have for similar sorts of research in future.

Contextualization

Globalization, glocalization and center versus periphery in scholarly publication

Globalization has been characterized by Waters (1995) as a process of increasing convergence on a global scale in the following three areas of social life: the economy, the polity and culture. According to Waters, the three categories are characterized by different systems of exchange: *material* (economic) exchange of goods and services, *political* exchange of support, security, coercion, etc. and *symbolic* (cultural) exchange by means of oral communication, publication, performance, teaching, etc. Academic publishing is, of course, a manifestation of symbolic exchange.

In general terms, globalization has it supporters and its detractors. Its supporters argue that the phenomenon is proof of the benefits to be gained from an international capitalist system of free trade (and, for some, Western parliamentary-style democracy), which has increased standards of living worldwide and is to the benefit of all, or nearly all. The detractors of globalization, in contrast, see it as a form of neoimperialism, culturally homogenizing, taking control away from individuals and countries in the way they live, and creating displacement, exploitative employment practices or loss of employment, often on a large scale.

To temper the view of globalization in terms of homogeneity, some have advocated the notion of 'glocalization', whereby it is argued that a global outlook has to be mitigated by local practices, and that the global and the local are mutually defining (e.g. Robertson, 1992, 1995). Glocalization is perhaps most visible in Waters' *symbolic* field, where symbols can easily be adapted to fit local cultural milieus. One just has to think about how popular music is adapted to local cultures or how recent trends in Hollywood cinema have demonstrated the adoption of elements of Hong Kong *Kung Fu* as just two examples. But this may also even include academic research and writing, where local elements may be grafted on to international practice, or vice versa.

Developing further Waters' theory of international symbolic exchange, in order for this to take place, a common language is required (something which he does not talk about). For historical reasons, English has taken on this role of an international lingua franca. But this leads to inequality, because English is the mother tongue of only a minority of the nations of the world, including the most powerful of them all, the USA. A barrier is thus created for those whose mother tongue is not English; they are required to learn it in addition to communicating and developing literacy in their first language.

A growing body of research on English as an additional language (EAL) scholarly literacy (e.g. Ammon, 2000; Belcher, 2007; Belcher & Connor, 2001; Burrough-Boenisch, 2003; Canagarajah, 1996, 2002; Casanave, 1998; Curry & Lillis, 2004; Flowerdew, 1999a, 1999b, 2000, 2001, 2008, in press; Flowerdew & Li, 2007; Gosden, 1995; Kaplan & Baldauf, 2005; Li & Flowerdew, 2007; Lillis & Curry, 2006; Liu, 2004) is providing a panorama of EAL scholars in various EFL/ESL (*periphery*) contexts struggling to cope with discursive, material and sociopolitical constraints to bid for scholarly participation at the international level, which usually means to get published in journals hosted by Anglophone (*center*) (Galtung, 1971; Wallerstein, 1979) countries. Such a panorama is needed because, as some have pointed out (Curry & Lillis, 2004; Salager-Meyer, 2008), there is a great disparity in the contexts in which EAL writers operate. Even among the peripheral countries there are tremendous differences in the degree to which these countries disseminate science.

The two sites for our research, Hong Kong and Mainland China, could both be described as peripheral territories, although they are in many ways very different. Hong Kong, at the time of the study, was still a British colony and, as such, it had traditionally been focused on its center, the UK. In terms of academic publication, it had been internationally oriented, but in the prehandover period during which the first stage of our project was under way, local academics had been under-represented at the expense of expatriates, although this was rapidly changing, and the focus of the study was uniquely on local scholars. Until relatively recently, Mainland China had undergone a period of self-imposed seclusion from the international sphere. But since the 1970s and the Four Modernisations policy of Deng Xiaoping, it has been making great strides to internationalize. In terms of academic research and publication, significant resources have been made available for elite research universities such as the one that was the focus of our study, with a strong requirement for international publication.

Although, at the outset, it was not a specific research goal to study the globalization process per se, the interaction between the global and the local and its theorization as set out earlier, provided important input into our focus for data collection, analysis and interpretation of our findings. In line with the spirit of 'glocalization' is a methodological tradition in anthropology and culture studies that highlights the importance of investigating 'local knowledge' through 'interpretive ethnography' or 'thick description' (Geertz, 1983; Hall, 1991). Such a methodology was an important aspect of the project. Here, the focus is not solely or even primarily on textual analysis, the traditional focus of writing research, but on how language is situated and appropriated by the Hong Kong and Mainland scholars.

Internationalization of higher education institutions

Of great importance to the interests of contemporary EAL academics are the policies adopted by individual institutions in the face of globalization, a response which commonly takes the form of 'internationalization', defined as 'the integration of an international dimension into the teaching, research and service function of higher education' (Knight & De Wit, 1995, as cited in Van Vught *et al.*, 2002: 106). It would seem to us that the great majority of major universities in non-Anglophone contexts (in our case Mainland China and Hong Kong) are set upon achieving a goal of an 'international' standard, as captured so well in a slogan on a banner in the main entrance of the university that was our main research site in the second stage of our project: 'Work hard to build ours into a comprehensive, research-oriented, and internationalized first-class university of the world'. Similarly, a recent headline on the home page of the web site at our home institution in Hong Kong – 'world ranking up 24 places' (a reference to the international ranking of universities by the *Times Higher Education Supplement*) – is further evidence of a university's drive toward internationalization. Research output, or the number and quality of publications by its academics is generally seen as an important index of the level of success of a university's internationalization programme.

According to Scott (1998: 122), universities may differ in the extent to which they are international, but 'all are subject to the same processes of globalisation – partly as objects, victims even, of these processes, but partly as subjects, or key agents, of globalisation'. As far as EAL academics are concerned, if as noted earlier, having to overcome various discursive, material and sociopolitical barriers to achieve equal participation in the international arena makes them 'victims', they are nevertheless also 'key agents' in determining the effectiveness of their institutions' internationalization processes.

Massification of higher education and publication requirement

In the past two decades or so, massification of higher education has been witnessed in many East Asian societies, including Mainland China and Hong Kong. Recent statistics indicate that 'about 30 percent of the 18–21 age group are admitted to colleges and universities in Hong Kong' compared with '13 percent in urban China' (Mok, 2006: 90). Implementing schemes of quality control to curb or counter the lowering of academic standards that may result from the massification process has become a major concern of many universities, especially when multiple universities are competing for limited government funding (Mok, 2006). In both Mainland China and Hong Kong (perhaps no different from elsewhere in the world), a mainstream of quality control schemes at higher education institutions has translated into publication requirements being set for both staff and graduate students.

In Mainland China, for example, publication has become a graduation requirement for Master's and PhD students. For science students at the PhD level in particular, the requirement often involves publication in English-medium overseas-based Science Citation Index (SCI) journals (see Li, 2006a). In Hong Kong, given its long-standing colonial history, it is perhaps no surprise that academics across various disciplines both in the hard sciences and in the HSS, are generally expected to write for publication in English (Braine, 2005; Flowerdew, 1999a, 1999b, 2000). (By contrast, in Mainland China, writing in English among HSS scholars is still only very sporadic, though clearly encouraged.) While unlike in Mainland China for PhD science students, English publication is not yet set in a written form as a graduation requirement for research students in Hong Kong, it is nevertheless an unwritten expectation.[1]

Local motivations for the first two stages of the present project

The motivation for the first stage of our work came from the impending change of sovereignty over Hong Kong from the UK to China and the very rapid expansion of tertiary education during the prehandover period. At the time, it was anticipated that the majority of expatriate academics working in the universities during the colonial period would be replaced by local counterparts and that these new entrants to the profession would face problems in publication.[2] Hence, the first stage of our project then was designed to investigate the ways Cantonese-first-language academics write for publication in English-language scholarly journals.

The very early inspiration for the second stage of the present project, the study of Chinese novice scientists (doctoral science students) writing for international publication, was Li seeing the doctoral science students in her English skills class (at a major university in Mainland China) facing difficulty in fulfilling the university's requirement of publishing papers in English. Meanwhile, the lack of pedagogical schemes and research efforts to address these students' needs seems a flagrant gap in ELT in China. Outside Mainland China, research on non-native English-speaking authors writing for publication was already building. In particular, Flowerdew's work in Hong Kong with Cantonese-speaking scholars confirmed to Li that studying the Chinese novice scientists' writing for publication scenarios would be a worthwhile scholarly undertaking.

Research Objectives

The overall research objectives in the first two stages of the present project can be stated as follows (see Flowerdew [2005: 67–68] for an outline of the research objectives of the first stage of the present project):

- to investigate Chinese scholars' attitudes toward and perceptions of being engaged in international publication in English;
- to understand the writing-for-publication scenarios of scholars across different disciplines, in particular, their problems and strategies;
- to investigate how these scholars engage in interactions with other members of their disciplinary communities, i.e. peers, supervisors and the gatekeepers of international journals, in their writing-for-publication process;
- to evaluate the implications of the English-language barrier to these scholars in their effort to be published in international journals.

With these research objectives, our research is characterized by multidimensional triangulations in terms of theoretical frameworks, issues and methods. Table 6.1 presents a complete picture of our decade-long efforts (1996–2006) to achieve the above stated research objectives (see Flowerdew [2005: 65] for a figure that summarizes the multiple 'methods' implemented in the first stage of the present project). As represented in Table 6.1, we categorize our research output from the

Table 6.1 Investigating Chinese scholars writing for publication in English (1996–2006)

The corresponding publications/ unpublished works	*Participants*	*The purpose/theme of the investigation*	*Data sources*	*Theoretical notions for framing purposes/ literature background*
Issue-driven studies				
Flowerdew (1999a, 1999b)	Cantonese-speaking Hong Kong scholars across disciplines	Attitudes, perceptions, problems and strategies of the scholars in writing for publication in English	Questionnaires, interviews, focus groups, official documents, emails, observation, informal conversation	English increasingly becoming dominant as the international language of research and publication
Li (2002)	Mandarin-speaking Chinese novice scientists across disciplines			*discourse community*, *disciplinary community*, *in-visible college*, *enculturation* and *legitimate peripheral participation*
Flowerdew (2001)	Eleven editors of 11 international journals in applied linguistics	The editors' attitudes to non-native speaker contribution	In-depth interviews	Work on issues of power, access and the social construction of knowl-edge, especially as it relates to non-native speakers of English

Table 6.1 (*Continued*)

The corresponding publications/ unpublished works	*Participants*	*The purpose/theme of the investigation*	*Data sources*	*Theoretical notions for framing purposes/ literature background*
Flowerdew and Li (2007)	Nine doctoral science students across disciplines and years of study	The students' beliefs and practices in language reuse	Interviews and student manuscripts	A genre perspective toward scientific writing addresses two gaps in the literature (1) no consideration given to the particular part of the text where the reuse occurs and (2) no attempt to investigate the motivations for the practices, i.e. testimonial evidence on the part of the writers
Li and Flowerdew (2007)	Twelve doctoral science students across disciplines and four professors in physics	Chinese novice scientists' research articles being shaped by correctors on their way to publication	Emails, interviews, blogs and manuscript drafts	A published research article, especially if it is written by an EAL (English as an additional language) author, needs to be viewed as a product involving a range of 'shapers' who participate in the editorial process

Table 6.1 (*Continued*)

The corresponding publications/ unpublished works	*Participants*	*The purpose/theme of the investigation*	*Data sources*	*Theoretical notions for framing purposes/ literature background*
Single-case case studies				
Flowerdew (2000)	A Hong Kong scholar in mass communication who recently returned from doctoral study in the USA	To describe and interpret the difficulties that the participant experienced in publishing a scholarly article in an international refereed journal	Interviews, manuscript drafts of a paper, editorial correspondence	*discourse community; legitimate peripheral participation*
Li (2005)	A doctoral student of physics, with particular difficulty in English	The enculturation experience of the student in the graduate school as seen in his interaction with the local community and his publication experience	Interviews and informal conversations, observation, emails, manuscript drafts and editorial correspondence	*enculturation; legitimate peripheral participation*

Table 6.1 (*Continued*)

The corresponding publications/ unpublished works	*Participants*	*The purpose/theme of the investigation*	*Data sources*	*Theoretical notions for framing purposes/ literature background*
Li (2006b)	A doctoral student of physics, whose paper eventually got published in a prestigious journal (with his two supervisors also involved)	To describe and interpret the student's publication story from a sociopolitical perspective	Interviews, emails, all major drafts of one manuscript, referees' reports and editorial correspondence	Written texts are sociopolitical artefacts
Li (2006c)	A doctoral student of computer science (two specialist informants, and several student informants were also involved)	The students' strategies and problems in negotiating knowledge contribution vis-a-vis multiple layers of discourse communities	Interviews, emails, the Chinese and English versions (with revisions) of one manuscript, referees' reports and other supporting documents	Knowledge construction in disciplines; *discourse communities*
Li (2007)	A doctoral student of chemistry	The student's multidimensional engagement with his *community of practice*	Process logs (in the form of blogs), interviews, emails and the first draft of one manuscript	*legitimate peripheral participation; community of practice*

Table 6.1 (*Continued*)

The corresponding publications/ unpublished works	*Participants*	*The purpose/theme of the investigation*	*Data sources*	*Theoretical notions for framing purposes/ literature background*
Li (2007b)	A doctoral student of biomedicine	To analyze the student's language re-use in citations	Interviews, email communication, Tong's developing text together with her source materials	Reading-to-write is a strategic process; citations often involve textual plagiarism in student writers' case

decade-long work into two main strands: (1) issue-driven studies (Flowerdew 1999a, 1999b, 2001; Flowerdew & Li, 2007; Li, 2002; Li & Flowerdew, 2007); and (2) single-case case studies (Flowerdew, 2000; Li, 2005, 2006b, 2006c, 2007a, 2007b). For each of the published studies, we specify participants, the purpose/theme of the investigation, data sources and theoretical notions for framing purposes or literature background.

Methodology

According to Denzin (1997), there are five basic types of triangulation in educational research: (a) data triangulation, (b) investigator triangulation, (c) theory triangulation, (d) methodological triangulation and (e) member-check triangulation. Others have suggested four (e.g. Patton, 1987), not including the last, i.e. member-check triangulation, or otherwise termed 'participant verification' (Sharpe, 1997). Our research fulfils all five types of triangulation specified by Denzin.

Here, we will provide a relatively detailed methodological account of our two main strands of research, i.e. issue-driven studies and case studies of publication stories, with particular focus on the latter, in the hope of providing insights for readers on how the 'general research methodology' issues work out in practice and how we refined them in the specific context of our study.

Sustaining issue-driven studies

By issue-driven we refer to studies that were motivated by specific research questions derived from issues that had been identified in the literature and through informal interviews. Flowerdew (1999a) reports on a quantitative survey that sought answers to such questions as: what exposure to English had the Hong Kong scholar participants had? What were their attitudes towards publishing in English? What were their problems? What were their strategies for successful publishing? And what change, if any, did they see accompanying the reversion of sovereignty over Hong Kong from the UK to China? In contrast to Flowerdew (1999a), Flowerdew (1999b) adopted a more qualitative, grounded approach (Strauss & Corbin, 1990) to the issues at hand. Through in-depth interviews, this paper identified a range of problems that confront Hong Kong Chinese scholars in writing for publication in English and which they felt put them at a disadvantage vis-à-vis native speakers of that language.

Similar to the first stage of the present project, our second-stage work, that with Mainland Chinese novice scientists, also began with surveys. A wide range of data was gleaned from a variety of sources – questionnaires, interviews, focus groups, official documents, emails, observation and informal conversation – to put together a general picture of Chinese novice scientists' attitudes toward and problems/difficulties and strategies in writing for international publication (Li, 2002, 2006a).

The early stage of survey-based work paved a way for the ensuing more focused research activities. Thus, in its overall procedure, our research resembles previous researchers' design of following up on a macroscopic investigation with a microscopic perspective (e.g. Belcher, 1989), or researchers being inspired to seek theoretical tools that could rationalize the data resulting from earlier studies (Prior, 1995).

The early surveys with the Hong Kong scholars connected to a study based on in-depth interviews with a group of *Applied Linguistics* and *Language Teaching* journal editors (Flowerdew, 2001), which was aimed at discovering these editors' attitudes toward non-native English speaker (NNES) contributions to their journals. In addition, surveys among Mainland Chinese novice scientists revealed two issues in particular that led to further concentrated research: that student writers commonly reuse (perhaps overuse) language from the literature in writing their own papers and that they seeks support from various sources in an effort to try to shape their manuscripts into a form potentially acceptable to the editors of their target journal. In addressing the two issues (Flowerdew & Li, 2007; Li & Flowerdew, 2007), we relied on building a rich database from a variety of sources over a prolonged period of time from numerous participants across disciplines, and analyzing the data in a *cyclical* pattern along with the collection process.

Negotiating theories, issues and methods in case studies

As indicated in Table 6.1, an important part of our research that effectively embodies such multidimensional triangulation is a series of six single-case studies, featuring, respectively, a Cantonese-speaking academic (Flowerdew, 2000) and a number of Mandarin-speaking apprentice scientists (Li, 2005, 2006b, 2006c, 2007a, 2007b). Except for Li (2005), which features a physics doctoral student's enculturation experience in the graduate school (including publication efforts), every one of the other five single-case studies was devoted to characterizing the particular case participant's writing-for-publication story.

A quote from the first of the case studies of five publication stories (Flowerdew, 2000) exemplifies our overall approach in the case-study series:

> Because this research is basically ethnographic in nature, it does not begin with a preestablished set of research questions; rather, the key issues are developed out of the data. As the ethnographic account will make clear, these key issues include the importance of knowing the rules of the publishing "game", the mediated nature of the publication process, the importance of adapting content to fit the expectations of the journal, the problem of distinguishing the dividing line between content and form, and the problems of geographic isolation. The article argues that the concepts of *discourse community* and *legitimate peripheral participation* are important in understanding these issues involved in the process of NNSs' scholarly apprenticeship. (Flowerdew, 2000: 128–129)

A salient point in the above quote is 'the key issues are developed out of the data', in the absence of 'a preestablished set of research questions'. Indeed, a principle that we have consistently practiced has been 'pulling out issues from case studies' (see Li & Flowerdew, 2008), a principle that is reminiscent of Stake's (2003) advice on carrying out case studies:

> To treat the case as an exemplar, they [the researchers] ask, Which issues bring out our initial concerns, the dominant theme? To maximize understanding of the case, they ask, Which issues seek out compelling uniqueness? (Stake, 2003: 143)

In all the five case studies of publication stories (Flowerdew, 2000; Li, 2006, 2006c, 2007a, 2007b), our initial concern was probably similar, that is to find out how best to characterize the particular publication story. However, to eventually decide 'what issues bring out our initial concerns', the theoretical framing we set for a particular study would be essential, as we saw in conducting and reporting the case studies. Davis (1995: 436) has enlightening observations of the role of theory in qualitative research: 'The first step in conducting a qualitative study is to determine the theories and views that are likely to affect the study'. While it is certainly advisable that we begin with certain 'theoretical guiding principles at the onset of the study' (Davis, 1995: 439; see also Flowerdew, 2002), what we would like to emphasize here is the idea that 'the specific theoretical perspectives the researcher begins with are likely to change as the study evolves (ibid)', or to be more exact, the idea that 'the specific theoretical perspectives the researcher begins with are likely to be modified or fine-tuned as the study evolves' (our words), presuming that the initial theoretical guiding principles are not a far cry from the theoretical framework eventually decided upon. In all of our five publication-story case studies, it was possible to begin with such broad-based theoretical notions as 'academic writing is socially mediated', 'writing for publication is a socio-political process', 'scholarly publication has to do with knowledge construction' and 'novice writing is a form of "legitimate peripheral participation" in the target "community of practice"' (e.g. Bazerman, 1988; Casanave, 2003; Knorr-Cetina, 1981; Lave & Wenger, 1991; Prior, 1998; Wenger, 1998). However, how to properly frame a particular case study with selected literature and the related theoretical underpinnings is something that researcher-writers can only arrive at through a *cyclic* and *reiterative* process of data collection, data analysis (which includes figuring out 'which issues seek out compelling uniqueness' [Stake, 2003: 143, as quoted earlier]) and refining the theoretical framing (Flowerdew, 2002; Li, 2006a; Li & Flowerdew, 2008).

No less of an evolving process are the methods of data collection. While it is useful and perhaps necessary to start out with a general scheme of 'methods' in mind, the scheme is an 'idealistic' one that has to be subject to the test of realities. In the second stage of our research, neither 'think-aloud' methodology nor 'Hallidayan textual analysis' (the latter as in Gosden's [1995] work on Japanese science students' research article drafts) was able to be implemented due to situational restrictions, though both were intended in our 'idealistic' scheme of 'multimethods' (i.e. contained in the 'processing strategies' and 'text analysis', see Flowerdew [2005: 65] for the summative figure). By contrast, diary, which had not been possible in the first stage of the project (see Flowerdew, 2005: 65) was successfully implemented through 'process logs' in the form of blogs, enthusiastically kept by a student of chemistry in the second stage (Li, 2007).

Main Findings

In the following eight points, we summarize the main findings of the first two stages of our ongoing project:

- The Chinese scholars in question (Cantonese-speaking Hong Kong academics and Mandarin-speaking Mainland Chinese novice scientists) are expending great effort to contribute their voice in international academia, despite potential discursive and nondiscursive obstacles.

- Major problems identified in Flowerdew (1999b), as expressed in interviews with the Hong Kong scholars and later corroborated in the course of the Mainland research, were as follows: they had less facility of expression than native English speaker (NES) writers; it took them longer to write; they had a less rich vocabulary; they found it difficult to make claims for their research with the appropriate amount of force; their process of composition may have been influenced by their L1; and the introductions and discussions to scholarly articles were particularly problematic parts.
- The two groups adopted various coping strategies (Canagarajah, 2003) to overcome the English-language barrier in writing for international publication. The strategies, in the case of the novice Mainland scientists, prominently include seeking 'textual mentorship' (Casanave & Vandrick, 2003) for learning the genre conventions of their disciplinary research articles and for reusing others' language in the specialist literature. The Hong Kong scholars, given that they were more experienced academics, and that they had greater access to English (see below), in addition to textual mentoring, tended to rely more on NES editorial assistance.
- In negotiating knowledge contribution to their target center-based discourse communities, Chinese scholars, as peripheral participants, while accommodating the expected conventions of academic writing and the criticisms of gatekeepers of their target journals, may do so with 'a critical awareness' and 'develop a cynical attitude' (Canagarajah, 2003: 208). They may do this, for example, by questioning certain English discourse conventions or by being cynical of feeling prejudice directed against them by gatekeepers in the *center.* This critical/cynical attitude, noticeably, is found in both senior and junior/novice scholars. However, these critical elements are not drastic or disruptive.
- Investigation of Chinese scholars' scenarios of writing for international publication confirmed the sociopolitical nature of scholarly writing and publication (Casanave, 2003; Casanave & Vandrick, 2003). The sociopolitical dimension resides in the power inequity between the peripheral scholars on the one hand, and the local specialist community, the institutional requirements and center-based gatekeepers of their target journals on the other. In the case of a novice scientist for example, the sociopolitical factors that shape the text and the writing and the publication process of a paper may

include: the interaction between the author and the peers/the supervisor (with the supervisor often having a particularly strong influence), the impact from the publication (graduation) requirement in the local institution and the negotiation (often with support from the supervisor) with the gatekeepers of the target center-based journal.

- Chinese scholars' self-perception of deficiency in English can be related to their self-perception as a 'stigmatized' group (Flowerdew, 2008; Goffman, 1968). While Hong Kong academics may obtain English editorial support from NES 'shapers' (Burrough-Boenish, 2003), Mainland Chinese scientists primarily rely on their EAL peers, professors and language professionals at the local level for the support. With regards to using professional editorial services, apart from the cost being a deterrent, uncertainty among Chinese scientists for the trustworthiness of such services – in terms of whether they can do an honest and professional job – may pose another setback. However, editorial services have a potential to develop in Mainland China (and develop further in Hong Kong) as they become more accessible (e.g. through enhanced online accessibility) and financially more affordable (e.g. with Chinese scientists' growing affluence) and as they establish a reputation for quality and reliability.
- Regarding the study conducted with the *Applied Linguistics* and *Language Teaching* journal editors in the first stage of the project, some of the key findings concern perceptions, problems and strengths. First, concerning perceptions, two stood out above all others: a questioning of the use of the term *non-native speaker* and a strong encouragement of submissions from Chinese and other NNES scholars and indeed for participation of such people on their editorial boards. Regarding problems, the editors did not find what they referred to as 'surface errors' of grammar and usage as problematic; aspects of EAL contributions that were referred to were the problem of parochialism – the need to make a study of interest to an international audience – and, especially for Asian authors, a perceived absence of a strong authorial voice. Regarding the strengths of EAL contributions, these included an awareness of cross-linguistic and cross-cultural issues, a testing mechanism for the dominant theories of the 'center', access to research sites and data where NESs would be intrusive and alerting 'center' scholars to research undertaken on the 'periphery'. It is important to emphasize that given the very specialized nature of this group of

research participants (*Applied Linguistics* and *Language Teaching* journal editors), their overall positive attitude to EAL contributors is perhaps not surprising – indeed such editors would be much more likely to be sensitive to the issues raised than editors from other disciplines.

- Finally, it is worth considering how our participants match up to the various categories of EAL 'periphery' scholars (Salager-Meyer, 2008). It is worth noting here that the Hong Kong scholars have certain advantages over their Mainland peers, not only in terms of superior material resources (Braine, 2005; Flowerdew, 2000). Most of Hong Kong scholars have been educated through English as the medium of instruction (although with Hong Kong characteristics [see e.g. Flowerdew *et al.*, 1998]), many have studied, and indeed, worked in English-speaking countries and collaborated with NES scholars in publication, while often having access to NES language editors. In contrast, the Mainland novice scholars are only beginning their careers in their home country and have no access to NESs, though of course, when having the advantage of working in a very prestigious research university (as with the novice scholars in our project), they may have leading scholars as mentors, some of whom give assistance with writing.

The significance of two strategies used by Mainland Chinese novice scientists (doctoral students), that is, language reuse and seeking editorial assistance, should not be underestimated, as our research has revealed (Flowerdew & Li, 2007; Li & Flowerdew, 2007). Heavy reliance upon the two strategies among the novice scholars indicates their tremendous difficulty in English writing. A wide range of novice text samples were provided in our published papers (in particular, Flowerdew & Li, 2007; Li, 2006b, 2006c, 2007a, 2007b; Li & Flowerdew, 2007), which illuminated the students' reuse of language from journal articles, often to the extent of textual plagiarism (Pecorari, 2003), and the transformation that the student texts underwent through reiterative editing by various language 'correctors' (Burrough-Boenisch, 2003), or especially through the decisive rhetorical reformulation by their supervisors. In the following examples, the first two examples illustrate the extent of language reuse among the students (with the overlaps between the student text and the source text underlined), and the third example indicates the potential text-transforming role of a supervisor in the novices' effort of writing for publication.

Example 1

Student A's text

Lunte [pseudonym] *et al.* instead look at the problem from a different perspective (see [15]). They maintain that the revision operation adopted by an agent itself evolves in light of new evidence.

Source text in Lunte et al. (i.e. [15] in student text)

We instead look at the problem from a different perspective. We maintain that the AGM framework can still be retained as is, however the revision operation adopted by an agent itself evolves in light of new evidence.

Example 2

Student B's text

3D models have received more and more attention in the applications in many fields, such as computer game, computer aided design, E-business, molecular biology, cultural relic preservation, etc. There are some classical manifold-based geometry representations (e.g. splines or polygon meshes) to describe a 3D model. However, in the internet many models are represented by point cloud, which is also a representation type of the 3D model. It uses particles, which can provide an expressive and intuitive approach to surface design, to represent and edit surfaces. It is a simple and versatile graphics primitive complementing conventional geometric elements.

Source text

3D models now play an important part in many applications, such as computer game, computer aided design, E-business, molecular biology, cultural relic preservation, etc. There are some classical manifold-based geometry representations (e.g. splines or polygon meshes) to describe a 3D model. However, recently it is common to represent the models in format of point cloud, which is a description of the models [4]. It uses particles to represent and edit surfaces, and the particle modeling provides an expressive and intuitive approach to surface design. Various researchers proposed the point cloud as a simple and versatile graphics primitive complementing conventional geometric elements, such as triangles or splines.

Example 3

Student C's text

As the heating temperature being increased the larger clusters are broken first and the smaller ones continue.

The supervisor's revision

As the temperature continues to increase, the internal pressure of the coated clusters increases further due to the confinement of the continuous expansion of its liquid core ...

Student C's text

The inner pressure starts to grow after melting and increases continuously because of temperature-dependent evaporation. The initial inner pressure is really large [9].

The supervisor's revision

cut the above

We found that although the Chinese novices' supervisors generally agree that imitation is necessary in the students' process of learning to write papers in English, they clearly have much more stringent criteria over what is and what is not *acceptable* borrowing from other texts. They do warn the students against 'copying'; but it is also true that they often overlook the students' copying so that textual plagiarism is detected in published papers first-authored by the students (see also Pecorari, 2006). Hands-on explicit teaching of writing by a supervisor (who has become a more 'expert' writer only through many years of writing for publication experience) to the students is limited, and a supervisor's editing is often taken by the students as is (as in the case of Student C in Example 3), not necessarily with a grasp on the latter's part of the essence of the expert reformulation.

Implications for ESL/EFL Writing Research and Teaching

Theorization of second language (L2) writing, or more specifically, L2 advanced academic literacy (AAL), has been a topic of much discussion in recent years (e.g. Grabe & Kaplan, 1996; Kroll, 2003; Leki, 2003; Matsuda, 1998). Our research contributes to this theorization by providing empirical evidence of L2 discursive activities in an EFL context. Toward the goal of theory building in L2 AAL, a crucial empirical basis would be studies conducted in a variety of instructional and disciplinary contexts, to investigate how people actually learn to write to achieve their varied academic goals (e.g. Kroll, 2003). Referring to a special issue of *Journal of Asian Pacific Communication* (*JAPC*) guest-edited by Kaplan (1995), on literacy and language planning in countries of the Pacific rim, Leki (2000: 107) observed that such efforts in AAL studies 'need to be expanded and supplemented with information from additional areas of the world and with more grounded descriptions of students' actual experiences'. Our research answers such a call.

Together with previous reports, our research reveals that this EAL phenomenon has a profound impact upon the professional lives of EAL scholars. It can perhaps be said that the overall attitude of these scholars toward English and English discourse conventions is accommodationist. National and institutional interests that prioritize scholars' international participation (e.g. with policies like 'publish English papers or no degree') certainly motivates this attitude; yet it is also clear that EAL academics themselves are increasingly feeling a need to publish in English. As previously mentioned, there are elements of cynicism and resistance, but they are not disruptive.

Methodologically, on the whole, we have adopted a 'problem-driven' principle in trying to achieve our research objectives, making methodological choices in light of the realities of the research process. This is perhaps in line with the proposal of those who advocate critical research practices (e.g. Sullivan & Porter, 1997). More specifically, our research attests to the value of a multidimensional approach and of naturalistic case studies. Long ago, Odell *et al.* (1983: 235) already talked of the need for 'a repertoire of research strategies' in research on writing. Two decades later, in a review article of research on L2 writing, Polio (2003: 59) reiterated, 'Just as multiple foci of L2 writing research are necessary, so are multiple approaches and techniques'. Indeed, it seems to have been a consensus among influential L2 writing researchers that multiple approaches and alternative perspectives are needed (e.g. Braine, 2002; Casanave, 2003; Connor, 1996; Swales, 2004). In our research, 'multiple triangulation' (Denzin, 1997) has shown its value by successfully offering multidimensional perspectives in the case of Chinese scholars writing for international publication.

Case studies potentially allow for varied research angles and methodologies, while providing researchers with opportunities for comparison and theory building (Casanave, 2003; Flowerdew, 2002). There have been calls for more case-study-based research to investigate educational contexts (e.g. Braine, 2002; Casanave, 2003; Merriam, 1988). Swales (2004) in particular, on reviewing extant case studies of PhD students' experience of dissertation writing, and concurring with Braine (2002: 131), noted that 'these studies have all been set in Anglophone environments' and 'we are in urgent need of case studies that address these key alternate contexts [in Asia and elsewhere]'. The cases studies in our research represent a step toward this goal.

Pedagogically, our research has confirmed the need for English for academic purposes (EAP) professionals acting as 'mediators of literacy', i.e. playing a role that bridges the gap between the students and the discourse expertise of the latter's target discourse community. Hyland and Hamp-Lyons (2002: 2) have stated as follows: 'English for Academic Purposes refers to language research and instruction that focuses on the specific communicative needs and practices of particular groups in academic contexts'. While highlighting 'specificity' as a primary feature of EAP, this conceptualization of EAP also points out a challenge inherent in EAP teachers' professional commitment. The challenge has a lot to do with the fact that EAP professionals 'are unlikely to belong to the same specialist fields as the writers they are supporting' (Curry & Lillis, 2004: 682). The proposal that EAP teachers act as 'mediators of literacy' seems a particularly promising solution to this dilemma (e.g. Curry & Lillis, 2004; Flowerdew, 2000; Flowerdew & Peacock, 2001; Johns, 1997).

Our research also points to the value of building a collaborative relationship between EAP specialists and subject specialists. The dialogue we have had in the past few years with the people in the alien 'tribes' (Becher & Trowler, 2001), i.e. our research participants, proved to be most worthwhile and fruitful. The subject specialists or the professors/supervisors of the science students in particular, have been most generously cooperative. It is in our dialogue with them that we realized how essential it is to involve the participation of subject specialists if EAP practitioners like ourselves want to achieve the pedagogical goal that we feel incumbent on us, i.e. 'equipping students with the communicative skills to participate in particular academic and cultural contexts' (Hyland & Hamp-Lyons, 2002: 2), and eventually, to help the disciplinary scholars/would-be scholars to contribute their voice in international academia in this new era of academic globalization.

Notes

1. Readers may feel that they would like to know where the authors of this paper stand on this issue, specifically as it relates to international publication. For a fuller discussion, see Flowerdew (in press). In brief, our position could be what has been described as a critical pragmatic one (Harwood & Hadley, 2004). This would mean encouraging training for EAL writers, on the one

hand, but on the other, emphasizing that there may be alternatives available to them to always writing in English and that EAL writers should be made aware of these options. This approach would encourage a critical mindset, but would alert EAL writers to the very high stakes in challenging the status quo. Some sort of language or languages is/are essential for the promotion of science, we feel, and, given that it has been established as English (at least for the foreseeable future, although Chinese might well be a candidate if current trends continue), then this might be considered as a necessity. However, this does not mean that its negative aspects should still not be drawn attention to. With regard to the imposition of (English) publication as a graduation requirement and for junior scholars to move forward in their careers, our position would be more critical. For the drawbacks of English as the lingua franca of science, see some of the literature referred to in this paper.

2. This has, to a degree, in fact now taken place, although there has also been a large increase in mainly US trained scholars originating from Mainland China.

References

Ammon, U. (2000) Towards more fairness in international English: Linguistic rights of non-native speakers? In R. Phillipson (ed.) *Rights to Language: Equity, Power and Education* (pp. 111–116). Mahwah, NJ: Lawrence Erlbaum.

Bazerman, C. (1988) *Shaping Written Knowledge: The Genre and Activity of the Experimental Article in Science*. Madison, WI: University of Wisconsin Press.

Becher, T. and Trowler, P.R. (2001) *Academic Tribes and Territories*. Buckingham: Open University Press.

Belcher, D. (1989) How professors initiate nonnative speakers into their disciplinary discourse communities. *Texas Papers in Foreign Language Education* 1, 207–225.

Belcher, D. (2007) Seeking acceptance in an English-only research world. *Journal of Second Language Writing* 16, 1–22.

Belcher, D. and Connor, U. (eds) (2001) *Reflections on Multiliterate Lives*. Clevedon: Multilingual Matters.

Braine, G. (2002) Academic literacy and the nonnative speaker graduate student. *Journal of English for Academic Purposes* 1, 59–68.

Braine, G. (2005) The challenge of academic publishing: A Hong Kong perspective. *TESOL Quarterly* 39, 707–716.

Burrough-Boenisch, J. (2003) Shapers of published NNS research articles. *Journal of Second Language Writing* 12, 223–243.

Canagarajah, A.S. (1996) "Nondiscursive" requirements in academic publishing, material resources of periphery scholars, and the politics of knowledge production. *Written Communication* 13, 435–472.

Canagarajah, A.S. (2002) *A Geopolitics of Academic Writing*. Pittsburgh, PA: University of Pittsburgh Press.

Canagarajah, A.S. (2003) A somewhat legitimate and very peripheral participation. In C.P. Casanave and S. Vandrick (eds) *Writing for Scholarly Publication: Behind the Scenes in Language Education* (pp. 197–210). Mahwah, NJ: Lawrence Erlbaum.

Casanave, C.P. (1998) Transitions: The balancing act of bilingual academics. *Journal of Second Language Writing* 7, 175–203.
Casanave, C.P. (2003) Looking ahead to more sociopolitically-oriented case study research in L2 writing scholarship (But should it be called "post-process"?). *Journal of Second Language Writing* 12, 85–102.
Casanave, C.P. and Vandrick, S. (eds) (2003) *Writing for Scholarly Publication: Behind the Scenes in Language Education*. Mahwah, NJ: Lawrence Erlbaum.
Curry, M.J. and Lillis, T. (2004) Multilingual scholars and the imperative to publish in English: Negotiating interests, demands, and rewards. *TESOL Quarterly* 38, 663–688.
Davis, K.A. (1995) Qualitative theory and methods in applied linguistics research. *TESOL Quarterly* 29, 427–453.
Denzin, N.K. (1997) Triangulation in educational research. In J.P. Keeves (ed.) *Educational Research, Methodology, and Measurement: An International Handbook* (2nd edn; pp. 318–22). Cambridge: Cambridge University Press.
Flowerdew, J. (1999a) Writing for scholarly publication in English: The case of Hong Kong. *Journal of Second Language Writing* 8, 123–145.
Flowerdew, J. (1999b) Problems in writing for scholarly publication in English: The case of Hong Kong. *Journal of Second Language Writing* 8, 243–264.
Flowerdew, J. (2000) Discourse community, legitimate peripheral participation, and the nonnative-English-speaking scholars. *TESOL Quarterly* 34, 127–150.
Flowerdew, J. (2001) Attitudes of journal editors to nonnative speaker contributions. *TESOL Quarterly* 35, 121–150.
Flowerdew, J. (2002) Ethnographically inspired approaches to the study of academic discourse. In J. Flowerdew (ed.) *Academic Discourse* (pp. 235–52). Harlow: Longman.
Flowerdew, J. (2005) A multimethod approach to research into processes of scholarly writing for publication. In P.K. Matsuda and T. Silva (eds) *Second Language Writing Research: Perspectives on the Process of Knowledge Construction* (pp. 65–77). Mahwah, NJ: Lawrence Erlbaum.
Flowerdew, J. (2007) The non-Anglophone scholar on the periphery of international publication. *AILA Review* 20, 14–27.
Flowerdew, J. (2008) Scholarly writers who use English as an additional language: What can Goffman's "*Stigma*" tell us? *Journal of English for Academic Purposes* 7, 77–86.
Flowerdew, J., Li, D.C.S. and Miller, L. (1998) Attitudes towards English and Cantonese among Hong Kong Chinese University Lecturers. *TESOL Quarterly* 32 (2), 201–259.
Flowerdew, J. and Li, Y-Y. (2007) Language re-use among Chinese apprentice scientists writing for publication. *Applied Linguistics* 28 (3), 440–465.
Flowerdew, J. and Peacock, M. (2001) Issues in EAP: A preliminary perspective. In J. Flowerdew and M. Peacock (eds) *Research Perspectives on English for Academic Purposes* (pp. 8–24). Cambridge: Cambridge University Press.
Galtung, J. (1971) A structural theory of imperialism. *Journal of Peace Research* 8, 81–117.
Geertz, C. (1983) *Local Knowledge: Further Essays in Interpretive Anthropology.* New York: Basic Books.
Goffman, E. (1968) *Stigma: Notes on the Management of Spoiled Identity.* Harmondsworth: Pelican. Original edition (1963) Englewood Cliffs, NJ: Prentice-Hall.

Gosden, H. (1995) Success in research article writing and revision: A social constructionist perspective. *English for Specific Purpose* 14, 35–57.
Grabe, W. and Kaplan, R.B. (1996) *Theory and Practice of Writing*. London: Longman.
Hall, S. (1991) The local and the global: Globalization and ethnicity. In A.D. King (ed.) *Culture, Globalization and the World-system: Contemporary Conditions for the Representation of Identity* (pp. 41–68). London: Macmillan.
Harwood, N. and Hadley, G. (2004) Demystifying institutional practices: Critical pragmatism and the teaching of academic writing. *English for Specific Purposes* 23, 355–377.
Hyland, K. and Hamp-Lyons, L. (2002) EAP: Issues and directions. *Journal of English for Academic Purposes* 1, 1–12.
Johns, A.M. (1997) *Text, Role, and Context: Developing Academic Literacies.* Cambridge: Cambridge University Press.
Kaplan, R. (ed.) (1995) *The Teaching of Writing in the Pacific Basin.* Special issue of *Journal of Asian Pacific Communication* 6 (1/2).
Kaplan, R. and Baldauf, R.B. Jr. (2005) Editing contributed scholarly articles from a language management perspective. *Journal of Second Language Writing* 14, 47–62.
Knight, J. and De Wit, H. (1995) Strategies for the internationalisation of higher education: Historical and conceptual perspectives. In H. De Wit (ed.) *Strategies for the Internationalisation of Higher Education* (pp. 5–32). Amsterdam: EAIE.
Knorr-Cetina, K.D. (1981) *The Manufacture of Knowledge: An Essay on the Constructivist and Contextual Nature of Science*. Oxford: Pergamon Press.
Kroll, B. (ed.) (2003) *Exploring the Dynamics of Second Language Writing*. Cambridge: Cambridge University Press.
Lave, J. and Wenger, E. (1991) *Situated Learning: Legitimate Peripheral Participation.* Cambridge: Cambridge University Press.
Leki, I. (2000) Writing, literacy, and applied linguistics. *Annual Review of Applied Linguistics* 20, 99–115.
Leki, I. (2003) Coda: Pushing L2 writing research. *Journal of Second Language Writing* 12, 103–105.
Li, Y-Y. (2002) Writing for international publication: The perception of Chinese doctoral researchers. *Asian Journal of English Language Teaching* 12, 179–193.
Li, Y-Y. (2005) Multidimensional enculturation: The case of an EFL Chinese doctoral student. *Journal of Asian Pacific Communication* 15, 153–170.
Li, Y-Y. (2006a) Writing for International Publication: The case of Chinese doctoral science students. Unpublished doctoral dissertation, City University of Hong Kong.
Li, Y-Y. (2006b) A doctoral student of physics writing for international publication: A sociopolitically-oriented case study. *English for Specific Purposes* 25, 456–478.
Li, Y-Y. (2006c) Negotiating knowledge contribution to multiple discourse communities: A doctoral student of computer science writing for publication. *Journal of Second Language Writing* 15, 159–178.
Li, Y-Y. (2007a) Apprentice scholarly writing in a community of practice: An "intraview" of an NNES graduate student writing a research article. *TESOL Quarterly* 41, 55–79.

Li, Y-Y. (2007b) Composing citations through language reuse: A doctoral student of biomedicine writing a research paper. *Asian Journal of English Language Teaching* 17, 1–27.

Li, Y-Y. and Flowerdew, J. (2007) Shaping Chinese novice scientists' manuscripts for publication. *Journal of Second Language Writing* 16, 100–117.

Li, Y-Y. and Flowerdew, J. (2008) Finding one's way into qualitative case studies in PhD thesis research: An interactive journey of a mentee and her mentor. In C.P. Casanave and X-M. Li (eds) *Learning the Literacy Practices of Graduate School: Insiders' Reflections on Academic Enculturation* (pp. 105–120). Ann Arbor, MI: University of Michigan Press.

Lillis, T. and Curry, M.J. (2006) Professional academic writing by multilingual scholars: Interactions with literacy brokers in the production of English-medium texts. *Written Communication* 23, 3–35.

Liu, J. (2004) Co-constructing academic discourse from the periphery: Chinese applied linguists' centripetal participation in scholarly publication. *Asian Journal of English Language Teaching* 14, 1–22.

Matsuda, P.K. (1998) Situating ESL writing in a cross-disciplinary contexts. *Written Communication* 15, 99–121.

Merriam, S.B. (1988) *Case Study Research in Education: A Qualitative Approach.* San Francisco, CA: Jossey-Bass.

Mok, K.H. (2006) *Education Reform and Education Policy in East Asia*. Abingdon: Routledge.

Odell, L., Goswami, D. and Herrington, A. (1983) The discourse-based interview: A procedure for exploring the tacit knowledge of writers in nonacademic settings. In P. Mosenthal, L. Tamor and S. Walmsley (eds) *Research on Writing: Principles and Methods* (pp. 221–236). New York: Longman.

Patton, M.Q. (1987) *How to use Qualitative Methods in Evaluation.* Beverly Hills, CA: Sage.

Pecorari, D. (2003) Good and original: Plagiarism and patchwriting in academic second-language writing. *Journal of Second Language Writing* 12, 317–345.

Pecorari, D. (2006) Visible and occluded citation features in postgraduate second-language writing. *English for Specific Purposes* 25, 4–29.

Polio, C. (2003) Research on second language writing: An overview of what we investigate and how. In B. Kroll (ed.) *Exploring the Dynamics of Second Language Writing* (pp. 35–65). Cambridge: Cambridge University Press.

Prior, P. (1995) Redefining the task: An ethnographic examination of writing and response in graduate seminars. In D. Belcher and G. Braine (eds) *Academic Writing in a Second Language: Essays on Research and Pedagogy* (pp. 47–82). Norwood, NJ: Ablex.

Prior, P. (1998) *Writing/Disciplinarity: A Sociohistoric Account of Literate Activity in the Academy.* Mahwah, NJ: Lawrence Erlbaum.

Robertson, R. (1992) *Globalization: Social Theory and Global Culture.* London: Sage.

Robertson, R. (1995) Glocalization: Time-space and homogeneity-heterogeneity. In M. Feathrestone, S. Lash and R. Robertson (eds) *Global Modernities* (pp. 25–44). London: Sage.

Salager-Meyer, F. (2008) Scientific publishing in developing countries: Challenges for the future. *Journal of English for Academic Purposes* 7, 121–132.

Scott, P. (ed.) (1998) *The Globalization of Higher Education.* Buckingham/Philadelphia, PA: Society for Research into Higher Education/Open University Press.

Sharpe, L. (1997) Participant verification. In J.P. Keeves (ed.) *Educational Research, Methodology, and Measurement: An International Handbook* (2nd edn; pp. 314–315). Cambridge: Cambridge University Press.

Stake, R.E. (2003) Case studies. In N.K. Denzin and Y.S. Lincoln (eds) *Strategies of Qualitative Inquiry* (2nd edn; pp. 134–164). London: Sage.

Strauss, A. and Corbin, J. (1990) *Basics of Qualitative Research*. Newbury Park, CA: Sage.

Sullivan, P. and Porter, J. (1997) *Opening Spaces: Writing Technologies and Critical Research Practices*. Greenwich, CT: Ablex.

Swales, J. (2004) *Research Genres: Exploration and Applications*. Cambridge: Cambridge University Press.

Van Vught, F., Van der Wende, M. and Westerheijden, D. (2002) Globalisation and internationalisation: Policy agendas compared. In J. Enders and O. Fulton (eds) *Higher Education in a Globalising World* (pp. 103–119). Dordrecht: Kluwer Academic.

Wallerstein, I.M. (1979) *The Capitalist World-economy: Essays by Immanuel Wallerstein*, Cambridge: Cambridge University Press.

Waters, M. (1995) *Globalization*. London: Routledge.

Wenger, E. (1998) *Communities of Practice: Learning, Meaning, and Identity.* Cambridge: Cambridge University Press.

Chapter 7

A Critical Evaluation of Writing Teaching Programmes in Different Foreign Language Settings

MELINDA REICHELT

Introduction

Over the last 15 years, my research into foreign language (FL) writing has involved investigation of FL writing in Germany, Poland and the USA, where I identified a range of factors shaping writing instruction. A search of the literature on FL writing instruction in other environments yielded information indicating that many of the contextual factors that shape FL writing instruction in the contexts I had investigated (Germany, Poland and the USA) have also been influential in China, Japan and Spain. In this chapter, by providing information about FL writing instruction in six contexts that differ considerably from each other, I attempt to contribute to an expanded, more global understanding of second language (L2) writing instruction.

The chapter begins with a description of research methodology issues, in which I outline how I gathered data on-site in Germany, Poland and the USA, and how the authors of works about China, Japan and Spain collected data in their research contexts.

In the remainder of this chapter, I report on my own research findings and those of others, describing FL writing instruction in these six places. For each context, I describe factors shaping FL writing instruction, pedagogical practices and teacher education regarding FL writing instruction. The chapter concludes with considerations regarding FL writing instruction for FL writing specialists, curriculum developers and language planners.

Methodology

While investigating FL writing in Germany, Poland and the USA, I gathered a variety of types of data, including information from curriculum guidelines, textbooks and other instructional materials, and published research and pedagogical descriptions regarding FL writing instruction in each environment; interviews with teachers, students, teacher trainers and curriculum developers; classroom observation; attendance at teachers' meetings; and responses from participants to working reports.

In 1994, I spent a year investigating English as a foreign language (EFL) and first language (L1) (German) writing instruction at a German *Gymnasium* (see Reichelt, 1997a, 1997b, 1999a), the most rigorous secondary school type in a three-level system. During this and several subsequent research projects, I investigated a range of writing issues (see Reichelt, 2003, 2005b) by employing a qualitative approach, focusing on writing instruction as it occurred naturally. I observed nearly 100 class sessions and conducted over 100 interviews with teachers, students, teacher trainers and curriculum developers. I also examined many relevant written documents and attended various teachers' meetings. Additionally, I elicited participant feedback by asking teachers for informal responses to my ideas and by asking my main research contact, a teacher, to read and respond to my working reports.

Later, I investigated EFL writing instruction at various educational levels in a central Polish city of approximately 780,000 inhabitants (see Reichelt, 2005a, 2006). I interviewed 13 English instructors drawn from the university's English Department, two secondary schools and the city's largest private foreign-language institute. These teachers provided me with access to their classrooms and teaching materials; I was also able to hold group discussions about writing instruction with approximately 70 students.

My next project looked into FL writing in the USA and included investigation of student and instructor perceptions of writing instruction in a US German classroom. This research involved classroom observation, student questionnaires and interviews with students and the instructor (Reichelt & Bryant, 2001). I also conducted a review of over 200 published works concerning FL writing in the USA (Reichelt, 1999b) and a critical analysis of 32 empirical studies of FL writing in the USA (Reichelt, 2001).

In my exploration of EFL writing instruction in China, Japan and Spain, I have drawn on work by authors who used a range of research procedures: classroom observation, including but not limited to reflection on one's own teaching experience (Chaudron *et al.*, 2005; Cummings, 2004; Dyer & Friederich, 2002; Heffernan, 2006; Martín Uriz & Whittaker, 2005; Ordóñez de Celis, 2005; Ordway, 1997; Sapp,

2001; You, 2004, 2005); interviews and questionnaires involving students and instructors (Chaudron *et al.*, 2005; Cummings, 2004; Dyer & Friederich, 2002; Heffernan, 2006; Martín Uriz & Whittaker, 2005; You, 2004); analysis of student texts (Cummings, 2004; Hirose, 2001, 2003; Kimura & Konda, 2002); and examination of curricular documents and teaching materials (Ordway, 1997; You, 2004, 2005).

In my own research and in my examination of others' work, in some cases, I was able to gather information about learners from a range of age groups, while in other cases, I was able to gather only information from primary/secondary levels or university levels.

EFL Writing Instruction in Germany

Factors shaping EFL writing instruction in Germany

English is by far the most commonly learned FL in Germany. From the 1960s on, all German students between the ages of 10 and 19 have received some English instruction (Bliesener, 1988). For Germans of all ages, knowledge and use of English serves as a status symbol. English is used in business, politics, law, advertising, research and the mass media (Berns, 1992). Many students are motivated to learn English, including written English, and English-language writing instruction tends to be quite rigorous (Reichelt, 1997a).

EFL writing instruction is shaped by German educational values that emphasize creativity, close reading of texts, a broad education, critical thinking and the German tradition of *Bildung*, or 'education'. *Bildung* emphasizes the overall formation of the individual and includes development of attitudes, views and values. According to Bliesener (1988: 11), *Bildung* 'serves to immunise people against totalitarianism, it opens windows to other points of view, it makes people independent and thus helps to preserve peace'.

The teaching of EFL writing in Germany

At the *Gymnasium* where I conducted my research, students in Grades 5 or 6 through 9 of German and English classes composed short narratives and texts about themselves; wrote text summaries; answered comprehension or opinion-related questions after reading, listening to or watching something; and composed texts with clearly instrumental functions, such as letters. In Grades 5–9 of German and Grades 7–9 of English, students also undertook 'creative-productive' writing, which involves writing in response to a text, usually with the stipulation of a specific context and audience. For example, students might read a short story and then write a letter from one character to another, fill a 'gap' in a story by writing a scene that is absent but could exist, write one part of a dialogue when the other part is provided, or write the end of a story after hearing the beginning (Reichelt, 1997a, 1997b).

In Grades 10–13 of English at this *Gymnasium*, students read and wrote about a broad range of texts chosen by their teachers to deepen their understanding of the cultures and important texts of English-dominant countries. By Grade 13, many were able to discuss, read and write about complex social and political issues in English; they were also held to rigorous standards for linguistic correctness (Reichelt, 1997a, 1997b). Students in Grades 10–13 of both English and German wrote arguments, literary interpretations and text analyses following a summary-application-personal opinion format. For exams, students typically received an unfamiliar reading and were asked to (1) summarize or describe the new material, (2) analyze it by applying what they had learned in class and (3) offer and justify an evaluation, comparison or personal opinion regarding the material. According to teachers at this *Gymnasium*, this three-part format was used to ensure that students responded to questions covering a range of cognitive demands (Reichelt, 1997a, 1997b).

Students typically did 'practice' writing assignments at home in preparation for their essay exams. They read their practice work aloud, and the teacher and students provided oral critique. Teachers scored exam writing according to content, style and grammatical accuracy (Reichelt, 1997a, 1997b).

While an emphasis on close reading of texts has held sway for several decades in German-language and EFL writing instruction at the *Gymnasium* level, newer ideas have brought the communicative function of EFL writing to the forefront. Recently, curriculum reforms for English instruction in secondary schools have called for writing tasks that are integrated into larger projects with communicative purposes (*Ministerium für Bildung, Wissenshaft, Forschung und kultur des Landes*, 2002). This approach moves students away from writing isolated text analyses that emphasize close, critical reading, and into writing produced for more immediate, context-embedded purposes. For example, students might write a guidebook in English about their city for American exchange students, create an English-language class newspaper or write and perform a play in English.

Teacher education in Germany

Secondary English teachers, almost always native Germans, undergo rigorous training, including training in teaching and correcting writing.

This training is based on a well-developed L1 (German) writing pedagogy. In general, younger teachers who had completed their education more recently were advocates of project-embedded writing activities, arguing that they were authentic, engaging and motivating, and that they helped students prepare for workplace writing in English. On the other hand, many older teachers appeared more committed to local (German) values, emphasizing that *Gymnasium* instruction should go beyond 'just' teaching students to communicate, and should also provide tools for students to engage in close reading, critical thinking and further learning (Reichelt, 1997a). Opponents of recent changes argue that it is difficult to ensure that each student has the opportunity to engage in writing tasks that demand a range of cognitive skills, that some students may need the help of the three-part format to guide them in their writing, and that the new types of writing assignments are more difficult to evaluate fairly than more traditional forms (Monika Meinhold, personal communication, 30 June 2001). These general differences in attitudes most likely stem, at least in part, from differences in the teacher education and in-service training that older versus younger teachers had received.

EFL Writing Instruction in Poland

Factors shaping EFL writing instruction in Poland

In Poland, learning a FL became compulsory at the secondary level and in higher education in the 1960s, and the popularity of English study increased in the 1970s and 1980s (Varney, 1984). After political and economic changes in Poland in the late 1980s and early 1990s, English emerged as the dominant FL taught (Lekki, 2003). In Poland, as in Germany, English enjoys prestige among all ages and is perceived as the language of professional and financial success. FL instruction – especially English instruction – was particularly important as Poland sought admission to the European Union (EU). (Poland became a EU member on 1 May 2004.) Oral skills have received the most attention in FL instruction in the past, and, unlike Germany, Poland lacks a strong tradition of L1 writing instruction. However, there is a growing sense of need for written FL skills, especially English skills, primarily for making and maintaining foreign business contacts, especially within Europe. FL writing is also considered useful in supporting overall FL learning by reinforcing grammar and vocabulary. The Polish government has recently mandated that graduating secondary school students select a FL as one of their written subjects; many choose English. Pressure to prepare for the FL written portions of the school-leaving exam has led to a greater focus on FL writing instruction. Similarly, at the university level, pressure to prepare English majors for written portions of year-end exams causes writing instructors to focus on essay types that typically appear on these exams.

The teaching of EFL writing in Poland

Schools have begun to offer English-language instruction at increasingly earlier ages, and compulsory FL instruction (with English as the most commonly chosen option) begins in grade four and continues through secondary school (Reichelt, 2005a). In the schools where I conducted my research, primary students (Grades 1–6) started writing in fourth or fifth grade and completed short writing tasks such as describing oneself, family, school and hobbies. At the *gimnazjum* level (Grades 7–9), students wrote other short descriptions (e.g. of a telephone, television, favorite place, friend, event or trip); stories; letters; dialogs; and essays, sometimes with instructions to use certain grammatical structures or vocabulary they had learned. At the *liceum* level (Grades 10–12), much of the writing instruction focused on preparing students for the standardized school-leaving exam – the *Matura* – which, at the 'basic' (required) level, included two writing tasks. For the short task, students had to write a text such as a postcard, a note or a notice about having lost something. The student was given information about the situation along with four pieces of information to convey, and one point was awarded for each piece of accurately conveyed information and one point for linguistic correctness. For the longer task at the basic level, students wrote 120–150 words, usually in the form of a letter. After completing the basic level of the *Matura*, students could opt to take an advanced level, including a longer composition. In class, students sometimes read their work aloud and received feedback from the teacher and classmates. Other times, teachers provided oral feedback to the class, covering common problems. Because of heavy teacher workloads, it was difficult for teachers to provide individual feedback to students (Reichelt, 2006).

At the university where I conducted my research, non-English majors received about one year of FL instruction from teachers in the university's language center and then had to pass an exam focusing primarily on grammar and translation. In contrast, English majors took EFL composition courses throughout all five years of their studies. For these students, pressure to prepare for the written portions of year-end exams shaped the EFL writing curriculum significantly. In the program

I investigated (Reichelt, 2006), the first two years of composition instruction for English majors were typically devoted to writing paragraphs, thesis statements, short narratives, descriptive pieces and business letters. Students also wrote a variety of essay types, e.g. for/against, definition, example, comparison/contrast and argumentative, which they practiced for year-end exams. Students typically took oral exams in their content-area courses rather than writing term papers, but if they did write papers for their other courses, they were rarely asked to use these essay formats. (Courses in linguistics, literature and culture were typically taught by native Poles, who preferred that students write in English but with the features of written Polish, which contrast considerably with the types of essays taught in English class.) These essay types are also perceived by students as irrelevant to on-the-job writing students might do after graduation, especially if they work outside of education. (While most English majors are training to become English teachers, many are also studying other subjects such as business, hoping that their knowledge of English will lead them to more lucrative careers.) In year three of their studies, students prepared for the third-year exam, in which they were asked to write a 600–800-word research paper based on sources they received in advance. Later work related to students' master's theses, which had to be written in English.

EFL writing instructors in this program for English majors have recently shifted away from a traditional, product-oriented approach, in which students wrote only one draft of each paper and received a grade with little feedback. (Several interviewees described this approach as typical of the experience students have with writing in Polish.) The techniques used nowadays vary from instructor to instructor, but common activities include those typical of process-oriented classrooms: use of sample texts, in-class prewriting activities, peer review, revision based on peer and teacher feedback, register work, grammar exercises and journal writing. According to instructors, students have responded positively to these changes (Reichelt, 2006).

Teacher education in Poland

At the primary and secondary levels, English teachers are typically native Poles trained to teach reading, listening and speaking skills, but not writing. Because of heavy workloads, and as the English-language portion of the old *Matura* (the school-leaving exam) taken by most students did not include a writing task, previously, English teachers experienced little motivation to emphasize writing. However, because of the new written FL portion of the *Matura*, teachers in the schools I investigated were beginning to focus more on writing. Teachers looked to textbooks for guidance, which typically integrate writing instruction with other skills and include communicative tasks in which students write for specific purposes and audiences, such as writing a postcard or note in order to convey specific information to a reader (Reichelt, 2006). Longman has produced several textbooks for use in Polish schools (see www.longman.pl), and Cambridge University Press also has some Poland-specific textbooks (see www.uk.cambridge.org).

At the university where I conducted my research (Reichelt, 2006), instructors from England, Ireland, Canada and the USA were often assigned to teach university composition courses, especially ones for upper level students. Writing instructors were responsible for finding or creating their own materials, and many had training in writing pedagogy from their home countries; not surprisingly, they tended to rely on pedagogies, materials and evaluation criteria from their home countries (see Casanave, this volume).

FL Writing Instruction in the USA

Factors shaping FL writing instruction in the USA

In Germany and Poland, the perceived importance of learning English provides concrete motivations for students to learn various English skills, including writing. In contrast, because of the role of English as a world language and the relative geographical isolation of the USA, there is generally less perceived need for FL learning in the USA and often less motivation and emphasis on FL than in many other countries. Therefore, FL instruction in the USA often occurs at beginner or near-beginner levels, even in colleges and universities, and there is typically a lack of clarity about FL students' writing needs.

FL writing instruction in the USA has been influenced to some degree by practices common in US ESL writing instruction (Hadley, 2001; Reichelt, 1999), which has itself been shaped by L1 writing instruction in the USA. Most US universities require incoming native English-speaking students to take one or more courses in L1 (English) composition, which has led to highly developed traditions of L1 writing scholarship and pedagogy. While approaches to teaching L1 composition vary widely, one especially influential aspect has been the process approach to writing, involving activities such as prewriting, use of multiple drafts, revision and teacher and peer feedback (Ferris & Hedgcock, 2005). While US students in L1 composition courses typically write longer pieces than most US FL students, many of these process approach practices have been adapted for FL writing instruction.

FL writing instruction in the USA is also shaped by the widespread availability of technology, especially at the university level. Many university FL programs have implemented Computer Assisted Language Learning (CALL) into their curricula (Pooser, 2004), often by providing students opportunities to visit language labs outfitted with computers and other media.

The teaching of FL writing in the USA

Common writing activities in US FL classes include guided composition and work at the sentence- or paragraph-level only or involve building compositions from the bottom up, progressing from words, phrases and sentences through paragraphs to whole essays. For lower-level and intermediate students, FL curricula often employ writing as a means of supporting overall target language (TL) development, especially in the areas of grammar and vocabulary (Reichelt & Bryant, 2001). For example, students might engage in dictation, sentence-length picture descriptions, postcard writing, present- and past-tense narrations and short essays on familiar topics (Hadley, 2001).

Because of the difficulty of identifying specific writing needs beyond the classroom, FL writing instruction in the USA often also includes creative and expressive writing tasks (Bräuer, 1997), designed to foster students' interest and motivation. Dialog journals are also used for this purpose (Peyton & Reed, 1990). For the relatively few students who take higher-level FL courses, writing is also used in analysis of literature (Hadley, 2001). Much of the FL literature also describes the use of the process approaches to writing (Lee & VanPatten, 2003) popular in North American English-language composition classrooms. These include practices such as planning activities, peer review, receiving teacher feedback and revision (Hadley, 2001).

Besides this, various authors describe their use of technology as part of their FL writing instruction, including email (Conroy, 2004) and the worldwide web (Pooser, 2004). Recently, literature about FL writing instruction has emphasized the development of integrated literacy skills. Kern (2004) describes literacy as focusing on 'relationships between readers, writers, texts, culture, and language learning', arguing that literacy can be used as an 'organizing principle' (p. 4) for teaching academic language. Kern provides descriptions of literacy activities, including storytelling followed by writing down of stories, and projects that integrate writing into them. While such literacy-based pedagogical recommendations exist, it is unclear to what extent they are actually being implemented in classrooms.

Teacher education in the USA

In the USA, a mix of native and non-native speakers of the TL is employed as instructors, at both the secondary and university levels. Most secondary-level instructors have majored in the FL in their university education, but some school districts employ teachers with a minor (or less) in the TL. Because US students – even those choosing to pursue FL teaching as a career – often enter university with low levels of TL proficiency, much of FL majors' coursework is devoted to building linguistic proficiency (Schulz, 2000). As FL majors must also meet requirements in literature and culture, subject matter courses must compete for time with education-related courses (Schulz, 2000), and FL majors intending to teach may take only one FL methods course. While published information is unavailable regarding how much such courses emphasize preparation for teaching FL writing, it is doubtful that it plays a central role, given the relative de-emphasis on writing skills in most US FL curricula.

Most textbooks used in methodology courses do include a chapter on writing instruction (Hadley, 2001; Lee & VanPatten, 2003). These chapters often draw from L1 English and ESL writing research and practice, sometimes extensively. Lee and VanPatten (2003), for example, advocate process writing instruction and assigning essay-length compositions even to beginner FL students. Hadley (2001) emphasizes that instructors should design writing tasks that support the development of grammar, vocabulary and discourse skills while allowing students to write for communicative purposes. However, in reality, FL instructors may be trained to focus more on grammatical structures and forms in writing rather than on issues such as content and audience (Reichelt & Bryant, 2001).

In university language departments with graduate FL programs, much of the lower-level FL instruction is provided by teaching assistants (TA), graduate students who are typically supervised by a faculty member but who often have sole responsibility for the course(s) they teach. TAs usually receive some form of preservice and inservice training, which may include training regarding writing instruction. Additionally, as graduate students, these TAs are likely to take courses in applied linguistics, especially those studying at the doctoral level (Schulz, 2000).

EFL Writing Instruction in China

Factors shaping EFL writing instruction in China

Today, English is the most studied FL in China. Since 2002, the Ministry of Education has required that English instruction begin in third grade (You, 2005). In 1989, a direct writing task was added to the university entrance exam (You, 2005). As in Poland, in China, the economic role of English is a significant factor in the motivation to learn English, including written English. As China became a center of manufacturing, English writing ability came to be seen by students as 'an indispensable skill in their professional development' (You, 2005: 135). Li (2007) writes that some doctoral students are required to publish articles in English-language journals in order to graduate.

As is true in Poland, the EFL writing curriculum in China is heavily influenced by the national syllabus and exam system (Sapp, 2001; You, 2004). The national syllabus for non-English majors prescribes that every university student must be able to write a short essay when given a certain topic or an outline (You, 2004). Achievement is measured almost exclusively by students' performance on the College English Test (CET) (Li, 2007), a standardized exam officially implemented in 1987. After receiving two years of English instruction, non-English majors typically complete their study of English by taking the CET-Band 4 examination at the end of their sophomore year (You, 2005). For the written portion, students are required to write a 100–120-word composition in 30 minutes on a topic related to general knowledge or daily life (Li, 2007). Correct form is emphasized over development of thoughts (You, 2004). Instructors receive financial rewards based on their students' performance, and high scores can open important doors for students (Sapp, 2001; You, 2004, 2005).

Another factor that impacts EFL writing instruction in China is large class sizes, often of 40 students or more (Yang *et al.*, 2006). Additionally, teachers' low salaries, combined with a high demand for English and a shortage of English teachers, lead many teachers to seek additional teaching employment outside of their colleges, which means that teachers are often too overloaded to provide individual attention to students' writing (Yang *et al.*, 2006; You, 2004).

The teaching of EFL writing in China

By the time students enter the university, they may have been studying English for quite some time. Since 2002, English has been a required subject in China, starting in third grade (Liu & Braine, 2005). Ellis and Yuan (2004) and Wang and Wen (2002) note that students in their empirical studies of EFL writing had received eight years of English instruction before entering university. Students in Wang and Wen's (2002) study entered university with the ability to write short compositions in English, although they had received no systematic training in EFL writing at the elementary or secondary level.

At the university level, all Chinese undergraduates are required to take English courses (Liu & Braine, 2005). In their two years of university-level English instruction, non-English majors typically receive one hour per week of English listening instruction and three hours per week of intensive reading instruction, which includes speaking, reading, writing and translation (You, 2004). However, in some cases, non-English majors may take a course devoted exclusively to writing (Yang *et al.*, 2006). English majors, of course, receive more overall English-language instruction, including more writing instruction. For example, Wang and Wen (2002) write that English majors at Nanjing University were required at the time of their study to take a four-year writing course that met two hours per week; year one focused on description and narration, year two on exposition, year three on argumentation, and year four on a research report and thesis.

University-level English writing instruction focuses initially on working up from sentences to paragraphs (Yang *et al.*, 2006; You, 2005). Later, it focuses on test-taking skills and language knowledge, including grammar and word choice, often via lectures in L1. Instructors focus on teaching students to write three- to five-paragraph essays with the format of introduction-body-conclusion (You, 2004, 2005); the focus of instruction is the written product, with students usually writing only one draft of a given paper (Yang *et al.*, 2006). Students often rely on model sentences, paragraphs and essays (Yang *et al.*, 2006), often memorizing essays on topics similar to those that commonly appear on the CET (You, 2004, 2005). While the approach may seem formulaic, large class sizes make it difficult for teachers to respond to multiple drafts of students' work (Yang *et al.*, 2006), or even to read all students' essays all of the time. Instructors may read just a handful of students' practice exam essays and discuss their strengths and weaknesses in class, assuming most other students have similar problems, and/or instructors may provide a model essay on a topic after students have written about it (You, 2004, 2005).

Because of large class sizes, small group activities can also be difficult to implement (Sapp, 2001). Sapp (2001), an American who taught university English in China, writes that the need to prepare students for national exams, large class sizes, and the traditionally dominant role of the teacher in the classroom made it difficult for him to implement student-centered, 'progressive' (Western) pedagogies, which he appeared to believe (perhaps somewhat uncritically) that he could import. However, You (2004) notes that, despite barriers to implementation, some Western teaching activities are slowly being introduced, including prewriting, group discussion, surveys, interviews, library research and process writing. Yang *et al.* (2006) also write that some university instructors are moving toward process approaches, including the use of feedback on intermediate drafts. In their study of peer versus instructor feedback at the university level, their results indicated that most of the teacher feedback and over half of the peer feedback was implemented and that peer feedback was more successful than teacher feedback, produced more meaning changes than teacher feedback and encouraged student autonomy. They thus argue that, especially given instructors' heavy workloads, peer feedback can play an important role in writing instruction in China.

In Hong Kong, English-language instruction, including writing instruction, differs from that of the rest of China because of Hong Kong's unique history. (Hong Kong was a British colony until 1 July 1997; Xiao, 2001.) Hong Kong secondary students are likely to receive more English instruction, including writing instruction, than other Chinese students, and may attend bilingual secondary schools. Secondary-level EFL writing instruction usually focuses on writing as a product because of the examinations required by the secondary-level system and the constraints of large class sizes (Xiao, 2001). All university courses in Hong Kong are conducted in either English or a combination of English and Cantonese. Students of all majors are typically required to take English courses and study writing (Braine, 2001; Xiao, 2001). Braine (2001) notes that students in a writing course at a university where he conducted research were required to write a 600-word expressive paper, a longer informative paper and a 1250-word persuasive paper based on library research. A process approach was employed.

Teacher education in China

Most university instructors educated in China do not receive training in ELT pedagogy. Instead, they learn about composition instruction through instructors' meetings regarding how to rate compositions written for the CET and are otherwise largely self-taught: when they are in high school, they learn how to compose in Chinese; as college students, they learn to write in English for the CET; and as college instructors, they learn by preparing their own students for the CET and by studying composition textbooks or CET reference books (You, personal communication, 25 May 2007).

EFL Writing Instruction in Japan

Factors shaping EFL writing instruction in Japan

After the Second World War, English became particularly influential in Japan because of the US impact on Japan's political, economic and social reform. While the Japanese Ministry of Education, Culture, Sports, Science and Technology has recommended that English-language instruction become more communicative (Casanave, this volume), large classes at both the secondary and university level, an emphasis on rote learning (especially at the secondary level) and little tolerance for error can foster a sense that English is an 'inert knowledge to be learnt and then forgotten' (Hyde, 2002: 16).

Attitudes about English and English-language learning in Japan apply, of course, to perceptions of EFL writing. Many secondary school students do not perceive EFL writing as important for their future study or careers, although in recent years, many public universities have added an English writing passage of 80–150 words to the university entrance exam (Rinnert & Kobayashi, this volume). At the university level, non-English majors often do not perceive a need for writing in English, perhaps because authentic purposes for EFL writing are sometimes difficult to identify (Hirose, 2001). However, at least some non-English majors do need to learn to write in English. For example, at the end of their studies, Cummings' (2004) computer science and computer engineering students were required to write a four- to six-page thesis in English, and required final reports in English as long as 20–30 pages. In contrast, English majors typically need to write in English for research papers in their EFL writing classes and content-area courses taught by non-Japanese instructors, as well as perhaps for their graduation thesis (Carol Rinnert, personal communication, 11 June 2007).

Japanese students gain experience in L1 writing that potentially impacts on their EFL writing. In elementary and secondary school, they engage in L1 expressive writing and write personal impressions of reading materials (Hirose, 2003; Rinnert & Kobayashi, this volume). Kobayashi and Rinnert (2002) argue that while little explicit Japanese writing instruction occurs in most regular classrooms, many secondary schools provide special courses or tutoring in L1 writing to help students prepare to write short argumentative essays for the university entrance exam. These essays require students to take a clear position and provide supporting evidence, and they value originality. Rinnert and Kobayashi (this volume) provide evidence that some Japanese writers transfer their L1 writing experience to their EFL writing, which indicates that this L1 writing instruction, at least in theory, could have a facilitating effect on EFL writing.

The teaching of EFL writing in Japan

While most Japanese students receive six years of English in secondary school, instruction typically focuses on translation at the sentence level from Japanese to English (Heffernan, 2006; Hirose, 2001, 2003). For secondary school students, there is little classroom attention to writing, although in some cases, teachers may devote a few minutes of class time to activities such as journal writing (Casanave, this volume). However, outside of class, some secondary students receive special preparation for the English-language writing task required by many universities as part of the university entrance exam.

Upon entering university, students may be preoccupied with accuracy, and many students will not have written in English beyond the sentence level (Hirose, 2001). Typically, students are not familiar with process approaches to writing (Dyer & Friederich, 2002), peer review (Hirose, 2001) or the requirements of writing a research report (Heffernan, 2006). Japanese university students usually learn first to write paragraphs in English, and then perhaps longer pieces (Dyer & Friederich, 2002).

Non-English majors study English for one or two years. The medium of instruction is often Japanese, and there is sometimes a heavy reliance on translation (Hyde, 2002: 16). Non-English majors may also take English writing courses (Carol Rinnert, personal communication, 11 June 2007). Such courses can vary in approach according to instructors' preferences and backgrounds, but students write at least paragraph-level pieces (Kobayashi, personal communication, 12 June 2007). According to Trokeloshvili and Jost (2007), starting in the 1990s, many composition instructors in Japan moved their courses into the computer lab because of the motivating aspects for students of using email and creating home pages.

Writing instruction for English majors seems to vary widely according to individual universities, programs and instructors. Many programs include preparation for writing the essay section of the Test of English as a foreign language (TOEFL), but often the curriculum also includes journal writing, research papers, other genres and training in using summary, paraphrase and citation conventions in preparation for writing the graduation thesis (Carol Rinnert, personal communication, 11 June 2007). Students may learn to write exposition and argumentative texts, and may complete assignments that focus on knowledge getting as well as practice writing. Courses may also include the use of multiple drafts and teacher and/or peer feedback (Kobayashi, personal communication, 12 June 2007). Hirose (2001) indicates that for the first-year English majors in her writing classes, besides activities that raised students' awareness of conventions of academic writing, fluency-aimed writing activities were important because students had so little experience of composing in English. She employed journaling because Japanese students are used to writing about their personal experiences and feelings in their L1.

University-level EFL writing courses for English majors often involve explicit instruction in the (perhaps stereotyped) differences between Japanese and English rhetorics. While some authors have problematized the generalizations made concerning the rhetorical differences between Japanese writing and English-language writing (Hirose, 2003), this topic features prominently in discussions of EFL writing instruction in Japan. Heffernan (2006) writes that the Japanese students in his university EFL writing course were unfamiliar with terms like *thesis statement, unity, coherence* and *support*. Kimura and Konda (2002) write that the notion of paragraph and other rhetorical features are different in Japanese and English. French (2005), for example, notes that because of his students' heavy workloads, he imposed Western rhetorical frameworks in his composition class for practical reasons.

It is not uncommon for native English speakers to be employed as composition instructors (French, 2005). Instructors trained in North America often import teaching approaches such as the use of multiple drafts and peer feedback. Many such approaches can be adjusted to fit the Japanese context and students' expectations (Carol Rinnert, personal communication, 10 June, 2007). Because of cultural differences, native English-speaking instructors may face significant challenges. For example, Cummings found that her students did not expect her to address them in English and could not understand her; intercultural clashes and inhibitions resulted in her and her students 'silencing each other' (Cummings, 2004: 26). (Faced with these difficulties, she successfully transformed the class into a computer-mediated course involving a great deal of online communication among students and with the instructor.)

Teacher education in Japan

Prospective secondary-level English teachers are required to participate in preservice training in an actual high school, guided by supervising teachers (Kobayashi, personal communication, 12 June, 2007). Published information on training for EFL writing instruction is unavailable, but it is likely that teacher candidates receive little such training, given the relative de-emphasis in the secondary level curriculum on EFL writing. University-level EFL writing instructors typically have an MA degree, but they are not required to participate in teaching practice in order to qualify as university instructors. Instructors vary in their disciplinary backgrounds, for example, literature, linguistics or translation, which can significantly impact their teaching approaches (Kobayashi, personal communication, 12 June, 2007).

Many native English speakers employed in Japan have an MA degree in TESOL and probably teach according to what they learned in these programs; however, application of such principles may be constrained by the teaching environment (Kobayashi, personal communication, 12 June, 2007). Casanave (this volume) describes the reactions of Japanese students in a MATESOL program in Japan to the pedagogical methods they learned in their program, as well as their beliefs about EFL writing instruction in Japan. (These students were unusual among their peers simply because they were enrolled in such a program.) Few of these students had taken a course in writing methods, but they believed that writing in English was important for their students because it could help them develop their ideas, express themselves, prepare for work outside Japan, broaden their vision and help them in English-dominant undergraduate and graduate programs. However, these MATESOL students struggled with whether the communicative, student-centered methodologies they had been taught could be implemented in Japan – especially at the secondary level – because of the exam-centered and teacher-centered nature of instruction in Japan; most felt that their program needed to devote more time to explicitly addressing how to implement these ideas in the Japanese context.

EFL Writing Instruction in Spain

Factors shaping EFL writing instruction in Spain

As in Poland and China, political and economic changes have led to greater emphasis on English instruction in Spain. When Franco's rule ended in 1975, an increasing openness on Spain's part, along with interest in joining the European Community, led to greater demand for

English for international relations, foreign investment, tourism and banking. During the 1980s, the number of English-medium schools and private language schools increased, and state-run official language schools (*Escuelas Oficiales de Idiomas*) offered English classes to adults (British Council, 1980, 1985) (alongside classes in some other languages, such as French, German, Italian, Arabic or Japanese). Due to a deficiency of English-teaching expertise, teacher shortages, large classes of mixed abilities and few resources, students' linguistic achievements were, in most cases, quite low (British Council, 1985). Despite intense interest in English, only 18% of Spaniards speak, read and write English with ease – as opposed to 31% of non-native English speakers in the European Union (EUROPA). Currently, interest in learning English is very strong, and students are beginning their study of English earlier and earlier, with students typically beginning by third grade, if not earlier (Ordway, 1997).

As is the case in Poland, in order to foster the mobility of Spanish students and workers within Europe, there is a perceived need to raise overall FL achievement levels, including achievement in EFL writing. In most of the autonomous communities of Spain, university entrance exams now require students to write a 45-minute FL composition in which they create a meaningful, unified text, addressing a reader with a communicative purpose (Chaudron *et al.*, 2005).

The teaching of EFL writing in Spain

As has been the case in Poland and Japan, writing has traditionally received little emphasis compared to other skills in EFL classes (Chaudron *et al.*, 2005). Similarly, Spanish students receive little explicit instruction in L1 composition (Victori, 1999) and EFL writing has been employed in primary education mainly as a means of reinforcing and supporting overall English learning, especially grammar and vocabulary. In primary schools, students progress from writing words and phrases to short, simple texts about themselves and other familiar topics (Peñate Cabrera & Bazo, 2002).

At the secondary level, curricula prescribe that students learn to write short, simple, reader-friendly messages about everyday topics, including narratives and letters. They are to use appropriate vocabulary, grammatical structures and cohesive devices. Students who undertake the optional two-year higher level of secondary education ('Bachillerato') are to add to their repertoire argumentative texts and written projects such as newspapers, leaflets and questionnaires. Teachers usually employ a product-centered approach to writing, including insistence on grammatical accuracy (Chaudron *et al.*, 2005). According to Ordóñez de Celis (2005), writing is often reduced to a grammatical exercise involving manipulation of structures in support of the TL or oral practice; rarely is it viewed as a creative process in which students can communicate personal information in an independent fashion.

Teacher education in Spain

Most secondary EFL teachers in Spain are native Spaniards with little or no training in teaching writing. In response to the addition of a communicative FL writing task to the university entrance exam, secondary teachers have become aware of a need to change their classroom treatment of FL writing to better prepare students for this task (Ordóñez de Celis, 2005). However, this presents significant challenges because of the lack of teacher education for EFL writing. Martín Úriz and Whittaker (2005), however, describe an example of the application of writing as a communicative process in secondary classrooms that was part of a collaborative study of secondary-level EFL writing undertaken by university investigators and secondary teachers. They describe ways in which limited experimentation with aspects of process approaches to writing instruction has begun at this level.

Discussion

These six contexts encompass a range of purposes and values regarding FL writing instruction. In China, Poland and Spain, FL writing is taught for instrumental reasons, as a means of upgrading students' overall FL proficiency in order to help them better compete for employment and higher education opportunities on an international level. Whether or not students have specific needs for FL writing *per se*, writing is used as a means of reinforcing overall TL skills, especially grammatical structures and vocabulary. In China, Poland and Spain, governmental initiatives to increase citizens' FL skills have led to the addition of a written FL portion on important standardized exams, producing a washback effect of an increased emphasis on writing in FL classrooms (see Leki [2001] for a discussion of the potential negative consequences of such testing.)

In some contexts, local educational values, including those emphasized in L1 writing instruction, have a significant impact on FL writing instruction. This is true, for example, in the USA, where L1 (English) process writing pedagogies have influenced FL writing instruction, and in Germany, where an emphasis in L1 (German) writing instruction on critical thinking and cultural literacy has impacted EFL writing instruction.

Many other factors have also impacted on FL writing instruction in these six contexts. Some of the most salient include the historical role of the FL and FL teaching in each context, which often correlates with learners' general level of overall FL proficiency – which, in turn, can affect how EFL writing is taught. Large class sizes and overloaded teachers also impact writing pedagogy significantly because these factors can make it difficult to employ various aspects of process approaches to writing (if desired) and can make it almost impossible for instructors to provide individualized attention to students' writing. At the university level, another influential factor concerns whether or not students are pursuing a degree in English. FL writing instruction for TL majors is typically more intense, and instructors have higher expectations for them than they do for nonmajors. The training that teachers have received in FL writing instruction also impacts how FL writing is taught. Teachers with little preparation in teaching FL writing may minimize FL writing instruction or focus primarily on grammatical form, while teachers who have learned about FL writing methods in English-dominant countries or programs may attempt to impose them in other contexts, perhaps inappropriately, or may struggle with whether doing so is realistic or desirable (Casanave, this volume).

Considerations for the Future of FL Writing Instruction

While the contexts described in this chapter differ in many respects, each provides evidence of the significant ways in which local contextual factors shape FL writing instruction. FL writing specialists, curriculum developers and language planners should consider the specifics of their particular contexts in making decisions about writing instruction. I would like to propose the following questions about FL writing instruction for decision-makers to reflect upon:

(1) What are appropriate purposes for classroom-based FL writing, given the particular setting? Possible purposes include the following, among others: reinforcing the TL; preparing students for exams; learning to write for future employment; writing to learn about cultural and political issues, especially of TL-dominant countries; and learning the rhetoric(s) associated with the TL. Decision-makers should examine these purposes critically, weighing what is to be gained and lost by emphasizing each. And, of particular importance, as Leki (2001) points out, decision-makers should consider what students' own purposes for FL writing might be.

(2) What should be the role of local educational values, practices and rhetorics? Should FL writing instruction draw on the practices of local L1 writing pedagogies, L2 writing pedagogies, or both – and in what proportion? Should Western rhetorics be emphasized, even if they displace local rhetorics? Should decision-makers encourage pedagogical practices of English-dominant countries, such as process approaches, even in contexts where local conditions such as large class sizes and heavy teacher workloads may make such practices unrealistically burdensome for teachers?

(3) If standardized FL exams include written portions, what are the consequences for the curriculum and for students, and are these consequences justified? As Leki (2001) points out, decision-makers need to carefully consider the outcomes of devoting resources to writing instruction, especially if doing so detracts from other aspects of the FL curriculum. Additionally, decision-makers must consider the consequences to students, for whom poor performance on such exams might have serious life consequences.

(4) How should L2 teacher education programs more adequately prepare their students for grappling with the local factors that shape EFL writing instruction around the world (See Casanave, in this volume)?

It is hoped that with these considerations in mind, decision-makers can develop locally appropriate practices regarding FL writing instruction.

References

Berns, M. (1992) Sociolinguistics and the teaching of English in Europe beyond the 1990s. *World Englishes* 11, 3–14.

Bliesener, U. (1988) Foreign language teaching in Germany. *Bildung und Wissenschaftt* 4, 2–32. (ERIC Document Reproduction Service No. ED436098).

Braine, G. (2001) A study of English as a foreign language (EFL) writers on a local-area network (LAN) and in traditional classes. *Computers and Composition* 18, 275–292.

Bräuer, G. (1997) Schreiben im Fremdsprachenunterricht? *Die Unterrichtspraxis: Teaching German* 30, 1–7.

British Council (1980) *English Language Teaching Profile: Spain.* London: English Language and Literature Division.

British Council (1985) *English Language Teaching Profile: Spain.* London: English Language and Literature Division.

Chaudron, C., Martín Uriz, A. and Whittaker, R. (2005) Innovación pedagógica: Los centros, los alumnus y los profesores. In A. Martín Uriz and R. Whittaker (eds) *La Composición como Comunicación: Una Experiencia en las Aulas de Lengua Inglesa en Bachillerato* (pp. 41–60). Madrid: Universidad Autónoma de Madrid.

Conroy, P. (2004) E-mail or blackboard: Teaching advanced French composition. *The French Review* 77, 550–559.
Cummings, M.C. (2004) "Because we are shy and fear mistaking": Computer mediated communication with EFL writers. *Journal of Basic Writing* 23, 23–48.
Dyer, B. and Friederich, L. (2002) The personal narrative as cultural artifact: Teaching autobiography in Japan. *Written Communication* 19, 265–296.
Ellis, R. and Yuan, F. (2004) The effects of planning on fluency, complexity, and accuracy in second language narrative writing. *SSLA* 26, 59–84.
EUROPA. Foreign language skills in the European Union. On WWW at http://europa.eu.int/comm/education/policies/lang/languages/index_en.html. Accessed 11.10.04.
Ferris, D. and Hedgcock, J. (2005) *Teaching ESL Composition: Purpose, Process, and Practice.* Mahwah, NJ: Lawrence Erlbaum.
French, G. (2005) The cline of errors in the writing of Japanese university students. *World Englishes* 24, 371–382.
Hadley, A.O. (2001) *Teaching Language in Context*. Boston, MA: Heinle & Heinle.
Heffernan, N. (2006) An integrated approach to teaching academic writing. On WWW at www.asian-efl-journal.com/Sept_06_nh.php. Accessed 27.2.07.
Hirose, K. (2001) Realizing a giant first step toward improved English writing: A case in a Japanese university. In I. Leki (ed.) *Academic Writing Programs* (pp. 35–46). Alexandria, VA: TESOL.
Hirose, K. (2003) Comparing L1 and L2 organizational patterns in the argumentative writing of Japanese EFL students. *Journal of Second Language Writing* 12, 181–209.
Hyde, B. (2002) Japan's emblematic English. *English Today* 71 (18), 12–16.
Kern, R. (2004) Literacy and advanced foreign language learning: Rethinking the curriculum. In H. Byrnes and H.H. Maxim (eds) *Advanced Foreign Language Learning: A Challenge to College Programs* (pp. 2–18). Boston, MA: Heinle & Heinle.
Kimura, K. and Konda, M. (2002) Effective writing instruction: From Japanese *danraku* to English paragraphs. *The interface between interlanguage, pragmatics and assessment: Proceedings of the Third Annual JALT Pan-SIG conference.* On WWW at http://jalt.org/pansig/2004/HTML/KimKon.htm. Accessed 27.2.07.
Kobayashi, H. and Rinnert, C. (2002) High school student perceptions of first language literacy instruction: Implications for second language writing. *Journal of Second Language Writing* 11, 91–116.
Lee, J.F. and VanPatten, B. (2003) *Making Communicative Language Teaching Happen.* Boston, MA: McGraw Hill.
Leki, I. (2001) Material, educational, and ideological challenges of teaching EFL writing at the turn of the century. *International Journal of English Studies* 1, 197–209.
Lekki, P. (2003) Watch your language. *The Warsaw Voice*, 10. On WWW at http://www.warsawvoice.pl/view/2875. Accessed 5.8.04.
Li, Y. (2007) Apprentice scholarly writing in a community of practice: An intraview of an NNES graduate student writing a research article. *TESOL Quarterly* 41, 55–79.
Liu, M. and Braine, G. (2005) Cohesive features in argumentative writing produced by Chinese undergraduates. *System* 33, 623–636.

Martín Úriz, A. and Whittaker, R. (eds) (2005) *La Composición como Comunicación: Una Experiencia en las Aules de Langua Inglesa en Bachillerato*. Madrid: Universidad Autónoma de Madrid.
Ministerium für Bildung, Wissenshaft, Forschung und Kultur des Landes Schleswig-Holstein. (2002) *Englisch* Kiel: *Lehrplan für die Sekundarstufe II: Gymnasium, Gesamtschule, Fachgymnasium*.
Ordóñez de Celis, L. (2005) Aplicación de conceptos teóricos de proceso you retórica a la enseñanza de la composición en bachillerato: Un ejemplo. In A. Martín Uriz, and R. Whittaker (eds) *La Composición como Comunicación: Una Experiencia en las Aulas de Langua Inglesa en Bachillerato* (pp. 155–168). Madrid: Universidad Autónoma de Madrid.
Ordway, H. (1997) Teaching English as a foreign language in Spain at the high school level. MA thesis, University of North Carolina at Chapel Hill.
Peñate Cabrera, M. and Bazo, P. (2002) Teaching the four skills in the primary EFL classroom. *The Internet TESL Journal* 8 (12). On WWW at http://iteslj.org.
Peyton, J.K. and Reed, L. (1990) *Dialogue Journal Writing with Nonnative English Speakers: A Handbook for Teachers.* Alexandria, VA: TESOL.
Pooser, C. (2004) Bringing the web to the foreign language writing class. *French Review* 78, 94–102.
Reichelt, M. (1997a) An investigation of first language and second language (English) composition theory and pedagogy at the secondary level in Germany. PhD Thesis, Purdue University.
Reichelt, M. (1997b) L2 writing instruction at the German 'Gymnasium': A 13th-grade English class writes the 'Abitur'. *Journal of Second Language Writing* 6, 265–291.
Reichelt, M. (1999a) A cross-cultural perspective on writing curricula. *International Education* 29, 16–42.
Reichelt, M. (1999b) Toward a more comprehensive view of L2 writing: Foreign language writing in the U.S. *Journal of Second Language Writing* 8, 181–204.
Reichelt, M. (2001) A critical review of research on FL writing classroom practices. *Modern Language Journal* 85, 578–598.
Reichelt, M. (2003) Defining "good writing": A cross-cultural perspective. *Composition Studies* 31, 99–126.
Reichelt, M. (2005a) English in Poland. *World Englishes* 24, 217–225.
Reichelt, M. (2005b) WAC practices at the secondary level in Germany. *The WAC Journal* 16, 89–100.
Reichelt, M. (2006) English language writing instruction in Poland. *Journal of Second Language Writing* 14, 215–232.
Reichelt, M. and Bryant, K. (2001) Writing in a second-year German class. *Foreign Language Annals* 34, 235–243.
Sapp, D.A. (2001) Globalization and "just" pedagogy: A description, interpretation, and critique of English composition pedagogy in China, Brazil, and Spain. PhD Thesis, New Mexico State University.
Schulz, R. (2000) Foreign language teacher development: MLJ perspectives—1916–1999. *Modern Language Journal* 84, 495–522.
Trokeloshvili, D. and Jost, N. (1997) The internet and foreign language instruction: Practice and discussion. *The Internet TESL Journal* 3 (8).
Varney, M. (1984) Poland: Another kind of hunger. *The Incorporated Linguist* 23, 155.

Victori, M. (1999) An analysis of writing knowledge in EFL composing: A case study of two effective and two less effective writers. *System* 27, 537–555.

Wang, W. and Wen, Q. (2002) L1 use in the L2 composing process: An exploratory study of 16 Chinese EFL writers. *Journal of Second Language Writing* 11, 225–246.

Xiao, M.K. (2001) The writing assistance programme: A writing center with Hong Kong characteristics. In Leki, L. (ed.) *Academic Writing Programs* (pp. 7–19). Alexandria, VA: TESOL.

Yang, M., Badger, R. and Yu, Z. (2006) A comparative study of peer and teacher feedback in a Chinese EFL writing class. *Journal of Second Language Writing* 15, 179–200.

You, X. (2004) "The choice made from no choice": English writing instruction in a Chinese university. *Journal of Second Language Writing* 13, 97–110.

You, X. (2005) Writing in the "devil's" tongue: A history of English writing instruction in Chinese colleges, 1862–2004. PhD dissertation, Purdue University.

Part 2

Looking Ahead. Issues in Theory, Research and Pedagogy

Chapter 8

The Contribution of Studies of Foreign Language Writing to Research, Theories and Policies

ALISTER CUMMING

Looking Back Three Decades

Two landmark studies in the history of applied linguistics, and indeed of educational research at large, were the comparative surveys of foreign language teaching and learning in schools coordinated by Carroll (1975) of French in eight countries and by Lewis and Massad (1975) of English in ten countries under the auspices of the International Association for the Evaluation of Educational Achievement (IEA). Teaching and learning a foreign language was touted to represent an exemplary instance of the direct impact of education on students' achievement in schools. Moreover, the researchers claimed to have 'proved' this point: their empirical results produced an almost perfect correlation between the time students in secondary schools spent studying a foreign language and their achievements on standard proficiency tests (Carroll, 1975; Walker, 1976). Instructional inputs through classroom teaching were said to neatly demonstrate the results of 'school effects' for foreign language education because – unlike other school subjects such as math, science or history – diverse knowledge sources or experiences in students' lives outside of classrooms did not, it was presumed, greatly influence students' learning of a foreign language. For foreign language education, teaching *inputs* corresponded directly to student *outputs* according to the time spent teaching and studying.

This conclusion led to policy recommendations, particularly to extend the time that students spend studying a foreign language in schools: more teaching time should, in principle, produce greater achievement among students. Moreover, sufficient time is required to learn a foreign language: The research evidence showed that 'relatively brief exposure to a foreign language given by non-intensive instruction over, say, a 2-year period, is relatively ineffective' (Carroll, 1977: 2). In turn, this time factor was paramount, overriding differences in the ages at which students began to study the foreign language: 'In neither the English or French study was there any clear evidence that it made a difference when a student started a foreign language, as long as the time devoted to it was held constant' (Carroll, 1977: 2).

However, the simple equation of *teaching input X time = achievement* proved to have added complexities, which surfaced as researchers began to inspect local educational and societal circumstances. Wolf (1977), for instance, analyzed data from Carroll's (1975) study for the USA, observing that the population of secondary school students of French consisted, not of a representation of American adolescents at large, but rather of a small, economically elite, mostly female population, almost entirely in academic streams (cf. Carroll, 1975: 142–143). The achievements of this subpopulation should, indeed, correlate to their time studying French because they were the academically successful subsection of the US school system (i.e. not representing vocational streams, lower socioeconomic classes, rural settings or school leavers). Lewis and Massad (1975: 53–55) acknowledged difficulties they had in establishing samples of student populations nationally because the extent of English studies varied by program types in many countries, and educators in some countries, such as Germany and Hungary, were reorganizing their school systems at the time of the survey. Moreover, the sociolinguistic variations in English achievement failed to produce the neat correlations that had appeared for Carroll's companion study of French. Ferencich (1980) demonstrated there were distinct regional differences within Italy in respect of students' attitudes toward and achievements in learning English. Husén (1977: 137) argued that students in such countries as Sweden and the Netherlands were able to make distinctive achievements in foreign language learning in part from their exposure to 'dominant international languages by TV, movies, travel, and other personal contacts'.

As educators began to act on these policy implications, further complexities appeared. In the UK, innovations to introduce French instruction in elementary schools encountered institutional and attitudinal barriers (related to unprepared or resistant teachers, lack of pedagogical and organizational resources, and social attitudes), and research indicated that older students were more efficient language learners than younger students – all leading to the abandonment of this innovation (Burstall *et al.*, 1974). Some educators also wondered if the then popular audiolingual pedagogy for foreign language education might be constraining students' learning to a limited set of (primarily oral and grammatical) language behaviors that were being uniformly evaluated, to produce correlations between instructional time and oral proficiency, but not adequately accounting for students' literacy development (Elley, 1991; Elley & Mangubhai, 1983). Concerns for the quality, in addition to the quantity, of foreign language instruction likewise spawned innovations such as immersion and other forms of content-based language teaching in Canada and elsewhere (Genesee, 1987; Swain & Lapkin, 1982). Stern (1983), while acknowledging the importance of time factors, charted a considerably more complex model of the various policy, institutional, resource and sociolinguistic factors that influence foreign language education and students' achievement.

Looking Here and Now

It is not just that, 30 years later, the focus of research on foreign language education and the situations of international communication have changed dramatically. What the chapters in the present book make clear is that the understandings we have of these matters now are that they are considerably more complex, extensive and nuanced, particularly for writing in foreign languages, than educators presumed at the start of the 1970s. Contributors to the present volume share the same concerns to relate empirical evidence, theoretical conceptualizations and educational policies as inspired John Carroll and his colleagues in their studies of foreign language education over 30 years ago. The research presented in Part 1 of this book is equally and impressively programmatic, as well. Four themes predominate in these seven chapters, echoing much of the other recent literature on second language writing. These themes assert the distinctiveness, importance and variability of: (1) foreign language education, (2) writing in English, (3) relations between micro- and macroprocesses and (4) reflexivity about research processes.

Distinctiveness of foreign language education

Foreign language education remains the situation, par excellence, to examine the effects of instruction and curricula on learning to write an additional language and to identify the pathways and trajectories of students' writing development in a second language. As Carroll and his IEA colleagues argued in the 1970s, learning in foreign language education programs can be presumed to arise mainly from the impact of instruction rather than from the many personal, home, community and societal factors that influence literacy development in the mother tongue or students' learning of most other school subjects. Opportunities to use and learn an additional language are, by definition in foreign language education, restricted to instructional contexts, as Ortega's review of studies of writing (this volume) attests. Student learner groups in foreign language education mostly have homogenous language and cultural backgrounds because they tend to be the majority population in a particular country and to be mainly in academic rather than vocational streams of education. As a result, they tend to possess similar (though often limited) attitudes toward, experiences with and aspirations for future uses of the foreign language.

In contrast are situations of so-called second language education, where students acquire the additional language in social contexts where that language is widely used outside of formal classroom instruction, for example, as the primary medium of communication in academic courses, at work and while interacting in the society at large. This is the case for visiting international students pursuing higher education degrees overseas, recent immigrants or in study- or work-abroad experiences. Second language education is characterized by diverse learner populations, often with mixtures of first languages and previous educational backgrounds as well as differing status, mobility and intergroup relations in respect to the majority language they are learning.

Silva and Brice (2004: 79–80) have documented how the frequency of research publications about writing in foreign language contexts has accelerated greatly over the past decade. The chapters in the present volume attest distinctively to this trend. Silva and Brice also observe the persistence of certain groups of researchers to pursue a long-term focus on foreign language writing, reflecting the inherent value of this research focus as well as the interests of educators, learners and populations at large in their home countries (e.g. Japan, Spain, China or the Netherlands). In this book, the work of these researchers features prominently.

In contrast, the vast majority of research on writing in additional languages that has burgeoned over the past 30 years has mainly involved learning and performance in second, rather than foreign language education (Grabe & Kaplan, 1996; Leki *et al.*, 2008; Matsuda, 2003). As a consequence, the main findings from this research are inextricably intermeshed with the complex and diverse sociocultural factors associated with learning and writing in second language settings. For this reason, it is difficult to establish precisely what the fundamental characteristics of second language writing are (notably, in contrast to the less complex situations of foreign language writing). Cumming and Riazi (2000), for example, concluded that their efforts to trace the effects of background, instructional and studial factors on the writing achievement of learners in one ESL university program in Canada were thwarted by the sheer variation in the learners' first languages, previous educational experiences and current learning styles and purposes.

Leki *et al.* (2008) have proposed that cultural factors figure so prominently in the research on second language writing that the social contexts of education constitute a fundamental basis for synthesizing this inquiry (i.e. by learners' age groups, types or levels of academic degree programs, and settlement, work or professional settings). The complexity of these sociolinguistic factors is evident in Hornberger's (2003) model of the many dimensions or continua on which literacy development in additional languages varies around the world. These variables relate, for example, to the differing status and uses of first and second languages in local contexts, the points in individuals' lives when they acquire literacy in first and in second languages, the extent to which people fully acquire either literacy or additional languages, and the formal characteristics of both (first and second) languages, their respective scripts and their similarity or differences between each other. Heath (1983) provided compelling evidence to demonstrate how literacy practices can vary extensively even between adjoining neighborhoods, according to such factors as race and social class, within the same language (English) and the same town (in the USA). Even more complex and varied (but much less well studied) are situations of learning to write in heritage or ancestral languages. For instance, the acquisition of bilingualism and written literacy among learners with backgrounds in Spanish or Indigenous languages in North or South America is complicated enormously by differences in learner populations, the language varieties and their vitality that prevail in local contexts, as well as their symbolic and cultural status (Hornberger, 2003; Ricento & Burnaby, 1998; Spener, 1994).

If the perception has remained intact of foreign language education as an enterprise primarily realized through classroom instruction (rather than arising from the many sociolinguistic variables that influence second or ancestral language and literacy development), what has changed over the past three decades is its image of consistency or universality. This shift in perspective follows from understanding the variability in second language writing (described in the previous paragraphs). But it has also arisen progressively from the understandings about writing in foreign language contexts established through the several long-term programs of research reported in the present book.

In the present volume, Reichelt analyzes writing in foreign language education within the sociohistorical contexts of six particular countries, showing how each has unique traditions of pedagogy and teacher education. Few assumptions are made about commonalities across these dimensions internationally, as had guided the research of Carroll (1975) or Lewis and Massad (1975). In turn, the present chapters by Rinnert and Kobayashi, by Sasaki and by Casanave focus on variation among learners of English in Japan – often assumed to be a prime example of homogeneity in student groups and conformity in a national educational system. These chapters, however, each demonstrate how Japanese students' differing experiences learning and using English (e.g. in classrooms or by sojourning or residing overseas), development of literacy in their mother tongue, and extent and quality of instruction all combine to produce varying attitudes, situations for teaching and teacher education, and stages of foreign language writing abilities, motivation as well as attrition.

Flowerdew and Li's research has started from the assumption that English, far from being a foreign language in Hong Kong, fulfills a major diglossic role in higher education and work throughout Hong Kong and, increasingly, in China, extending as well to professional, institutional and business networks that span the world. These situations impact distinctly on learners' attitudes and abilities as well as the future situations of work and academic study for which education needs to prepare them, particularly in respect to writing for academic and professional purposes. In turn, Celaya and Navés offer analyses of student populations who, while learning English as a foreign language, are already bilingual in Spanish and Catalan – realizing the European policy aim of plurilingualism (rather than simply bilingualism, cf. Council of Europe, 2001) or the realistic goal of attaining multicompetence (Cook, 2003) – yet who differ in their ages of starting foreign language instruction. The present chapters by Manchón, Roca de Larios and Murphy and by Schoonen, Snellings, Stevenson and van Gelderen also demonstrate how students' attentional and linguistic resources for composing develop as they acquire proficiency in the foreign language, displaying differences in qualities of ability in addition to strictly linear progressions in achievement (as Carroll's 1975 results had implied).

As these examples indicate, there are numerous sources of variation in foreign language education, writing processes and texts, and qualities of achievement and ability. These variations exist not only between but also within countries, student populations, educational systems, text types, language varieties and societal circumstances, as has been emphasized in policy-oriented analyses of language education around the world (Dickson & Cumming, 1996; Hornberger, 2003; Kaplan & Baldauf, 1997). The status of certain languages taught and learned in schools might now be better termed 'lingua franca' than 'foreign' in view of the uses of, for example, English, French, German, Japanese, Russian, Spanish, Chinese or Arabic as media for international communications, business relations, pop culture or religious affiliations (McGroarty, 2006). One striking aspect of the present book is the extent to which all chapters (with the exception of sections of Reichelt's chapter concerning the USA) focus on English as the so-called foreign language of instruction.

Writing in English

Chapters in the present book reflect two major, interrelated changes in education internationally over the past few decades: the global spread of English and the increasing prominence and value of written communications. English is, by far, the most extensively studied foreign language in education around the world, though eight or nine other international or lingua franca languages (listed above) are also widely taught and used in many countries, each related to postcolonial influences as well as current economic or labor opportunities (Dickson & Cumming, 1996; McGroarty, 2006). Cummins and Davison's recent, two-volume *International Handbook of English Language Teaching* (2007) analyzes the many forces, issues and implications related to the global spread of English and its continuing increase as both a subject and medium of education and of communications in business, technology and research.

Along with the increasing prominence of English has been a corresponding expansion in expectations for and about writing in foreign language education. Carroll's (1975, 1978) research required students to produce written compositions in French: 'to write a short composition comparing the merits of living in the country and in a big city', following several prompted phrases. But Carroll's examinees were only asked to compose for 10 minutes, and their resulting compositions were evaluated for the quantity of clauses they produced as well as their grammatical and lexical correctness. Since the 1980s, the burgeoning research on mother tongue and second language writing has greatly expanded professional knowledge about writing abilities. These expanded definitions of the construct of writing have, in turn, increased the standards for students' performance and achievements in writing as well as the scope and nature of methods for assessing writing abilities.

Notably, Purves and colleagues' (1992) comparative study of writing in secondary schools in 14 countries demonstrated that valid assessments of mother tongue writing require students to display their abilities to compose extended texts in several different genres (e.g. narrative, description, argumentation), each of which need to be evaluated holistically and quantitatively on numerous analytic dimensions. Moreover, Purves and colleagues (1984, 1992) determined that the criteria for effective writing vary inherently by languages and the norms of education in each country, and so require that panels of expert writing educators in each country establish unique, national norms. As Flowerdew and Li observe in the present book, along with the globalization of uses of English writing around the world are accompanying trends to promote the localization of literacy standards, language varieties and writing practices within specific regions or cultural or professional groups.

Around the same time, in the 1980s and 1990s, the tests for screening the English proficiency of the increasing flow of international applicants to English-medium universities in North America, the UK, Australia and New Zealand (i.e. Test of English as a foreign language [TOEFL], Michigan, International English language testing system [IELTS] and various Cambridge exams) began to add writing components. These involved writing extended compositions scored on sophisticated holistic rating schemes, above and beyond existing assessments of reading and listening comprehension as well as grammar and vocabulary knowledge in these tests (Cumming, 1997, 2007; Spolsky, 1995; Weigle, 2002). By the 1990s, effective writing in English – indeed, writing in any language and in foreign language proficiency overall – was conceived to involve mastery of high skill levels in complementary, literate processes of linguistic, cognitive, rhetorical and social construction (Cumming, 1998). A distinctive point of contrast is to compare (a) Rivers' (1968) influential view of writing as an add-on skill, suitable only for the most advanced learners of a foreign language who had mastered the fundamentals of oral communication, grammar and vocabulary with (b) the considerably expanded view of writing as a multifaceted rhetorical, cognitive and social construct promoted in recent chapters in Uso-Juan and Martinez-Flor (2006). In the 2000s, writing remains one of four language 'skills' for the purposes of foreign language teaching, learning and assessment (as it was for Carroll, 1975 or Rivers, 1968), but the scope, substance and significance of writing have now expanded greatly (Cumming, 1997; Kunnan, 2008). Simply, learning to write in a foreign language, particularly English, is more important and consequential for academic study, work and professional communications than it was 30 years ago.

Micro and macro components and processes

As with other studies of writing (conducted primarily in first or second language contexts), the studies in the present book show how foreign language writing in English consists of multiple components and processes. Foreign language writing may represent one set of skills, distinct from reading, listening or speaking as they are commonly considered in curricula and assessments. But the dimensions of this 'skill' entail numerous micro and macro components and processes that complement and interact with one another at multiple levels of texts, language systems, individual writers, and educational and social contexts. Understanding these elements and their relations points toward what might need to be learned to acquire writing abilities in a foreign language.

At a microlevel are the linguistic elements, text forms, attitudes and thinking processes that a person must acquire and learn to control to produce written texts in a foreign language. Most of the chapters in this book address these microaspects of text production and skill acquisition for students at schools or universities, though the respective authors have approached their inquiries from differing perspectives, each yielding unique viewpoints on phenomena of foreign language writing and learning. At a macrolevel are educational and professional policies (both nationally and institutionally), the resources and standards applied to implement these policies (such as teacher education, curricula and instructional materials, pedagogical practices, or requirements to publish or report on work in writing), norms for written genres of established discourse communities, and international trends such as the increasing spread and local diversification of lingua franca languages like English.

The upshot of this inquiry into micro- and macroprocesses is an appreciation of the differing levels of variability associated with foreign language writing. In respect to individual development, the present research affirms Cook's (2007) argument that bilinguals should be thought of as multicompetent users of two (or many) languages, and expected to attain variable levels of writing proficiency in foreign languages rather than compared to monolingual norms. In turn, contributing to individual variation are differences in the educational policies and the resources and contacts for foreign language writing, which differ across nations, levels and systems of education, as well as subcultures within them. Further, in respect to global discourses, are changing uses of and expectations for foreign language writing associated with the increasing dominance of a few lingua franca languages as well as the countervailing establishment of local norms regionally in professional, academic and technical communications.

Rinnert and Kobayashi recount how they began their studies with a focus on the influences of first language writing on second language writing, attending particularly to evidence of these influences in Japanese students' written texts in English. Their approach follows from theories about, and much other empirical inquiry into, the genres of second language writing (Connor, 1996; Hyland, 2004; Johns, 1997; Swales, 1990), extending Kaplan's (1966) observations about contrastive rhetoric and Cummins' (1984) hypotheses about the cross-linguistic transfer of cognitive-academic skills. Rinnert and Kobayashi's unique contribution, however, has been to explore and demonstrate how the educational experiences of Japanese students have, both in writing in English and in Japanese, influenced their rhetorical choices and tendencies in both languages. Their chapter concludes that first language influences prevail at the beginning stages of learning to write in a foreign language whereas writers with advanced skills in foreign language writing tend to transfer the rhetorical repertoires they have acquired in the foreign language (English) back onto their writing in their first language (Japanese). Transfer in foreign language writing is bidirectional and results in variable multicompetences, not static abilities in either first or second languages.

Sasaki takes up similar microlevel issues about composing processes, educational and writing experiences, and writing abilities among Japanese learners of English, but she does so from the vantage point of longitudinal interview data, extending the findings from her previous studies into the factors that contribute to foreign language writing abilities. Here, Sasaki adopts sociocognitive and sociocultural theories (e.g. Cumming, 2006; Lantolf & Thorne, 2006) to explain the influences of writing and language experiences on Japanese students' motivation and English writing abilities. Sasaki concludes that extended experiences living and studying in foreign language contexts positively influence students' motivations to improve their writing in the foreign language. In turn, motivation to improve one's writing in a foreign language may not be feasible or profound for students who do not have such intensive experiences of language contact and the resulting opportunities to construct imagined communities or audiences for their writing. The implication of this difference is that it may explain why students in truly foreign language situations may not be motivated to develop high levels of writing ability in a foreign language unless they have had personally meaningful experiences in a society that uses that language.

Manchón, Roca de Larios and Murphy explain how their research has focused on the time, attention and language resources that students in Spain (at differing levels of English proficiency and, correspondingly, different ages) use while planning, formulating and revising their texts as they compose in English and in Spanish. The researchers observe that writing in the foreign language is considerably more demanding of cognitive resources than writing in the mother tongue, particularly in searching for and verifying lexical choices. But, as people gain proficiency in the foreign language, have greater experiences writing, and mature, they learn to plan and revise their writing more extensively (rather than simply to compose by sequentially formulating ideas then writing them down), to direct their thinking toward improving the quality of their writing (rather than simply to compensate for problems as they encounter them), and to balance and diversify the control that they have over strategic uses of their first and second language resources (rather than simply to think in the first language then translate into the second). These results confirm and extend findings from other studies that have closely examined the thinking processes, language switching and ability differences among people writing in both their first and second languages (cf. Cumming, 1990; Qi, 1998; Wang, 2003; Whalen & Menard, 1995; Woodall, 2002).

The chapter by Schoonen, Snellings, Stevenson and van Gelderen documents how they have sought to define the linguistic skills and the cognitive dimensions of writing abilities and composing processes through a set of unique, complementary studies over the past decade with adolescent Dutch students writing in English as a foreign language. Schoonen *et al.* draw on cognitive models of composing, such as Hayes (1996) and Bereiter and Scardamalia (1987), as well as the psycholinguistic speech production model of Levelt (1989). Their results show that all relevant linguistic, literate and conceptual abilities contribute effectively to writing performance, but in the foreign language, attention to linguistic matters dominate (as Manchón, Roca de Larios and Murphy also conclude). This attention to language can inhibit conceptual performance while writing (or, as they demonstrate, experimentally, be facilitated through training to speed up retrieval of words in the foreign language). In addition to developing a holistic account of the factors that facilitate writing in a foreign language, an interesting by-product of these studies is a concern that different research or analytic methods produce different research results in this domain. For instance, different writing tasks can yield different results about the microprocesses of composing as do different units of analyses, such as frequencies of revision compared to episodes of processing time while revising.

The preceding chapters recount investigations into the microprocesses of foreign language writing and learning, embedded implicitly within the policy contexts of education in Japan, the Netherlands and Spain, respectively. In contrast, Celaya and Navés' chapter starts from a macrolevel of policy issues in foreign language education. They demonstrate how evidence about students' English language writing development can inform policy debates about the appropriate age to begin foreign language instruction in Spain. Their analyses are informed by (the often conflicting) results of previous psycholinguistic research on age factors in the development of bilingualism as well as measures of text features that have become conventional in studies of writing development. Celaya and Navés' findings hearken back to the conclusions of Carroll (1975, 1977) and Burstall *et al.* (1974). Interpretations recently made about the superiority of beginning early in second language contexts do not seem to hold for foreign language education because of differences in the quality and intensity of instruction in each type of educational context, uses of the additional language in school and other sociolinguistic contexts, and the skills and knowledge already acquired by older compared to younger students. Analyses of their written texts show that Catalonian students who begin English language study at an older age appear to be more efficient and effective writers of that foreign language compared to counterparts who started English language study at an earlier age.

The macrocomponents of educational policies assume the foreground of Reichelt's chapter. She describes and compares foreign language writing in Germany, Poland, the USA, China, Japan and Spain from the viewpoint of influential sociohistorical factors as well as traditions and common practices for pedagogy and teacher education, as she or others have observed them. In each country, the characteristics, resources and organization of these elements differ according to sociolinguistic, historical and economic factors as well as the relative importance of foreign languages, and thus foreign language writing, in educational policies and the respective societies. Where educational systems have recently placed greater emphasis on foreign language writing, particularly in English, trends are also evident toward national-level curricula, earlier starting ages for foreign language studies, and the transfer to or popularization in foreign language education of research and theories about writing and literacy in the mother tongue. There are also increasing emphases on pedagogies involving composing processes and realistic academic or communication tasks (in addition to more conventional text analysis and rhetorical models), intensification of programs for English majors in higher education and extensions of contacts with users of the foreign language, both within and outside of the local country.

Flowerdew and Li's chapter describes how, and helps to explain why, some of the macro- and microprocesses of foreign language writing interrelate through the ongoing interactions of practicing writers along their career paths, for their institutional roles and interests, and through their international networks. Focusing on the writing practices in English of mature scholars in China – rather than students in schools or universities (as in the previous chapters) – Flowerdew and Li broaden the perspective on the microprocesses of individual abilities in foreign language writing performance as well as the macroprocesses of national educational policies and practices. They appeal to theories at several levels. At the level of international sociology, Flowerdew and Li draw on theories of glocalization, the changing intersections of global and local interests, to observe that the demands of knowledge production and international competitiveness require scholars in countries such as China, while working at universities primarily in Chinese, to publish the results of their work in leading peer-reviewed journals in North America or Europe (Canagarajah, 2002, 2005; Graddol, 1999; Robertson, 1992). At the level of individual development, Flowerdew and Li's research addresses two complementary tendencies. One is the tendency of professional discourse communities to establish normative genres of writing, to which members who aspire to enter that discourse are expected to conform – in this instance, to adopt genre conventions of scientific writing in English (Berkenkotter & Huckin, 1995; Hyland, 2004; Johns, 1997). The second tendency is to conceive of learning to write in a foreign language, not through academic tasks in school, but as negotiated through processes of 'legitimate peripheral participation' situated in work-related tasks, in collaboration with, mentored through and scaffolded by successful peers, private tutors or hired editors, peer reviewers and journal or book editors (Flowerdew, 2000; Lave & Wegner, 1991).

Reflexivity about research

What I found most interesting about the present chapters are the authors' reflections on their long-term development of their programs of research. Inquiry in education seldom, if ever, involves a single, one-shot study that unambiguously resolves the issues that researchers have set out to address. More commonly, one study generates further questions, exposes new aspects on an issue or reveals interactions between elements. These, in turn, warrant and even spawn further inquiry. The initial seven chapters in this book, therefore, tell us as much about foreign language writing as they do about the efforts, achievements and challenges of doing research on this topic. Each author or group of collaborating authors have devoted up to a decade or more to investigating foreign language writing. As they look back on their own studies in these chapters, we receive unique insights from the researchers' reflective syntheses of their own progressive developments.

The authors all acknowledge that they progressively changed or adopted theoretical perspectives, analytic methods and/or data sources to understand better the objects of their inquiry. Sasaki, for instance, observes herself shifting to sociocognitive theories about motivation to more fully comprehend phenomena that she had previously analyzed as cognitive processes of composing and language proficiency. Celaya and Navés bring new views to a long-standing debate (about age effects on bilingualism) by contributing extensive data from written compositions, whereas previous studies had mostly limited their inquiry to spoken data or grammar assessments. Flowerdew and Li are most explicit about their long-term efforts to investigate a particular problem of multilingual writing through increasingly varied methodological, situational and theoretical analyses. Rinnert and Kobayashi as well as Schoonen, Snellings, Stevenson and van Gelderen recount devising an impressive series of new experimental-type studies and innovative analytic methods to account more fully for their developing understanding of key aspects of foreign language writing and the assessment of it. Manchón, Roca de Larios and Murphy, in turn, explain how they progressively and more intensively probed into different aspects of their data to understand key dimensions of them. Reichelt describes how her focus of inquiry expanded from studying situations in one or two countries to encompass and compare situations in other, related countries.

In the process of these reflections, a full array of research designs and analytic methods emerges. The resulting image is two-fold. First, diverse research approaches are complementary in helping to reveal multiple aspects of foreign language writing. Second, certain methods of inquiry are suited to investigate certain aspects of foreign language writing. For instance, cross-sectional research designs and within-subject analyses can reveal notable points of difference between proficiency groups, ages of learners and abilities across languages (Rinnert & Kobayashi; Celaya & Navés; Manchón, Roca de Larios and Murphy; Schoonen, Snellings, Stevenson and van Gelderen). Longitudinal designs and training studies can indicate how learning progresses (Sasaki; Schoonen *et al.*). Comparative analyses can show fundamental similarities and differences between situations (Reichelt). Mixed-methods approaches can build and confirm interpretations from a variety of perspectives, combining case studies, policy analyses, interviews, surveys, document analyses and observations (Flowerdew & Li). Foreign language writing can – indeed, needs to – be studied from multiple viewpoints, including composing processes, cognitive skills, linguistic knowledge, text and genre characteristics, attitudes and motivation, transfer, learning, development through the lifespan, curriculum policies and resources, teaching and assessment practices, sociolinguistic variation, intergroup relations, institutional organizations and communications systems.

Looking Forward to Future Directions

Where should inquiry into foreign language writing go from here? On the one hand, the present chapters themselves chart future trajectories. Individual research groups will surely continue their inquiries into foreign language writing for years to come. There is every reason to build on these accomplishments and to pursue them to further conclusions. Moreover, a collective trajectory is also now established, through the present volume, elucidating the multiple components of foreign language writing, each of which warrants further study as well as comprehensive and critical syntheses of their relations together.

On the other hand, the fundamental issues motivating past, recent and probably future research on foreign language writing remain akin to those that Carroll (1975) had taken up: what educational and societal variables positively influence achievement in foreign language writing? How do these vary by populations, educational systems and regions? What recommendations can be made to improve educational policies and instructional practices? The difference is that 30 years later – as Luke (2005) has argued for educational policy in general – new, multiple and diverse forms of evidence need to be considered and critically evaluated to establish educational policies. Moreover, this needs to be done uniquely in each local jurisdiction, because no universal policy could ever account for the diversity of elements that come into play in education, even for as seemingly pure a taught ability as foreign language writing, even in one language such as English.

If the purpose of inquiry into foreign language writing is to address these issues systematically in order to help improve local educational policies and conditions, what future directions might this inquiry usefully take? I see promise in three directions. First, the micro- and macrocomponents of foreign language writing need to be interrelated rather than conceived in isolation from each other. A second direction is to expand definitions of literacy, of which composition writing in a foreign language is but one component. A third direction concerns enhancing the pedagogical functions of writing assessment.

Consolidating the micro and the macro

Consolidating the micro- and macrocomponents of foreign language writing requires theories to link together their psycholinguistic and sociolinguistic dimensions as well as to explain the processes of learning and variability that account for individual and group change. As Schoonen, Snellings, Stevenson and van Gelderen propose, a 'blueprint' is gradually accumulating to describe the psycholinguistic components of individual abilities to write in a foreign language. At the same time, Reichelt shows – from a decidedly empirical and impressionistic, rather than theoretical, perspective – how education in foreign language writing differs by sociohistorical and policy conditions from country to country. To reconcile these polar perspectives, sociocultural theory (e.g. Lantolf & Thorne, 2006) offers a method to explain learning and the development of functional capacities to write in a foreign language. Capitalizing on this point, Sasaki draws on activity and goal theories to explain individual differences in students' motivation, as do Flowerdew and Li in addition to genre theory to explain writing development in professional contexts.

It is tempting to suggest that studies of foreign language writing should examine both psycholinguistic and sociolinguistic variables together. But cognizance of either dimension may be all that is feasible. It is difficult to conceive of even large-scale investigations that could realistically achieve this dual scope – without, for instance, greatly reducing the construct of writing and a foreign language to simple tests and questionnaires to survey representatively across countries, as Carroll (1975) did, or conversely, to focus indepth on just a few cases, as Flowerdew and Li or Sasaki have done, and thereby neglect issues of generalizability or breadth of scope. One research approach that links individual and sociohistorical variables is learner autobiographies or life histories, of which numerous precedents exist (Belcher & Connor, 2001; Braine, 1999; Pavlenko, 2007). The interview methods associated with this approach can also include text analyses, highlighting how personal, academic and professional writing marks status and ability as well as accessibility and identity (Gentil, 2005; Ivanic & Camps, 2000). The political dimensions of individual writing and mass education also warrant analysis, as Flowerdew and Li and Celaya and Navés have suggested in this volume, and are particularly evident for writing in postcolonial countries (Canagarajah, 2002, 2005; Ramanathan, 2004).

Expanding definitions of literacy

Writing is but one aspect of literate abilities, just as foreign languages are but one facet of communication or individual competencies. Future studies of foreign language writing need to expand their definitions of literacy and consider the situations of various languages other than English. Obvious directions to pursue are advocated in the new literacy studies (Cope & Kalantzis, 2000; Hamilton *et al.*, 1994; Street, 2005), multimedia communications and concepts of literate design (Cummins & Sayers, 1995; Kern, 2000; Kern & Warschauer, 2000) and cross-cultural analyses of standards for writing (Connor, 1996; Li, 1996). Students now, and surely in the future, will in addition to conventional school tasks, exchange text messages, create blogs, interact in chat sessions and mediate verbal and visual texts on the Internet. Relations need to be pursued, as well, between students' reading and writing in foreign languages, assuming that is where literate knowledge is situated, and thus develops (Albrechtsen *et al.*, 2008; Belcher & Hirvela, 2001; Carson & Leki, 2003; Grabe, 2003; Hirvela, 2004; Krashen, 1993; Lee, 2005).

Pedagogical functions of assessment

On the pedagogical front, educational policies for foreign language writing need to adopt new orientations to assessment, beyond the proficiency-based, testing approach that has dominated this domain internationally (Cumming, 1997; Kunnan, 2008). This is but one way to address the issues of motivation that presently constrain learning and teaching in this domain (Leki, 2003; Sasaki, this volume). One has only to consider the impoverished, error-dominated approaches to responding to students' writing, and their impact on students' writing in a foreign language, as described by Porte (1997), compared to the rich array of responding techniques catalogued by Ferris (2003) for comparable students in second language contexts. But as Rea-Dickins (2008) cautions, we are only now beginning to document and know how to guide the complex functions of formative assessment practices in language classrooms. Alderson (2005), elaborating on the European Union's DIALANG project, demonstrates the value of diagnostic and self-assessment approaches. Poehner and Lantolf (2005) argue for methods of dynamic assessment that link instruction directly to learning and writing improvement, as demonstrated in Aljaafreh and Lantolf (1994). Canagarajah (2006) appeals for standards of assessment that recognize international as well as local norms. Such reorientation also calls for teachers' professional development, a dimension which, as Reichelt and Casanave observe in the present book, has received little attention in respect to foreign language writing internationally (Clachar, 2000; Pennington *et al.*, 1996, 1997).

In conclusion, future inquiry into foreign language writing is bound and obliged to address three interfaces that have emerged from previous inquiry, and in the process, to expand current definitions of how foreign language writing develops, what it involves and how it should be taught and assessed. One interface is through theories that link individual, psychological variables and development to personal-historical, socio-structural and cross-cultural factors. A second interface is through expanded conceptualizations of literacy that link conventional school-based and academic tasks to new technologies, multimedia communications and diverse notions of literacy at work and in society. The third interface is through approaches that link assessment closely to pedagogy, promote the development of learners' self-awareness and abilities through the lifespan, and enhance teacher education, ongoing professional development and cross-cultural understanding.

References

Albrechtsen, D., Haastrup, K. and Henriksen, B. (2008) *Vocabulary and Writing in First and Second Languages: Processes and Development*. Houndmills, UK: Palgrave Macmillan.

Alderson, J.C. (2005) *Diagnosing Foreign Language Proficiency: The Interface between Learning and Assessment*. London: Continuum.

Aljaafreh, A. and Lantolf, J. (1994) Negative feedback as regulation and second language learning in the zone of proximal development. *Modern Language Journal* 78, 465–483.

Belcher, D. and Connor, U. (eds) (2001) *Reflections on Multiliterate Lives*. Clevedon: Multilingual Matters.

Belcher, D. and Hirvela, A. (eds) (2001) *Linking Literacies: Perspectives on L2 Reading-Writing Connections.* Ann Arbor, MI: University of Michigan Press.

Bereiter, C. and Scardamalia, M. (1987) *The Psychology of Written Composition*. Hillsdale, NJ: Lawrence Erlbaum.

Berkenkotter, C. and Huckin, T. (eds) (1995) *Genre Knowledge in Disciplinary Communication: Cognition/Culture/Power.* Hillsdale, NJ: Lawrence Erlbaum.

Braine, G. (ed.) (1999) *Non-native Educators in English Language Teaching*. Mahwah, NJ: Lawrence Erlbaum.

Burstall, C., Jamieson, M., Cohen, S. and Hargreaves, M. (1974) *Primary French in the Balance*. Windsor: National Foundation for Educational Research.

Canagarajah, S. (2002) *The Geopolitics of Academic Writing and Knowledge Production*. Pittsburgh, PA: University of Pittsburgh Press.

Canagarajah, S. (ed.) (2005) *Reclaiming the Local in Language Policy and Practice*. Mahwah, NJ: Lawrence Erlbaum.

Canagarajah, S. (2006) Changing communicative needs, revised assessment objectives: Testing English as an international language. *Language Assessment Quarterly* 3, 229–242.

Carroll, J.B. (1975) *The Teaching of French as a Foreign Language in Eight Countries*. New York: John Wiley and Sons.

Carroll, J.B. (1977) The IEA studies in English and French as foreign languages: Implications for educational planning. *Studies in Educational Evaluation* 3, 1–5.

Carson, J. and Leki, I. (eds) (1993) *Reading in the Composition Classroom*. Boston, MA: Heinle & Heinle.

Clachar, A. (2000) Opposition and accommodation: An examination of Turkish teachers' attitudes toward Western approaches to the teaching of writing. *Research in the Teaching of English* 35, 66–100.

Connor, U. (1996) *Contrastive Rhetoric: Cross-cultural Aspects of Second-language Writing*. New York: Cambridge University Press.

Cook, V.J. (ed.) (2003) *Effects of the L2 on the L1*. Clevedon: Multilingual Matters.

Cook, V.J. (2007) The goals of ELT: Reproducing native-speakers or promoting multicompetence among second language users? In J. Cummins and C. Davison (eds) *International Handbook of English Language Teaching* (pp. 237–248). New York. Springer.

Cope, B. and Kalantzis, M. (eds) (2000) *Multiliteracies: Literacy Learning and the Design of Social Futures*. London: Routledge.

Council of Europe (2001) *Common European Framework of Reference for Languages: Learning, Teaching, Assessment*. Cambridge, UK: Cambridge University Press.

Cumming, A. (1990) Metalinguistic and ideational thinking in second language composing. *Written Communication* 7, 482–511.

Cumming, A. (1997) The testing of second-language writing. In C. Clapham (ed.) *Language Assessment*, Vol. 7 of the *Encyclopedia of Language and Education* (pp. 51–63). Dordrecht: Kluwer.

Cumming, A. (1998) Theoretical perspectives on writing. *Annual Review of Applied Linguistics* 18, 61–78.

Cumming, A. (ed.) (2006) *Goals for Academic Writing: ESL Students and Their Instructors*. Amsterdam: John Benjamins.

Cumming, A. (2007) New directions in testing English proficiency for university entrance. In J. Cummins and C. Davison (eds) *International Handbook of English Language Teaching* (pp. 473–485). New York: Springer.

Cumming, A. and Riazi, A. (2000) Building models of adult second-language writing instruction. *Learning and Instruction* 10, 55–71.

Cummins, J. (1984) *Bilingualism and Special Education: Issues in Assessment and Pedagogy*. Clevedon: Multilingual Matters.

Cummins, J. and Davison, C. (eds) (2007) *International Handbook of English Language Teaching*. New York: Springer.

Cummins, J. and Sayers, D. (1995) *Brave New Schools: Challenging Cultural Illiteracy*. Toronto: OISE Press/University of Toronto Press.

Dickson, P. and Cumming, A. (eds) (1996) *Profiles of Language Education in 25 Countries*. Slough: National Foundation for Educational Research.

Elley, W. (1991) Acquiring literacy in a second language: The effect of book-based programs. *Language Learning* 41, 375–411.

Elley, W. and Manguhbahi, F. (1983) The impact of reading on second language learning. *Reading Research Quarterly* 19, 53–67.

Ferencich, M. (1980) English as a foreign language in Italy. *Studies in Educational Evaluation* 6, 53–55.

Ferris, D. (2003) *Response to Student Writing: Implications for Second Language Students*. Mahwah, NJ: Lawrence Erlbaum.

Flowerdew, J. (2000) Discourse community, legitimate peripheral participation, and nonnative-English-speaking scholars. *TESOL Quarterly* 34, 127–150.

Genesee, F. (1987) *Learning Through Two Languages: Studies of Immersion and Bilingual Education*. New York: Harper and Row.

Gentil, G. (2005) Commitments to academic biliteracy. Case studies of Francophone university writers. *Written Communication* 22, 421–471.

Grabe, W. (2003) Reading and writing relations: Second language perspectives on research and practice. In B. Kroll (ed.) *Exploring the Dynamics of Second Language Writing* (pp. 242–262). New York: Cambridge University Press.

Grabe, W. and Kaplan, W. (1996) *Theory and Practice of Writing: An Applied Linguistic Perspective*. Harlow: Longman.

Graddol, D. (1999) The decline of the native speaker. *AILA Review* 13, 57–68.

Hamilton, M., Barton, D. and Ivanic, R. (eds) (1994) *Worlds of Literacy*. Clevedon: Multilingual Matters.

Hayes, J.R. (1996) A new framework for understanding cognition and affect in writing. In C.M. Levy and S. Ransdell (eds) *The Science of Writing: Theories, Methods, Individual Differences and Applications* (pp. 1–27). Mahwah, NJ: Lawrence Erlbaum.

Heath, S.B. (1983) *Ways with Words: Language, Life, and Work in Communities and Classrooms*. New York: Cambridge University Press.

Hirvela, A. (2004) *Connecting Reading and Writing in Second Language Writing Instruction*. Ann Arbor, MI: University of Michigan Press.

Hornberger, N. (ed.) (2003) *Continua of Biliteracy: An Ecological Framework for Educational Policy, Research, and Practice in Multilingual Settings*. Clevedon: Multilingual Matters.

Husén, T. (1977) Policy implications of the IEA findings and some of their repercussions on national debates on educational policy. *Studies in Educational Evaluation* 3, 129–142.

Hyland, K. (2004) *Genre and Second Language Writing*. Ann Arbor, MI: University of Michigan Press.

Ivanic, R. and Camps, D. (2001) I am how I sound: Voice as self-representation in L2 writing. *Journal of Second Language Writing* 10, 3–33.

Johns, A. (1997) *Text, Role, and Context: Developing Academic Literacies*. New York: Cambridge University Press.

Kaplan, R. (1966) Cultural thought patterns in inter-cultural education. *Language Learning* 16, 1–20.

Kaplan, R. and Baldauf, R. (1997) *Language Planning: From Practice to Theory.* Clevedon: Multilingual Matters.

Kern, R. (2000) *Literacy and Language Teaching*. Oxford: Oxford University Press.

Kern, R. and Warschauer, M. (eds) (2000) *Network-based Language Teaching: Concepts and Practice.* New York: Cambridge University Press.

Krashen, S. (1993) *The Power of Reading*. Englewood, CO: Libraries Unlimited.

Kunnan, A. (2008) Large scale language assessments. In E. Shohamy (volume ed.) and N. Hornberger (series ed.) *Encyclopedia of Language and Education* (2nd edn), Volume 7, *Language Testing and Assessment* (pp. 135–155). New York: Springer.Lantolf, J. and Thorne, S. (2006) *Sociocultural Theory and the Genesis of Second Language Development*. Oxford: Oxford University Press.

Lave, J. and Wenger, E. (1991) *Situated Learning: Legitimate Peripheral Participation.* Cambridge: Cambridge University Press.

Lee, S-Y. (2005) Facilitating and inhibiting factors in English as a foreign language writing performance: A model testing with structural equation modeling. *Language Learning* 55, 335–374.

Leki, I. (2003) A challenge to second language writing professionals: Is writing overrated? In B. Kroll (ed.) *Exploring the Dynamics of Second Language Writing* (pp. 315–331). New York: Cambridge University Press.

Leki, I., Cumming, A. and Silva, T. (2006) Second-language composition teaching and learning. In P. Smagorinsky (ed.) *Research on Composition: Multiple Perspectives on Two Decades of Change* (pp. 141–169). New York: Teachers College Press.

Leki, I., Cumming, A. and Silva, T. (2008). *A Synthesis of Research on Second Language Writing in English*. London: Routledge.

Levelt, W.J.M. (1989) *Speaking: From Intention to Articulation.* Cambridge, MA: MIT Press.

Lewis, E.G. and Massad, C.E. (1975) *The Teaching of English as a Foreign Language in Ten Countries*. New York: John Wiley and Sons.

Li, X-M. (1996) *'Good Writing' in Cross-cultural Context*. Albany, NY: SUNY Press.

Luke, A. (2005) Evidence-based state literacy policy: A critical alternative. In N. Bascia, A. Cumming, A. Datnow, K. Leithwood and D. Livingstone (eds) *International Handbook of Educational Policy* (Vol. 2; pp. 661–675). Dordrecht: Springer.

Matsuda, P. (2003) Second language writing in the twentieth century: A situated historical perspective. In B. Kroll (ed.) *Exploring the Dynamics of Second Language Writing* (pp. 15–34). New York: Cambridge University Press.

McGroarty, M. (ed.) (2006) *Lingua Franca Languages*. Special issue of *Annual Review of Applied Linguistics* 26.

Pavlenko, A. (2007) Autobiographical narratives as data in applied linguistics. *Applied Linguistic* 28 (2), 163–188.

Pennington, M., Brock, M. and Yue, F. (1996) Explaining Hong Kong students' response to process writing: An exploration of causes and outcomes. *Journal of Second Language Writing* 5, 227–252.

Pennington, M., Costa, V., So, S., Shing, J., Hirose, K. and Niedzielski, K. (1997) The teaching of English-as-a-Second-Language writing in the Asia-Pacific region: A cross-country comparison. *Regional English Language Centre Journal* 28, 120–143.

Poehner, M.E. and Lantolf, J. (2005) Dynamic assessment in the language classroom. *Language Teaching Research* 9, 1–33.

Porte, G. (1997) The etiology of poor second language writing: The influence of perceived teacher preferences on second language revision strategies. *Journal of Second Language Writing* 6, 61–78.

Purves, A. (1984) In search of an internationally-valid scheme for scoring compositions. *College Composition and Communication* 35, 426–438.

Purves, A. (ed.) (1992) *The IEA Study of Written Composition II: Education and Performance in Fourteen Countries*. Oxford: Pergamon.

Qi, D. (1998) An inquiry into language-switching in second language composing processes. *The Canadian Modern Language Review* 54, 413–435.

Ramanathan, V. (2004) *The English-vernacular Divide: Postcolonial Language Politics and Practice*. Clevedon: Multilingual Matters.

Rea-Dickins, P. (2008) Classroom-based language assessment. In E. Shohamy (volume ed.) and N. Hornberger (series ed.) *Encyclopedia of Language and Education* (2nd edn), Volume 7, *Language Testing and Assessment* (pp. 257–271). New York: Springer.

Ricento, T. and Burnaby, B. (eds) (1998) *Language and Politics in the United States and Canada: Myths and Realities*. Mahwah, NJ: Lawrence Erlbaum.

Rivers, W. (1968) *Teaching Foreign-language Skills*. Chicago, IL: University of Chicago Press.

Robertson, R. (1992) *Globalization: Social Theory and Global Culture*. London: Sage.

Silva, T. and Brice, C. (2004) Research in teaching writing. *Annual Review of Applied Linguistics* 24, 70–106.

Spener, D. (ed.) (1994) *Adult Biliteracy in the United States*. McHenry, IL: Delta Systems and Center for Applied Linguistics.

Spolsky, B. (1995) *Measured Words: The Development of Objective Language Tests*. Oxford: Oxford University Press.

Stern, H.H. (1983) *Fundamental Concepts of Language Teaching*. Oxford: Oxford University Press.

Street, B. (2005) Recent applications of New Literacy Studies in educational contexts. *Research in the Teaching of English* 39, 417–423.

Swales, J. (1990) *Genre Analysis: English in Academic and Research Settings.* New York: Cambridge University Press.

Swain, M. and Lapkin, S. (1982) *Evaluating Bilingual Education: A Canadian Case Study.* Clevedon: Multilingual Matters.

Uso-Juan, E. and Martinez-Flor, A. (eds) (2006) *Current Trends in the Development and Teaching of the Four Language Skills.* Berlin: Mouton de Gruyter.

Walker, D. (1976) *The IEA Six Subject Survey: An Empirical Study of Education in Twenty-One Countries.* New York: John Wiley and Sons.

Wang, L. (2003) Switching to first language among writers with differing second-language proficiency. *Journal of Second Language Writing* 12, 347–375.

Weigle, S. (2002) *Assessing Writing*. Cambridge: Cambridge University Press.

Whalen, K. and Menard, N. (1995) L1 and L2 writers' strategic and linguistic knowledge: A model of multiple-level discourse processing. *Language Learning* 45, 381–418.

Wolf, R. (1977) *Achievement in America: National Report of the United States for the International Educational Achievement Project*. New York: Teachers College Press.

Woodall, B. (2002) Language-switching: Using the first language while writing in a second language. *Journal of Second Language Writing* 11, 7–28.

Chapter 9

Studying Writing Across EFL Contexts: Looking Back and Moving Forward

LOURDES ORTEGA

Introduction

Learning to write in foreign language (FL) contexts is different from learning to write in second language (SL) contexts in several unique ways. Some of the differences arise because learning an additional language (L2) in an FL setting versus an SL setting itself is different. FL learners can be expected to exhibit generally lower levels of L2 proficiency than is typically the case for SL learners (e.g. Hirose & Sasaki, 1994; Kasper, 1997), and their competencies also develop less fully in FL than in SL instructional settings, as shown, for example, in L2 areas as varied as pragmatic competence (Bardovi-Harlig & Dörnyei, 1998) and writing complexity (Ortega, 2003). Without prospects to use the L2 beyond the confines of the classroom or in their immediate future, FL learners may find it difficult to imagine reasons why they may want to write, and to write well, in the L2. This is perhaps why many teachers and educators often characterize FL writing as a less purposeful and needs-driven enterprise than SL writing. Not all differences imply a disadvantage for FL contexts, however. The widely varying kinds and degrees of literacy that can be assumed of L2 learners in SL settings (Bigelow & Tarone, 2004) can greatly complicate L2 writing development. In many FL settings, by contrast, a rather uniform familiarity and even maturity with literacy practices in the L1 can often be assumed. Under such premises, potentially positive roles for L1 literacies arise that can nourish the development of L2 writing.

These differences are insufficiently recognized in the wider field of L2 writing. Furthermore, in many reports, knowledge about English as a second language (ESL) writing gets naturalized inadvertently as being about L2 writing more generally, with the implication that it is universally valid and easily generalizable across writing contexts, including FL and English as a foreign language (EFL) contexts. Thus, we cannot but recognize a decided ESL bias in much L2 writing scholarship (Ortega, 2004). Yet, the academic, professional, international and virtual (internet-related) demands for English writing across non-English-dominant contexts are enormous, and they are not likely to diminish in the future. As the importance of English writing gains momentum, so does the need to make space for EFL findings. We can only hope that knowledge about L2 writing will eventually be built on a broader base that includes insights from a wide range of school, university, workplace and virtual settings in varied FL contexts. As part of this forward-looking move, I would like to explore two main questions in this chapter: what are the prominent themes in current EFL writing research? What research will be needed in the future if the goal is to 'arrive at a situated understanding of writing practices in FL instructional settings' (Manchón, this volume: 4)?

Sixteen Years of EFL Writing Research in Two Flagship Journals

In order to identify the prominent themes that have been investigated with regard to L2 writing in FL contexts, it is useful to examine the publication patterns in the *Journal of Second Language Writing* (*JSLW*) during its first 16 years (1992–2007). In addition, I also examine publications about writing that have appeared in *TESOL Quarterly* (*TQ*) during the same time period. In what follows, I will make no reference to L2 writing in FL contexts pertaining to languages other than English, given that too few of such studies were found: only six in the *JSLW* and (as is to be expected) none in *TQ*. Therefore, I concentrate on the EFL writing research. (Reichelt [2001] offers a comprehensive review of L2 writing in non-English FL contexts; see also the annotated bibliography offered by Reichelt, this volume.) The resulting empirical corpus comprises 72 EFL writing studies out of a total of 202 empirical studies that dealt with L2 writing.

Between 1992 and 2007, 56 or 36% of all empirical L2 writing studies in the *JSLW* ($n = 154$) were conducted in an EFL context. As Manchón and de Haan (2008) observe, 75% of them have been published since 1999. Table 9.1 shows a summary of the countries and institutional contexts investigated. The table shows that most of the studies were conducted in Japan and Hong Kong. In addition, five of six EFL writing studies conducted in China were published just in the last five-year span,

Table 9.1 EFL writing studies published in the *Journal of Second Language Writing*, 1992–2007

Countries	*Institutional contexts*			
	School system	*Higher education*	*Other*[a]	*Total*
China		6		6
Colombia			1	1
Croatia			1	1
Ecuador			1	1
French Canada	1		1	2
Germany	1			1
Hong Kong	4	9		13
India	1			1
Israel		1		1
Japan		13		13
Korea		1		1
Morocco	1			1
Poland	1[b]			1
Puerto Rico		2		2
Singapore		3		3
Spain		3		3
Taiwan		3		3
The Netherlands	1			1
Ukraine		1		1
Total	10	42	4	56

Note: This table presents a tally of $n = 56$ out of 154 total primary research studies published (36% of all primary studies published).

[a]Other institutional contexts comprised nonstudent adult populations writing in the work place and in scientific journals.

[b]This study (Reichelt, 2006) was conducted in Poland and covered both the K-12 school system and higher education.

pointing at the likely rise of writing research in this country in years to come. It is also noteworthy that the majority of EFL studies (75%) have concentrated on college writers, mirroring a similar preference for higher education contexts in ESL writing studies. Thus, knowledge about EFL young writers in elementary or secondary schools, and even more so about EFL adult writers in professional, academic or virtual contexts beyond the school system, is scarce.

Table 9.2 offers the same information for *TQ*. Sixteen or 33% of all empirical studies about L2 writing published in this journal between 1992 and 2007 ($n = 48$) focused on EFL writing. As was the case in the *JSLW*, most (10 of 16) have appeared since 1999 and have explored college-level writers (11 of 16). No particular geography seems to be more heavily represented in these publications.

Looking Back: Things we know about EFL Writing, in a Nutshell

An inspection of the topical areas represented across the 72 studies in Tables 9.1 and 9.2, as well as in the studies included in the annotated bibliography by Reichelt (this volume), yields a wealth of themes

Table 9.2 EFL writing studies published in *TESOL Quarterly*, 1992–2007

Countries	*Institutional contexts*			
	School system	*Higher education*	*Other*	*Total*
China		2	1	3
French Canada	1			1
European countries (several)			1	1
Germany		2		2
Hong Kong		3	1	4
Japan		1		1
Singapore	1			1
South Africa		3		3
Total	2	11	3	16

Note: This table presents a tally of $n = 16$ or 33% out of $n = 48$ empirical studies on L2 writing.

investigated by EFL writing scholars. The bibliographical exercise offers us an opportunity to reflect on what knowledge has been generated to date about EFL writing, and to ask ourselves: what do we know thus far about the cognitive, textual-linguistic, social and educational dimensions of EFL writing? As a way to answer this question broadly, I would like to take readers through a selective but representative journey across what I consider to be central themes in EFL writing scholarship.

Cognitive processes of composing

The characterization of processes that expert writers engage in, including recursive and nonlinear mental strategies organized into three broad stages of planning, formulating and revising, was first advanced by Hayes and Flower (1980) for L1 English writing. The Spain-based research program led by Manchón (see Manchón *et al.*, this volume) has perhaps contributed the most robust findings in this area. These researchers have investigated the nature of problem-solving strategies undertaken during argumentative and narrative one-hour essay writing. In such time-compressed tasks, at least, and whether during L1 or L2 composing, Manchón *et al.* note that about 60% of total composing time is likely to be devoted to formulation. On the other hand, at the lowest L2 proficiency level, EFL writers may spend more time overall in formulation processes, and it is only after a certain threshold in L2 expertise that they may be more able to strike a balance between formulation and the other two cognitive activities of planning and revising. This finding is consonant with similar results yielded by several cognitive studies of the L2 writing processes of novice and expert Japanese EFL writers, undertaken by Sasaki and Hirose and discussed by Sasaki (this volume).

Manchón *et al.* (this volume) conclude that FL writing as an activity draws more heavily on already chunked or automatized language than on new, novel language creations, in that text generation is made up of predominantly fluent outbursts of language. In this they concur with claims made by Ellis (2002) and Wray (2002) that at the most fundamental level all language knowledge and use, including first and additional, rests on 'structural regularities that emerge from learners' lifetime analysis of the distributional characteristics of the language input' (Ellis, 2002: 144). However, the amount of fluent formulation segments dramatically decreases for a given writer when composing in their FL, as compared to their L1. Along the L2 proficiency continuum, on the other hand, only qualitative differences in fluency were uncovered. Specifically, more advanced FL writers are likely to experience disfluencies because they pose themselves more challenging problems that have the goal of *upgrading* their text, often in terms of higher-level (ideational and textual) dimensions. By comparison, FL writers with lower L2 proficiency levels may be more disfluent because they are more consumed by the goal to solve formulation problems that demand *compensation* of gaps and holes, particularly in terms of lower-level (linguistic) dimensions such as lexical searches and effortful application of grammatical rules.

Another notable FL writing research team, led by Schoonen in The Netherlands, has also produced complementary findings regarding writing as a cognitive phenomenon. Schoonen *et al.* (this volume) make the theoretical prediction that linguistic variables (vocabulary knowledge, vocabulary fluency and grammatical knowledge) are more heavily implicated in FL writing proficiency than in L1 writing proficiency, whereas the latter may be made up of many more nonlinguistic dimensions, such as background knowledge. More specifically, they propose the Inhibition Hypothesis, which predicts that the high demands of linguistic aspects of FL writing will consume resources and inhibit attention to conceptual aspects of FL writing, such as content elaboration, monitoring and higher-order revisions. In their fine-grained cognitive model of L2 composing, they also include specific measures of declarative versus procedural linguistic knowledge as well as multiple measures of L1 and L2 writing by the same writers. Given the well-known dissociation among FL students between knowledge of grammar and vocabulary (declarative or explicit L2 knowledge) and the ability to retrieve it for use (procedural or implicit L2 knowledge), a distinct contribution of these two facets of L2 proficiency to L2 writing is highly plausible. However, the findings to date have not supported the prediction, nor have they supported the hypothesis that improving lexical fluency improves the fluency and the quality of EFL writing (Snellings *et al.*, 2004). Overall, and as the authors acknowledge, the writing tasks employed in these studies are simple and the EFL writers involved are young. These two circumstances may explain why the writing generated tends to be simple in content and why the writers engage in equally few higher-order revisions and conceptual elaboration across their languages (L1 Dutch and FL English). Thus, the Inhibition Hypothesis merits future investigation with more cognitively mature writers and more challenging writing tasks.

Textual-linguistic studies of EFL products

Slowly but surely, findings from the textual-linguistic analysis of written EFL products are accumulating, particularly in three areas that complement the cognitive approach just reviewed: the use of the L1, fluency and revision.

The shifting roles that the L1 may play in the development of FL writing are a topic that lends itself particularly well to complementary cognitive and linguistic-textual investigation. Thus, in support of cognitive process findings reported by Manchón *et al.* (this volume) and Wang and Wen (2002), among others, Celaya and Navés (this volume) also found evidence of a greater and more direct reliance on L1 lexical knowledge in the texts produced by their younger-aged EFL learners as well as their lower-proficiency EFL learners. It is not, however, that the L1 ceases to play a role in EFL writing with increased cognitive maturity (i.e. age) and linguistic expertise (i.e. L2 proficiency). Rather, the evidence suggests that at higher levels of proficiency and cognitive maturity, the L1 is less often used for compensatory purposes or to generate more text and instead begins to serve as a mediational tool for the purposes of enabling higher-quality planning, revising and monitoring processes.

Fluency is another area where processes and products of composing can help triangulate theoretical interpretations, as the construct can (and should ideally) be measured both cognitively and textually. Manchón *et al.* (this volume) remark that lower-proficiency EFL writers express anxiety caused by the need to generate text and worry about sheer length. This observation accords well with repeated ESL findings that essay length is predictive of writing placement and writing quality ratings at low and low-intermediate levels of proficiency (e.g. Jarvis *et al.*, 2003). The centrality of fluency in early FL writing development also resonates with the findings reported by Celaya and Navés (this volume) that, in terms of textual products, essay length and overall amount of production were the only areas in which EFL learners in Barcelona schools who had started studying the L2 early (at age 8 or Grade 3) were seen to catch up and surpass their peers who had started three years later (at age 11 or Grade 6). The converging findings amount to evidence for a fundamental role for fluency-aimed intervention in the teaching of FL writing, particularly at incipient levels of proficiency. Casanave (1994) and Ishikawa (1995) suggested this idea over a decade ago, but few if any FL writing researchers have pursued it formally.

Self-initiated revision is another promising area where cognitive process and linguistic product meet to yield potentially important insights about the nature of FL writing. In their research program, Schoonen *et al.* (this volume) view self-initiated revision as involving at least three levels: conceptual, linguistic and orthographic. They submit for future research the question of whether attention to lower-level, linguistic revision may inhibit attention to higher-level, conceptual revision in EFL writing, a prediction included in their Inhibition Hypothesis. The use of key-stroke logging software may prove to be a particularly important tool to aid FL writing researchers in these future efforts to understand textual revision as it unfolds in real time (see Stevenson *et al.*, 2006; Sullivan & Lindgren, 2006).

Teacher feedback and peer response in EFL writing

If revision from a textual-linguistic and cognitive perspective pertains to composing behaviors that are self-initiated during the act of writing, revision can also be more social and collaborative in nature when it is prompted by others (e.g. a teacher or a peer) via writer feedback and response. Several sources of other-prompted revision have attracted attention from EFL writing researchers. For example, we have detailed knowledge about preferences and strategies adopted by secondary Hong Kong teachers when providing error correction, thanks to the work by Lee (2004). She found that the use of error codes was widespread among the 206 teachers she studied, but she also suggested that this practice may not be as useful as teachers and students assume. Another important area of inquiry is whether EFL teachers should provide feedback on grammar, content or both, and how the foci for the feedback should be sequenced in the writing-and-redrafting cycle. Ashwell (2000) discovered that such details may matter little if the EFL writers in question rely heavily on feedback on grammar and neglect to take feedback on content seriously enough. A comparison of teacher versus peer feedback and their relative value by Miao *et al.* (2006) showed that even in a so-called collectivist and authority-oriented country like China, EFL writers can see the benefits of peer as well as teacher feedback when they are offered as complementary options rather than mutually exclusive alternatives. Training for peer response has come to be viewed in recent years as an essential need in EFL contexts, and a feasible practice that can lead to successful peer response among writers who share the same L1 (Hu, 2005; Min, 2005).

Pedagogical and curricular landscapes of L1/L2 composition across EFL contexts

EFL writing scholars have been instrumental in creating a wide recognition that composing pedagogies should be based on an understanding of the nature of writing instruction that writers experience in their own mother tongue during regular schooling. The impetus for innovative research in this area has been initiated by scholars working specifically in EFL contexts who have paid close attention to what Cumming (this volume) calls the macrocomponents of educational policies that affect EFL writing.

The program developed over the years by Reichelt (this volume) in the USA has been comparative and transnational and has involved the documentation of English writing instruction and curricular climates in countries as diverse as Germany, Japan, Poland, Spain and the USA. Other researchers have investigated programmatic practices in EFL contexts at a more general level, sometimes in contexts where L2 writing instruction was being introduced into a curriculum that had been predominantly oriented towards oral and reading practice (e.g. Tarnopolsky, 2000, in Ukraine) or other times in settings where the undue influence of high-stakes writing assessment has placed new constraints on classroom practices (e.g. You, 2004). Cumming (this volume) offers an extended commentary on the value and future of these lines of FL writing research.

Dynamic EFL writing development across contexts of engagement

Another notable innovative direction in recent years has been to place emphasis on understanding the changes that texts undergo from a dynamic perspective, as the contexts EFL writers traverse change, making them grow in training and experience in different ways. Rinnert and Kobayashi (this volume) present findings that help piece together an understanding of EFL writers in Japan as they experience L1 and L2 writing instruction from elementary and secondary school, to extracurricular enrichment instruction (e.g. tutorials, cram schools) available to only special students, all the way to higher education in their own country. These researchers have concentrated on studying the interplay among three factors: (a) the metaknowledge accrued by formal instruction about L1 as well as L2 writing, (b) the changes that stem from differing amounts of practice and experience with L1 as well as L2 writing and (c) the textual choices exhibited in L2 essay writing, particularly in argumentative essays. The research program developed by Sasaki (this volume) has also addressed some of the same issues, while she has recently turned to the longitudinal documentation of changes in EFL writers over the full length of their undergraduate studies.

Both Japan-based EFL research programs have also begun to account for the impact of college-level studies abroad, an experience that implies a radical change of context, and a practice that has become increasingly extended in many countries in the Asia-Pacific region and recently also in Europe. Interestingly, both Rinnert and Kobayashi (this volume) and Sasaki (this volume) note that the impact of study abroad differs depending on the length of stay, with three years affording more encompassing benefits than one year of residence abroad. Sasaki (this volume) shows that when Japanese EFL writers temporarily live in a context where the L2 is the medium of instruction, important changes in L2 writing motivation and confidence take place for many of them, provided the length is substantial. The changes are probably propelled by three factors that were found in the study abroad context she investigated: (a) the demand to write extensively, (b) the authentic audience and immediate needs that such a context affords EFL writers perhaps for the first time and (c) the explicit instruction about L2 writing that was also part of the study abroad experience.

Four central variables can be singled out from the work by these two EFL research teams: motivation, confidence, metaknowledge and practice. These variables are shown to affect the textual and rhetorical choices of L2 writers and, in turn, to be deeply affected by changing, dynamic contexts. For these reasons, they are worthy of sustained future study.

Rhetorical repertoires available to EFL writers across their languages

Contrastive rhetoric (Connor, 2002) has been the target of recent criticisms for embracing an uncritical notion of culture as fixed and essential, and as entailing objective differences rather than differences that are constructed socially and historically (Kubota & Lehner, 2004). This critique has been contributed by EFL writing scholars, who are naturally more sensitive than SL writing scholars to L1–L2 cross-rhetorical influences and to how they position groups of EFL writers. For example, Kubota (2004: 34) warns against the dangers of stereotyping and othering that result from 'cultural dichotomies between the West and the East, as seen in applied linguistics scholarship which often contrasts individualism with collectivism, directness with indirectness, logic with emotion, linearity with circularity, creativity versus memorization, and so on'.

An associated development is the burgeoning of cross-rhetorical transfer studies in which Japanese university EFL students are asked to write in both their mother tongue and English in order to compare the processes and products of such bilingual writing acts (e.g. Hirose, 2003; Kubota, 1998). The results in these studies point at a complex picture in which rhetorical differences across languages and cultures are less than straightforward and where negative transfer of assumed rhetorical preferences often does not occur. Even more recently, transfer of rhetorical preferences from the L2 to the L1 has been uncovered, a phenomenon that Rinnert and Kobayashi (this volume) call 'bidirectional transfer'.

An important insight that has emerged in these lines of research is that we cannot take for granted that what our students know is a static knowledge-base deterministically stemming, as we might have it, from their cultural affiliation. Canagarajah (2006) provides a striking illustration. He analyzed three research publications by the same Tamil L1-English L2 senior scholar in Sri Lanka. The rhetorical differences were largest between the paper written in Tamil for a local, nonacademic audience, and the two papers written in Tamil and English, respectively, which were designed to be read by scholarly experts in the local and international community, respectively. In other words, differences in context and audience made a deeper impact on the rhetorical choices made by this multicompetent writer than language differences *per se*. Canagarajah reasons that what shapes and informs the rhetorical choices made across a writer's multiple languages are not the culture or language one has been born to, imagined as fixed attributes of the writer. Rather, rhetorical repertoires can be best understood as emerging from the changing, multiple contexts and communities that the writer simultaneously inhabits. He urges writing scholars to focus more on the multiplicity of a writer's contexts rather than on his or her texts.

The struggle to write for scholarly publication in English

In a problem-driven and triangulation-guided research program, as they characterize it, Flowerdew and Li (this volume) have examined how EFL writers experience the symbolic as well as material power of English in their quest to write for international publication. As they note, the internationalization of higher education in many parts of the world has catapulted English writing to the status of pressing need for professional survival for many scientists and academics in non-English-speaking countries. The undercurrent of power differentials is clear between the center, defined as English-speaking regions where much scholarly and technological knowledge production takes place, and the periphery, defined as non-English-speaking regions that are viewed as consumers rather than generators of such knowledge. The double standards of international scholarship are poignantly described by Makoni (2005: 717): 'Scholars working in non-Western contexts are under pressure to constantly refer to Western scholarship because Western scholarship serves as an all pervasive and silent but salient referent for their work. However, Western scholars do not feel similar pressure, even if they are writing about non-Western contexts. Indeed, the quality of Western scholarship does not seem to be compromised when it is unaware of non-Western scholarship'.

For many scholars the motivation to publish in English is experienced as an externally imposed institutional requirement in order to get a degree (Flowerdew & Li, this volume) or for job security and promotion purposes (Curry & Lillis, 2004; Flowerdew, 1999). However, many others are themselves alumni from English-speaking institutions (Shi, 2003) who, having been socialized into their disciplines in English-dominant academic worlds, have internalized the need to publish in English as an ambivalent personal choice. For example, these scholars may have grown convinced that in order for their work to count in their academic communities, they had better publish in English (and, if possible, in so-called international periodicals, which in fact are simply periodicals published in center contexts). In either case, the stakes are very high both in terms of pressures and rewards (Curry & Lillis, 2004; Li, 2007).

A number of dimensions that have turned out to be important when writing for scholarly publication in English are culturally contested as well. Among others, Flowerdew and Li (this volume) identify voice (e.g. being able to make claims with appropriate force, being able to affirm the authority and expertise of the writer) and intertextuality (or what they call 'reusing others' language', such as citing and building on other published texts in order to build an authoritative argument, and so on). These are dimensions of academic writing that have been studied extensively by now in the ESL literature, but remain relatively unexplored across EFL contexts.

The hindsight of 16 years of EFL scholarship

In sum, the themes reviewed in this section reveal an undeniable predilection among EFL writing scholars for cognitive and textual-linguistic dimensions of EFL writing and in associated process pedagogies. However, also discernable is an incipient concern with writer's creativity, voice and audience as culturally contested notions, and an increasing presence of context as dynamic influence. Both trends are likely to be amplified in future scholarship. But I would be remiss if I did not confess that it is in the latter front where EFL writing researchers would appear to be particularly uniquely equipped to continue making important contributions. This is because of their privileged insider position as teachers, writers and scholars. This position may afford many of them a double vision and an interstitial perspective (Bhabha, 1994/2004), which can be exploited productively to understand varied bicultural and bilingual experiences right from the heart of the periphery.

Moving Forward: Needed Knowledge about EFL Writing

An awareness of the themes that have most intensely engaged EFL writing researchers in recent years affords us a window into future needs for the field of FL writing. In what follows, I sketch some critical reflections about the kinds of research that will be needed in the future in order to keep advancing our knowledge of EFL writing in both the theoretical and the applied fronts.

Researching what we value in EFL writing pedagogies: Language development, motivation and feedback

For many educators and teachers, a main purpose for writing in a FL is to practice and learn the L2. If we accept the importance of this widespread perception, then a priority for future EFL scholarship is to strengthen our knowledge about how language develops through L2 writing. Arguing that L2 writing can be an ideal site for pushed output in FL pedagogy, Manchón and Roca de Larios (2007: 106–109) have made explicit the theoretical connection between Swain's (1985) Output Hypothesis and the problem-solving cognitive processes that writing in an L2 conjures up. They reason that engaging in L2 production through writing offers several advantages over oral pushed output. One is that writing and rewriting can be done without the pressures of oral online production, allowing more room for hypothesis testing, in the form of self-monitoring, evaluation of the goodness of match between intention and expression and external feedback. They also remind us that other features of the cognitive processes engaged in writing offer great potential for fostering metalinguistic awareness and noticing of gaps and holes (Schmidt & Frota, 1986; Swain & Lapkin, 1995). These include the cyclical and recursive nature of composing processes, with constant scanning of the already written text, or *backtracking*, and the effortful nature of generating text in the L2, which often forces writers to search for alternatives to a syntactic plan that is evaluated as unviable or unsatisfactory, or *restructuring*. Vygostkian sociocultural L2 scholars have offered an additional rationale for claiming writing as an ideal site for L2 learning, because it encourages graduated, contingent and collaborative scaffolding (Aljaafreh & Lantolf, 1994; de Guerrero & Villamil, 2000) and it promotes meta-awareness of language issues (Swain & Lapkin, 1995).

Writing for the sake of language practice, however, is often in difficult compatibility with writing for engagement and pleasure, and motivation may enter into tension with accuracy in many FL writing classrooms. For example, Lo and Hyland (2007) discovered that certain innovations they introduced in the curriculum experienced by primary students in a Hong Kong classroom resulted in much greater writing engagement and in what could be considered pushed output. At the same time, they also observed unintended consequences, including a drop in language accuracy and an increased reliance on L1 textual solutions. When the content of the writing that EFL writers are willing to attempt becomes more involved, complex and challenging, teachers may feel that their pedagogical goals for accuracy-oriented practice are compromised. Thus, on the one hand, we need to understand how we can foster writing tasks that motivate and engage EFL students and make them want to pose themselves sophisticated problems as writers, as well as to persist and spend as much time as needed in writing. On the other hand, we will also need to understand better how such increased investment in writing may affect linguistic development, and whether and how, in such cases, accuracy goals may need to be balanced in special ways. In both areas, Casanave (this volume) rightly reminds us of contextual constraints that will need to be taken into consideration.

The study of feedback on language forms (as distinct from content, organization, voice and so on) should be another important concern for researchers working in EFL writing contexts, because error correction is highly valued by EFL teachers and students. Despite heated interest in feedback and response among L2 writing researchers (see Ferris, 2004), the contributions of EFL researchers discussed in an earlier section, while valuable, have not had the wider impact one would expect. For example, Truscott (2007) in a recent meta-analytic synthesis of 15 writing studies of teacher-provided error correction included only one from an EFL context (Robb *et al.*, 1986), by comparison to five conducted with Spanish, German or French FL writers and nine more conducted with ESL learners. Given that feedback on language is a central practice in much FL pedagogy, EFL writing research in this area has only begun to broach the issues. Approaching the study of feedback while better accounting for the sociocultural context in which it happens would also be of great value, as Hyland and Hyland (2006) have argued from an SL perspective (see also Casanave, this volume).

The nature of metaknowledge about (L1 and L2) writing: Explicit, implicit, affective, social?

Although we have begun to collect evidence regarding the kinds of knowledge about L1 and L2 composition that EFL writers have formed across previous experiences and contexts, the research to date seems to assume that choices made by L2 writers are always bolstered by metaknowledge that is fully verbalizable. In this volume, both Rinnert and Kobayashi and Schoonen *et al.* appear to favor a model in which metaknowledge is explicitly encoded, albeit not always available for actual use. However, it may be that some textual-linguistic and rhetorical choices are intentional and explicit, whereas others are the result of knowledge that is implicit and virtually nonverbalizable. This is an empirical question well worth investigating.

In the same vein, we will need to understand better the relative importance of cognitive versus affective and attitudinal influences on the knowledge that informs writer choices. Indeed, some of those choices may be motivated by intuitions and aesthetic preferences rather than metacognitive knowledge of a reasoned kind. For example, Rinnert and Kobayashi (this volume) note that writers occasionally make textual and rhetorical decisions partly depending on how similar or different they perceive the conventions and styles of the two languages to be. Furthermore, in their studies, they captured instances when EFL writers made actual use of some of the rhetorical knowledge they did possess only if they held positive attitudes towards it. Some of the influences on metaknowledge are also likely to be social in nature, as we are reminded by Canagarajah's (2006) admonition to view rhetorical repertoires as emergent from the multiplicity of contexts that a writer travels, rather than as a fixed property of his or her originary languages and cultures. Surely, what shapes such perceptions of similarity and difference, and of usefulness or appropriateness, resides in social and affective forces that need to be better understood. Thus, we will need to go beyond investigating the content of the knowledge about writing that FL writers bring to the task, by also probing its nature (e.g. implicit as well as explicit, affective and social rather than purely cognitive) and by explicating how that knowledge is a tool that writers use to exercise their agency.

The nature of EFL writing instruction: Explicit, implicit, formulaic?

A related question that would be worth exploring is the extent to which the L2 writing instruction EFL writers receive is explicit (e.g. via actual explanation of rhetorical and linguistic rules and patterns, delivery of explicit feedback and provision of controlled practice) or implicit (e.g. via the reading and responding to good models, delivery of content-oriented feedback and provision of holistic practice). Furthermore, it may be useful to ask ourselves in the future: where along the explicit-implicit pedagogical continuum should optimal L1 and L2 writing instruction fall, for whom and in which cases?

Rinnert and Kobayashi (this volume) appear to endorse a preference for explicit instruction, as they note that their findings probably suggest 'that unless such knowledge is taught, writers are unlikely to employ these specific features when writing L1 or L2 essays' (Chapter 1: 39). Yet, very different routes exist to developing L2 writing competencies, each possibly enabling different kinds of metaknowledge and writing self-awareness. For example, Manchón *et al.* (this volume) note that in the EFL context of Spain, formal writing instruction (in either L1 or L2) is less commonly and less broadly provided during schooling and therefore EFL writers develop competencies mostly through experiential implicit processes afforded by 'repeated engagement with writing assignments and some form of response from their teachers' (Chapter 4: 117). In the future, then, cross-national research along the lines of Reichelt's work (this volume) could be designed in a more targeted fashion in order to compare the metalinguistic and metacognitive knowledge about writing that students accrue under educational systems in which writing instruction in the L1 or L2 is typically abundant and explicit and under systems in which no writing-specific instruction is typically available in the L1 or the L2.

In investigations of ESL contexts where L2 writing instruction was explicit, Atkinson and Ramanathan (1995) and Yoshida (2007) have documented the undesirable outcome of formulaic knowledge. At the same time, other researchers have noted greater diversity and variety of content in L1 writing instruction. For example, Kubota and Shi (2005) reported that junior high school textbooks in Japan and China contain a great diversity of L1 text models and, in the same vein, Kobayashi and Rinnert (2008) found that more diverse types of discourse are used by writers who enjoyed L1 writing instruction. It may be unhelpful to see the issue as a property of specific language-and-culture constellations and conclude, for example, that English writing instruction is more formulaic, and Japanese and Chinese writing instruction is more subtle and richer. It might be, for example, that L1 writing teachers may more often assume that their students can learn the subtleties of writing, free from low-level linguistic concerns. By contrast, in a self-fulfilling belief in the Inhibition Hypothesis (Schoonen *et al.*, this volume), perhaps L2 writing teachers may more often make the assumption that their students can only understand and do so much amidst the linguistic constraints of writing in their L2. This tension between explicitness and formulaic knowledge calls for more attention in the future.

Expanding methodologies for the investigation of EFL writing

In order to answer questions about the cognitive, textual-linguistic, social and educational dimensions of EFL writing, researchers will want to continue using (and triangulating across) the methodologies employed thus far: (a) think-aloud methodologies, (b) linguistic and textual analyses of the written products and (c) surveys of writers, teachers and other actors involved in FL writing education. However, an expansion of the kinds of evidence brought to bear on EFL writing research would greatly help augment the theoretical import of the insights that have accumulated to date.

In-depth ethnographic observations over long periods of time have produced important insights in the field of L1 writing (e.g. Chiseri-Striter, 1991) and the same methodology would greatly advance EFL writing research. Some scholars have included classroom observation in their suite of research methods to study L2 writing in FL contexts (cf. Reichelt, 1997; You, 2004). However, as Cumming (this volume) notes, the purpose seems to have been the portrait of an overall survey-like or broad-stroke picture of implementations and approaches in FL contexts. Systematic and close classroom observational data would be ideal to probe fundamental questions about EFL writing instruction, such as those surrounding the explicitness and quality of L1 and L2 writing instruction.

Likewise, a number of seminal qualitative case studies of ESL writers have allowed the in-depth exploration of evolving L2 writers' lived experiences, motivations and choices (e.g. Leki, 2007; Spack, 1997). No comparable descriptions of EFL writers exist, and the scarce and valuable longitudinal case studies that do exist (Li, 1996; Sasaki, 2004, this volume) have so far adopted a generic level of description of individual cases. Flowerdew and Li's (this volume) call for methodologies that allow for more grounded descriptions of cases, points in this direction. The field of

L2 writing stands to gain much if the stories of diverse EFL writers are made visible through interpretive-qualitative longitudinal case studies (Duff, 2008; Harklau, 2008).

Understanding (and contesting) globalization

Material, sociopolitical and cultural challenges in the teaching of writing in any FL are many, but they are particularly pressing when the FL is English, given the singular role of English as a global language in our contemporary world. Quite simply, EFL writing as a phenomenon is enmeshed with globalization as a phenomenon, and the study of the former cannot be complete without taking the study of the latter into account. Therefore, the investigation of writing in English as a FL needs to be more fully conceptualized in light of material, cultural and sociopolitical forces associated with globalization.

One area in which globalization profoundly affects EFL writing is in the interpenetration of pedagogies and values between center and periphery. Casanave (this volume) poignantly discusses how, with globalization, the English-speaking center (USA, UK, Australia, Canada, New Zealand) propagates knowledge and pedagogies that may or may not be appropriate for application in so-called FL and other periphery contexts. In the same vein, Leki (2001: 197) suggests EFL writers and their teachers have 'the right to resist center imposed materials and methods'. Yet, to date, we have scant empirical evidence as to how this right may be felt or exercised across varied EFL contexts, although work by Reichelt (this volume) and others (e.g. You, 2004) has helped make visible a serious mismatch between the construction of L2 writing pedagogies depicted in center publications and their portraits of many lived EFL realities.

Casanave (this volume) takes the position that teachers are best served by acting upon a double awareness of 'their local realities' and 'an idealistic view of their work' (Chapter 10). This difficult blend of realism and idealism resonates with what Bhabha (1994/2004) has described as a double vision or an interstitial perspective that allows us to reach beyond binaries. It also echoes Allwright's (2005) recommendation that language teachers must pursue lived understandings and put the quality of classroom life first, thinking globally and acting locally (after a lemma coined by the late David Brower in 1969, when he founded the largest environmental organization in the world, Friends of the Earth). Most likely, a blend of realism and idealism is our best hope to deliver successful L2 writing instruction across EFL contexts. Investigations of how EFL writing teachers make sense (or not) of the pressures of material, sociopolitical and cultural challenges that arise from powerful global trends would greatly illuminate our understanding of ways to nurture the difficult blend Casanave envisions.

Contextualizing and using the 'FL' label with caution

Several other areas are important to consider in the future, many of them associated with the need to understand L2 (including EFL) writing as a site of multicompetence rather than deficiency (see Ortega & Carson, 2009). However, due to space constraints, they must be left out of these reflections. Instead, I would like to finish by emphasizing an important thread that runs across many of the other themes discussed in this chapter: the research imperative of contextualization.

In future research, we should take great care to avoid the pitfall of treating teachers, writers and writing contexts across studies as belonging to an undifferentiated, homogeneous contextual class of 'FL' or 'EFL'. The FL label is convenient and allows FL researchers to gain a broader base and a deeper impact in their pursuits. But it should not blind us to the great diversity it hides, as the research programs represented in this collection attest. As much as we must use commonalities across FL (and English as a FL) contexts in order to build strength across research communities, we must also not forget that research is always built on contingent, context-specific data. As Duff (2006) has usefully discussed, depending on our ontological and epistemological affiliations, we may strive to generate knowledge that aims at generalizability (in quantitative and postpositivistic research approaches) or particularization (in qualitative and interpretive research approaches), but in either case contextualization is a prerequisite for gauging the validity of our inferences and interpretations. When EFL researchers provide descriptions of the contexts for EFL writing they investigate, they should make it clear for readers that each context comes with its own history and its own cultural and social values and constraints, not to mention its own national and societal symbolic relationship towards English (or other target languages). Good EFL writing research demands the mounting of knowledge about writing in a FL that is fully contextualized and capitalizes on diversity.

Conclusion

Educators and researchers interested in writing in a FL face formidable challenges all over the world. The academic, professional, international and personal demands for English writing are enormous, and they are not likely to diminish in the future. The inclusion of EFL findings and insights in the official history of the discipline of L2 writing is therefore of the essence. The substantive wealth of the EFL writing research programs gathered in this collection, and the diversity and importance of the themes investigated in flagship publications over the last decade and a half, point at felicitous conditions of expansion. In the not so distant future, the community of L2 writing scholars who work in EFL contexts will be ready to join forces and offer coherent and wide-encompassing knowledge that advances theories and practices for L2 writing. Preferably, such knowledge about EFL writing should be generated from a wide range of school, university, workplace and virtual settings across diverse geographical and institutional contexts. With the increasing importance of English writing for academic, professional, international and virtual purposes and the burgeoning of research on and educational knowledge about L2 writing, it is time to seize the opportunity to maintain the existing wide-encompassing research programs and initiate new ones that can advance our theories of L2 writing as much as our educational policies and practices for EFL writing.

References

Aljaafreh, A. and Lantolf, J.P. (1994) Negative feedback as regulation and second language learning in the Zone of Proximal Development. *The Modern Language Journal* 78, 465–483.

Allwright, D. (2005) Developing principles for practitioner research: The case of Exploratory Practice. *Modern Language Journal* 89, 353–366.

Ashwell, T. (2000) Patterns of teacher response to student writing in a multiple-draft composition classroom: Is content feedback followed by form feedback the best method? *Journal of Second Language Writing* 9, 227–257.

Atkinson, D. and Ramanthan, V. (1995) Cultures of writing: An ethnographic comparison of L1 and L2 university writing/language programs. *TESOL Quarterly* 29, 539–568.

Bardovi-Harlig, K. and Dörnyei, Z. (1998) Do language learners recognize pragmatic violations? Pragmatic versus grammatical awareness in instructed L2 learning. *TESOL Quarterly* 32, 233–262.

Bhabha, H. (1994/2004) *The Location of Culture*. New York: Routledge.

Bigelow, M. and Tarone, E. (2004) The role of literacy level in second language acquisition: Doesn't who we study determine what we know? *TESOL Quarterly* 38, 689–700.

Canagarajah, A.S. (2006) Toward a writing pedagogy of shuttling between languages: Learning from multilingual writers. *College English* 68, 589–604.

Casanave, C. (1994) Language development in students' journals. *Journal of Second Language Writing* 3, 179–201.

Chiseri-Strater, E. (1991) *Academic Literacies. The Public and Private Discourse of University Students*. Portsmouth, NH: Heinemann, Boynton/Cook.

Connor, U. (2002) New directions in contrastive rhetoric. *TESOL Quarterly* 36, 493–510.

Curry, M.J. and Lillis, T. (2004) Multilingual scholars and the imperative to publish in English: Negotiating interests, demands, and rewards. *TESOL Quarterly* 38, 663–688.

de Guerrero, M.C. and Villamil, O.S. (2000) Activating the ZPD: Mutual scaffolding in L2 peer revision. *The Modern Language Journal* 84, 51–68.

Duff, P. (2006) Beyond generalizability: Contextualization, complexity, and credibility in applied linguistics. In M. Chalhoub-Deville, C. Chapelle and P. Duff (eds) *Inference and Generalizability in Applied Linguistics: Multiple Perspectives* (pp. 65–95). Amsterdam: John Benjamins.

Duff, P. (2008) *Case Study Research in Applied Linguistics*. New York: Lawrence Erlbaum Taylor & Francis.

Ellis, N. (2002) Frequency effects in language processing. *Studies in Second Language Acquisition* 24, 143–188.

Ferris, D.R. (2004) The "grammar correction" debate in L2 writing: Where are we, and what do we go from here? (and what do we do in the meantime?). *Journal of Second Language Writing* 13, 49–62.

Flowerdew, J. (1999) Writing for scholarly publication in English: The case of Hong Kong. *Journal of Second Language Writing* 8, 123–145.

Harklau, L. (2008) Developing qualitative longitudinal case studies of advanced language learners. In L. Ortega and H. Byrnes (eds) *The Longitudinal Study of Advanced L2 Capacities* (pp. 23–35). New York: Routledge.

Hayes, J.R. and Flower, L.S. (1980) Identifying the organization of writing processes. In L.W. Gregg and E.R. Steinberg (eds) *Cognitive Processes in Writing* (pp. 31–50). Hillsdale, NJ: Lawrence Erlbaum.

Hirose, K. (2003) Comparing L1 and L2 organizational patterns in the argumentative writing of Japanese EFL students. *Journal of Second Language Writing* 12, 181–209.

Hirose, K. and Sasaki, M. (1994) Explanatory variables for Japanese students' expository writing in English: An exploratory study. *Journal of Second Language Writing* 3, 203–229.

Hu, G. (2005) Using peer review with Chinese ESL student writers. *Language Teaching Research* 9, 321–342.

Hyland, K. and Hyland, F. (2006) Interpersonal aspects of response: Constructing and interpreting teacher written feedback. In K. Hyland and F. Hyland (eds) *Feedback in Second Language Writing: Contexts and Issues* (pp. 206–224). Cambridge: Cambridge University Press.

Ishikawa, S. (1995) Objective measurement of low-proficiency EFL narrative writing. *Journal of Second Language Writing* 4, 51–69.

Jarvis, S., Grant, L., Bikowski, D. and Ferris, D. (2003) Exploring multiple profiles of highly rated learner compositions. *Journal of Second Language Writing* 12, 377–403.

Kasper, G. (1997) The role of pragmatics in language teacher education. In K. Bardovi-Harlig and B.S. Hartford (eds) *Beyond Methods: Components of Language Teacher Education* (pp. 113–136). New York: McGraw-Hill.

Kobayashi, H. and Rinnert, C. (2008) Task response and text construction across L1 and L2 writing. *Journal of Second Language Writing* 17, 7–29.

Kubota, R. (1998) An investigation of L1-L2 transfer in writing among Japanese university students: Implications for contrastive rhetoric. *Journal of Second Language Writing* 7, 69–100.

Kubota, R. (2004) The politics of cultural difference in second language education. *Critical Inquiry in Language Studies* 1, 21–39.

Kubota, R. and Lehner, A. (2004) Toward critical contrastive rhetoric. *Journal of Second Language Writing* 13, 7–27.

Kubota, R. and Shi, L. (2005) Instruction and reading samples for opinion and argumentative writing in L1 junior high school textbooks in China and Japan. *Journal of Asian Pacific Communication* 15, 97–127.

Lee, I. (2004) Error correction in L2 secondary writing classrooms: The case of Hong Kong. *Journal of Second Language Writing* 13, 285–312.

Leki, I. (2001) Material, educational, and ideological challenges of teaching EFL writing at the turn of the century. *International Journal of English Studies* 1, 197–209.

Leki, I. (2007) *Undergraduates in a Second Language: Challenges and Complexities of Academic Literacy Development*. Mahwah, NJ: Lawrence Erlbaum.

Li, X-M. (1996) *"Good Writing" in Cross-cultural Context*. Albany, NY: State University of New York Press.

Li, Y-Y. (2007) Apprentice scholarly writing in a community of practice: An "intraview" of an NNES graduate student writing a research article. *TESOL Quarterly* 41, 55–79.

Lo, J. and Hyland, F. (2007) Enhancing students' engagement and motivation in writing: The case of primary students in Hong Kong. *Journal of Second Language Writing*, 16, 219–237.

Makoni, S. (2005) Introduction to: Toward a more inclusive applied linguistics and English language teaching: A symposium. *TESOL Quarterly* 39, 716–719.

Manchón, R.M. and de Haan, P. (2008) Writing in foreign language contexts: An introduction. *Journal of Second Language Writing* 17, 1–6.

Manchón, R.M. and Roca de Larios, J. (2007) Writing-to-learn in instructed language learning contexts. In E. Alcón Soler and M.P. Safont Jordà (eds) *Intercultural Language Use and Language Learning* (pp. 101–121). Dordrecht: Springer.

Miao, Y., Badger, R. and Zhen, Y. (2006) A comparative study of peer and teacher feedback in a Chinese EFL writing class. *Journal of Second Language Writing* 15, 179–200.

Min, H.T. (2005) Training students to become successful peer reviewers. *System* 33, 293–308.

Ortega, L. (2003) Syntactic complexity measures and their relationship to L2 proficiency: A research synthesis of college-level L2 writing. *Applied Linguistics* 24, 492–518.

Ortega, L. (2004) L2 writing research in EFL contexts: Some challenges and opportunities for EFL researchers. *Applied Linguistics Association of Korea Newsletter*. On WWW at www.alak.org.kr.

Ortega, L. and Carson, J.G. (2009) Multicompetence, social context, and L2 writing research praxis. In T. Silva and P.K. Matsuda (eds) *Practicing Theory in Second Language Writing*. West Lafayette, IN: Parlor Press.

Ramanathan, V. and Atkinson, D. (1999) Individualism, academic writing, and ESL students. *Journal of Second Language Writing* 8, 45–75.

Reichelt, M. (1997) L2 writing instruction at the German 'Gymnasium': A 13th-grade English class writes the 'Abitur'. *Journal of Second Language Writing* 6, 265–291.

Reichelt, M. (2001) A critical review of foreign language writing research on pedagogical approaches. *The Modern Language Journal* 85, 578–598.

Reichelt, M. (2006) English language writing instruction in Poland. *Journal of Second Language Writing* 14, 215–232.

Robb, T., Ross, S. and Shortreed, I. (1986) Salience of feedback on error and its effect on EFL writing quality. *TESOL Quarterly* 20, 83–95.

Sasaki, M. (2004) A multiple-data analysis of the 3.5-year development of EFL student writers. *Language Learning* 54, 525–582.

Schmidt, R. and Frota, S. (1986) Developing basic conversational ability in a second language: A case study of an adult learner of Portuguese. In R.R. Day (ed.) *Talking to Learn: Conversation in Second Language Acquisition* (pp. 237–326). Rowley, MA: Newbury House.

Shi, L. (2003) Writing in two cultures: Chinese professors return from the west. *The Canadian Modern Language Review* 59, 369–372.

Snellings, P., van Gelderen, A. and De Glopper, K. (2004) The effect of enhanced lexical retrieval on L2 writing: A classroom experiment. *Applied Psycholinguistics* 55, 175–200.

Stevenson, M., Schoonen, R. and de Glopper, K. (2006) Revising in two languages: A multi-dimensional comparison of online writing revision in L1 and FL. *Journal of Second Language Writing* 15, 201–233.

Spack, R. (1997) The acquisition of academic literacy in a second language: A longitudinal case study. *Written Communication* 14, 3–62.

Sullivan, K.P.H. and Lindgren, E. (eds) (2006) *Computer Keystroke Logging and Writing*. Amsterdam: Elsevier.

Swain, M. (1985) Communicative competence: Some roles of comprehensible input and comprehensible output in its development. In S.M. Gass and C.G. Madden (eds) *Input in Second Language Acquisition* (pp. 235–253). Rowley, MA: Newbury House.

Swain, M. and Lapkin, S. (1995) Problems in output and the cognitive processes they generate: A step towards second language learning. *Applied Linguistics* 16, 371–391.

Tarnopolsky, O. (2000) Writing English as a foreign language: A report from Ukraine. *Journal of Second Language Writing* 9, 209–226.

Truscott, J. (2007) The effect of error correction on learners' ability to write accurately. *Journal of Second Language Writing* 16, 255–272.

Wang, W. and Wen, Q. (2002) L1 use in the L2 composing process: An exploratory study of 16 Chinese EFL writers. *Journal of Second Language Writing* 11, 225–246.

Wray, A. (2002) *Formulaic Language and the Lexicon*. New York: Cambridge University Press.

Yoshida, M. (2007) *Beliefs about Academic Writing: Where do they all come from?* Paper presented at the Sixth Symposium of Second Language Writing, 15–17 September, Nagoya Gakuin University, Nagoya, Japan.

You, X. (2004) "The choice made from no choice": English writing instruction in a Chinese university. *Journal of Second Language Writing* 13, 97–110.

Chapter 10

Training for Writing or Training for Reality? Challenges Facing EFL Writing Teachers and Students in Language Teacher Education Programs

CHRISTINE PEARSON CASANAVE

Introduction

I am guessing that, like me, thousands of first language (L1) and second language (L2) graduates of language teacher education programs go abroad full of lofty ideas on how to improve the teaching of English in places still 'burdened' by tradition and convention. 'Enlightened' as we are by the latest in Western research and pedagogy, we set out to reform the system and open the eyes of willing students to the joys and benefits of L2 writing. Surprise! The realities of local English as a foreign language (EFL) contexts often constrain what teachers are able to enact from their L2 teacher education programs and from their personal beliefs about writing instruction.

Leki (2001) has underscored this mismatch in her critique of the unexamined enlightened vision, one that includes our commitment to process approaches, peer response, minimal error correction, instruction in the Western concept of plagiarism and the development of voice, by asking what local EFL realities and purposes are. Without asking the hard 'why' questions and attending to the local realities of our writing instruction, we risk fomenting ideological clashes and spreading Western hegemony and arrogance. This is a significant problem, given that most graduates of MA and certificate programs in Teachers of English to speakers of other languages (TESOL) work outside English-dominant countries.

In this chapter, I discuss some of the realities of teaching writing in foreign language (FL) contexts and the implications these realities have for the education of writing teachers in English-dominant teacher education programs. Building on Leki (2001), other literature and on my own examples from Japan, I ask EFL teachers and teachers' educators to balance their local realities with an idealistic view of their work. After reviewing some existing literature that addresses aspects of the problem, I provide some concrete views of a number of students in TESOL programs who were also working teachers in Japan. I conclude the chapter with some suggestions for language teacher education programs, most of which are preparing teachers to work in non-English-dominant settings, whether they realize it or not.

An Ecological Framework

A thought-provoking perspective from which to view the issues brought up in this chapter is an ecological view of learning, derived from sociocultural theory and explored in language learning contexts by Van Lier (2002, 2004) and Tudor (2003; see also the edited collection on ecological perspectives in language study by Kramsch [2002]). In contrast to cognitive and linguistic perspectives, and also to technological approaches, this view emphasizes the complex, messy, interrelated and contextually situated (or local) nature of all learning, including language learning (Larsen-Freeman, 2002; Tudor, 2003; Van Lier, 2002, 2004) and writing (Casanave, 1995b). As Van Lier (2002: 144) reminds us, the primary requirement of an ecological view of learning is 'that the context is central, it cannot be reduced, and it cannot be pushed aside or into the background'. As we will see, the main issues that writing teachers and educators of future teachers of writing face concern our need to understand, be sensitive to, and adapt to local conditions of learning and teaching. In this view, teachers of L2 writing need to work with the interrelated nature of what have, in the past, been considered separable components of language and writing instruction.

The Suitability of 'Western' Methodologies

A major issue facing language teacher education programs has to do with the suitability of so-called 'Western' (usually North American) methodologies. For many years, some scholars have questioned whether innovative language-teaching methods, based as they are on research in English-dominant settings, should be applied uncritically in EFL contexts. The critique does not just concern English language imperialism (Canagarajah, 1999, 2002; Pennycook, 1994; Phillipson, 1992), but also which methodologies can be incorporated into or should replace traditional ones, by which is usually meant grammar-translation methods of FL learning. A long-standing debate, for instance, concerns the appropriateness of communicative and task-based language teaching in educational systems that are exam-oriented, grammar-focused and staffed by teachers who may not be fully proficient in the L2 (e.g. Sheen, 1994; Swan, 2005). Although the pressure to innovate may be influenced by English-dominant teacher education programs, it is also experienced in some Asian countries as a mandate from ministries of education that hope to educate students in communicative and functional English (mainly oral skills) so that they can participate more effectively in a global society (see, e.g. McDonough & Chaikitmongkol [2007] who discuss mandates from the Thai government).

The reports of how nontraditional instruction is received in EFL settings, particularly in Asia, tend to condemn wholesale applications of communicative, task-based and process writing methodologies as inappropriate for a number of reasons. For instance, in a testing-oriented curriculum, oral and written communication skills may not be needed or valued as much as traditional grammar and translation skills. Also, teachers, educated in such a curriculum, may not have the requisite language proficiency to teach communicatively (Ellis, 1996; Li, 1998; Liu *et al.*, 2004). Further, although some scholars promote communicative language teaching (CLT) in countries such as China (e.g. Liao, 2004), others note that the broad recommendations do not consider the many contextual factors, for example, differences between more and less developed regions (Hu, 2003, 2005) and particular needs for English that may require mainly reading and translation of important documents (Liu, 1998). Other widespread limitations to implementing communicative, process writing and task-based approaches include: large classes in which teachers, in particular novice ones, have trouble maintaining discipline; inadequate teacher preparation; persistent use of L1; resistant teacher and student beliefs and attitudes; and unclear or unrealistic governmental policies (Burnaby & Sun, 1989; Li, 1998; Liu *et al.*, 2004; Nunan, 2003). Some, however, remain generally optimistic about task-based instruction (Carless, 2002, 2004; Ellis, 2003; Nunan, 2004; Skehan, 2003). In Thailand, for example, McDonough and Chaikitmongkol (2007) experimented successfully with a carefully designed task-based curriculum that included grammar instruction at a university that was under a government mandate to provide a more communicative curriculum. In one of the few studies focused on the teaching of writing, You (2004a) found that in China some of the same constraints apply that have been reported elsewhere: when a syllabus is nationally unified and exam-oriented, teachers have little time or incentive to enact 'Western writing pedagogies' that, for example, ask students to develop their thoughts. Interest in EFL writing in China, however, is growing, in spite of constraints (You, 2004b). In another study from Hong Kong, Pennington *et al.* (1996) found mixed reactions to process writing lessons among secondary students and teachers. The teachers worked under similar constraints as those described in other studies (e.g. large classes, heavy work loads, little contextual support). In Japan, some of us regularly used uncorrected journal writing in both secondary school (Duppenthaler, 2002, 2004) and university (Casanave, 1994, 1995a) with positive results (e.g. cases of better motivation, greater fluency, fewer errors, better thinking over time). I was not, however, constrained by a top-down curriculum or testing, grading and exam preparation requirements, as are many teachers in Japan, China and Korea who work at secondary and tertiary schools and at commercial for-profit language schools. (For other perspectives on writing in the Asia Pacific area see Kaplan [1995], Li & Casanave [2005] and Reichelt, this volume; for students' experiences with academic writing in Japan, see Rinnert & Kobayashi, this volume, and Sasaki, this volume.)

In Europe, English is increasingly being used as a lingua franca for business and other professional reasons, although responses to instruction seem to differ by country and by type and level of schooling. In Poland, Reichelt (2005) documented a very positive attitude toward EFL, where teachers and students she interviewed did not see English as a threat to their identity or values. Still, parallel to the situation in Asia, much writing instruction was aimed at exam preparation. In her other work in Germany (reviewed in this volume), Reichelt found that English functions as a status symbol, where it is used in many walks of professional life, and that motivation to learn English, including writing, is high. In her review of published work about Spain, Reichelt (reviewed in this volume) notes that the study of English is gaining in importance, given the competition in European markets, but that instruction parallels that in Asia in some ways: large, mixed proficiency level classes and a great deal of exam preparation. Neither L1 nor L2 instruction that focuses specifically on writing is common. In Ukraine, Tarnopolsky (2000) reported that there was great interest in EFL, in particular in business English, but that the students in his commercial language school dropped out if they were bored, which they apparently were by the process writing methods he was using. Another study reported more ambivalent attitudes on the part of seven Turkish teachers of English (Clachar, 2000). Trained to use Western (process, rhetorical) writing methodologies, four of the teachers felt they were being asked to teach in ways that were not appropriate for Turkish students, who expected more traditional, explicit and authoritative instruction from teachers. The other three teachers, though ambivalent, saw the need for internationally minded students to develop ways of thinking, critiquing and writing typical of Western scholarship. In short, the reception by students and teachers of EFL and nontraditional Western writing pedagogies differs widely. Critique has been more vocal in Asian contexts, where opportunities to practice nontraditional teaching methods seem more limited by contextual constraints than in some, but not all, European contexts. From his Asian perspective, Swan (2005) points out that most of the world's EFL learners are low-level learners, the '3hpw' variety (three hours per week, totaling only 600 hours of instruction over many years), who need (he claims) a great deal of explicit grammar and lexical instruction.

If we consider the teaching of writing within these and other constraints, and the fact that rarely are entire classes devoted to writing, then 'communicative' and task-based writing, peer reading and teacher-student conferences, free and uncorrected writing, and multiple revision might be difficult, or even unreasonable, to practice in some settings. Although interest in EFL for functional purposes, including writing, is greater in Europe, attitudes and practices differ widely from one context to another, requiring that teachers learn about and be sensitive to local constraints and traditions (see Reichelt, this volume). Blanket imposition of nontraditional writing instruction won't do, but neither will blanket acceptance of traditional methods. Both need to be examined thoughtfully and critically for their appropriateness, and teachers need to be prepared to listen, learn and adapt within the contexts and dynamics of their local teaching-learning situations (Tudor, 2003: 9).

Language Teacher Education Programs

In a second body of work, the questions concern whether graduates of language teacher education programs from English-dominant universities are being prepared to deal with the ecological realities of teaching writing in EFL settings.

In a strongly worded argument, Liu (1998, 1999) accuses TESOL teacher education programs in North America, the UK and Australia of being ethnocentric because they neglect the needs of international students who will return to their home countries to teach, as well as the needs of native English speakers who plan to teach abroad. He states that 'this neglect may stem from an urge to make international TESOL students learn and practice back home the "new" teaching methodologies' (Liu, 1998: 4). However, such an approach disregards the ideas and values in students' home cultures. He points out that in Asia (using China as an example), English is an academic subject given limited class time, not a survival tool, and that English education is run by top-down, test-oriented policies. Liu weakens his argument by using broad stereotypes of Asian and Western cultures (Asia: cultures with 'a long tradition of unconditional obedience to authority'; the West: 'teaching is a process or discovery oriented' in which interaction and small student-centered classes predominate; Liu, 1998: 5). Nevertheless, his point that TESOL programs don't prepare students to teach outside English-dominant countries stands.

Govardhan *et al.* (1999) make the same point. These authors took a different approach. They looked at job ads and descriptions for jobs abroad (in this case, outside the USA) and at descriptions of US MATESOL programs, and found great diversity of requirements, titles and offerings. In general, they felt that the MA programs offered too much theory and did not reflect enough practical realities for jobs that are increasingly opening up throughout the world. 'It is intellectually and pedagogically naive to believe that teaching English abroad is no more than an extension of ESL at home', they conclude (Govardhan *et al.*, 1999: 124). Finally, the two US MATESOL programs described by Ramanathan *et al.* (2001) do not seem to have any focus at all on teaching English abroad, but to be shaped by local and departmental links and needs. The unstated assumption seems to be that graduates from these programs will take jobs in the USA or that methods and principles based on 'center' research can be applied universally.

Even if a TESOL teacher education program is offered in an Asian context, this is no guarantee that students can apply what they learn to the realities of their own teaching. In Hong Kong, Richards and Pennington (1998) discovered that five novice BA-TESL teachers quickly resorted to whatever techniques they could use in order to maintain order in their classes and to cover required material. This meant a great deal of teacher-fronted instruction, use of students' L1 and close adherence to textbooks. In a case study of a preservice English teacher in Singapore, Farrell (2007) found that a student who failed her practicum was overwhelmed by the harsh realities in her first teaching experiences and resorted to unproductive 'maxims' from her own previous learning experiences (Richards, 1996).

A fairly consistent message emerges from this brief review, in spite of the cultural overgeneralizations made by some authors. From an ecological perspective: (1) so-called 'Western' methods of English language teaching (communicative, task-based, student-centered, process-oriented) cannot be applied wholesale to EFL contexts, where traditions of large, teacher-fronted, exam-oriented classes persist in Asia and in many European countries; and (2) English-dominant TESOL teacher education programs do not pay nearly enough attention to the needs of students to know how to adapt to local teaching conditions in diverse EFL settings.

I turn now to some concrete experiences and beliefs of students in L2 teacher education programs who were EFL teachers in Japan or who were planning to become teachers in Japan. Some were particularly interested in writing. These concrete experiences make vivid some of the needs for educating future teachers of EFL writing.

Experiences of Working Teachers in L2 Teacher Education Programs

In a small study I did with students in an American university MATESOL program in Japan (Casanave, 2004) where I was teaching Writing Methods, Research and Practicum, I observed classes that my students were teaching. Some of these classes, at the high schools in particular, left me wondering whether students could apply what they were learning. At the time, I was not sure. But some students told me later that the MA program had helped them see areas of possibility even within constraints. It is on this positive note that I now describe somewhat less encouraging details of what confronts teachers in Japan who have been educated in English-dominant TESOL programs. In spite of some harsh realities, I do not want to lose sight of the potential for idealism.

As a first look at some experiences of L2 teacher education students who would be working in Japan after graduating, I turn to a study by Sandra McKay (2000) of five Japanese students studying in a MATESOL program in San Francisco. McKay learned from the students that going back to Japan and implementing what they had learned would be very difficult. Their learning logs demonstrated that they wrestled with questions about whether similar methods could be used in both the USA and Japan. Throughout their MA program, they had come to believe in the importance of communicative, student-centered methodologies. But in spite of the Japanese Ministry of Education's pronouncements about making English language instruction more communicatively oriented, the students worried, with good reason, about whether they could implement what they had learned when they returned home, in great part because of exam- and teacher-centered instruction.

McKay asked the students in a group interview how they might be able to make their future classrooms in Japan more student-centered, given the likely lack of support from colleagues and students. The students, recognizing they would lack power and authority as young, new employees, said they would be quiet – that they would wait the many years it took for them to be promoted. Even the one student-teacher who experimented most with innovative methods in the USA context admitted that trying to instigate a student-centered high school class in Japan would go against students' expectations. He saw himself as making small changes, over time, one step at a time (McKay, 2000: 64). One of the students said he would be prepared to wait five years before trying anything new, and another said she would be 'quiet' so as not to be considered 'naughty' by her senior colleagues (McKay, 2000: 58).

In my own experiences in two US university L2 language teacher education programs in Japan, I faced these dilemmas first hand. Innovations and 'enlightened' teaching of writing was possible in only a few of the elite, private high schools and universities. At the risk of exaggerating and generalizing, let me characterize what I learned about the more typical, primarily public high schools (and junior high schools and even some universities) where some of the MA teachers that I observed worked.

English classes, required of all students, met two or three times a week for only 50 minutes at a time. In these classes, many students showed little interest in lessons. Students of all proficiency levels were put in the same class, often 40 or more students, in the belief that it was not fair to segregate better from poorer ones. Curricula were controlled by the Ministry of Education in the sense that only approved textbooks were allowed and the Ministry published, for nationwide consumption, the guidelines for what was to be accomplished in each skill area. Textbooks tended to depict cultural, gender and ethnic stereotypes. A group at a school, and not the individual teachers, decided the specific schedules, lessons, tests and activities. Teachers who were not senior by virtue of age and experience lived in fear of making decisions or mistakes that might go against established policy. Innovation by individual teachers tended to be looked down upon because it might signal that the teacher believed he/she knew more than the others. Along the same line, I had several students who were in the MA program secretly, because they feared being reprimanded by higher ups in their schools and shunned by colleagues for setting themselves apart as better. Tests and exams controlled much of the high school curriculum, particularly as students neared the time for the dreaded university entrance exams. The teachers of Japanese nationality were given a great deal of extra work (committees, club and sports monitoring) as well as grammar and reading classes (language of instruction: Japanese; main activity, translation from English to Japanese – Gorsuch, 1998), while the native-English speakers tended to be given conversation classes. Classroom management – getting students to stop chattering and attend to the day's work – was a major problem. And perhaps most challenging for the teachers that I worked with, classes dedicated to writing generally did not exist.

EFL students thus lacked opportunities for the extended practice so essential to learning how to write – the grammar-translation-reading-oriented curriculum had too strong a hold on teachers in such classes. In high schools, this focus is almost inevitable: teachers, administrators, parents and even students themselves, even though they are often bored, feel they must prepare for entrance exams. Motivation for writing as communication or creative production was therefore anathema in the exam-burdened atmosphere of the high school. In other words, it was challenging to enact even the fundamentals of what we have come to consider good writing instruction.

However, in some classes in the better schools, successful teachers (who were also better class managers) were able to allow perhaps 10 minutes at the end of a class for a writing activity. They did this regularly and even managed to find time to read and put at least one mark or comment on students' journals. These teachers moved constantly around the class and had hawk-like eyes for any students not paying attention. They also tended to be the ones who had a theoretically more consistent basis for their instructional activities, and who used a mix of Japanese and English in their instructional language. Finally, they were able to find clever ways to adapt required text materials that achieved the dual purpose of covering the material and sparking students' interests.

There is hope. But in my writing methods and practicum classes, I did not initially understand the severe constraints that the lower tier high school teachers in particular worked under. In our MA course, we spent a lot of time reading about and discussing issues such as contrastive rhetoric, the process-product debate, issues in and methods of feedback and assessment, fluency and risk-taking activities such as journal writing, and so on, as though they could apply unproblematically to their own teaching contexts. But this part of the class, while building valuable background knowledge on issues raised in published literature, felt unhelpful for the hands-on problems that the teachers faced in their own classes.

Let me now turn to some specific comments by some working teachers from the two US university L2 teacher education programs that I was working at. In a follow-up study to Casanave (2004), I asked another group of graduate students who were interested in L2 writing to comment specifically on several aspects of their work and its relation to their graduate program (Casanave, 2005).

Commentary by Working Teachers

I spoke with 16 master's and doctoral students, 12 of whom were Japanese, and 12 of whom were female. They were all working teachers, many at the high school level. We communicated by email, online discussion and open class discussion. The main questions came from five sets of email questions and responses exchanged between January and March 2005. The questions, in five categories, asked about respondents' backgrounds, coursework in their MA programs, beliefs about L2 writing, application of beliefs and coursework to their teaching, and actual teaching practices. I learned that their coursework in their graduate programs varied rather widely and that few had taken any courses in the teaching of writing (an elective, when offered, which was rare). In what follows, I offer a selection of their commentary, in four areas: their beliefs about writing, the application of their beliefs and coursework to their teaching, the effectiveness of their MA program and their suggestions for change.

Beliefs about the value of teaching and learning writing

In general, the graduate students told me that they believed that EFL writing was important for students to learn, for their personal development, future work and possible future study. They noted some of the following reasons: (a) writing is a tool for developing thought and self-expression, which students have rarely practiced even in Japanese; (b) it prepares them for future work in a world beyond Japan's borders, or at the very least broadens students' visions of the world; (c) it is required for students in English-dominant undergraduate or graduate programs (present and future) and for English majors. However, several people, including one teacher at a technical school, mentioned that students don't need to learn academic writing in English unless they will need this kind of writing in other courses. According to one person, more important are the kinds of writing that students may actually already be doing, especially on the internet:

> I don't think they need to study academic writing unless they wish to go to graduate school or study abroad. What they need to study is more casual online writing (e.g. email, online shopping, making inquiries online, etc.) because using internet and email internationally is getting more and more popular among young people. (EI, email questionnaire)

The respondents were uniform in their beliefs that students did not need grammar-translation exercises except as exam preparation. Rather, they needed writing that built confidence, fluency, and expressive and communicative skills, along with a lot of practice – all of which contribute to language learning in general (see Harklau's [2002] and Manchón and Roca de Larios's [2007] discussions of how writing can contribute to learning and L2 acquisition). However, they said that it was difficult to escape the exam pressure. Two respondents wrote that they were pessimistic about the examination system changing to one that was more communicative because the government was too deeply invested in 'existing views and sources of power and income' (SR, email questionnaire; RY, email questionnaire).

Application of MA coursework to teaching

The participants' responses to a question on whether they could apply what they learned in their master's programs to their own teaching situations varied greatly, but many felt very constrained. As expressed by one respondent, 'The reality we experience [in the MATESOL program] does not always translate into the reality we face in the classroom' (SR, online discussion). The primary constraints concerned rigid test-oriented curricula, including time constraints, and lack of student motivation or reasons to write in L2.

At the curricular level, several respondents, particularly those teaching at public high schools, noted that the problems stemmed from expectations at many levels (Ministry, schools, teachers, students, parents) that students improve test scores in English, and that material be covered in an approved curriculum that itself focused on correct grammar and accurate translation. MK stated that when she was teaching high school, 'the curriculum and the syllabus were rigidly fixed by the school (and the students' expectations), and the extent to which I can apply what I learned about L2 writing generally was very limited' (MK, email questionnaire). SR said that the expectation in high schools is to have students 'produce good translations' that are identical to each other, rather than to have them become fluent writers (SR, email questionnaire). One high school teacher commented that her Ministry-approved textbook had the word 'writing' in the title, but that the portion of the book devoted to writing was merely 'lip service'. Another high-school teacher mentioned the constraints of time in a curriculum where she was under pressure to cover the required material and to prepare students for exams. She tried to give students some freewriting activities five times a year (about once every two months), but noted that 'it will be difficult to spend 10 to 15 minutes on just writing' (HF, e-mail questionnaire).

Although constraints are less severe at the university level because the entrance exam pressure is off, they still pose problems for teachers. These constraints often have to do with students' lack of purpose or motivation for writing. In her MA program, EI learned about 'learners' aspects' such as motivation, beliefs and aptitudes, and tried to incorporate these ideas into her syllabus. However, she noted that 'we can't expect students who are not good at writing in Japanese to write well in English', particularly if they have no real reasons or purposes for writing and no real readers. MK (e-mail questionnaire) also mentioned that students' English proficiency levels were so low that she 'found it of higher priority to teach them basic English grammar than spend time on writing'.

Another university teacher who taught non-English majors also felt constrained by students' lack of purpose in communicating and writing, noting that he could apply little of what he had learned in his MA program. Although he had learned about CLT in his TESOL methods course, he found that 'it is like pulling teeth' to use CLT practices with many of his students who lacked motivation, so he tried to concentrate on those students who made some effort. 'It is not realistic to expect everyone to like communicative English when they perceive no need for using English in their future' (CB, email questionnaire).

The other side of this rather bleak picture was expressed by respondents who felt more positive about being able to apply what they had learned in their graduate teacher education to their own teaching. In these cases, the curricular constraints were less severe, and students had some purpose for learning to write in English. A few of the teachers, particularly those at private universities and high schools, were actually teaching writing courses rather than general English courses. Teachers who had taken an elective course in methods of teaching writing in their MA programs were especially enthusiastic about the chance to teach writing. RY said: 'I'm teaching L2 writing at the college level, so I can do whatever I like. I can use many kinds of materials such as newspapers, articles, videos, etc. I can apply what I learned about L2 writing instruction such as dialogue journals, freewriting/quickwriting, academic writing, etc.'. She taught academic writing only to those students who would need this kind of writing for the future, such as for study abroad (RY, email questionnaire). One teacher who worked at a public high school managed to teach writing in spite of pressures and expectations to prepare students for college entrance exams. At her school there was a class called 'Writing 1' in which the textbook contained many grammar exercises. Using a pedagogy of flexibility that she learned in her MA program, she supplemented the textbook with activities such as journal writing, postcard writing to Korean students, haiku contests, plans for her students to teach English to elementary children and essays for essay writing contests. She hoped to convince students that they could enjoy writing as a way to communicate with people – that there was more to English than learning how to pass entrance exams (SS, email questionnaire).

If this diversity of responses is at all representative of other teachers who have studied in US- (or British, Australian, etc.) sponsored TESOL programs, we can get a sense of the complexity of teaching situations and local demands (Larsen-Freeman, 2002; Tudor, 2003). To say that the constraints are cultural (e.g. beliefs in Asia conflicting with those in the West) is to vastly oversimplify the local contexts of teachers' work and their own backgrounds, beliefs and experiences.

Effectiveness of the MA program in preparing teachers to deal with constraints

Many respondents in my small study, particularly those who were teaching in junior and senior high schools, claimed that their master's programs did little or nothing to directly prepare them for the realities of their lives in the Japanese classroom. There were two main issues: undue condemnation of traditional teaching in favor of communicative classes, and the lack of specificity of instruction to Japan.

In the first case, in learning what the latest theories were, the respondents felt that the message from their MATESOL program was that students would not learn English, or to write English, by doing grammar exercises, translations and exam preparation exercises. The condemnation of 'traditional' ways of teaching in Japan struck some students as quite strong. One respondent wrote that 'In [U.S.] college and

MA courses, the students are persuaded that their traditional ways of teaching are not effective and valid' (HF, journal entry). Another student wrote in a journal entry that she felt that her professors wanted the TESOL students to confirm the validity of nontraditional methods:

> In some TESOL methodology courses I took here, it seemed to me that professors wanted each of TESOL students to do action research in order to validate a success story like this: 1) The current Japanese EFL education is bad (e.g., grammar translation, teacher-centered approaches); 2) Apply SLA theory and TESOL methods (e.g., interactionism, CLT, cooperative learning, task-based learning) to change the situation; 3) The situation will be improved. (MM, journal entry)

She was not able to 'swallow this story' in full, because she saw the benefits of traditional grammar- and exam-oriented instruction. She stated further: 'When I was in high school I really enjoyed them, and general linguistic awareness I acquired through such approaches often benefitted me later in L2 and L3 acquisition'.

The second area of effectiveness (or lack of) of the MA program – specificity of instruction to Japan – brought mixed responses from the teachers. Even though the two graduate programs were located in Japan, the emphasis seems to have been on general theories and practices rather than on specific issues concerning language teaching in Japan. Many students noted that ways to apply what they had learned came out in class discussion, but others found this inadequate. As one woman said, 'I think there is few opportunities to discuss these constraints and realities. I think that TESOL program focus on how to teach English in communicative language teaching but it doesn't seem to focus on what to teach in Japan' (RY, email questionnaire). MK concurred, commenting that it was very hard for her to apply the theories she had learned, because too 'little research in SLA and ELT is conducted in a similar situation to Japan's secondary school' on topics such as the effectiveness of feedback (MK, email questionnaire). Another MA graduate noted that 'My strongest criticism to the program is that it focuses far too much on theory and studies done in other [i.e., nonJapanese] contexts' (SR, email questionnaire). He added bluntly that 'The MA program did not prepare me for dealing with school management' in the Japanese context.

Not all teachers condemned this lack of specificity to Japan, feeling that generally they were on their own to adapt what they knew to their local settings. In particular, their views about the value of learning about theories differed from those of the more critical students. EI said:

'I learned a lot of theories which support what I actually do in the class. Knowing theories I can apply them to various situations. I learned how to find a way to adjust things to have successful classes even though we usually have lots of constraints' (EI, email questionnaire). HF agreed, saying that 'even though it is hard to apply everything in classes, I know about the current theories and can try to find some time to put into action' (HF, email questionnaire).

In sum, the teachers I worked with responded in diverse ways to the question of what might be applied from their education to their own teaching, but, in general, in accordance with an ecological perspective, they felt much more attention needed to be given to specific EFL settings in their discussions and readings.

Respondents' recommendations for changes in TESOL programs

All the respondents who communicated with me recommended that some aspects of their MA programs be changed, primarily by shifting more attention to Japan contexts, and addressing school-wide issues beyond the English class. Although they discussed general changes, all of their views apply to the teaching of writing and the training of writing teachers.

Most respondents commented that they would like their programs to focus more on the realities of teaching English in Japan, where the education system is linked closely to governmental and corporate influences. The realities include differences between teaching at junior-senior high school levels and in colleges and universities, large classes in which it is impossible to assign and comment on many writings, classroom management problems, and few classes and little time devoted to writing. But the most formidable of these realities is the test-oriented curriculum – entrance exams for entering university and, more recently, the pressure to prepare university students for TOEIC, which more and more companies are requiring of applicants. In the context of these realities, a number of respondents questioned their MA programs' focus on communicative and fluency-oriented language teaching, wondering whether 'this teaching approach fits for English education in Japan' (RY, email questionnaire). This finding is consistent with some of the literature reviewed in the first part of this chapter.

Several other respondents, like RY, felt pessimistic about the possibility of changing the Japanese government's powerful role in influencing how English is taught, particularly in high schools. Although the

Ministry now recommends a shift to CLT, the entrance exam system remains in place and government approved textbooks continue to drive curricula and methods. At the university level, as well, exam-driven curricula are spreading due to the influence of TOEIC (McCrostie, 2006). Exam preparation is now an enormous, lucrative business for private for-profit schools and publishers, who continue to expand their influence. This profit motive, and the high-stakes nature of testing, will be difficult to counter, even with well-supported pedagogical arguments by educators. Japanese teachers, some not fully proficient in communicative English, and not wishing to counter governmental policies, thus easily justify exam preparation classes.

Looking beyond the English class, some respondents recommended that MATESOL programs offer more general courses in philosophy, education, sociology, politics and linguistics that focus on broad educational, social and language issues that pertain to the larger school setting. These include questions about purpose, attitude, motivation, and classroom and school management. These larger issues are institutional, social and political, and deeply affect the quality of teachers' lives and the decisions they make in local contexts, whether these contexts are ESL or EFL. In other words, in addition to knowing the whys and hows of teaching process writing (for example), teachers need to be prepared *not* to have opportunities to teach writing, let alone process writing, and to have an idea of what they can do, or will be required to do, instead. They need, in short, to learn how to negotiate the local institutional culture (Tudor, 2003; Van Lier, 2004), which can include the reality of teachers' having little power within a system to be able to make changes of any kind without risking losing their jobs. Moreover, because so few opportunities may exist for these teachers to instruct students in the specifics of writing, taking a writing-to-learn approach, in the sense of helping students build fluency and confidence in their L2 and of interacting with particular content, may make more sense than a learning-to-write approach (Harklau, 2002; Manchn & Roca de Larios, 2007). Such an approach, although not specifically articulated by my informants, might alleviate some frustration that teachers feel at not being able to pursue a focused writing agenda within the realities of the local institutional culture.

These suggestions came from teachers who were working in public and private high schools and universities. Not represented in this discussion is another large group of teachers that TESOL programs and writing teachers need to pay attention to, namely, teachers who work within the growing for-profit language-school industry. Graduates from language teacher education programs need to know that they may end up in one of these commercial schools, in which all materials and methods are prescribed by the organization. In general, it will not be possible to teach writing in such settings in ways they have learned about in their programs.

To conclude this section, let me say that in my MATESOL classes in Japan on writing, I tried to convince students to continue developing their own intellectual and educational attitudes, beliefs and knowledge, regardless of the day-to-day constraints in their own classes. As changed people, perhaps they could then change the lives of their own students, simply by being/modeling who they had become. If students are bored by a test-oriented curriculum, and many are, teachers have an obligation to help students discover the pleasures of reading and writing, and idealistic teachers can help do this. Idealism should be part of every L2 teacher education program, along with an exploration of many local possibilities.

Conclusion: Some Hard Questions and Some Suggestions

L2 teacher education programs need to address the dilemma of the mismatch between their current pedagogical ideals and research findings on the one hand, and the very diverse realities of local EFL contexts for writing instruction on the other. In what follows, I pose some of the hard questions that writing teacher educators face in the coming years and I make a few suggestions.

(1) Do we standardize MATESOL and certificate programs more than is currently the case, as a way to ensure consistency in language teacher education programs? What courses or issues, if any, should be considered core for language teacher education programs?

With Liu (1998, 1999) and others, I believe that one or more courses need to be included that address specific issues in EFL teaching and that acquaint students with some of the pedagogical and political realities they may encounter. Even if a teacher education program is not heavily theoretically oriented, students can be introduced to sociocultural and ecological views of learning that will help them understand how to work flexibly within the local contexts of their teaching (Van Lier, 2004). Specific examples of the diversity of issues can be provided in the form of readings and discussion, based on the work of scholars such as Reichelt and others who are represented in this volume. The question as to whether all programs should require graduates to learn methods and materials of L2 writing is more difficult, given that writing courses may be rare in EFL settings, and traditional kinds of essay and academic writing seem to be needed only in specific cases, such as when students are preparing to study abroad in English-dominant universities (see Reichelt's [2005] comments on writing instruction in Poland, and this volume). At the very least, teachers need to understand the kinds of exam-oriented writing used in local settings, to practice adapting all kinds of materials and finding ways to slip in writing instruction where possible. By shifting their focus only slightly, teachers may be able to see their instruction as hands-on practice with language and content, rather than just as instruction in writing. In fact, without even calling attention to the fact that they are teaching writing, teachers can learn how to use writing to support many other kinds of learning. The need for courses in how to do this kind of adaptive work seems fundamental in teacher education programs. Likewise, courses need to pay greater attention to ways the Internet can be used creatively for L2 literacy activities. This can be accomplished by including threads on multimodal literacy (Cope & Kalantzis, 2000; Kress, 2003) across a broad range of courses.

Additionally, every program needs rigorous attention to future teachers' knowledge of the grammatical and lexical systems of English: L1 speakers need to know their own language inside and out, and L2 speakers need to be as proficient in their L2 as possible (Liu [1999] recommends a 'language improvement' component for L2 speakers, but I think many L1 speakers need this as well). Finally, every program needs to incorporate a reflective element into every class and every practicum (Bailey *et al.*, 2001; Freeman & Richards, 1996; Gebhard & Oprandy, 1999; Richards, 1996; Zeichner & Liston, 1996). Specifically, future writing and EFL teachers need to see themselves as 'reflective practitioners' rather than just technicians (Schön, 1983, 1987), who know their beliefs and attitudes well, and who are always on the lookout for ways to adjust their agendas to the realities that they encounter.

(2) Do we give up or modify our idealistic portrayals of L2 writing?

All of the respondents in my study, and graduate students I have had since then, believe that many kinds of nontraditional writing activities can help students build confidence and fluency in using English, and can help reduce the boredom so often experienced in traditional grammar classes. Students in L2 education programs need to nourish this idealism, while simultaneously trying to cope with realities. Instruction in L2 (and L1) writing research, and inquiry into further innovations, should continue. Additionally, to the extent possible, I believe that writing teachers themselves need to write, and come to see themselves as writers. Teachers' sense of idealism, enthusiasm and possibility will thus be passed on to students. However, bandwagon fads, and innovation for the sake of innovation, rather than for principled reasons, must be resisted – a difficult challenge when pressure to innovate comes from the institution itself. Traditional teaching methods need to be studied as well, and not simply dismissed as outmoded (Swan, 2005).

(3) What kinds of research on L2 teacher education programs are needed in the coming years?

Perhaps most important is the need for more research on EFL teaching and writing that includes more documented cases of teaching and learning language in EFL settings, including in elementary, junior high and high schools and in for-profit language schools. This decentering of L2 research from its traditional English-dominant university settings, and the continued participation of multilingual scholars who can do research in students' L1, are essential in the coming years, given the proliferation of EFL instruction in school, business and for-profit contexts. Findings from case studies, in particular, of EFL teachers and learners in action, can then feed into language teacher preparation programs. L2 writing scholars, in particular, need to look closely at the kinds of writing activities that EFL students may need in the future and to balance research and instruction on these realities without losing their own idealism and enthusiasm about the power of writing to enrich lives in personal and professional ways.

This chapter has reviewed some issues related to the education of teachers of EFL writing by relying on experiences and commentary by a small number of teachers in one context, that of Japan (itself made up of diverse local contexts). My point is not to generalize from this specific discussion, but to emphasize the need for all EFL writing educators and teachers to observe closely the local needs and realities of their particular settings rather than prescribing fixed teacher education curricula for future EFL writing teachers.

References

Bailey, K.M., Curtis, A. and Nunan, D. (2001) *Pursuing Professional Development: The Self as Source.* Boston, MA: Heinle & Heinle.

Burnaby, B. and Sun, Y. (1989) Chinese teachers' views of Western language teaching: Context informs paradigms. *TESOL Quarterly* 23 (2), 219–238.

Canagarajah, A.S. (1999) *Resisting Linguistic Imperialism in English Teaching*. Oxford: Oxford University Press.
Canagarajah, A.S. (2002) *A Geopolitics of Academic Writing*. Pittsburgh, PA: University of Pittsburgh Press.
Carless, D. (2002) Implementing task-based learning with young learners. *ELT Journal* 56 (4), 389–396.
Carless, D. (2004) Issues in teachers' reinterpretation of a task-based innovation in primary schools. *TESOL Quarterly* 38 (4), 639–662.
Casanave, C.P. (1994) Language development in students' journals. *Journal of Second Language Writing* 3 (3), 179–201.
Casanave, C.P. (1995a) Journal writing in college English classes in Japan: Shifting the focus from language to education. *JALT Journal* 17, 95–111.
Casanave, C.P. (1995b) Local interactions: Constructing contexts for composing in a graduate sociology program. In G. Braine and D. Belcher (eds) *Academic Writing in a Second Language: Essays on Research and Pedagogy* (pp. 83–110). Norwood, NJ: Ablex.
Casanave, C.P. (2004, April) *Creating misfits or adjusting to the cultural status quo? Dilemmas in applying what we know about writing instruction in a foreign language setting*. Paper presented in the Colloquium: Preparing Teachers of Second Language Writing, at TESOL, Long Beach, CA.
Casanave, C.P. (2005, March) *Applying in Japan what is learned in a U.S. MATESOL program about L2 writing*. Paper presented in the Colloquium: Preparing Teachers of Second Language Writing (Part 2), at TESOL, San Antonio, TX.
Clachar, A. (2000) Opposition and accommodation: An examination of Turkish teachers' attitudes toward Western approaches to the teaching of writing. *Research in the Teaching of English* 35 (1), 66–100.
Cope, B. and Kalantzis, M. (eds) (2000) *Multiliteracies: Literacy Learning and the Design of Social Futures*. London: Routledge.
Duppenthaler, P.M. (2002) The effect of three types of written feedback on student motivation. *JALT Journal* 24 (2), 130–154.
Duppenthaler, P.M. (2004) Journal writing and the question of transfer of skills to other types of writing. *JALT Journal* 26 (2), 171–188.
Ellis, R. (1996) How culturally appropriate is the communicative approach? *ELT Journal* 50 (3), 213–218.
Ellis, R. (2003) *Task-based Language Learning and Teaching*. Oxford: Oxford University Press.
Farrell, T.S.C. (2007) Failing the practicum: Narrowing the gap between expectations and reality with reflective practice. *TESOL Quarterly* 41 (1), 193–201.
Freeman, D. and Richards, J.C. (eds) (1996) *Teacher Learning in Language Teaching*. New York: Cambridge University Press.
Gebhard, J.G. and Oprandy, R. (1999) *Language Teaching Awareness: A Guide to Exploring Beliefs and Practices*. Cambridge: Cambridge University Press.
Gorsuch, G. (1998) Yakudoku EFL instruction in two Japanese high school classrooms. *JALT Journal* 20 (1), 6–32.
Govardhan, A.K., Nayar, B. and Sheorey, T. (1999) Do U.S. MATESOL programs prepare students to teach abroad? *TESOL Quarterly* 33 (1), 114–125.

Harklau, L. (2002) The role of writing in classroom second language acquisition. *Journal of Second Language Writing* 11 (4), 329–350.

Hu, G. (2003) English language teaching in China: Regional differences and contributing factors. *Journal of Multilingual and Multicultural Development* 24 (4), 290–318.

Hu, G. (2005) 'CLT is best for China' – An untenable absolutist claim. *ELT Journal* 59 (1), 65–68.

Kaplan, R.B. (ed.) (1995) The teaching of writing in the Pacific Basin. Special issue of the *Journal of Asian Pacific Communication* 6 (1 & 2).

Kramsch, C. (ed.) (2002) *Language Acquisition and Language Socialization: Ecological Perspectives*. New York: Continuum.

Kress, G. (2003) *Literacy in the New Media Age*. London: Routledge.

Larsen-Freeman, D. (2002) Language acquisition and language use from a chaos/complexity theory perspective. In C. Kramsch (ed.) *Language Acquisition and Language Socialization: Ecological Perspectives* (pp. 33–46). New York: Continuum.

Leki, I. (2001) Material, educational, and ideological challenges of teaching ESL writing at the turn of the century. In R. Manchón (ed.) *Writing in the L2 Classroom: Issues in Research and Pedagogy*. Special issue of *International Journal of English Studies* 1 (2), 197–209.

Li, D. (1998) 'It's always more difficult than you plan and imagine': Teachers' perceived difficulties in introducing the communicative approach in South Korea. *TESOL Quarterly* 32 (4), 677–697.

Li, X. and Casanave, C.P. (eds) (2005) Multiple perspectives on L1 and L2 academic literacy in Asia Pacific and Diaspora contexts. Special issue of the *Journal of Asian Pacific Communication* 15 (1).

Liao, X. (2004) The need for communicative language teaching in China. *ELT Journal* 58 (3), 270–273.

Liu, D. (1998) Ethnocentrism in TESOL: Teaching education and the neglected needs of international TESOL students. *ELT Journal* 52 (1), 3–10.

Liu, D. (1999) Training non-native TESOL students: Challenges for TESOL teacher education in the West. In G. Braine (ed.) *Non-native Educators in English Language Teaching* (pp. 197–210). Mahwah, NJ: Lawrence Erlbaum.

Liu, D., Ahn, G-S., Baek, K.S. and Han, N-O. (2004) South Korean high school English teachers' code switching: Questions and challenges in the drive for maximal use of English in teaching. *TESOL Quarterly* 38 (4), 605–638.

Manchón, R.M. and Roca de Larios, J. (2007) Writing-to-learn in instructed language learning contexts. In E. Alcón and P. Safont (eds) *The Intercultural Speaker. Using and Acquiring English in Instructed Language Contexts* (pp. 101–121). Dordrecht: Springer.

McCrostie, J. (2006) Why are universities abandoning English teaching for TOEIC training? *On Cue* 14 (2), 30–32.

McDonough, K. and Chaikitmongkol, W. (2007) Teachers' and learners' reactions to a task-based EFL course in Thailand. *TESOL Quarterly* 41 (1), 107–132.

McKay, S. (2000) An investigation of five Japanese English teachers' reflections on their U.S. MA TESOL practicum experience. *JALT Journal* 22 (1), 46–68.

Nunan, D. (2003) The impact of English as a global language on educational policies and practices in the Asia-Pacific region. *TESOL Quarterly* 37 (4), 589–613.

Nunan, D. (2004) *Task-based Language Teaching*. Cambridge: Cambridge University Press.

Pennington, M.C., Brock, M.N. and Yue, F. (1996) Explaining Hong Kong students' response to process writing: An exploration of causes and outcomes. *Journal of Second Language Writing* 5 (3), 227–252.

Pennycook, A. (1994) *The Cultural Politics of English as an International Language*. Harlow: Longman.

Phillipson, R. (1992) *Linguistic Imperialism*. Oxford: Oxford University Press.

Ramanathan, V., Davies, C.E. and Schleppegrell, M.J. (2001) A naturalistic inquiry into the cultures of two divergent MA-TESOL programs: Implications for TESOL. *TESOL Quarterly* 35 (2), 279–305.

Reichelt, M. (2005) English-language writing instruction in Poland. *Journal of Second Language Writing* 14 (4), 215–232.

Richards, J.S. (1996) Teachers' maxims in language teaching. *TESOL Quarterly* 30 (2), 281–296.

Richards, J.C. and Pennington, M. (1998) The first year of teaching. In J.C. Richards (ed.) *Beyond Training* (pp. 173–190). New York: Cambridge University Press.

Schön, D. (1983) *The Reflective Practitioner: How Professionals Think in Action*. New York: Basic Books.

Schön, D. (1987) *Educating the Reflective Practitioner: Toward a New Design for Teaching and Learning in the Professions*. San Francisco, CA: Jossey-Bass.

Sheen, R. (1994) A critical analysis of the advocacy of the task-based syllabus. *TESOL Quarterly* 28 (4), 127–151.

Skehan, P. (2003) Task-based instruction. *Language Teaching* 36, 1–14.

Swan, M. (2005) Legislation by hypothesis: The case of task-based instruction. *Applied Linguistics* 26, 376–401.

Tarnopolsky, O. (2000) Writing English as a foreign language: A report from Ukraine. *Journal of Second Language Writing* 9 (3), 209–226.

Tudor, I. (2003) Learning to live with complexity: Towards an ecological perspective on language teaching. *System* 31 (1), 1–12.

Van Lier, L. (2002) An ecological-semiotic perspective on language and linguistics. In C. Kramsch (ed.) *Language Acquisition and Language Socialization: Ecological Perspectives* (pp. 140–164). New York: Continuum.

Van Lier, L. (2004) *The Ecology and Semiotics of Language Learning: A Sociocultural Perspective*. Dordrecht: Kluwer Academic.

You, X. (2004a) 'The choice made from no choice': English writing instruction in a Chinese university. *Journal of Second Language Writing* 13 (2), 97–110.

You, X. (2004b) New directions in EFL writing: A report from China. *Journal of Second Language Writing* 13 (4), 253–256.

Zeichner, K.M. and Liston, D.P. (1996) *Reflective Teaching: An Introduction*. Mahwah, NJ: Lawrence Erlbaum.

Part 3

Coda

Chapter 11

Bibliography of Sources on Foreign Language Writing

MELINDA REICHELT

This bibliography includes sources published since 1997 about foreign language (FL) writing. During this period, there has been a very rapid increase in publications in this area. An attempt has been made to include a broad range of published sources, including works from areas of the world and instructional levels that are often neglected in the literature. Due to space constraints, sources already addressed in other chapters in this volume, as well as master's theses and dissertations, have not been included.

The bibliography contains an annotated and an unannotated section. Both sections include empirical studies categorized under three headings: *Texts*, which includes studies of written texts produced by FL writers; *Individual Differences*, which includes primarily studies comparing the characteristics of individual FL writers; and *Processes/Strategies*, which includes studies investigating what writers actually do as they compose. The unannotated section includes studies falling under these and three additional categories: *Contexts*, which includes descriptions of how writing instruction is practiced in different countries; *Effects of Pedagogical Procedures*, which includes empirical studies investigating the impact of various teaching practices; and *Pedagogical Practices and Issues*, which includes sources devoted to describing pedagogical practices. While the sources in the last category are not rigorous empirical studies, they provide important information about the concerns, practices and contexts of FL writing instruction in a range of settings, including many settings that are not represented in the research literature.

Annotated Bibliography

Texts

Albrechtsen, D. (1997) A discourse analysis of narrative essays written in English by Danish students. In K. Pogner (ed.) *Writing: Text and Interaction. Odense Working Papers in Language and Communication* 14, 1–40.

The author applied a narrative analysis to 78 narrative essays written by 16 to 19-year-old Danish students. Three factors were found to account for 67.9% of the total variance in holistic assessments of the texts: degree of evaluation (purpose for telling the story); sophistication in structure and character description; and degree of orientation.

Aliakbari, M. (2002) Writing in a foreign language: A writing problem or a language problem? *Pan-Pacific Association of Applied Linguistics* 6, 157–168.

Thirty-three university English majors in Iran wrote comparison/contrast essays in both Persian (L1) and English and took an English proficiency test. Essays were scored for language, content and organization. L2 proficiency rather than L1 writing ability was found to be a better predictor of L2 writing ability.

Chiang, S. (1999) Assessing grammatical and textual features in L2 writing samples: The case of French as a foreign language. *The Modern Language Journal* 83, 219–232.

Three native-French-speaking instructors of French rated 172 one-page essays written by beginning and intermediate US university students of French, based on morphology, syntax, cohesion, coherence and overall quality. In rating, raters relied heavily on discourse features, especially cohesion. The rating scale exhibited content validity and reliability, but not the desired construct validity.

Chiang, S. (2003) The importance of cohesive conditions to perceptions of writing quality at the early stages of foreign language learning. *System* 31, 471–484.

Fifteen native-English-speaking professors of English and 15 native-Chinese-speaking professors of English evaluated 60 English essays written by Taiwanese university students, based on 10 discourse features, 10 grammatical features and overall quality. Coherence and cohesion ratings correlated with ratings of overall quality, and cohesion was a strong predictor of quality of the 20 discourse/grammatical features.

de Haan, P. and van Esch, K. (2005) The development of writing in English and Spanish as foreign languages. *Assessing Writing* 10, 100–116.

The researchers collected English- and Spanish-language argumentative essays written by Dutch university students, and L1 essays written by Spanish university students. Holistic ratings were compared with syntactic and lexical analyses, and students' writing development after one year was measured. More advanced students were more fluent writers than less advanced students and used longer sentences and longer words.

Guillot, M-N. (2005) *Il y a des gens qui disent que...* 'there are people who say that...' Beyond grammatical accuracy in FL learners' writing: Issues of non-nativeness. *International Review of Applied Linguistics* 43, 109–128.

The researcher compared writing by advanced FL French learners at a British university with a corpus of French and English texts written by native speakers. Focusing on the issue of vagueness in academic writing, the researcher explored speech-writing relationships, linguistic transfer and the interrelatedness of discourse and psycholinguistic factors.

Hawes, T. and Thomas, S. (1997) Problems of thematization in student writing. *RELC Journal* 28, 35–55.

In a corpus of 100 essays written by lower-intermediate to advanced Malaysian students, the authors examined various theme types used, thematic progression strategies and rhetorical purpose. The authors conclude that students' writing, when measured against the writing in two British newspapers, uses too few or too many of any given type of thematization, and uses the types inappropriately.

Hyland, K. (2002) Authority and invisibility: Authorial identity in academic writing. *Journal of Pragmatics* 34, 1091–1112.

The author compared the use of first person personal pronouns in 64 undergraduate theses written by Hong Kong students, comparing them with a corpus of research articles. The results of this analysis, along with interviews with students and their supervisors, indicated a preference for avoidance of first person, especially when making arguments or claims.

Hyland, K. (2004) Disciplinary interactions: Metadiscourse in L2 postgraduate writing. *Journal of Second Language Writing* 13, 133–151.

Hyland explored the use of metadiscourse in 240 dissertations and theses written in English by Hong Kong students. He proposed a model of metadiscourse that illustrates how academic writers represent themselves and their work, which varies according to discipline and genre.

Kamimura, T. and Oi, K. (2001) The effects of differences in point of view on the story production of Japanese EFL students. *Foreign Language Annals* 34, 118–130.

Japanese college EFL students wrote first-person and third-person narratives, based on the same series of pictures. Low-proficiency students' third-person narratives were lower in quantity and quality, while high-proficiency students' third-person narratives were only slightly lower in quality.

Kang, J. (2005) Written narratives as an index of L2 competence in Korean EFL learners. *Journal of Second Language Writing* 14, 259–279.

Kang compared L1 and English-language narratives of university-level Korean EFL writers with English-language narratives of native English speakers. While the Koreans' EFL writing exhibited some specifically Korean linguistic strategies (e.g. frequent use of demonstrative references and repetition), it also diverged somewhat from Korean writing in the direction of English-language norms.

Khuwaileh, A. and Al Shoumali, A. (2000) Writing errors: A study of the writing ability of Arab learners of academic English and Arabic at university. *Language, Culture and Curriculum* 13, 174–183.

English- and Arabic-language essays were written by 150 native-Arab-speaking students in Jordan. Analysis of essays indicated that poor writing in English correlated with poor writing in Arabic.

Kuiken, F. and Vedder, I. (2008) Cognitive task complexity and written output in Italian and French as a foreign language. *Journal of Second Language Writing* 17, 48–60.

Dutch university students ($n = 167$) studying Italian or French wrote two tasks of differing cognitive complexity. Texts written in response to the cognitively more demanding task were more linguistically accurate. No differences were found between task types of measures of syntactic complexity or lexical variation.

Liu, M. and Braine, G. (2005) Cohesive features in argumentative writing produced by Chinese undergraduates. *System* 33, 623–636.

The authors investigated the use of cohesive devices in 50 EFL argumentative essays written by Chinese non-English majors in Beijing. Lexical devices were used most frequently, followed by references and conjunctives. Quality of essays correlated with the number of lexical devices and the number of cohesive devices.

Makalela, L. (2004) Differential error types in second-language students' written and spoken texts. *Written Communication* 22, 368–385.

The author compared transcripts of oral presentations given by 50 South African university students with two-page essays that they had written. Written compositions exhibited more nonstandard morphosyntactic forms than oral presentations, while oral presentations contained more nonstandard discourse forms.

Mei, W.S. (2006) Creating a contrastive rhetorical stance: Investigating the strategy of problematization in students' argumentation. *RELC Journal* 37, 329–353.

The author analyzed 27 geography essays written by first-year university students in Singapore, focusing on how writers problematized issues. Writers of high-rated essays used evaluative resources more effectively than writers of low-rated essays, employing such strategies as setting up contrasting positions early in their essays, asserting/reiterating their own positions and posing rhetorical questions.

Ruiz-Funes, M. (2001) Task representation in foreign language reading-to-write. *Foreign Language Annals* 34, 226–234.

The author analyzed reading-to-write tasks composed by third-year US university students of Spanish, examining the relationship between types of task representation and the papers' linguistic characteristics. Students interpreted the same task in different ways, but neither grammatically correct nor syntactically complex sentences correlated with sophistication in composing strategies or the ability to express highly developed ideas. However, grammatically correct sentences did, in some cases, correlate with syntactic complexity.

Simpson, J.M. (2004) A look at early childhood writing in English and Spanish in a bilingual school in Ecuador. *International Journal of Bilingual Education and Bilingualism* 7, 432–448.

English and Spanish writing samples from first graders in an Ecuadorian bilingual school were analyzed. The children used similar amounts of topical repetition in both languages, and analysis indicated developmental stages in narrative strategies.

Way, D.P., Joiner, E.G. and Seaman, M.A. (2000) Writing in the secondary foreign language classroom: The effects of prompts and tasks on novice learners of French. *The Modern Language Journal* 84, 171–184.

The study analyzed the effects of descriptive, narrative and expository writing tasks in combination with bare, vocabulary and prose model-writing prompts. A total of 937 writing samples written by 330 novice learners of French were analyzed. The descriptive task was easiest and the expository task was most difficult; prose model prompts produced the highest scores and bare prompts the lowest.

Individual differences

Cheng, Y-S. (2002) Factors associated with foreign language writing anxiety. *Foreign Language Annals* 35, 647–656.

This study investigated FL writing anxiety. Perceived FL writing competence predicted anxiety better than writing achievement did; female students experienced more anxiety than male students; anxiety increased according to length of study; and L2 writing anxiety was distinct from L1 writing anxiety.

Ferenz, O. (2005) EFL writers' social networks: Impact on advanced academic literacy development. *Journal of English for Academic Purposes* 4, 339–351.

Through questionnaires and interviews, the author investigated the interpersonal relationships graduate student EFL writers in Israel develop to acquire academic literacy. Results indicated that students' identities and goals impact their social networks, which in turn affect students' development of literacy skills, including writing skills.

Haneda, M. (2005) Investing in foreign-language writing: A study of two multicultural learners. *Journal of Language, Identity, and Education* 4, 269–290.

Two Canadian university students, one who spoke Japanese at home and one who had learned Japanese through a one-year immersion in a Japanese high school, were interviewed and given questionnaires. Their approach to writing in Japanese was closely linked to their histories, identities and agencies.

Kamimura, T. (2000) Integration of process and product orientations in EFL writing instruction. *RELC Journal* 31, 1–28.

Thirty-five Japanese college students wrote an argumentative essay, and, based on scores, were categorized as skilled or unskilled. Students also completed a retrospective questionnaire and a test of knowledge of English academic texts. Skilled writers had more knowledge of academic texts and more advanced composing strategies. Both characteristics were deemed important for writing success.

Lee, S-Y. (2005) Facilitating and inhibiting factors in English as a foreign language writing performance: A model testing with structural equation modeling. *Language Learning* 55, 335–374.

Writing apprehension, writer's block, voluntary reading, self-initiated writing, and student beliefs and attitudes were investigated among 270 Taiwanese university students, who completed questionnaires and wrote a 40-minute essay. Voluntary reading was the only predictor of EFL writing performance.

Leibowitz, B. (2004) Becoming academically literate in South Africa: Lessons from student accounts for policymakers and educators. *Language and Education* 18, 35–52.

South African students' literacy biographies and a set of their essays were examined. Their acquisition of academic literacy was shaped by their English proficiency, access to literacy materials, ways with words and participation in literacy events. Implications for educators and policy makers are discussed.

Li, Y. (2007) Apprentice scholarly writing in a community of practice: An intraview of an NNES graduate student writing a research article. *TESOL Quarterly* 41, 55–79.

This study investigates a Chinese doctoral student of chemistry writing a research article for publication in English. The student's process logs, developing text and message exchanges were examined, and the student was interviewed. Findings indicate that key factors shaping the student's experience included his engagement with research communities, his data and his own experience.

Roca de Larios, J., Manchón, R., Murphy, L. and Marín, J. (2008) The foreign language writer's strategic behaviour in the allocation of time to writing processes. *Journal of Second Language Writing* 17, 30–47.

Twenty-one native Spanish speakers with 6, 9 or 12 years of English instruction wrote an argumentative task in one hour and participated in think-aloud protocols. The researchers measured the time that participants used during the initial, medial and final stages of writing, noting the amount of time participants devoted to seven composing processes. For all three groups, the process of formulation took up the most amount of time. Writing processes were distributed differently across the three stages of writing, depending on the writer's proficiency level.

Processes/strategies

Armengol-Castells, L. (2001) Text-generating strategies of three multilingual writers: A protocol-based study. *Language Awareness* 10, 91–106.

Through think-aloud protocol, the author compared the L1 (Catalan), Spanish (L2) and EFL writing of three Spanish university students. For each student, planning and other text-generating strategies were consistent across languages, and each student approached writing in the three languages in a similar way that reflected that student's individuality.

Chimbganda, A.B. (2000) Communication strategies used in the writing of answers in biology by ESL first year science students of the University of Botswana. *English for Specific Purposes* 19, 305–329.

The author examined strategies used by first-year university students in Botswana who wrote answers in biology. Use of L2-based strategies such as circumlocution, generalization and paraphrase were commonly used but did not contribute to successful writing because of the precision necessary for scientific writing. Risk avoidance and semantic simplification also did not correlate with better writing, but risk-taking, regardless of grammatical correctness of constructions, did.

Cohen, A. and Brooks-Carson, A. (2001) Research on direct versus translated writing: Students' strategies and their results. *Modern Language Journal* 85, 169–188.

Thirty-nine intermediate learners of French wrote one essay directly in French and one in L1, then translating into French. Two-thirds of students did better writing directly in French on all evaluation scales. Differences were found on evaluations of expression, transitions and clauses, but not on grammar. Retrospective reports indicated that students often thought in English while writing in French.

Ellis, R. and Yuan, F. (2004) The effects of planning on fluency, complexity, and accuracy in second language narrative writing. *SSLA* 26, 59–84.

The authors investigated the effects of three types of planning on the written narratives of 42 EFL university students in China. Pretask planning resulted in better fluency and syntactic variety; unpressured online planning resulted in greater accuracy; and no planning resulted in comparatively less fluency, complexity and accuracy.

Hatasa, Y. and Soeda, E. (2000). Writing strategies revisited: A case of noncognate L2 writers. In B. Swierzbin, F. Morris, M. Anderson, C. Klee and E. Tarone (eds) *Social and Cognitive Factors in Second Language Acquisition: Selected Proceedings of the 1999 Second Language Research Forum* (pp. 375–396). Sommerville, MA: Cascadilla Press.

Four university-level native English speakers in fifth-year Japanese wrote one argumentative essay each in English and Japanese, thinking aloud while writing. There was no correlation between fluency and essay quality; writers used generally similar strategies when writing in L1 and L2; and L1 use facilitated L2 writing.

Kobayashi, H. and Rinnert, C. (2008) Task response and text construction across L1 and L2 writing. *Journal of Second Language Writing* 17, 7–29.

Twenty-eight first-year Japanese university students wrote essays in Japanese and English and were interviewed about their processes and L1 (Japanese) and L2 (English) writing background. Students' training in L1 versus L2 writing had been different, but findings indicated that writing competence can transfer across languages.

McDonough, J. and McDonough, S. (2001) Composing in a foreign language: An insider-outsider perspective. *Language Awareness* 10, 233–247.

Over five months, an adult learner of Modern Greek completed nine writing tasks, engaging in think-aloud protocol. Data was analyzed from two different perspectives, that of the writer herself and a strategies researcher. The authors juxtapose these analyses in order to illustrate their varying awarenesses and perceptions of writing processes and strategies.

New, E. (1999) Computer-aided writing in French as a foreign language: A qualitative and quantitative look at the process of revision. *The Modern Language Journal* 83, 81–97.

Five native-English-speaking university students enrolled in intermediate French completed a two-part writing task, using a software tracking program. Analysis of student texts, computer records, videotaped writing sessions and completed questionnaires indicated that writers revised but that surface-level changes were more common than content changes.

Porte, G. (1997) The etiology of poor second language writing: The influence of perceived teacher preferences on second language revision strategies. *Journal of Second Language Writing* 6, 61–78.

Seventy-one underachieving Spanish EFL university writers were interviewed over a nine-month period regarding attitudes toward revision and possible effects on students' revision strategies. Revision was often perceived as a proofreading task, and teaching strategies may have reinforced this perception.

Ruiz-Funes, M. (1999) The process of reading-to-write used by a skilled Spanish-as-a-foreign-language student: A case study. *Foreign Language Annals* 32, 45–62.

A skilled third-year US university student of Spanish completed a reading-to-write task. Data consisted of stimulated-recall interviews, and reading and writing logs. Based on the results, a preliminary model of the reading-to-write process was developed.

Stevenson, M., Schoonen, R. and de Glopper, K. (2006) Revising in two languages: A multi-dimensional comparison of online writing revisions in L1 and FL. *Journal of Second Language Writing* 15, 201–223.

The authors compared the Dutch and EFL online revisions of 22 Dutch junior high school writers, using think-aloud protocol and keystroke logging. While students made linguistic revisions more often in EFL, they also made higher-level revisions. There was no relationship between revision frequency and text quality.

Thorson, H. (2000) Using the computer to compare foreign and native language writing processes: A statistical and case study approach. *The Modern Language Journal* 82, 155–170.

US university students studying German wrote two letters and two articles, one each in FL (German) and L1 (English). Students composed directly on the computer, and their writing processes were analyzed via a tracking program. Students wrote less but revised more in their FL than in their L1.

Victori, M. (1999) An analysis of writing knowledge in EFL composing: A case study of two effective and two less effective writers. *System* 27, 537–555.

The metacognitive knowledge of two strong and two weak EFL writers in Spain was investigated through interviews, think-aloud protocols and examination of their written texts. The weaker writers had limited and inadequate metacognitive knowledge, while the stronger writers had a more appropriate and comprehensive view of the writing process.

Wang, W. and Wen, Q. (2002) L1 use in the L2 composing process: An exploratory study of 16 Chinese EFL writers. *Journal of Second Language Writing* 11, 225–246.

Sixteen Chinese EFL learners thought aloud while writing narrative and argumentative texts. More L1 use was found in the narrative task. Students relied more on L1 when managing writing processes and generating and organizing ideas, and more on L2 when examining the task and generating text. L1 use decreased with L2 proficiency.

Wong, A.T.Y. (2005) Writers' mental representations of the intended audience and of the rhetorical purpose for writing and the strategies that they employed when they composed. *System* 22, 29–47.

This study investigated the strategies used by four advanced writers in an academic setting. Writers were videotaped and engaged in think-aloud protocols, and follow-up interviews were conducted. Writers used a generally similar range of cognitive, metacognitive and affective strategies, but they made use of these strategies to different extents, for different purposes and at different points in the writing process.

Woodall, B. (2002) Language-switching: Using the first language while writing in a second language. *Journal of Second Language Writing* 11, 7–28.

Eleven ESL, nine FL Japanese and eight FL Spanish learners in a US university engaged in think-aloud protocol while writing. Less proficient learners switched to L1 more often than higher-proficient learners; the more difficult the task, the longer the duration of L1 use. For students of a cognate L2, language-switching facilitated higher-quality writing; the opposite was true for students of a noncognate L2.

Nonannotated Bibliography

Texts

Al-Khatib, M.A. (2001) The pragmatics of letter-writing. *World Englishes* 20, 179–200.

Bacha, N. (2001) Writing evaluation: What can analytic versus holistic essay scoring tell us? *System* 29, 371–383.

Castro, C.D. (2004) Cohesion and the social construction of meaning in the essays of Filipino college students writing in L2 English. *Asia Pacific Education Review* 5, 215–225.

Kenworthy, R. (2006) Timed versus at-home assessment tests: Does time affect the quality of second language learners' written compositions? *TESL-EJ* 10. On WWW at http://tesl-org/ej37/toc.html

Khalil, A. (1999) The role of cross-linguistic influence in Palestinian EFL students' English compositions. *INTERFACE: Journal of Applied Linguistics* 13, 99–112.

Kiany, R. and Khezri Nejad, M. (2001) On the relationship between English proficiency, writing ability, and the use of conjunctions in Iranian EFL learners' compositions. *ITL Review of Applied Linguistics* 133/134, 227–241.

Olsen, S. (1999) Errors and compensatory strategies: A study of grammar and vocabulary in texts written by Norwegian learners of English. *System* 27, 191–205.

Petric, B. (2005) Contrastive rhetoric in the writing classroom: A case study. *English for Specific Purposes* 24, 213–228.

Vergaro, C. (2004) Discourse strategies of Italian and English sales promotion letters. *English for Specific Purposes* 23, 181–207.

Yi, J. and Kellogg, D. (2006) Beneath higher ground: Vygotsky, Volosinov, and an archaeology of reported speech in primary EFL writing. *Language Awareness* 15, 38–52.

Individual differences

He, T-H. (2005) Effects of mastery and performance goals on the composition strategy use of adult EFL writers. *Canadian Modern Language Review* 61, 407–431.

Mahfoudhi, A. (2001) Teaching EFL writing: Students' hidden agenda. *Cahiers Linguistiques d'Ottawa* 29, 19–49.

Rubin, B., Katznelson, H. and Perpignan, H. (2005) Learning for life: The potential of academic writing courses for individual EFL learners. *System* 32, 17–27.

Processes/strategies

Belcher, D. and Hirvela, A. (eds) (2001) *Linking Literacies: Perspectives on L2 Reading-Writing Connections.* Ann Arbor, MI: University of Michigan Press.
Christianson, K. (1997) Dictionary use by EFL writers: What really happens? *Journal of Second Language Writing* 6, 23–43.
Grainger, P. (2005) Second language learning strategies and Japanese: Does orthography make a difference? *System* 33, 327–339.
Khaldieh, S. (2000) Learning strategies and writing processes of proficient versus less-proficient learners of Arabic. *Foreign Language Annals* 33, 522–534.
Olivares-Cuhat, G. (2002) Learning strategies and achievement in the Spanish writing classroom: A case study. *Foreign Language Annals* 35, 561–570.
Parera, M.T. (1997) Computers and communication in the classroom: Learning to write in a foreign language. *RESLA* 12, 95–114.
Schwarzer, D. (2004) Student and teacher strategies for communicating through dialogue journals in Hebrew: A teacher research project. *Foreign Language Annals* 37, 77–84.
Victori Blaya, M. (1997) EFL composing skills and strategies: Four case studies. *RESLA* 12, 163–184.

Contexts

Allison, D. and Mei, W.S. (2001) Academic writing: Whose expectations? *RELC Journal* 32, 52–72.
Bacha, N. (2002) Developing learners' academic writing skills in higher education: A study for educational reform. *Language and Education* 16, 161–177.
Braine, G. (2005) The challenge of academic publishing: A Hong Kong perspective. *TESOL Quarterly* 39, 707–716.
Clachar, A. (2000) Opposition and accommodation: An examination of Turkish teachers' attitudes toward western approaches to the teaching of writing. *Research in the Teaching of English* 35, 67–100.
Glenwright, P. (2002) Language proficiency assessment for teachers: The effects of benchmarking on writing assessment in Hong Kong schools. *Assessing Writing* 8, 84–109.
Mustafa, Z. (1997) The effect of the academic culture on producing genres in L1 and L2. *Grazer Linguistische Studien* 48, 41–51.
Rainville, A. (2000) EFL and the writing process in Bulgaria. *TESOL Matters* 10, 10.
Strong, R. and Fruth, J. (2001) The Spanish Writing Center at the University of Minnesota. *ADFL Bulletin* 32, 33–36.
Tarnopolsky, O. (2000) Writing English as a foreign language: A report from Ukraine. *Journal of Second Language Writing* 9, 209–226.
Xiao, M.K. (2001) The writing assistance programme: A writing center with Hong Kong characteristics. In I. Leki (ed.) *Academic Writing Programs* (pp. 7–19). Alexandria, VA: TESOL.

You, X. (2005) Ideology, textbooks, and the rhetoric of production in China. *College Composition and Communication* 56, 632–653.

Effects of pedagogical procedures

Akyel, A. and Kamisli, S. (1997) Composing in first and second languages: Possible effects of EFL writing instruction. In K. Pogner (ed.) *Writing: Text and Interaction, Odense Working Papers in Language and Communication* 14, 69–105.

Al-Jarf, R.S. (2004) The effects of web-based learning on struggling EFL college writers. *Foreign Language Annals* 37, 49–57.

Amores, M. (1997) A new perspective on peer-editing. *Foreign Language Annals* 30, 513–522.

Braine, G. (2001) A study of English as a foreign language (EFL) writers on a local-area network (LAN) and in traditional classes. *Computers and Composition* 18, 275–292.

Duppenthaler, P. (2002) The effect of three types of written feedback on student motivation. *JALT Journal* 24, 130–154.

Duppenthaler, P. (2004) Journal writing and the question of transfer skills to other types of writing. *JALT Journal* 26, 171–188.

Gascoigne, C. (2004) Examining the effect of feedback in beginning L2 composition. *Foreign Language Annals* 37, 71–76.

Ghahremani-Ghajar, S-S. and Mirhosseini, S.A. (2005) English class or speaking about everything class? Dialogue journal writing as a critical EFL literacy practice in an Iranian high school. *Language, Culture and Curriculum* 18, 286–298.

Hansen-Thomas, H. (2003) A case study of reflective journals in a university-level EFL writing course in Hungary. *English Teaching Forum* 1, 22–29.

Hirose, K. and Sasaki, M. (2000) Effects of teaching metaknowledge and journal writing on Japanese university students' EFL writing. *JALT Journal* 22, 94–113.

Jones, R., Garralda, A., Li, D.C.S. and Lock, G. (2006) Interactional dynamics in on-line and face-to-face peer-tutoring sessions for second language writers. *Journal of Second Language Writing* 15, 1–23.

Kehagia, O. and Cox, M. Revision changes when using wordprocessors in an English as a foreign language context. *Computer Assisted Language Learning* 10, 239–253.

Kubota, R. (1999) Word processing and WWW projects in a college Japanese language class. *Foreign Language Annals* 32, 205–218.

Kuiken, F. and Vedder, I. (2002) Collaborative writing in L2: The effect of group interaction on text quality. In S. Ransdell and M. Barbier (eds) *New Directions for Research in L2 Writing* (pp. 169–188). Dordrecht: Kluwer.

Lee, I. (2002) Teaching coherence to ESL students: A classroom inquiry. *Journal of Second Language Writing* 11, 135–159.

Levine, A., Ferenz, O. and Reves, T. (1999) A computer-mediated curriculum in the EFL academic writing class. *ReCALL* 11, 72–79.

Levine, A., Oded, B., Connor, U. and Asons, I. (2002) Variation in EFL-ESL peer response. *TESL-EJ* 6. On WWW at http://www-writing.berkeley.edu/TESL-EJ/ej23/a1.html.

Liaw, M.L. (1998) Using electronic mail for English as a foreign language instruction. *System* 26, 335–351.

Liaw, M.L. and Johnson, R. (2001) E-mail writing as a cross-cultural learning experience. *System* 29, 235–251.
Manley, J. and Calk, L. (1997) Grammar instruction for writing skills: Do students perceive grammar as useful? *Foreign Language Annals* 30, 73–83.
Matsumura, S. and Hann, G. (2004) Computer anxiety and students' preferred feedback methods in EFL writing. *Modern Language Journal* 88, 403–415.
Martinez-Gibson, E.A. (1998) A study on cultural awareness through commercials and writing. *Foreign Language Annals* 31, 115–139.
Min, H-T. (2005) Training students to become successful peer reviewers. *System* 33, 293–308.
Min, H-T. (2006) The effect of trained peer review on EFL students' revision types and writing quality. *Journal of Second Language Writing* 15, 118–141.
Moon, Y-I. (2002) Korean university students' awareness of plagiarism in summary writings. *Language Research* 38, 1349–1365.
Nakayama, T. (2002) Learning to write in Japanese: Writing contexts, student performance, and instructional approach. *Babel* 37, 27–37.
O'Sullivan, I. and Chambers, A. (2006) Learners' writing skills in French: Corpus consultation and learner evaluation. *Journal of Second Language Writing* 15, 49–68.
Pérez-Sotelo, L. and González-Bueno, M. (2003) IDEA: Electronic writing in L2: Accuracy vs other outcomes. *Hispania* 86, 869–873.
Sagasta-Errasti, M.P. (2003) Acquiring writing skills in a third language: The positive effects of bilingualism. *International Journal of Bilingualism* 7, 27–42.
Saito, H. and Fujita, T. (2004) Characteristics and user acceptance of peer rating in EFL writing classrooms. *Language Teaching Research* 8, 31–54.
Stapleton, P. (2005) Using the web as a research source: Implications for L2 academic writing. *The Modern Language Journal* 89, 177–189.
Taylor, A., Lazarus, E. and Cole, R. (2005) Putting languages on the (drop down) menu: Innovative writing frames in modern foreign language teaching. *Educational Review* 57, 435–455.
Tseng, Y-C. and Liou, H-S. (2006) The effects of online conjunction materials on college EFL students' writing. *System* 34, 270–283.
Tsui, A.B.M. and Ng, M. (2000) Do secondary L2 writers benefit from peer comments? *Journal of Second Language Writing* 9, 147–170.
Warden, C. (2000) EFL business writing behaviors in differing feedback environments. *Language Learning* 50, 573–616.
Yang, M., Badger, R. and Yu, Z. (2006) A comparative study of peer and teacher feedback in a Chinese EFL writing class. *Journal of Second Language Writing* 15, 179–200.

Pedagogical practices and issues

Abu Rass, R. (2001) Integrating reading and writing for effective language teaching. *English Teaching Forum* 39, 30–33.
Atari, O.F. and Triki, M.A. (2000) The formal features of oral and literate strategies of communication: Their implications for EFL writing revision. *IRAL* 38, 95–107.
Becker, C.A. (2003) The benefits of associative activities for writing in German as a foreign language. *Die Unterrichtspraxis* 36, 56–66.

Bräuer, G. (ed.) (2000) *Writing across Languages*. Stamford, CT: Ablex.

Breiner-Sanders, K., Swender, E. and Terry, R. (2002) Preliminary proficiency guidelines—writing: Revised 2001. *Foreign Language Annals* 35, 9–15.

Byrnes, H. and Sprang, K.A. Fostering advanced literacy: A genre-based, cognitive approach. In H. Byrnes and H.H. Maxim (eds) *Advanced Foreign Language Learning: A Challenge to College Programs* (pp. 47–85). Boston, MA: Heinle Thomson.

Conroy, P.V. (2004) E-mail or blackboard: Teaching advanced French composition. *The French Review* 77, 550–559.

Coombe, C. and Barlow, L. (2004) The reflective portfolio: Two case studies from the United Arab Emirates. *English Teaching Forum* 42, 18–23.

Daoud, S.A. (1998) How to motivate EFL learning and teaching of academic writing by cross-cultural exchanges. *English for Specific Purposes* 17, 391–412.

Ducate, L. and Lomicka, L. (2005) Exploring the blogosphere: Use of web logs in the foreign language classroom. *Foreign Language Annals* 38, 410–421.

Flowerdew, J. (2001) Toward authentic, specific-purpose writing at the lower levels of proficiency. In Leki, L. (ed) *Academic Writing Programs* (pp. 21–33). Alexandria, VA: TESOL.

French, G. (2005) The cline of errors in the writing of Japanese university students. *World Englishes* 24, 371–382.

Green, A. (2006) Washback to the learner: Learner and teacher perspectives on IELTS preparation course expectations and outcomes. *Assessing Writing* 11, 113–134.

Greene, D. (2000) A design model for beginner-level computer-mediated EFL writing. *Computer Assisted Language Learning* 13, 239–252.

Habulembe, S.H. (2007) A classroom response to HIV/AIDS—Project proposal writing. *English Teaching Forum* 45, 36–42.

High, J., Hoyer, J. and Wakefield, R. (2002) Teaching process editing skills with computers. *Die Unterrichtspraxis* 35, 153–165.

Huang, J. (1998) English corner and EFL extracurricular writing. *English Teaching Forum* 36, 29–31.

Hyland, K. and Anan, E. (2006) Teachers' perceptions of error: The effects of first language and experience. *System* 34, 509–519.

Kern, R. (2003) Literacy as a new organizing principle for foreign language education. In P. Patrikis (ed.) *Between the Lines: Perspectives on Foreign Language Literacy* (pp. 40–59). New Haven, CT: Yale University Press.

Kern, R. and Schultz, J.M. (2005) Beyond orality: Investigating literacy and the literary in second and foreign language instruction. *Modern Language Journal* 89, 381–392.

Koltay, T. (1997) Teaching technical writing to Hungarian students of translation. *Issues in Writing* 8, 192–199.

Landolfi, L. (1998) Children writing in a foreign language: Dream or reality? *Rassegna Italina di Linguistica Aplicata* 1, 99–118.

Lee, I. (2004) Error correction in L2 secondary classrooms: The case of Hong Kong. *Journal of Second Language Writing* 13, 285–312.

Leki, I. (2001) Material, educational, and ideological challenges of teaching EFL writing at the turn of the century. *International Journal of English Studies* 1, 197–209.

Liu, L. (2005) Rhetorical education through writing instruction across cultures: A comparative analysis of select online instructional materials on argumentative writing. *Journal of Second Language Writing* 14, 1–18.
Muncie, J. (2002) Finding a place for grammar in EFL composition classes. *ELT Journal* 56, 180–186.
Nemati, M. (2003) The positive washback effect of introducing essay writing tests in EFL environments. *Indian Journal of Applied Linguistics* 29, 49–62.
O'Brien, T. (2004) Writing in a foreign language: Teaching and learning. *Language Teaching* 37, 1–28.
Paesani, K. (2006) *Exercices de style*: Developing multiple competencies through a writing portfolio. *Foreign Language Annals* 39, 618–639.
Plonsky, L. and Mills, S.V. (2006) An exploratory study of differing perceptions of error correction between a teacher and students: Bridging the gap. *Applied Language Learning* 16, 55–74.
Pooser, C. (2004) Bringing the web to the foreign language writing class. *The French Review* 78, 94–102.
Porte, G. (1999) Where to draw the red line: Error toleration of native and non-native EFL faculty. *Foreign Language Annals* 32, 426–434.
Roebuck, R.F. (2001) Teaching composition in the college level foreign language class: Insights and activities from socio-cultural theory. *Foreign Language Annals* 34, 206–213.
Ruiz-Funes, M. (1999) Writing, reading, and reading-to-write in a foreign language: A critical review. *Foreign Language Annals* 32, 514–526.
Shi, L., Wang, W. and Wen, Q. (2003) Teaching experience and evaluation of second-language students' writing. *The Canadian Journal of Applied Linguistics* 6, 219–231.
Simpson, J. (1998) Research writing in a foreign language. *English Teaching Forum* 36, 34–37.
Simpson, J. (2000) Derby writing in classes. *English Teaching Forum* 38, 33–34.
Worthington, L. (1998) Let's not show the teacher: EFL students' secret exchange journals. *English Teaching Forum* 36, 2–7.

Index